The Maxwells of Montreal

Middle Years 1923–1937
Late Years 1937–1952

Also in this series:
The Maxwells of Montreal: Early Years 1870–1922

*William Sutherland Maxwell,
Hand of the Cause of God and architect of the superstructure of the Shrine of the Báb.
An account of his outstanding achievements in the art and architectural world
is given by Nancy Yates in Volume I, Appendix II*

The Maxwells of Montreal

Middle Years 1923–1937
Late Years 1937–1952

by

Violette Nakhjavani

with the assistance of Bahiyyih Nakhjavani

GEORGE RONALD
OXFORD

George Ronald, Publisher
Oxford
www.grbooks.com

© Violette Nakhjavani 2011
All Rights Reserved

First printed in hardcover 2012
This edition 2022

*A catalogue record for this book is available
from the British Library*

Hardcover ISBN 978–0–85398–561–7
Softcover ISBN 978–0–85398–656-0

Cover design: Steiner Graphics

CONTENTS

Middle Years
1923–1926   3
1927–1930   71
1930–1934   139
1935–1937   209

Late Years
1937–1940   269
1940–1952   381

Bibliography   429
Index   431

MIDDLE YEARS

1923–1937

1923–1926

May left New York for Haifa on 7 March 1923, very weak and ill, in mourning and inconsolable. She was travelling with her 12-year-old daughter and a maid, Athala Burke, on the French liner *S. S. Paris*. Shortly before the sailing date, she received a loving cable from her husband, Sutherland, whom she had left behind in Montreal:

> I HOPE YOU ARE BETTER, AS ALL HELPED AS REQUESTED. PLEASE SEND DAY LETTER WITH NEWS, ALSO DATE OF SAILING AND BOAT SO I MAY LEAVE IN TIME TO SEE YOU OFF. ALL WILL GO WELL HAVE NO FEAR – MUCH LOVE S.

She was quite ill on her arrival in Paris. The following cable sent by Shoghi Effendi to Hippolyte Dreyfus-Barney on 21 March indicates that she might even have to cancel her pilgrimage altogether at this point:

> PRAYING MAXWELLS RECOVERY ENABLE VISIT HOLY LAND NAWRUZ GREETING

She could not travel fast. She proceeded at a painstakingly slow pace by train, from Paris to Marseilles, and then by steamer across the Mediterranean to Egypt. She was also delayed there for a while, arriving in Haifa almost eight weeks after she had left home. In later years Rúḥíyyih Khánum often mentioned that as a child of 12 she had found herself responsible for all the travel arrangements during this interminable journey.

1922 and 1923 had not been easy years for either mother or daughter. When the death of 'Abdu'l-Bahá intervened and May lost her will to live altogether, the daughter found herself responsible for her mother from one day to the next.

It is very touching to see how Mary tried to comfort May during this difficult period. The natural pragmatism and instinctive common sense of the 12-year-old was a source of immense help to May. The young girl had her feet planted firmly on the ground; she was able to keep her mother anchored at those times when she was threatened by waves of despair. On one occasion, Mary painstakingly copied out for May a poem by Sir Walter Scott entitled 'Pharos Loquitur' about the Bell Rock lighthouse, but the pure light that shone from her own clear brow was surely what kept her mother going:

> *Far in the bosom of the deep*
> *O'er these wild shelves my watch I keep*
> *A ruddy gem of changeful light*
> *Bound on the dusky brow of Night*
> *The Seaman bids my lustre hail*
> *And scorns to strike his tim'rous sail.*

By the time they embarked on the last lap of that never-to-be-forgotten voyage to the Holy Land in the spring of 1923, Mary had become her mother's closest helpmate and companion. May depended on her for everything and could not have undertaken the trip without her. Although they were accompanied by Athala, the maid, Mary was to all intents and purposes in charge of all practical matters. The guest book of the Pilgrim House in Haifa records the historic date of their arrival:

April 29th, 1923	Montreal Canada May Ellis Maxwell
April 29th, 1923	Montreal Canada Athala Burke
April 29th, 1923	Montreal Canada Mary Maxwell

Soon after their arrival in Haifa, May received from the beloved Guardian the last Tablet of 'Abdu'l-Bahá to her. It had been translated by Dr Lotfullah Hakim, with the following explanation typed underneath the translation: 'The above Tablet was found amongst the papers of the Master and Shoghi Effendi gave it to me (Lotfullah S. Hakim) in Haifa on March 29th, 1922 in the Western Pilgrim House until Mrs Maxwell (the owner of the Tablet) comes to Haifa.' It must have been amongst the last Tablets revealed by 'Abdu'l-Bahá and did not get posted to its recipient. Upon receiving it, May surely was overwhelmed with joy and gratitude to her beloved Master.

> *O thou dear daughter!*
> *Thy letter hath been received. Its contents were full of cheerfulness, for it was an indication that the friends and the handmaidens of the Merciful have arisen in the regions of Canada in spreading the Word of God with pure intention, a paramount desire and a strong purpose. This news became the cause of great happiness. It is certain that if such a rising up is taken (by the friends) the region of Canada will become like unto a sublime heaven.*
> *God says in the Qur'án: 'His knowledge is extremely powerful.' That is, those souls who spread the Divine Teachings are taught the spiritual doctrine which is strong and powerful. That is, the breaths of the Holy Spirit assist them.*
> *However, it is my hope that each one of the friends may breathe a spirit of life in the inhabitants of Canada so that the light of the Kingdom may illumine the east and the west of that clime, that the Divine Teachings may spread (there), and that universal peace may become the cause of rest for the world of humanity.*
> *Convey my respected greeting to thy dear husband.*
> *Upon thee be greeting and praise.*

Rúḥíyyih Khánum often described her first encounter with the youthful Guardian. The day after their arrival in Haifa, she and her mother were in the old Pilgrim House opposite the home of 'Abdu'l-Bahá on Persian Street, where they were staying, when a visitor came to the door. Mrs Maxwell, who had suffered from insomnia on the voyage over, was finally sleeping after several broken nights, and Mary, in her concern for her mother, was determined that no one should disturb her. When the door opened a young man stepped into the hall and asked to see Mrs Maxwell. Rúḥíyyih Khánum recounts: 'I pulled myself up to my full height and said, "Mrs Maxwell is resting; who is it who wants to see her?"'

'I'm Shoghi Effendi,' was the young man's bemused reply – at which young Mary gasped and fled into her mother's room. Quite forgetting her concern to allow May an uninterrupted sleep, she dived beneath the pillows, 'like a puppy', as she always put it, and woke her up. When her mother asked her what on earth was the matter, Mary could only manage to say, 'He's here! He's here!' and, burrowing her head further into the pillows, point to the hall behind her. Upon realizing the situation, May said to her daughter, 'Now Mary, pull yourself together and go and tell him I am coming.'

Whether or not Mary's behaviour was quite as dreadful as she imagined, her mother must have sensed there was room for improvement. Some time during the spring of 1923 when she remained a little longer in Bahjí to recuperate, she sent Mary on ahead to Haifa, with strict instructions about her social conduct. During their few days' separation she sent several notes to her daughter:

> I know that you will behave in every way so that the Holy Family and everyone will see as Kitty did that you are the 'most changed girl she ever saw'.
> I know that you will do this . . .
> I am resting quietly in the sun and although I miss you very much I know this will do me good and that you will have a very happy time and make others happy as well. Give my love to the Holy Leaf and other members of the Holy Family, also to . . . Edith Sanderson, and to Edna and ask her for my sake to look after you a little just like two loving chums.
> <u>Be sure</u> and go to bed early, have your hot water bottle filled and <u>sleep warm . . .</u>
> P. S. Do not spend any money until my money arrives but get the <u>rubbers immediately</u> and do not spoil your shoes, and take some good pictures.

In another letter written to Mary from Bahjí, which May was later to describe in a letter to Sutherland as the 'one place I improved the most spiritually, mentally and physically' in the course of her pilgrimage, May's words indicate how much she depended on her daughter's help and cooperation at this time:

> My darling little Girl,
> I hope you slept well last night and that you will have a nap to-day because this heat is very exhausting and sleep and food will keep up your strength.
> Tomorrow Pisharo is going to bring me some things from Haifa and I would like you to write me a nice little letter and send by him

telling me if you saw Tewfik, if you play with the young girls at the Holy Household, and if you are getting enough to eat.

Please tell me everything, Darling, and be happy and contented so that Mother will have a good chance to get stronger and better for a few days longer . . .

With tender love
From Mother

In addition to her anxious exhortations regarding her daughter's behaviour and eating habits, and despite her own physical weaknesses, May still found the energy to share with Mary in this letter two glimpses of a dazzling contrariety:

> Today a beggar with a large monkey came and another one with a long black snake wound around his neck. Two nuns came to the house and asked permission to visit the Holy Shrine of Bahá'u'lláh! This filled me with a wonderful joy to see how from all people, nations and creeds they come to worship and adore at His holy Threshold.

Contrarieties were what May herself was experiencing at this time. She was subject to mood swings that alternated between hope and despair according to her fluctuating strength and feebleness. Day after day she struggled with her grief. Day after day the Guardian tried to lift her depression, to fill her heart and mind with optimism. Rúhíyyih Khánum would often speak of the way in which Shoghi Effendi treated her mother's spiritual ailments during that pilgrimage, like a doctor. He knew that she was brooding over the loss of the Master and was mourning that she would never see Him again. He was aware of her heartsickness, her propensity to succumb to dark thoughts of despair. He did his utmost to remind her that an obsession with annihilation and fear was conducive to the dispersion of her spiritual powers, the degradation of her thoughts. He did everything to help her rise above such negative notions and bent his energy and will in the direction of her positive encouragement. He knew that only the Faith could provide the ultimate healing for May's soul.

It is very moving to see how in notes written to herself during this pilgrimage May reiterates such ideas, in an attempt to echo the force and clarity of Shoghi Effendi's logic and to capture the references he was giving her to the Writings:

> 'There is naught in the Universe save God.'
> Reality of Man – Immortality – Page 24 'Conception of annihilation'
> 'It has been conducive to <u>dispersion weakening</u> of human thought.'
> Duality of thought world – all creation based on law of <u>opposites</u>.
> Man must believe in <u>truth</u> not in <u>error</u> – because the plane of <u>thought</u> leads to the plane of spirit in reality (see Divine Philo. page 121) 'so that he may <u>advance upward</u> and <u>higher</u> to spiritual <u>perception</u> of the continuity of the human reality'.
> 'Desire rules the darkness mind (thought) rules the light.' 'As a man thinketh in his <u>heart</u> so is he.' 'Ye believe in God believe also in Me,' 'He that believeth in Me' etc.
> Belief – faith – spirit of Faith – Faith is <u>conscious</u> knowledge. Mind is the means – the power – the emanation of the soul that lifts the soul from the earth, the body – sense etc. upward –.

She noted that Shoghi Effendi had told her that her depression was 'the result of my severe illness', that when she was physically weak she was naturally more 'susceptible' to psychological weaknesses too. In order to rise above such conditions, he urged her to throw herself into active service, to teach the Cause which she so loved and treasured. Day after day, in an attempt to change her perspective on life, he would turn towards her at dinner table and say, 'Mrs Maxwell, the thoughts you are thinking are <u>not</u> true!'

* * *

The first two months of her pilgrimage marked a significant change in the life of May Maxwell. They signalled the turning of a page, the beginning of a new chapter. But the complete transformation would take longer.

When Shoghi Effendi left for Europe that summer, he advised May to go to Egypt for a period of rest and recuperation. He did not tell her he would see her on his return, and she did not know, when he bade her farewell, whether he intended that she should come back to Haifa or not. She obeyed him as best she could, but did not get very far. The first time she had passed through Cairo had been in Lua's footsteps; the last time had been in the company of Sutherland, going to visit her beloved 'Abdu'l-Bahá. And now the Master was no more, and Shoghi Effendi was away in Europe. May was engulfed in woe once more. Writing to the beloved Guardian from Alexandria where she was a guest in the home of one of the believers, she admitted that she was ailing again. In fact, she was unable to travel any further than Port Said and stayed in the summer resort of Ramleh from July until September. On 7 September 1923, she forewarned her husband that she would not be back for Christmas:

> Mary and I have hoped and longed to be with you but it is impossible.
> The real Christmas for all of us will be when we meet. Our thoughts and love will be with you that Day and you must spend it as happily as you can with your family and I will try to make Mary happy too.

One month later, May was still grounded in Ramleh. On 14 October 1923, she confessed to Sutherland how weak and hopeless she was feeling:

> Two days ago I received your beautiful cablegram which refreshed my whole being and gave me new strength and as a result I have had two splendid nights sleep and feel much better . . .
> About ten days ago I wrote you a most lugubrious letter telling you about my condition and my terrible longing for you, and my pity for your lonely condition.
> Altho [sic] it is all true yet I know it is not right to send you such a letter, but rather we should try to strengthen and encourage one another in the cruel separation.
> This you always do, you never lose hope and courage, and you remind me of the Words of the Blessed Beauty Bahá'u'lláh Who says we must always hope, that even in the darkest hour we must have hope because this attracts to us the infinite Mercy and Bounty of God.

What made matters more complicated was that wherever May went, her daughter was bound to go, and wherever Mary went, a whole menagerie of animals was sure to follow. In a charming letter written to her father from Alexandria a month later, on 16 November, Mary told him that they were going to be travelling the following day, and added, 'we will take the zoo and baggages: 1 cat 1 rat 2 dogs 1 hen, we ate the other one'. May endured the onslaught of pets with her usual tolerance, however difficult it was to share her hotel room with birds, a pet snake, a cat and finally 'a white rat with red eyes'.

Sutherland depended on his daughter's cooperation, support and above all communications at this difficult time. It is evident from his letter to her written on 23 October 1923 that he relied as much on his young daughter as her mother did:

> My darling Mary, Daddy has been a hopeless writer of letters because he has 'been working' very hard but is well. I do think you should send me a letter every week telling all about you and Mother, because Mother sometimes cannot write. I know that you are a great help to her and cheer her up and support her when she so needs help. So please do everything you can and be sure and write me regularly . . .
>
> Uncle Eddie's bull and cow went with Gordon to Syracuse in New York State and were exhibited at Jersey Cattle Show open to the whole of the States and Canada. They each got second prize which is great triumph for Gordon, and of course Uncle Eddie was pleased . . .
>
> I have had the outside of the house painted, also the basement. I put in a new gas stove, it's a beauty and is waiting for you to make candy.
>
> Today I went to Senneville to Forget's place. The new farmer's house is just finished and is really very nice indeed. Gyp [Mary's dog] went with Pitts and me and had a fine time. He is very well and a great pal of me. I can hold Polly under my coat now. She does not talk – queer, as she is a girl parrot . . .
>
> Well, darling, I suppose you are riding donkeys and camels now? Wish I were there to learn how.
>
> The Chateau looks fine. When are you coming home? I send a great deal of love to you and Mother and kisses.
>
> Remember – write me many letters. My regards to Atla [Athala]. Saw her mother today, she is well. Daddy.

Sutherland himself had indeed been overwhelmed with work and anxieties during his family's absence in the Middle East. In addition to all the work he had to do for the Chateau Frontenac, as well as the arrangements that he had to make for the continuation of the Maxwell firm, he was also carrying several administrative responsibilities in the Baháʼí community at this time. He was not only recorded as a member of the League of Nations Society in Canada in January of 1923, but had been serving as chairman of the Teaching Committee, and on the Temple, Music Arts Exhibitions, Ways and Means, and Finance Committees for the previous year. In his little note to May, just before she left for the Holy Land, he sends her this assurance regarding his Baháʼí work:

> Had very nice meeting last night 12 men and 4 women present. Read your letter at meeting and shall report after tomorrows Committee meeting.

In fact, as one of her old friends, Anne Savage, wrote to May a year later, although her absence from Montreal was deplored, it made her husband assume a far less passive role in the community and he began to participate in Baháʼí activities as never before:

> We miss you dear, more than I can tell you – no one can harmonize different elements as you can . . . (but) Sutherland is perfectly fine. I cannot tell you how the responsibility of taking your place on the Spiritual Assembly has brought him out . . .

The Prospectus of weekly programmes of the Montreal Baháʼí community, for example, notes his name among the speakers from 15 October 1922 to 29 April 1923:

January 21/23	Randolph Bolles	*Some aspect of Architecture*
March 4/23	Sutherland Maxwell	*Japanese Art*
April 15/23	Suzor-Cote	*Great French Artists*
April 29/23	Mr Mountfort Mills	*The Changing Lights of Human Progress*

But by the summer of 1923, Sutherland had only one overriding concern. His brother Edward was forced, because of his deteriorating health, to stop working in the firm altogether. After a richly creative collaboration of twenty years the firm of the Maxwell brothers was no more; Mr George Pitts, another Montreal architect, was the new partner. On 7 June 1923, *The Montreal Gazette* announced the change in the firm officially, in recognition of

> the architectural firm of Edward and W. S. Maxwell, one of the oldest and best known throughout Canada, having carried on a successful practice for over thirty years. Among the buildings it has executed are the Parliament Building, Regina; the Dominion Express Building, Montreal; the Montreal High School; the Victoria Hospital Nurses' Home; the Montreal General Hospital and numerous other important works, including many well-known city residences and country houses. The new firm is known as Maxwell and Pitts and is carrying on the work of its predecessor, including the extensive additions to and remodeling of the old building, together with the furnishings and decorations of the Chateau Frontenac, Quebec, for the Canadian Pacific Railway Co. This 20-story structure will be the largest hotel in this company's world-famous chain of hostelries and one of the most modern, perfectly appointed and picturesque hotels on the continent.

The early 1920s were a hard time, both personally and professionally, for William Sutherland Maxwell. To have endured the collapse of his beloved wife in 1921–2, only to then have to watch his dear older brother fading away before his eyes at a time when May and Mary were so far away, left him very much alone. On 14 November 1923, Sutherland's birthday, Edward passed away and one can only surmise how keenly his younger brother felt the blow.

May's health had been improving slightly just before she heard the news. When she learned of Sutherland's loss, she was plunged into sorrow once more. Some days later, she sent Mary ahead of her to Cairo together with Athala the maid, and remained behind in Port Said in solitude. Her health continued to deteriorate. After months of being bedridden she now found herself unable to walk, and felt herself to be a burden on everyone. She was sick with worry for her husband who was carrying such grief in his heart as well as work on his shoulders at this time. She was concerned about the Bahá'í community in Canada, which she had abandoned for so long. And she was increasingly anxious about her daughter, waiting for her in Cairo, going to visit the pyramids with no one but an Irish maid for a chaperone. May brooded on death incessantly at this time. Even her pragmatic daughter picked up on her mood in a melancholy little note she sent to her father after hearing about her Uncle Edward's passing:

> I wish you were [here] for we miss you all the time. Sometimes I think you will be the one to take us home. Dear Daddy I am so sorry you were alone when Unkle [sic] Eddie died, Mother told me about it. I was so sorry . . .

The Greatest Holy Leaf sent May several messages, letters and cables during her sojourn in Egypt, inquiring about her health, asking of her well-being. She must have sensed the fragility of May's spirit and was probably not surprised to hear that her dear friend from Canada had fallen seriously ill again in Egypt that autumn. Sutherland was so worried that he sent a cable to Mrs Schopflocher, who was going to Haifa at this time, and begged for her assistance. May could not travel alone and was obviously far too weak to return to Canada that winter. As Lorol ('Kitty') Schopflocher explained to May in a letter written on 8 November 1923:

> I wired Haifa at the instigation of Sutherland, who was very upset over your helplessness over there alone, and if I hadn't done this he was going over after you. He visualized you over there dying all alone with no one to look after you, with you too ill and proud to call for help: something like happened to Lua. I begged him to wait and let me go and see how you were and promised to cable him immediately. He thinks you are more ill than you will admit, etc. So he said if the reply from the family pointed to no immediate trouble he would wait until I went over, and then he might come for you in January, but he said his work was in such a critical state just now that it would necessitate great loss if he went flying off just now or during the next two months.

The result of her wire was that the Guardian, who had just returned from Europe, heard of May's condition and summoned her straight back to

Haifa. In a letter sent to Sutherland from Ramleh on 20 November, May wrote:

> My dearest,
>
> In the past few days we have received two beautiful and interesting letters from you telling all about the visit of Jenabe Fazel, until I was so thrilled with happiness at all this good news in the Cause that I felt like a new being.
>
> In fact I have felt much stronger in the past week, and this change for the better in my health came quite suddenly the result I believe of several combined factors.
>
> I wrote you last week that I was in a drier and warmer house, then I learned that the Master had lived here for months which accounted for the beautiful atmosphere . . .
>
> But the real fundamental change came simultaneously with the return of our beloved guardian [sic] to Haifa, and as though the heart began to throb once more with the divine life and energy the whole body of the believers must have felt the sacred influence.
>
> No words can express my thankfulness to God for this improvement in my condition especially for your sake and Mary's.

There is no doubt that May's sense of well-being was directly related to the fact that she had just received a telegram from Shoghi Effendi. On 19 November he had cabled her in Ramleh with permission to return to the Holy Land. 'MOST WELCOME,' he wrote. Ten days later, on 30 November, having learned of her condition, he sent another cable to Port Said. 'DESIRE TO SEE YOU. WISER TO BRING WITH YOU MARY AND ATHALA.'

A postcard dated 28 November 1923, which May sent from Port Said to her daughter in Ramleh, touchingly reminds her of the passing of the Master barely two years before:

> Am much better. Mother sends her deepest love and greeting on this blessed Ascension Day. Take care of yourself my darling.
> Mother

On her long, slow journey back to Haifa through Beirut, May received another cable from the Guardian, dated 28 December: 'MOST WELCOME,' he repeated. 'EAGER TO MEET YOU.' Upon receiving this message, she sent a letter to her daughter, instructing her on how to pack up all their affairs in Ramleh. Not only were all the down-to-earth obligations involved in their travel arrangements placed on young Mary's shoulders, but she was also drilled by her mother on the various acts of courtesy that were expected of her before her departure, on the necessary gestures of generosity that were required in order to forge spiritual bonds as well as express gratitude to all the people they had stayed with and had met during their sojourn in Egypt.

My Darling,
 I am just dictating these few lines through Abdur-Rahim in haste to catch the train and write more fully to-morrow.
1. Have Athala do all the packing immediately keeping all my things in the Brown Trunk and yours in the Black Trunk.
2. Have her put all the clothes you wear everyday and dresses you usually wear in your new basket suit case.
3. Take a complete inventory of everything Athala & I made a list of & see that nothing is lost or broken and send me by return mail a list of anything we have to replace.
4. Please get rid of your birds, pack the rat carefully at the last moment. Have you got your snake?
5. Take the book to Mr. Skandar [sic], give him my cordial greetings & be very nice to him. Tell him how much I regret leaving without seeing him again and that I would like to leave with him, the Book of Abdul Baha's Talks as a souvenir of the beautiful talks I had with him.
6. Be sure and give the bracelet and hat pin to Epiniki [sic] & her sister, because you told them you had these little gifts for them, and while you are there stop for a few moments & speak to Husni Bey & ask him if he ever received my note and the money enclosed, and if he did not you get it from Epiniki yourself & take it to him and do this <u>without fail</u>.
7. Did you get the box of paints for Charles?
8. Give my love to Victoria and tell her how much I hope & pray for her welfare & happiness . . .

 The reasons I am giving you all these instructions is because I received the following wire from Shoghi Effendi: 'Desire to see you.

Wiser to bring with you Mary & Athala (Sgd) Shoghi.'

I have since heard that our Dear Guardian wants me to go home as soon as I am able & he thought of sending us all I understand on the boat with Mrs. Morton, but I have not felt well enough yet to go to Haifa, although each day I am a little better . . . Now my darling little girl when you get this letter please dictate a letter to me through Athala & tell me how long it will take you to attend to all these things, without of course tiring yourself all out and tell me also just how you feel.

We must all work together in a sensible harmonious way so that we may please our Beloved Guardian & go home to the Daddy who is so longing for us.

There must be no strain or forcing, but we must all get ready, then I will communicate with Mr. Whitfield & have him give you the money to pay the rent & all the expenses, and I will send you a wire to meet me here.

I think the best way is to come by the morning 9 o'clock train 2nd class and I will have you met at the station.

I want you to tell me exactly how you are in your health & if you are sleeping well. Give my love to Athala, I hope she is feeling well & rested . . .

Mary responded to these varied demands with admirable maturity. In a letter dated 21 January 1924, she wrote from Bahjí to her father on the state of May's health and general well-being after their return to the Holy Land:

> I think Mother is improving very much. She walks a little every day and one day when Shoghi Effendi came here and went to the Tomb we all went with Him and Mother walked about 200 yards without any help. She was a little tired the next day but got right over it.

The freedoms given to this young girl were clearly tempered by her responsibilities and both, in retrospect, appear to have an astonishing range. They confound all stereotypes regarding how a girl should be brought up, whether in the East or in the West. Apart from requiring her to balance a remarkable degree of autonomy with considerable practical and financial duties, Mrs Maxwell also taught her daughter to take on her share in human relations too. This teamwork between mother and daughter was to characterize all their teaching efforts in the future, but it is wonderful to see how early it began.

* * *

For the next two months, Mrs Maxwell, her daughter and their maid stayed in the old Pilgrim House, across the street from 'Abdu'l-Bahá's home on Persian Street, as Shoghi Effendi's guests. Their extended pilgrimage lasted through January and February 1924. In essence the Guardian was May's 'true physician' during this period; he had diagnosed her condition and prescribed the cure. He sat her next to him at the dinner table and at every meal she received instruction in Bahá'í administration. He not only changed her thoughts from negative to positive ones, but turned them away from herself to the needs of the Cause. He inspired her with Bahá'u'lláh's vision of world order; he enabled her to see the spiritual basis of the institutions of the Faith; he charged her to teach the North American believers about this new stage of development in the Cause. And she fulfilled her pledge to him on her return, in the administrative as well as teaching fields, through hardship and hope, through trials and triumphs, for the rest of her days.

The Schopflochers, Montreal Bahá'ís, were visiting the Holy Land at the same time, and Siegfried Schopflocher (later to be appointed a Hand of the Cause of God) wrote the following letter about mother and daughter to Sutherland Maxwell on 5 February 1924:

> The cable I sent you surely met you in the best of health and I was glad to have the privilege to give you the glad tidings of May's much improved health upon her arrival from Bahajee [sic] . . . Mary arrived the following day with a regular menagerie, including rats, cats, owls and chickens, so she had to leave a number of dogs in Bahajee. However you will be glad to know, she has developed beautifully and promises to combine the love and charm of her mother's with the freshness of youth. In a letter, which Shoghi Effendi gave me to mail, he says, 'I am glad to convey to you the glad news of the improving health of that loved one of God, our dear Mrs. Maxwell. That pioneer worker of the Cause, so precious an asset to the Movement in Canada, will soon be in your midst, refreshed and restored.'

May says, this settles it, since it is our Beloved Guardian's wish, she will take one of the first direct steamers to America, <u>if not the first</u>.

Despite her expressed readiness to leave, however, May did not manage to catch the first steamer. Nor was it direct. It took her another two weeks to obtain a berth, first to Port Said to collect her luggage, and then to go on to the United States.

It was May's life-long habit to write notes and letters. She wrote them compulsively, first to 'Abdu'l-Bahá and now to the Guardian; in fact Shoghi Effendi encouraged her to write to him regularly and she complied, with short and ardent expressions of her love, even before she had left the Holy Land. There are many such notes among her papers and a rich storehouse of longer letters too, written while she was staying across the road from 'Abdu'l-Bahá's house, and just two steps away from him. The two following examples, written while she was in Haifa, portray her deep love for the Guardian as well as her longing for his good-pleasure. The first one, dated 22 February 1924, concerns her arrangements to return home and her guilt over her delay:

> I want you to know that yesterday I felt deeply your disappointment in my not having made an earlier effort to go home, that the sorrow and pain I have felt for you has awakened in me a feeling of shame and responsibility that I have not known since the Master's Ascension, because I had no hope of being able or worthy to serve you.
>
> As you have permitted me to draw nearer to you, and my health also has improved, a new life of service has opened . . . what I knew yesterday was more deep and indefinable, but so poignant as to create an intense longing, an immediate urge for action, such as I have not felt since my illness.
>
> I have made every endeavour to find out about all boats leaving immediately for America or England so that I might submit them to your advice, and by leaving Haifa tomorrow on an Italian boat, or Tuesday on another boat going directly to Port Said, we can connect with boats leaving immediately either way.

A few days later she wrote another note to Shoghi Effendi:

> I have just read your last general letter to America a second time

with an impression so deep that I am silent... It has given wings to my homeward journey and a new disregard for myself and my condition. There is something pent up in my heart longing for escape, for expression, and my last wish and prayer is that it may speak to you from America in the language you want to hear.

I hope that you are much better today, but I beg of you not to come here for our sakes, if it is the least exertion. We have received such bounties and blessings whose priceless value will become better known when we leave this dear home, now we are ready to sacrifice even the joy of seeing you if it is best for you, and we shall always abide in the shelter of your mighty love and tender protection. Humbly yours.

In a longer letter written to him just before leaving Haifa, May asked if he wished her to stay a while in Egypt on her way home and do some travel teaching there. When she was en route, in Port Said on 1 March 1924, she received the following cable from the Guardian in answer to her question:

CONCENTRATE EFFORT ON NEEDY AMERICA. AFFECTIONATE GRATITUDE. FEELING BETTER SHOGHI

Mrs Maxwell and her daughter did, however, stop in London, England, on their way back to America. It was a visit about which she wrote in glowing terms to the 'Blessed Ladies of the Holy Family' one month later. In a few vivid strokes of the pen she described for them the souls she had met there on her way home:

We had the most beautiful visit in London with such Bahá'ís as I have not met anywhere, Mrs. Cropper, whose very existence imparts life and light wherever she is, as 'Abdu'l-Bahá Himself told me; Lady Blomfield who is active, a flame and a most eloquent speaker; Doctor Esslemont who is so rare and precious that one longs for a thousand more such souls; and a number of others, all so sincere, so devoted to the Cause and united that the Cause seems to me to be making greater progress in England relative to the number of believers than it has been doing here.

Two years later, on 26 February 1926, she wrote the following note to the British friends themselves, summarizing the importance of this visit to her:

> I can see now on looking back the wisdom of our beloved Guardian when he said to us as we left his dear Presence: 'I want you to go directly to London. Do not stop anywhere. You will find the friends there very united, illumined, active and steadfast.' There was something about our visit in London, after those months of profound realization in Haifa, which seemed to establish our spiritual lives in a new way and served as a link between that most Holy Spot and the Western world.

While in London, Mary wrote a little triumphant note to her father, on 23 March, reassuring him that they were on their way home at last:

> Last night we went to a meeting and Mother did not take her chair [wheelchair]. Love Mary. We will be home soon.

* * *

London may have been May's link between 'that Holy spot' and 'the Western world' but once she was back in that world, she herself became the link. She became a channel through which Shoghi Effendi instructed the believers about the form and function of Bahá'í administration. She had a mandate from him, and a message to give. All the lessons she had learned at his table, all his counsels on the spirit and purpose of the Bahá'í institutions, now bore fruit. In her letter to the 'Ladies of the Holy Family' written on 11 April 1924, the anniversary of the day on which 'Abdu'l-Bahá had arrived in the United States, she bore witness to the bond she felt with Haifa:

> Every stage of this journey which has taken me further and further away in body from that blessed, beloved Spot, has brought me nearer in spirit to its sacred beauty, righteousness and glory and like a divine touchstone every soul I have encountered on the way possessing a single trace of capacity has felt that mysterious influence of which Professor Brown[e] in his book says that once felt it can never be forgotten.

MIDDLE YEARS 1923–1926

She returned from her third pilgrimage not only physically refreshed but spiritually restored. At Riḍván of 1924 she attended the 16th Annual Convention held in Worcester, Massachusetts, at which a letter from the Greatest Holy Leaf was read aloud as a prelude to the talk she gave to the North American friends. She seized on this chance to address the assembled delegates directly about the vision of Shoghi Effendi and the significance of the new Order he was erecting in the Bahá'í world, which most of them still did not understand and many of them were criticizing. An unsigned excerpt from an account of this Convention reads:

> In the stillness that followed the reading of this letter the Chairman called upon Mrs. Maxwell to speak and she said, 'Dear friends, I do not feel that I can speak just now but I have a message for you all from Shoghi Effendi sent to you the last day before we left Haifa.
>
> 'During the last two weeks of our stay certain conditions in the Cause were troubling him very much and we could see a shadow falling upon him, gradually eclipsing the joyous light and radiance of his beautiful young countenance, until he became almost stern in his gravity and endurance. Day by day we saw him breaking under a burden of conditions too heavy to bear, and as he left the pilgrim house the last day before he was confined to his room and I saw the stoop of his young shoulders, suddenly a shadow seemed to fall over me, the shadow of disgrace. I felt disgraced. We did not see him again as he was confined to his bed, but in the grief-stricken faces of the members of the Holy Family we saw reflected his suffering. Just before we left he sent for us to say good-bye and I found him in his room, pale and agitated, his eyes showing the great strain under which he was labouring. He told me that he was not physically ill, that he was not exhausted from his overwhelming work, but he said, "When the progress of the Cause is affected by the unhappy and unharmonious conditions existing among the friends I am plunged into this agitation – my work suffers, I become weak and ill, I cannot work, thus the Cause suffers greatly." Then he added these words: "I do not judge anyone, I have no criticism for any person, I do not condemn. It is myself I am taking to task here day by day, alone with God. If there were not some great lack in me the friends would not be in this condition."

'Later he asked the Greatest Holy Leaf to make this attar of rose for you, and he sent it to you with his love, not to any special one, but to each and every one of his dear ones in America, and he asked me to anoint you with this attar if this is acceptable to you.'

That year May began her administrative services in earnest. She was elected to the National Spiritual Assembly; she was also appointed to serve on the National Teaching Committee. Her presence on these embryonic bodies of the Administrative Order became crucial to their proper functioning during the mid-1920s. Although her dominating passion in life continued to be the propagation of the Faith, the range and scope of her Bahá'í activities expanded during the Guardian's ministry from the individual realm of teaching to the collective dimension of administration. The fire of her ardour was fed by her devotion to the Centre of the Covenant, 'Abdu'l-Bahá, and after Him to His Chosen Branch, Shoghi Effendi. For she knew that the essence of her faith and her ability to share it with others depended entirely on her obedience to the Covenant.

On 11 May 1924, she wrote to Shoghi Effendi about the gradual evolution in the character of the institutions on which she was serving.

> The first meeting of the National Spiritual Assembly held immediately after the Convention was somewhat tentative in character. New adjustments were being made and preliminary consultation on the vast work of the coming year. But during the meeting of the past two days a new power was bestowed, a sacred influence drew us together and trust and confidence, open and frank discussion, deep sincere consultation and a sensitive consideration for the feelings of all were the abiding spirit among us.

In addition to attending the Green Acre Summer School during the month of August 1924 where Sutherland joined her for a visit, May was busy throughout that summer, taken up with the pressure of Committee meetings, going back and forth to National Spiritual Assembly meetings. As Alfred Lunt, a fellow member of the National Spiritual Assembly, acknowledged in the following note written to her at the end of that year, in December of 1924, she had become an indispensable source of harmony and a fountain-head of spirituality for these fledgling administrative bodies:

I always think of you after an Assembly meeting as the inspirer of pure and noble deeds by the Assembly, and as one who always lays the emphasis upon the tender, sacrificial action which best typifies the Cause of God.

Since the Guardian had invited her to write to him about her activities, she was keeping him informed of everything, of course. And her letters blazed with love and praise for her fellow co-workers. The following note, written in March of 1925, is an example of her generosity towards others. Having been blessed by Shoghi Effendi's spiritual attentions, she longed to share them:

Dearest Shoghi Effendi,
    Although it is the middle of the night, I cannot sleep because the fire of love in my heart does not let me rest, and I see you palpably before me as in those blessed ineffable days when I was in your adored presence.
    With you it is nine o'clock and you are in your room, the point from which the wireless messages of the Spirit are transmitted to the longing hearts everywhere – the spot from which issue forth your written words imparting life, energy, motion, administrating and coordinating all the vast intricate affairs of the Cause of God . . . As for the little group who are privileged to serve on the National Assembly, you have caused our cup to overflow with the wine of your praise and we are overwhelmed by your loving kindness! Surely we have not merited the sweetness of your good pleasure, but like the burning rays of the sun your words have unfolded our capacities, imparting new life, joy and inspiration.
    Your very love and thoughts for a soul cause them to progress and I see how wonderful our gifted secretary has become under this sacred influence. You can hardly imagine the joy and serenity, the deep overflowing happiness and tranquility emanating from him since your recent letters came.

She was a true lover and her heart sang when she wrote to her beloved Guardian:

You remember the day last summer you told me, almost with

severity, that I must not adore you. Oh! I have tried so hard to obey you – to know just what you wished and intended, and to conform my whole being to your wish and instruction. But in spite of every effort, the more this love goes out to others, the more I love and draw the hearts by this magnet – the more intensely does this fire burn within. I see you ever before me – every dear aspect of those divine days when I could see your face and hear your voice. Forgive me – this love has become the substance of my life – perhaps because my Beloved went away, and came again to me in this new guise – but the heart cannot be deceived – that soul-captivating Beauty is one. Whatever I am doing or saying I am inwardly occupied with some thought of you – some means to carry out your deepest hopes and wishes – to be just a sensitive tool in your strong hand moved only by you.

May's whole-hearted devotion to Shoghi Effendi and her unqualified commitment to erect the foundations of a firm Administrative Order under his guidance was all the more significant given the radical shift of emphasis in the work of the Cause after the passing of 'Abdu'l-Bahá. It was a time of change, and many of the early believers clung to the old ways. It was also a time of nostalgia and old memories, and some of the friends felt the absence of 'Abdu'l-Bahá keenly, missed Him terribly. On 9 July 1925, May wrote to Mariam Haney saying:

> This morning Juliet [Thompson] came here and we made a little pilgrimage to the home in New York of our blessed Master, which I always visit every time I come.

Amatu'l-Bahá Rúḥíyyih Khánum often mentioned how her mother would stand outside the door of 'Champney House', where 'Abdu'l-Bahá had stayed while in New York, reciting prayers quietly, in her heart. Shoghi Effendi was well aware of such sensitivity and recognized the spiritual importance of such gestures towards the past as well as their value for the future. In a letter of his dated 28 May 1926 addressed to May Maxwell he writes, regarding the Champney House:

> I have urged the National Spiritual Assembly to give their earnest consideration to the choice of the Master's house in New York as a

national executive centre. I heartily endorse the idea if it be found feasible and practicable. Its destiny is assured and nothing can mar its unique significance.

During the year 1925, too, May was engaged in this new field of administrative responsibility. She travelled ceaselessly across North America to fulfil these administrative duties, crossing the border from Canada to New England, back and forth at least twice and sometimes three times a year. She was an alternate member of the National Spiritual Assembly, a member of the Green Acre Program Committee, the History of the Cause in America Committee, and the National Teaching Committee. She was also the chairman of the Teaching Committee in Canada, the Green Acre Publicity Committee and Resolution and By-Laws Committee! And Shoghi Effendi encouraged her continuously. How it must have revived her spirits to receive letters such as the following, written on 6 March 1925:

> Your marvellous magnificent efforts in the days of my absence from the Holy Land are indelibly engraved upon my grateful heart. Every step you took with your characteristic determination & passionate fervour has been guided by our beloved Master to Whom in His hour of need you have rendered memorable service. I congratulate you on your splendid achievements, on your undaunted courage, on your exemplary devotion & self-sacrifice. I am so glad to know you are so actively engaged in the all-important work of the National Spiritual Assembly...

May had been greatly marked by the young Guardian's indefatigable spirit, his unstinting energy and his undeviating dedication to his work, and she yearned to follow his example. She was passionately concerned about the need to educate the Bahá'ís so that their involvement in the electoral process of Bahá'í administration might be more mature and systematic. Writing to Sutherland on 16 June 1925, she confessed:

> It is so hard to train the people in the understanding of this Divine Organization and to get the true balance between a wise conservatism on the one hand and a progressive breadth of action on the other. Neither extreme is safe nor wise but of the two I prefer the

progressive attitude to that narrow and tight spirit which still dominates so many assemblies, stifling all growth.

That same summer of 1925 she organized a 'community kitchen' at Green Acre 'for Bahá'ís of small means' and the success of this too depended greatly on Sutherland. It was an invitation catering to over 200 people and supplying them with a communal meal, which must have been a challenge in practical logistics quite apart from anything in the spiritual realm. A few weeks earlier, on 28 June, she had written a letter from Green Acre with the salutation 'My dear [Bahá'í] brother', but no name or address:

> We are all . . . working hard in preparation for the coming Bahá'í Convention to be held here July 6th to 8th. The Banquet will be on Saturday night – July 4th – and a public Congress Sunday afternoon and Monday.

And in her letter of 16 June to Sutherland, she sent a long list of instructions regarding the silver and linen she wanted him to bring to Green Acre:

> You know that I am cooperating with some members of the National Assembly in having a community kitchen at Greenacre so that the poorer Bahá'ís may be able to come – & since they know about it they are coming in hordes! I am so happy about this so darling will you please bring our real silver . . . and *all* the Woolworth stuff for the community kitchen. Do not fail or I shall have to buy it here.

The secretary of the Bahá'í Publishing Committee, Annie B. Romer, wrote to her afterwards, thanking her for the event whose great success was '. . . largely due to your efforts. Congratulations.' Sutherland's efforts too, she might have added!

As for the Convention itself, it was a historic occasion. Just one month before it took place, Shoghi Effendi's letter of 3 June to the 'delegates and visitors' challenged them to realize that upon them 'now rests the responsibility of achieving the universal recognition of the Bahá'í Faith, of fulfilling 'Abdu'l-Bahá's fondest hopes':

Will it be America, will it be one of the nations of Europe, that will seize the torch of Divine Guidance from Persia's fettered hands and with it set the western world aflame? May your Convention, by its spirit, its resolutions and its accomplishments, give to that country's urgent call a noble and decisive answer.

May spent the rest of the month of July that year in New York. The Committee for the *Star of the West* had been temporarily transferred from Chicago to that city because it had, in her words, 'gone to pieces'. It needed to be put on a sound footing and a more secure working foundation and, as a member of that Committee, she soon became involved in the business of gathering material, corresponding, editing, and producing issues of this very important international Bahá'í publication.

'I have never been so overwhelmed with work in my life', she wrote to one of the Guardian's temporary assistants on 10 July, 'as since I returned from Haifa.' She does not complain about the workload, however; she sees it as the logical outcome of the bounties she received from Shoghi Effendi during her stay. '[T]his is only natural,' she continues. '[M]y long stay in the Holy Land made it essential and befitting that I should contribute more actively to the Cause than I have done for many years.' It is clear that she feels she owes her life to the Guardian. Her services to the Cause are the least she can do to express her gratitude for 'the renewing of my health and strength in the presence of our dear Valeye [Guardian], in association with the Holy Family and repeated visits to those sacred Shrines which impart Eternal life'.

Summer was the time when Shoghi Effendi usually went to Europe for a period of recuperation. That year, however, he left the Holy Land in a state of nervous prostration, for he was extremely overworked. He had, as Rúḥíyyih Khánum so vividly portrays in *The Priceless Pearl*, been seeking for a competent and trustworthy helper in Haifa for some time but had so far found no one who could relieve him of some of his work. The temporary assistants whom he sometimes had to depend on were either unable or unwilling to meet his high standards. By 1925, his need for a good secretary had become urgent. Although Dr Esslemont had responded to his call, this 'dear friend of his student days' was himself unfortunately too weak to help and suffering from a ravaging disease which would kill him in November. And May must have known it. On 3 July 1924 she wrote a beautiful letter to Dr Esslemont.

> My relation to you is more like spiritual communion. Because, although I am so far beneath you in this great Cause, yet we love and adore the same Beloved and our hearts are burned with the flame of His beauty. You can well believe how deeply we have been grieved over the departure from Haifa of our beloved Shoghi Effendi and our prayers and longing and unceasing effort in servitude is to bring him back to that sacred home where he belongs . . .

Galvanized by her empathy for the young Guardian, she threw herself into the work of the Cause. The one way she could try to alleviate his burdens and relieve the load on his shoulders a little was by assuming her share of the administrative work. A few months later, in another letter to Dr Esslemont, she confessed:

> . . . the stress of activity has been so great, that although I have a stenographer half a day, I cannot keep up with my work, and the rest of the time must be devoted to teaching and meetings.

In fact, one of May Maxwell's most significant contributions to the establishment of the Administrative Order in the North American continent was her correspondence, the quality and quantity of which must surely stand as an example for all time. She was in constant communication with the friends – either through their Assemblies or on an individual basis – helping to arrange or assist with the logistics of meetings, as well as generally organizing, encouraging, guiding and advising them in their local teaching efforts. In her role as Secretary she had the responsibility of translating the plans of the National Teaching Committee for the year into inspiring and motivating actions, involving both Assemblies and the friends around the country. She also drafted the annual reports for the Committee, having, through her loving correspondence, invited friends from near and far to submit to her their local news. Her letters of guidance to the various communities in the United States and Canada, and the reports of the National Teaching Committee that she drafted, always reflected with clarity the goals and programmes to be pursued and won. And the friends were spurred on to deeds of sacrifice through the pure and unadulterated language of love which she employed, a language that always exquisitely reflected the hope and vision of her beloved Guardian as well as the Assembly.

She wrote literally volumes of letters, which were a source of unstinting love and praise to those who were privileged to receive them, and kept up a steady flow of correspondence with communities large and small in the United States and Canada. Although the pressure of this correspondence expanded over the years, the tone of courteous love never diminished. Indeed her epistolary etiquette alone is a model for the future. It was an often-expressed desire and hope of Amatu'l-Bahá that one day a selection of her mother's letters during her period of service on the National Teaching Committee would be chosen and published in a book, as a manual for secretaries.

May's participation in Bahá'í administration would continue till her death. From the moment she returned to North America after her third pilgrimage until she drew her last breath sixteen years later, she shared the Guardian's lessons with the believers and taught them all that she had learned. In the mid-twenties she even circulated a mimeographed collection of notes which were essentially on Bahá'í administration, an eight-page account of what became known as:

CONVERSATIONS WITH SHOGHI EFFENDI
From informal notes taken by Mrs. May Maxwell at Haifa in
1924.
Produced for information of the Bahá'í friends with the permission of the National Spiritual Assembly

* * *

The five years between 1924 and 1929, when May was doing all she could to help the friends understand the Administrative Order, proved to be the most challenging period in relation to her daughter's schooling.

In later years Rúhíyyih Khánum often referred to the fact that she had not had a conventional formal education. Her schooling during her childhood and early teens was both irregular and unorthodox. It included several private governesses, as well as attendance as a young girl in Montessori classes – a highly progressive and advanced teaching system.[1] This education pattern was partly due to the customs of her class and times, when it was usual for a young lady to have private

---

[1] One of the first Montessori schools in Canada was set up in Montreal by Mrs Maxwell in 1914, in her home. See vol. 1, p. 320.

tutors rather than go to school, and no doubt partly due to her mother's uncertain health which had made any kind of routine difficult to maintain and which, as Amatu'l-Bahá herself often pointed out, had placed a great deal of responsibility on her own shoulders.

In 1923, when May was immobilized in Egypt in the course of her third pilgrimage, and Mary, now 13 years of age, was away from her home and schooling for an indefinite period of time, May became acutely concerned about Mary's education. Writing to Sutherland on 14 October that year she expressed her worries:

> The thing that troubles me most apart from my separation from you is Mary's education. Her lack of education at her age is becoming an actual crime against the child, especially as the Master says that no excuse of <u>any</u> kind is accepted by God for not giving a thorough education to our children.
>
> When I realized that I am not able to travel I wanted to send her home then you would be both happier and she could go to Miss Gascoigne's or Trafalgar school, but she did not feel at all happy to leave me in my present health and she said you would not like it. However I have decided to make a temporary arrangement with a teacher by the week so that she may have instruction at least until she can attend a good school.

After their return from pilgrimage, Mary was soon placed under the tutelage of a new teacher, Miss Doreen Barwick.[2] On 3 July 1924, May wrote to Mary from Portsmouth, New Hampshire about her adjustment to the personal nature and characteristics of her new governess:

> My darling Mary,
> Your dear letter touched me very much and I realize that it is difficult for you and Miss Barwick to be really congenial.
> But I am seeing more & more since I came home from Haifa that every Bahá'í – young or old – must now live up to the standard of this Great Cause. We have to <u>understand</u> with our mind & our heart that other people – like Miss Barwick are not responsible to

---

[2] Mary's latest governess during this period came from New Zealand; she remained in touch with the family over the years and cabled congratulations to 'Mary' on her marriage, as well as condolences upon the passing of Shoghi Effendi.

God for their actions in the same way that we are. If Miss Barwick is not considerate, if she does not try to make you happy and to be sweet and harmonious with you this is her misfortune and she is simply allowing her ego to grow big and strong – but if <u>you</u> act in this wrong way toward her you are <u>displeasing God</u> and hurting the heart of our Beloved young Guardian. Therefore we, who are the chosen people of God, and He has chosen us to bring the light of His love and goodness to every soul, must obey His commands, be kind when others are unkind – sweet when others are cross & trying, patient, forgiving and unselfish under <u>all conditions</u> and then a great light, joy and happiness will come to us more & more. I know how dearly you love Shoghi Effendi, & how hard you try for His sake – while He is living alone in <u>one room</u> – in the broiling summer heat of Egypt on <u>one meal a day</u> suffering every spiritual and physical privation so that we may learn to <u>love one another</u> – and be <u>kind & loving</u> to every human being. He says when we have <u>all done this He will</u> come back! I know how hard you try my darling – & Mother will help you – & will soon be home – & in the meantime Paul Haney[3] is coming to visit you! So be happy & hopeful & live for Shoghi Effendi! as He is living for us!

Jeanne & Randolph send you their love – & I send all mine & kisses

Your own Mother

A few days later, on 8 July, she wrote to her daughter again, from New York.

. . . I am here working in this hot city but very very happy because there is a new love and unity – and harmony among all of the friends and all are working together to make Shoghi Effendi happy, so that he will soon return to Haifa.

I hear you have a new rabbit and some ducks and I hope the hedge-hog and rat are well and that the parrot is enjoying the country.

What are you reading – dear, and does Miss Barwick read out loud to you? Tell her I would like her to do this, especially the

---

3   A lifelong friend of Amatu'l-Bahá Rúḥíyyih <u>Kh</u>ánum from her childhood, Paul Haney was appointed a Hand of the Cause by the Guardian on 19 March 1954.

Gree[k] and the Roman History a little each day, which will save your eyes, and which you will find very very interesting, and she has a most agreeable voice so I am sure that you will enjoy it.

. . . Just think in one month is your birthday and what a lovely time we shall all have, and I think that Elizabeth Coristine[4] will be with you at that time. I have written her mother begging her to let her come.

Give my love to Miss Barwick and thank her for her sweet little letter and love to Daddy. With my heart full of deep and tender love to my darling little girl whom I miss all the time and pray for constantly

And writing from Chicago on 22 October 1924, having learned from Sutherland that Mary was 'getting on splendidly', May expressed her happiness to her daughter:

I want you to write to me, Mary darling, and tell me all that you are doing and just how you feel. In a telegram I received from him [Sutherland] yesterday he told me that you are getting on splendidly in your school and with your home lessons, and it made me so happy. You know nothing could make me happier than this. I hope you are practicing your piano every day and that you have asked Miss Olga[5] to give you some music which you enjoy, because you make your best progress when you are interested and happy in your work . . . Do you go horseback riding two or three times a week? Please, darling, do not spend the afternoons in the movies because you will ruin your health if you spend your mornings in school and your afternoons in the house . . . I hope you are getting enough sleep and that you are keeping that balance of health and happiness so that everyone receives the sunshine of your lovely, radiant spirit and your beautiful, clear mind, and thus, you are actively a Bahá'í. I recall Shoghi Effendi's last letter! The friends here are deeply touched by it and are all striving to live according to his standards and thus,

---

4   Elizabeth was the daughter of Mary Coristine, an early Montreal Bahá'í. She and Mary Maxwell had shared the honour of unveiling the two Tablets of the Divine Plan to Canada at the ceremony in New York in 1919. See vol. 1, p. 347, and illustration facing page 365.
5   Some time in 1980, when this piano teacher came to Israel, Rúḥíyyih Khánum invited her to the Master's House for a visit. Although she was admittedly never keen on learning the piano, she maintained friendships faithfully.

nourish his heart and spirit as the Master told us to do, bringing him the strength and happiness for his great, world-wide work . . . I miss you very much, my precious, and I know that you miss me, but we are so united in service to our dear Guardian and I shall soon be home. In the meantime, I never forget, in the midst of all my strain and fatigue, how you took me in your arms and kissed me so softly and sweetly that last day – you were just like a lovely flower, and the perfume of your spirit is with me always, Mary. God bless you, my darling, and pray for mother that she may really serve Him in Chicago among these dear and faithful souls and strengthen the bonds of love and unity, which alone can give life to the world today.

As for Mary's Bahá'í education, it could not have been more rigorous. Her mother drew her attention constantly towards her treatment of visitors, other members of the family, as well as the poor and the sick in the community. In this same letter written on 22 October 1924, she instructs her daughter:

My darling:
   I have just written to Daddy and told him how happy I am that you and he are making preparations for Mr. Randall's visit to Montreal, and you and he will have to give him all the warmth and welcome that I so long to give him, but which is impossible on account of my work here . . .
   I hope you have not forgotten your promise to take dear old Mrs. Pomeroy out at least twice a week. You have so much to give and share with others, and this is the greatest happiness in life, and poor, old Mrs. Pomeroy is old and sick and very poor, and I know how she would appreciate these drives, especially if you sometimes go with her yourself . . .
   Be sure and telephone your cousins the Maxwells, Mary Stewart and Tillie and anyone else you may think of about Dr. Randall's lecture on Friday night, so that as many people as possible may have the joy and inspiration of hearing him . . . Give my love to Aunt Janne [sic] and Uncle Randolph, and call up Annie Savage for me on the telephone and give her my special love and tell her how sorry I was not to have a minute to call her up to say goodby [sic].

It is fascinating, during these years, to see just how much responsibility young Mary was given in the running of her mother's house, in the hiring and firing of cooks and maids. When she was in New York the following winter, Mrs Maxwell received this letter from her daughter, then aged only 14, written on 26 January 1925:

> I am very sorry not to have written to you before, but so many things have happened since you left that I have not had a minute to write before now. In the first place the cook affair is in an awful mess because that perfect JEM [sic] of a scotch cook you engaged didn't come until last night anyway, and when she did turn up, she said you told her that the chauffeur would wait on the table. Of course I informed her very gently that she was entirely mistaken and that we would talk it over after dinner; as Mr. de Trembly was coming to dinner I was in a hurry but still showed her where everything was and was very nice to her . . . After dinner I went down stairs and gave her clean linen and talked to her about the house and said I thought she would get on all right and that if there was anything at all she wanted I would be very glad to show her where it was . . . After the meeting was over some one phoned up and said that her sister did not like the place and was spending the night with her and would call for her things in the morning!!!!!!!!
>
> Never mind I think God must have come to our aid or some good spirit, because tonight a young (she says she is thirty) girl came to the door and said that our furnace man had told her we needed a servant, so I had a very nice talk with her and am going to get a reference tomorrow from the lady she worked for before and if every thing is all right she will come Monday, the arrangement will be this: if I take her, she will do the cooking and the beds and light housework, and I will have Mrs. Bennet twice a week to do the very heavy work, I will pay her 50$ a month, now is that all right? . . .
> P. S. I nearly forgot to tell you that we got a reference of that girl which was very good and that she is coming this afternoon, she is French.

For such a young girl to be managing their house, hiring and firing housemaids, was remarkable, as indicated in the following letter of 28 January 1925 written by May from New York:

I hope that you and Daddy received my telegram last night because I was so delighted to get your letter and so interested in all that you wrote. Now I will answer one by one the points that you brought up:

First – I must congratulate you on your good management of the household and with regard to the cook. You are a very capable girl and I am sure that by the time I get back home, I shall find a far better housekeeper than myself. May I suggest that you or Daddy, once or twice a day or late in the evening, just take a look around downstairs and in the refrigerator in order to keep track of things. Since this cook was sent to us through Cloutier, I think we should be a little careful . . .

On the same day, she wrote to her husband on the subject of a 'fast' party:

Please ask Mary to read you just what I wrote her about JF's party. Unless there is going to be a lot of drink and vulgarity, I do not mind Mary going if GS will look after her, but she simply cannot go without an older person and of course J would not want you because it evidently is for younger people.

Does Mary practice the piano and go to bed early? We must hold her up to a standard now that the Boarding School is given up.

This little exchange was characteristic of many long-distance consultations between father and mother about their daughter during these growing years. May would often send her daughter a letter and tell her to share it with her father, and then, writing separately to Sutherland, she would ask him to read the letter she had just written to their daughter on the subject of parties, food, exercise, health and Mary's education, both spiritual and intellectual. Whenever May was travelling, all through Mary's childhood and adolescence, and during all the years of correspondence between herself and her husband, the Maxwells maintained this united spirit in the way they raised their daughter. It would have been impossible, of course, without Sutherland's undeviating loyalty and total acquiescence to May's opinion.

By the time Mary was 14 years old, Mrs Maxwell must have decided that if her daughter could take all the stress of the household management on her shoulders, she could probably cope with formal education too. And so Mary was sent to the Weston School, for a short period between 1924–5. However, this experiment proved short-lived. She missed a great deal of time from her classes during her mother's absence that winter, which greatly distressed May. Nevertheless, Mary's performance of Titania in *A Midsummer Night's Dream* at Christmas of 1924 must have been a memorable one. The thespian art was always of great interest and attraction to her, as was poetry, and she evidently spent more time writing poems during her stay at Weston School than on her studies. On 13 February 1925 she wrote to her mother:

> Dearest Mother
>   . . . I will send you some of my poems in this letter. I have written quite a few, my teacher says that some of them are quite good.
>   I have made three heads of wax, you know that stuff daddy had? . . . don't you?, one is a woman's head and the face is about one inch high, the second one is the head of a Frenchman and Daddy says it is very good, third is a chinaman and looks just like one, I am going to name him Lin Chung Sue, don't you think that is an interesting name? It came to me in a dream a few nights ago.
>   O Mother! did you get that snake? PLEASE get it for me, Mother.
>   Well I will say goodbye now and have my lunch,
>   Your loving Mary.
> P. S. It said in the papers last [night] that all the hospitals are full on account of scarlet feaver [sic] and measles, so I am going to be very careful, and not go in any public places.

All through her life, through the encouragement of her father, Mary was keenly interested in sculpture. Many years later, when Shoghi Effendi and Amatu'l-Bahá were travelling in Europe and Sutherland was 'holding the fort' in Haifa, he wrote to her on 7 September 1947:

> Dearest
>   I am delighted about the Helen of Troy you are doing – you have a real talent for sculpture, stick to it – and have at least a cast made in plaster. Take good care of it – (send a snapshot of it to me).

In response, on 12 October Rúḥíyyih Khánum wrote:

Dearest Dad

It's eleven PM and I am sitting looking at Helen – on whom I have worked for 1½ hours. Her forehead and nose now look as if they really could have 'launched a thousand ships' – but her chin wouldn't launch a row boat!

She is a lot of trouble to me and causes me much inconvenience and artistic pangs. But I am beginning to love her! All this is done solely for your sweet sake to please you – so let's hope I get her done. She begins to look as if she deserved to be finished and she begins to be really lovely. Shoghi Effendi is admiring her a little and that's a good sign!

May must have phoned home after the receipt of Mary's letter of 13 February 1925, as she wrote to Mary on 23 February from New York:

It made me very happy to hear the clear tones of your dear voice on the telephone last night and after all the days of longing and loneliness, it brought me such sweet relief and comfort to speak to you, to find you so helpful, cheerful and selfless. I thought of the words of the beloved Master about you when he [sic] said: 'God gave her to you to be a comfort to you.'

I cannot make this letter very long as I have already dictated 8 or 10 letters in connection with my work and I am packing to go out to Rye. I am sure I shall feel rested and refreshed in that beautiful fresh air, then later we shall have a lovely time in Burlington together.

It is a great comfort to know that you are stronger and able to go to school, and I know you have done your very best in this connection because it has distressed me beyond words to have you miss so much time at this critical age. However, you could not help it, darling, and I know you are very faithful about going to bed and doing your best to keep in condition for your studies.

In regard to the snake, do you not think it is better for me to have it properly caged, or boxed with a strong wire top and bring it with me when I come? I have not yet got it but it is promised for this week and as I think I wrote you, it will be about five feet long, or a little longer, and larger round than a broomstick. The man says that a seven foot snake is out of the question, that they only import them for zoos or large circuses. They are very expensive and much too heavy for you to handle. He said you could not even lift one. How I am ever going to make up my mind to go and look at the beast I do not know, but I suppose I can do anything for you! And then comes the problem of breaking the glad tidings to daddy! You see if I bring it to Burlington we can let him down easy and yet I cannot bear to really go against his will. In fact, I do not think it is right because he does everything in the world for us. Therefore, we must manage it so that he will regard this as an experiment, which indeed it is and gradually he may become reconciled.

Soon the weather will be milder and we can keep the creature in the roof house because it is <u>absolutely impossible</u> to have that snake in the house and you must make up your mind to this from the very start.

. . . Please write to me General Delivery, Post Office Rye, N. Y., and tell me everything and how you are and give me the assurance that you will stick it out this week at school no matter how tired you get because, darling, you are young and strong and there is nothing the matter with you, and although I know it is very hard yet I also know what a strong will and firm character you have.

. . . with all my tender love, my precious, my own . . .

The appeal to 'stick it out this week at school' must not have provoked the hoped-for result because in May's next letter, written on 27 February, instead of lecturing or reprimanding the young girl for laziness, she commiserated with her daughter, blamed herself, and dangled a six-foot reward under Mary's nose:

Dearest,

It is so sweet to hear your voice on the telephone and as I wrote Daddy, it is the only thing that comforts me in this terrible longing I have for you both. I know how tired it makes you, darling, to have to be waked every day to go to school, and I blame myself so much for not having brought you up to sleep and rise early because there is nothing harder in life than not to conform to the common life of humanity; to be an exception, to be different in all those things, which pertain to our every day life is a great mistake. Although it is so hard for you now to get up and go to school, yet some day when you have your own home, your husband, your children, your servants, you will be glad to be up in the mornings bright and cheerful setting all the forces of your home in motion, bringing happiness, support and encouragement to all . . .

Why do you not write some more poems? They are so beautiful and interesting.

Now you must not be disappointed when I tell you that I am having an awful time with that London Dog Shop about the snake. They keep putting me off saying that the steamer is delayed, so in case they are deceiving me and no snake is forthcoming, I have discovered a man downtown in the Bowery who has promised me a very large, handsome, six foot snake not later than the end of March, a strong wild snake, but not dangerous. He is a special dealer and, although the snake will cost twice as much as the one at the London Dog Shop, I am sure that in the end it will be more satisfactory. However, I expect to hear by Monday about the one on Fifth Ave., and will let you know.

Please write me, darling, how you are getting on with your studies and your piano. I hope you are able to practice. I am mailing you today a charming French book, which I know you will enjoy as much as Le Bouchon de Crystal.

Why do you not tell me anything about Mr. de Tremblay? I have asked you in every letter. I know all about Roger because you have him all sewed up.

Dr. Funk is very anxious to fill your tooth because he says you are the best looking girl he knows.

My little sweetheart, I think of you every day all the time and just what you are doing and I fairly ache to be with you.

Are you saying the beautiful nineteen day prayer for Shoghi Effendi?

I send you my kiss and tender and devoted love,
From Mother.

Both parents did everything possible to stimulate their daughter's love of the arts. Not only was she offered the most wonderful collection of fairy stories by her father, beautifully illustrated by Kay Nielsen and Arthur Rackham, but she was also given every kind of encouragement by her mother to write her own stories. She wrote four plays, as well as performing in several others at Green Acre in her early youth, one of which she dreamed of turning into a movie. Poetry, drama, painting and sculpture were second nature to her. School, however, remained a challenge and it is salutary to observe that by this stage, neither reprimand nor reward seemed to have much effect on Mary. Writing to her on 12 March 1925, May struggled to find another way to approach this awkward subject:

> I know how hard it was for you to get up and go to school this morning, and although I may have seemed a little hard and determined with you, I nevertheless felt the most tender sympathy.
>
> Mary, dear, every one has to learn, at some time in their lives, what a powerful part the human imagination plays in everything. I am convinced that nine-tenths of all our bad feelings, fatigue, nervousness, sleeplessness – or anything else – is due to the unconscious domination of the imagination. You know how much I have talked to you about this already, and it is only because I want so much to help you to be one of those women controlled by reason and your will, and not by temperamental ideas and sensations.
>
> I must just tell you a little story that this wonderful eye specialist I saw yesterday, told me:
>
> He had a patient, a young girl, who had so much trouble with her head and eyes and nose that she lost four years of schooling, and no doctor could help her; at last she was brought to him. He found that the muscles of her eyes did not make her eyes focus correctly. He explained to me that whenever we look at anything we see two images, and there is a wonderful little brain inside our big brain, whose only function is to make these two images into one, by muscular control. He trained these muscles by use of various pictures before the eyes; then he sent the girl home, and made her practice these exercises alone each day. Besides this treatment, he explained to her the power of her own mind – that big psychology which made her believe that she could not use her eyes. He built up her self confidence, and after a few weeks he called her on the telephone and asked her how much she was reading a day. She said – 'Five minutes'. The Doctor laughed, 'Why,' he said, 'you are going to California this year, and you will be six days on the train. I expect you to use your eyes 12 hours a day.' Of course the girl nearly had

a fit, but the doctor was serious. He told her that God had created us with an inexhaustible strength; that the human eyes are created in perfection to work 12 hours at least in the 24 without any strain whatever. He told her that the power of the imagination can be turned either way – for or against the thing we wish to do. He said, for instance, that a person may feel all tired out and almost ill from doing a little work, yet that same person, the same day, can dance 4 hours without fatigue. All this is due to a psychic element in the human mind, over which we must gain the control. Well, finally, this girl went to California, and read the whole way on the train without any eye strain whatever, and yet, due to her imagination, she lost four precious years of her education.

Now, darling, you have nothing the matter with your eyes, so this does not apply to you, except in the sense that it applies to each of us, and it is certain that although it is harder and less agreeable for you to sit on a hard chair at school and study for several hours than it is to drive in the automobile and spend the evening with Mary Harrison, yet one will not hurt you any more than the other. As you are a very intelligent girl, you can grasp this great truth at once, and be master of your own destiny and your own life.

I told the doctor how you say it exhausts you to study, and he said it is imagination. That the brain is equipped for many, many, many hours of hard concentrated work, and that far from tiring us, the more we use it, the stronger it grows. He said the people who become mentally or nervously exhausted, do so because they are ignorant and do not know the wonderful innate, inexhaustible powers of the human soul, mind and body.

Mary, darling, I have taken the trouble to write you all this with the utmost love, and I want you to take the trouble to read it carefully and thoughtfully, and let Daddy read it too, and keep this letter, because it will help us both in the future.

This doctor is having a wonderful effect upon me, because he explains things in a scientific way that I can understand.

We all have to cooperate with God and with Nature if we are going to amount to anything; otherwise we simply remain on the plane of ease, ignorance and self-indulgence, and never rise above the level of the millions of . . . people who know nothing of the realities of life.

You know, dearest, how I seek always your happiness, even before my own, and that it is only out of the greatest love that I write you so earnestly; otherwise, our souls are not united, and our relationship to each other is very shallow, and not deep, divine, and enduring . . .

With great pleasure I am looking forward to seeing you in Boston on the 28th, and meantime, I hope you will not miss another day from school. And just a little secret, which Daddy will not understand even when he reads this letter, – I expect to have a BIG surprise for you when we meet. You know what I mean.

Three months later, on 13 June 1925, at the end of the academic year, Mr Maxwell wrote a brief note about Mary's achievements to his wife in Green Acre:

Dearest

This is just a little greeting to tell you how nice it was to hear you talk over the phone Sunday and to know that nice sensible Mrs. Morton tucked you in bed for 3 days and got you rested – a bit.

It will be lovely to meet you in Greenacre, if that turns out to be the solution and the Prime cottage is just about far enough from the centre of activities.

Miss Stone phoned this morning that she would like Mary at 10.30 to receive a prize. She got the poetry prize for work in the school magazine. Miss S. says she is talented. It was very nice news and Mary reversed gear and 'humped' herself to school. . . .

We are busy with the Cowan's stable and garage and I have about finished the Meredith decorations . . .

Well Darling it's nice to think that you stopped work for a while. Quite a good plan –

Un baiser et beaucoup d'amour, ton Sutherland.

*   *   *

William Sutherland Maxwell was himself very busy during the twenties. He was the Chairman of the Montreal Spiritual Assembly during these years and active in the Bahá'í community despite his many professional commitments. When the young 16-year-old son of President Coolidge died in 1924, it was W. S. Maxwell who received a letter from the American Consul General thanking him for his condolences and expressing gratitude for his sympathy on behalf of the Assembly. When Dr John Herman Randall, the well-known historian and philosopher from Columbia University in New York, spoke at the Montreal Ritz-Carlton – where he stated that 'he had never felt a more responsive audience',[6] – it was again Mr Maxwell who chaired the meeting. In addition to his architectural work in the new firm, he was also painting; one scene he drew in a small sketch book was of Green Acre and is dated 'August 1924'.

But it must not have always been easy for this intensely private and naturally reticent man to find himself thrust into the limelight as a Bahá'í. On one occasion, during the winter months of 1924–5 when May herself was away in New York and he was alone in Montreal with his daughter, the strain entailed in his services to the Faith must have been considerable. Although his daughter did not know what was 'the matter with him' during this period, his 'crankiness' evidently had a more serious cause than the 'devilish' cold. In her letter to Shoghi Effendi dated 29 January 1925, May requested prayers on Sutherland's behalf:

> My husband has been so noble lately in a great trial through which he has passed and in which he has been forced into public position in connection with the glorious Cause, to which he is utterly dedicated. I humbly beg for great joy and confirmation for him.

The 'great trial' she refers to concerned the attempt of a mentally disturbed Bahá'í to commit suicide in their Montreal home. Elizabeth Josselyn had for some years been cared for and helped by a variety of different believers in the North American community, including Sarah Farmer. It was while she was a house guest of the Maxwells that she tried to take her life, on 19 December 1924. The poor woman was hospitalized immediately and was on the way to recovery when she died. Since, as Mary wrote to her mother at the end of February that year, there was an epidemic taking place in Montreal and 'all the hospitals are full on account of scarlet fever', this poor Bahá'í was thought at first to have succumbed to the disease. But the newspaper account[7]

---

6 *Bahá'í News*, no. 1 (December 1924).
7 *Montreal Star*, 3 February 1925. The story had also been reported in the *Gazette* the previous day.

stated that '[w]hat appeared to be natural death from a weak heart, due to an attack of scarlet fever, was found in the autopsy . . . to be death caused by the poison of a bullet that penetrated the lung close to the heart'. Quite apart from the shock of finding the poor woman shot in his own house, it must have been very difficult indeed for Sutherland Maxwell to have to give evidence in court about this sad event. The suicide caused something of a scandal.

There is no doubt about the qualities of endurance, of patience, of high integrity and of long-suffering evinced by William Sutherland Maxwell all through his life, at the end of which he was named a Hand of the Cause of God by the Guardian. May's achievements were, to a large part, due to his active support. She would never have been able to embark on this new chapter in her life – of playing a major part in establishing the Administrative Order in North America, of travelling to communities on both sides of the border, of participating in a thousand and one Bahá'í committees – without the full backing of her husband. In letter after letter which she sent to him in the 1920s, her gratitude towards Sutherland, her dependence on him, and her communion with his spirit when they were apart is demonstrably evident. She also went out of her way to keep in close touch with his professional activities and praise him to the skies for his achievements as well as his services to the Faith. On 9 February 1925 she wrote to him from New York:

> About an hour after I spoke to you and Mary on the telephone last night, your letter came, telling about the Arts' Club Ball, and in spite of your warning to be careful of my eyes, I read every word of the enclosed clipping. It was too interesting for words, all the people, many of whom I know, by name at least, and the descriptions of all their costumes, made me feel as though I had been there and it was just as good as a show. What a brilliant success it was! I should think representing a fine class of people in Montreal, not social 'snobs' but real people with some temperament and charm. Of course I see you as one of the central figures of the whole event and I know that without your wonderful talent, executive ability, and hard work, this would not have been such a delightful event in Montreal. How I wish I might have been there and the next time the Arts' Club thus distinguishes itself, I hope you may count on me.

> I am so glad that your cold is well, Darling, and that Mary is getting better. I noticed last night she was a little irritable, but never mind Sweetheart, her nerves are naturally weak as the result of the grippe, and she will be her own sweet affectionate self in a few days. Whatever happens, you never lose your equanimity and your insight and your understanding, seems to me, to increase all the time. I just wrote Shoghi Effendi about you last week and . . . told him how desperately hard it is for us all to be so much separated. I did not complain to him, but simply stated facts and I am sure that he will regulate our lives in a more balanced way.

Their separations were not always due to May's travels for the Faith, however. At the end of that same summer, Sutherland wrote to his wife, who was in Green Acre with their daughter, to announce his departure for Europe. The break was long overdue. It was to be an architectural trip, an art trip, a trip involving exhibitions and auction houses, of course, and therefore justifiably a professional trip, but above all a time for Sutherland to rest, to relax and to be replenished in those ways that mattered most to him aesthetically, after several years of overwork, stress and grievous loss. This was to be one of the very rare occasions that he indulged himself in this manner. The last time he had passed through Europe in 1909, in the wake of his pilgrimage with May, he had forgone the opportunity to visit the sights of beauty so dear to him. And he would not have another chance again for many years to come, as a result of the economic crises of the late twenties and early thirties. So this trip in 1925 stands out as a landmark.

He had already passed the necessary medical tests for his crossing before writing on 31 August 1925 to announce his imminent departure to his family, and it is clear from the eagerness of his tone how ready he was for this brief respite, which promised a renewed acquaintance with old English buildings and antiques:

> I have my passage booked for Sept 11th, and my passport arranged . . . Other details incidental to the trip are well under way. Prof. Nobbs lent me 5 maps on which he indicated delightful short tours of England, with particular reference to the smaller and more interesting churches. It was awfully nice of him.

But how could he leave on his jaunt across the Atlantic without first saying goodbye to his wife and only daughter in Maine? His invitation to meet up with them for this farewell is very droll:

> Now kids the question is: what are your plans? And when and where do we meet – can go to you and say au revoir. Of course I couldn't go without such a performance. Let me know.

On 17 September 1925, aboard the *S. S. Montroyal*, he wrote another letter to his wife, telling her all about his voyage and the people he had met en route:

> Tomorrow at noon I shall be in Liverpool. The trip has been enjoyable and I have slept well and have not missed a meal – no suggestion of sea-sickness.
>
> I have not done much reading, have played shuffle-board each afternoon. The first afternoon out we anchored off the Island of Orleans because the tide was out and the water low, after about five hours the voyage was resumed and for two days we were in sight of land – a splendid preparation. The following few days the ship corkscrewed her way in a fairly heavy sea – not a gale – but I proved to be a good sailor, somewhat to my surprise.
>
> They have only about ninety first [class] passengers on board and they are a nice lot of people. I have been at the pursers table – four of us, he is a Scot named MacDonald, about 40 or thereabouts, cheery, very humorous with a fund of stories – wonderful ones. At the table sit Mr. Levine, about 40, a Scotch Jew – nice chap – a whisky maker – nice natural and my regular partner at shuffle-board. Also an English chap about 30, named Dowing. He is sallow but nice, has been sick most of the trip . . .
>
> I have had many conversations with Mr. Willie Birks of Montreal and he introduced me to Sir Andrew Rushton who was Lord Mayor of Liverpool last year. Sir A. is about Uncle Rich's size and a very nice man. He has given me three or four letters of introduction to The Liverpool Cathedral Deans and others, and it will be very interesting to avail myself of the special privileges, etc.
>
> A chap named Smith – about 26 and a very clean cut Englishman of good family is going to telephone Mr. Walter Brierly, an

architect in York, that I shall call on him on Monday. This will be an interesting experience for me and useful indeed. A Cambridge man (age about 20) named MacDougal, from Ottawa, asked me to look him up when there – and so it goes.

I am refreshed from the sea trip, and look forward to a splendid time now that I am here – which means within a few hours of the coast of Ireland. I would like to have you and Mary with me, but you will go each step in my company and I shall have so much to show and talk over on my return. It's a rare feeling to have that extra two weeks, it means time for loafing whenever I choose. I do hope your ankle healed quickly, it was the hardest kind of luck – I am to go to shuffle-board – With a great deal of love to you both and kisses, Your Sutherland.

As he set sail, May was with him, as she always was, in spirit. Her first letter to him, written on 18 September 1925, confirmed that all her thoughts were hovering close:

Dearest:

It is strange that although I know you are far away on the Sea yet you seem near enough to almost speak to me. Always when I have been separated from you I have felt near to you in spirit, as though the world has shrunk, the Atlantic Ocean seems small and near and your little boat riding cheerfully over the waves almost within touch of my hand. I have felt this difference in my relation to the world and everything in it, it is the comparative smallness and accessibility ever since my last pilgrimage to Haifa. I have sent you two wireless messages, just a little greeting of love, to which you have not replied, although I feel the response in my heart . . .

There is not an hour of the day that Mary and I do not think of you and speak of you, and we are hoping and praying that you are not having this awful weather we have here, rain from morning to night, which you know I love, but which I know is depressing to you. I am sure you are laid down and relaxed and having a wonderful rest and loafe [sic], with nothing to think about and not a care on your mind, and you do not know how happy and rested this makes me feel. I just want you to stay in that utter state of 'happy-go-lucky' care free enjoyment, pleasure and happiness during your entire trip and you will come back like a new being. Of course we are longing for your first letter telling about your journey and safe arrival, but even these letters you must make short and not waste any time from all that you have to do.

England will be beautiful now and should not be too wet as early in the season as this, and you must take the most comfortable car you can get and enjoy this great architectural trip with all your heart and soul. It is just as though I am there with you and sharing every moment of it, while the world here is jogging along comfortably. I am getting stronger and better every day. Mary is well, and life is delightfully uneventful after the strenuous summer in Green Acre . . .

. . . How pathetic humanity is! People only learn to live together in loving kindness, generous forbearance, harmony and real beauty of life about the time they are ready to die, and the majority never learn at all, and yet this is the only purpose of their creation . . .

. . . Mary is missing you terribly. She has even reproached me saying 'I do not understand you at all, you do not seem to miss Daddy the way I do'. I have assured her of my real feeling which she understands – although I miss you outwardly in one way I feel nearer to you even than that, in living with you and sharing with you this splendid trip which I have so longed for you to have. Mary understands now that this [is] a deeper relation and she talks about you all the time. We both send you our hearts full of love and devotion and our utmost longing for your great joy and happiness which we share with you.

Once he arrived in England, Sutherland sent a postcard to his wife on 21 September from the historic city of York:

Dearest, having wonderful time. Sunday Mr. Smith, a chap of about 23 with whom I played shuffle-board on ship took me to his home, Oxton Hall at Tadcaster. Delightful English people living in a Georgian House filled with old furniture. A wonderful experience. They want me to go tonight and stay a day. Will show me other houses. York is remarkable, English people very nice. Sun yesterday and today. Am comfy and well – too much to see but get up late and have breakfast in bed. Much love, Sutherland.

He sent another to his daughter saying:

> Wish I had you here to see one of the most interesting cities I have seen.

He spent several days in London on three different occasions, visited the British Empire Exhibition at Wembley in north London and then left for Paris on 14 October. On the continent, he did a great deal of sightseeing and bought quite a number of art books, several of which remained in his library until the end of his life. May wrote another letter to him on 14 October, full of love and encouragement and characteristic generosity. Although she did not mention it until the end, she could not refrain from wishing that he might visit the Guardian while he was in Europe and from reminding him about the Bahá'ís he might also meet in Paris:

> Mary and I have been receiving your delightful postcards at intervals keeping us in close touch with you, but last night I got your perfectly thrilling letter from London telling all about your trip, the Chesshire [sic] Cheese, the traveling bag you bought, the dress suit you ordered! and all the charming times you are having. Oh dear it is all so exciting and of course we both long to be with you, in fact we would like to take the next boat and join you in Paris although I hate to think of crossing that sea.
> Well you certainly are having a wonderful time and I can feel by the tone of your letter that you are spiritually, mentally and physically attuned and are enjoying life with a new zest and vital contact which is exactly what I foresaw when I persuaded you to take this trip. We all become stale and fall into a habit of gray monotonous reactions from time to time and to seek an entirely new cheerful and inspiring environment not only renews all the forces of life but greatly prolongs life in a much more vital way. I am glad you have stopped speeding and are just going to enjoy yourself without any conscientious scruples in London and in Paris, like a boy let out of school for this is exactly what you need, to get your mind off architecture and start some new brain cells and refresh all your being . . .
> . . . Don't skimp yourself my darling just get whatever you need and let me know if you want any more money.

> How I wish you would go to Haifa and see Shoghi Effendi! But I suppose you could not spare the time . . .
>
> . . . Now if you have time and want to see Mountfort Mills or the Dreyfus-Barneys or Edith Sanderson or any others, you can address Hippolyte a line to 15 rue Greuze, Paris.
>
> Mary sends her love and kisses to her daddy and I send my heart full and we feel that it will be a great day, and many days! when you arrive feeling so well, looking so happy and loaded with photographs, etc.

Sutherland did not visit the Holy Land on this trip, however. It is uncertain that he met with the friends in Paris either. His time was indeed short before he had to return to the pressing demands awaiting him in Montreal. He was back in London by early November and ready to return to Canada on the 6th of the month.

* * *

1926 was another busy year for the Maxwells. May's movements indicate that she was continuously on the road. Throughout this period, the National Teaching Committee, of which she was an active member, focused the attention of the North American Bahá'í community on 'circuit' teaching programmes, on the holding of 'Amity' and 'World Unity' conferences. A year later, all these activities were cast within the framework of the 'Plan of Unified Action', with its focus on the building of the Temple, and May was wholeheartedly engaged in its implementation. In February of 1926, she corresponded with the Bahá'ís in London, in the United Kingdom, and shared with them the news from Montreal:

> Now we are planning a World Unity Conference, for sometime in early April when we shall hold a round table dinner conference, for representatives of international thought, modern education, League of Nations Society, our large local Forum and other representative people who may discuss freely and harmoniously the most urgent problems of the times.

Between 29 April and 2 May she attended the 18th Annual Convention of the Bahá'ís of the United States and Canada in San Francisco. And after that she went to Seattle, Washington, on her way to Vancouver, British Columbia. During the months of June and July, May and Elizabeth Greenleaf engaged in intensive teaching activities together in the city of Vancouver. Her notes about this trip reflect her ceaseless activity, her constant exertions. She met with

> groups, individuals, public meetings, from 9 in the morning till 12 or 1 at night, scarcely time to eat and very little to sleep . . .

She wrote, with excitement, that

> a number of souls have become attracted and are starting their first study class tonight and a few have become quickened and enkindled with a spark of divine fire.

She also listed the associations she contacted during this period, including the New Thought Society, the Soroptimist Club, British Women's League, Absolute Scientists, and several other groups that she met at the home of Mr and Mrs Harvey. She also attended classes at the Vancouver Hotel in order to meet souls who might be attracted to the Faith. She used every ounce of energy, every minute of time, with the result that the Spiritual Assembly of Vancouver was formed during this remarkable trip. In July and August, after achieving this goal, she made her way back across Canada through Winnipeg, Manitoba, to Portsmouth, New Hampshire, and finally on to the haven of Green Acre.

As a result of all this effort, she suffered a decline in health that summer. Shoghi Effendi was in Europe at the time and so she wrote to the Greatest Holy Leaf, asking for prayers to overcome the 'nervous disorder' to which she admitted that she was often prone whenever physically exhausted:

> The Beloved Master used to tell me to say to Him whatever was in my heart and in this spirit I turn to you always, and now tonight I open my heart to you who, after our Guardian are nearest to Him – He in the invisible – you in the visible world.
>
> Shoghi Effendi has on his blessed shoulders the burden of the Cause in its infinite aspects and manifold responsibilities – I long to

bear for him my humble share of this weight – and never to lay so much as a feather of my own on his dear soul.

You are too holy for me to approach – even in my thoughts yet I guide my steps and surround my life with that sacred influence I felt in your beloved presence in Haifa so to you I dare to turn in the hour of need – when my frail footsteps falter – I know that if I can open my heart to you for a moment – <u>all will be well</u>.

I have striven with all the faith of my soul to respond by my life and humble service to your appeal when we left you – after being so blessed beyond all comprehending in that Holy Spot. Now after two years of almost unceasing work in which I have grown steadily stronger, I find myself once more somewhat exhausted, my vital forces low, and a certain nervous disorder to which I become subject at such times recurs making my recovery to normal still more difficult.

I earnestly and humbly beg – thro your sacred prayers at the Holy Threshold – that I may find the necessary rest and recuperation, freedom from peculiar disorders, and equilibrium, to enable me to continue to serve, bringing love and joy to the hearts, a quickening spirit to the souls and a wider and deeper grasp and penetration of this mighty Cause in its manifold aspects and phases. The Cause is so mighty and powerful – the conditions and need of the world so overwhelming – and we are such tiny atoms!

The Guardian had explicitly instructed May, when she left the Holy Land after her third pilgrimage, to pace herself wisely so that she might maintain her services in the long term. He warned her repeatedly about this, as May had tried to remind Sutherland the previous year: 'The Guardian <u>told</u> us what to do – to put my health before everything – & it is dangerous to disobey him – we are being cruel to Mary who <u>trusts</u> us.'[8] His advice had always been to ensure that her services were sustainable and systematic, lasting and efficient. The correspondence between them over the years illustrates how often May suffered setbacks and how frequently Shoghi Effendi concerned himself with her well-being, how many times she collapsed under pressure and how solicitously he recalled to her the importance of balance. Writing to her husband on 30 March 1926, from Boston, where she was with her daughter, May repeated to him the Guardian's advice, perhaps as a way of implementing it herself:

---

8   Undated letter in the 1925 Estate papers.

I do hope, Darling, that you have been able to fix everything all right at the office with a good draftsman to take the burden off of you. You and I are both very strong and vigorous for our age, but it is my belief that this time of life is a turning point with most people; they can either shorten or prolong their lives according to the degree of care and common sense during these few years. So many people die around the age of sixty for no other reason than the utter expending of their forces between the age of 50 and 60, when the energies may somewhat decline, but the body and mind can take on a new lease of life by proper rest, sleep, air, exercise and general harboring of their forces. I feel that I am not doing this and I have made up my mind that I shall work in moderation and throw the balance on the side of my health during the next few years if God spares my life, and I hope, Darling, that you will do the same. You are looking splendid.

But May could not hold back from serving the Faith with every sinew of her being. She had always been prone to excess, from her earliest days of service in Paris when she tried to respond to the injunctions of 'Abdu'l-Bahá. The Guardian was not the only one to express his concern about her. As early as October 1924, after her return from pilgrimage, Keith Ransom-Kehler was cautioning her against too strenuous a programme:

> I am simply heart-broken to learn of your condition. May, you simply must not give yourself as you do. At present you are absolutely indispensable to the Cause and you have to be spared . . . nobody seems to realize how restricted your energy is.

The following February, she herself had been obliged to admit to the Guardian that

> Often it has been impossible to obey your parting instruction to take care of my health, but perhaps the essence of obedience has lain in whatever little service I may have rendered, for I have found rest in work, healing in union of the hearts, and strength in the true progress of the Cause . . .

The trouble was that although she knew that she had to guard against over-exertion, the Guardian's example was ever before her. May had never met anyone who worked as hard! How could she ignore his example? Her love for Shoghi Effendi was such that even when she was depleted she longed to lift the burden off his shoulders. She was not alone in being thus galvanized by Shoghi Effendi to transcend her limitations, but she was one of the first to put into practice what would in later years be a veritable race among the Bahá'ís to vie with one another to fulfil the goals of his worldwide plans. The minute she recuperated from one set of meetings, she would renew engagements for another. She would start travelling, she would begin attending Bahá'í events as soon as she was able, maintaining a punishing schedule of conferences on both sides of the border. And as a result, after a short period, she would collapse once more. This pattern of crisis and victory, on both a physical and emotional level, was to continue throughout the 1920s and 30s.

After the summer of 1926, May became busy again and started giving a series of public talks in Montreal that fall. She was also very active with her membership in the Progressive Education Association. And in December, while in Boston, she wrote to the Guardian about a plan that she and Elizabeth Greenleaf had conceived to extend their teaching plans from Vancouver to Toronto the following year:

> It is our ardent wish to go together to Toronto not later than February, and in the meantime I shall spend a little time in New York, where I hope to become more rested and renew all my forces for another intensive period of activities.

Shoghi Effendi had earlier reminded her that he too paused in his exertions from time to time and had expressed his hopes for her collaboration with Mrs Greenleaf. On 10 August 1926 he wrote:

> My dear and most precious May,
> Though resting in the calm and invigorating atmosphere of the Swiss mountains I can always find time to correspond with you, which I assure you is a great pleasure to me. I have read your letter and am deeply grateful to learn of the services which you are continuing to render to our beloved Cause. All I ask you is to consider your health for it is the prerequisite of lasting and efficient service. I have great hopes in your collaboration with that radiant and beautiful

soul Mrs. Greenleaf and shall expect to hear of the progress of your joint efforts in that promising country . . .

* * *

May yearned for the mythic calm of hearth and home whenever she was on the road. In 1926, when Sutherland joined her briefly during her stay in Boston with Mary, there had been a respite. On his return, she wrote on 30 March:

> Mary and I already miss you very much and we hope you had a good trip home and found everything all right. It was so lovely to be together here, and there was some deep and radiant quality about this little holiday together while listening to those inspiring conferences.

But such 'little holidays', sweet as they were, invariably took place in the context of Bahá'í activities, and perhaps Sutherland would have sometimes preferred a more private time with his wife and daughter, or a re-creation of dear old Dinan? Or maybe he was dreaming of a canoeing holiday that year, in the company of his family, alone? Writing to him on 19 May 1926, his wife promised that, 'When I get home, we will look for a little house along the lake where you can drive out every night and we can all spend the summer together.' She would sound this idyllic theme again and again, looking forward to their reunion with eager anticipation. 'I send you a whole heart full of [love] dearest,' she wrote on 18 August, 'and would give anything to be with you and Mary instead of here.' However, the dream of a family holiday in the summer of 1926 had come to naught, a fact which May deplored at the conclusion of that same letter:

> It made me a little lonesome to think of you sitting out in that canoe all by yourself and it makes me so discouraged when I think how the summer has worked out after all.

The truth was that Sutherland's choice of holiday was not exactly May's cup of tea. Canoeing in Canada was very different from spending summer on the beaches of Brittany and there was certainly no comparison between renting a house in Dorval and staying in a charming villa in Dinard. Besides, May had a bothersome cough that year, so Mary joined Sutherland without her, accompanied by several of her friends. This did not, however, lessen May's remorse at letting her husband down. It was just as well that over the next decade Bahá'í needs usually took precedence over holidays. On 4 May 1934, for example, during her long trip in California, May wrote of her longing to be back home and contradicted herself with the next breath:

> God, if I ever get you both in my arms and myself into that house we shall just sit and bask in the sunshine of united love and happiness, well – for ever! Another consideration is that I would like to do some travelling through Canada and teach, in fact I feel that I must do so before the winter sets in again for this is the field that the Master gave me and I shall never be right well and strong on every plane until I fulfil this destiny . . .

Since May's periods at home were rare, Sutherland was often left with the responsibility of running the house on Pine Avenue as well as being a partner in the firm on Beaver Hall Square. In addition, he was a pillar of the fledging Bahá'í community and also the parent-on-site who had to keep an eye on young Miss Mary Maxwell, whose premature appearance of wisdom teeth wreaked havoc on her school attendance that spring. May consulted with Sutherland on all matters related to their daughter's well-being, and on 19 March 1926 she sent him anxious instructions:

> About Mary, it is all wrong for her to be living on eggnogs and such stuff, especially with the spring coming on. She will get very much run down, and there is no use in locking the barn door after the horse is stolen. I think we should take some radical measures about Mary's teeth, and the first thing will be for you to mail me the X-Ray pictures you had taken, and I will show them to an expert here or in New York, explain what Doctor Hutchinson said and get an opinion. I understand it sometimes takes a year for a wisdom tooth to come through, even 18 months, and she is getting hers very early – so by the time she has had this pressure and nerve pain a few months longer, she will be in a far worse condition to have any operation on the tooth than she would if she had it now. Do you not agree with me, Sutherland, and that we should not allow Mary to linger on in

this condition, detrimental to her health and her studies? – because Miss Smith wrote me, and she does not consider that Mary can do her best work by having some one read all her lessons to her.

Mary's studies were certainly not a priority that year but she graduated from snakes in 1926, and took up with a bear. With his wife away, it was Sutherland, again, who was left principally responsible for it. May gave him detailed instructions about its care:

> I had a bad dream about the bear the other night, and I am sure you and Mary do everything you can to make the poor creature happy. Give him a few hours of freedom every day, see that he has a variety of food, fresh water and petting.
> Also, have Polly with you sometimes – because these servants are not like Marguerite and Henri, who were so devoted to the pets.
> Now, I want to write to Mary, and this letter is altogether too long – but read it over carefully and take time to answer the important points, about the money, the X-Ray films, etc. I would like to know about your own teeth and if you are having them properly put in order.
> Did you get my letter, in which I told you how homesick I am for you – because it is your duty to be a little miserable, too, sometimes.
> I want to know how little Randolph is, and give my best love to Brother.
> The doctor – a big Boston specialist – says the reason M. R. is so run down is because she does not get sufficient exercise in the open air. Is Mary skating or tobogganing every day for an hour or more? Can you not arrange to have her go horseback-riding with R. R.? I will pay for the rides, as it will save doctors' bills in the future. Please let me know about this?
> Well, good-bye, my darling. I hate Sundays because I am always so homesick.

Two weeks later, on 30 March, May was still worrying about the bear:

> I hope you will find some time to give the bear a little petting and exercise, and let Randolph and Jeanne come up and see him and not frighten him, but give him a little companionship.

Sutherland followed orders cheerfully. Early that winter, he reassured May about the condition of their daughter, her friends and all the animals in the house:

> I was delighted to receive your 'wire' and to know that you are getting rested. Mary slept later than usual Thursday morning – I did not know about waking her.
> She had a sliding time Thursday with Y. and Mary Harrison . . .
> Today – as I wired you the Marys and Joe went to the Motor Show and tomorrow Ginger and the Ceylonese will go to slide etc. –
> The animals are fed, the new cage in the house. The size you gave nearly caused the house to be torn down to get it in –
> Ball receipts in cash – are over $1000 to date and going strong. Decorations are very fine in every way.
> I think everything will go along OK here so don't worry – just rest and enjoy yourself – am a bit hurried and send a great deal of love in which I know Mary joins me.

A few months later, on 13 May 1926, when May was on the West Coast during her 1926 circuit teaching trips and Mary was away too, he wrote again:

> Here I am after holding the attitude of mind that I could only reach you by night letters . . . I figured that after two weeks my writing would be useless as the letters would only reach you on your return to Montreal. Well here goes – a storm chase as the nautical men say – but it may catch up with you . . .
> It was lovely of you to remember the wedding anniversary – it is such a happy marriage that we both like to dwell on it and I send you a hug and a kiss dated May 8th.
> News, washerwoman is not coming back does not like to wash.
> Animals all well, including one cat which the furnace man reports is living a few doors away – and satisfied. The cat had poor toilet habits and is stupid so I do not begrudge the neighbours her acquisition.
> Randolph . . . and family going to France in June – very sensible indeed . . .
> I am well and not working so hard – weather is fine – cash is

satisfactory – Randolph has just called and I am late for a meeting so I must go.

Well Darling it's a great world if you don't weaken. So here's to your happiness health and the meeting we all look forward to.

May was thrilled with her husband's letters, as her reply of 19 May to his letter attests:

> Now I am going to prove to you how mistaken you are about the difficulty in catching up with me with your letters. Here I have your letter which came last night and delighted my soul, and I am going to send your reply by air which you will receive in three days.
>
> However, I feel this will be the end of our quick communications as they do not have this air service from other points and I am leaving tonight for Portland, then in a couple of days for Seattle and by Sunday or Monday I expect to be at Victoria – in Canada at last!
>
> Somehow I shall feel much nearer to you then, and then on my homeward way for that blessed and happy re-union with you and Mary a few weeks later. But of course I expect to be home before she arrives.

She was effusive about his humour, which she found 'simply killing', and praised 'your refreshing way of looking at people and at life which has made you such a charming companion'. She was also full of praise and encouragement about Sutherland's Bahá'í activities:

> I was delighted in reading your telegram this afternoon, when I came back from the doctor's, to see that you are going to be chairman for Mr. Snow, which I know you will do beautifully and I hope you will make some reference to the great evolution of thought and broad-mindedness that has taken place in Montreal since his ministry and the establishing of such a universal forum.
>
> I consider that he has been one of the greatest evolutionary factors in that city . . .
>
> Montreal always lets her best man go – they have done the same at McGill, this stuffy, reactionary element is hard to work against – thank God, it is being swept away all over the world by the ever rising mighty tide of Ideal Divine Progress.

I am also very proud and happy that you are going to preside at the young people's debate. You are young yourself, full of vigor, enthusiasm and a vital interest in all that is highest and best.

* * *

Just as she had wanted to ensure that her husband forged his own independent relationship with the Covenant during the early years of her marriage, so too one of May's priorities during the mid-twenties was to make sure her daughter did the same. She felt that when Mary reached the age of spiritual maturity, she should go on pilgrimage without her parents. It was typical of her to be so generous in her trust, and typical of Sutherland to support her initiative and give it his wholehearted approval. As their daughter set sail from New York in April 1926, he wrote to Mary from Montreal:

> Dearest Mary, I am writing to you this time because you are going to have a wonderful trip that will do you a great deal of good and bring you much happiness.
>
> It is fortunate that you will have Juliet with you. You will have so much in common and together will appreciate the many artistic sights and things; and you will see so much more in these things than you did on the previous voyage.
>
> Mother and I will be perfectly sure the trip will be a happy one for you and we will be contented and enjoy it with you. It's hard luck that we cannot go too but we all have occasion to experience such luck –
>
> All goes smoothly here – and the bear is well looked after by the servants. On Sunday to my surprise I found him perched on the basement staircase with a bar to play on – he is fat and sleek and good natured.
>
> Gyp is too fat but OK. I am disappointed at not going to see you off but think of you very often and you don't seem so far away after all. Give my greetings and love to all the dear Ones in Haifa.
>
> I had Y. to lunch at St James Club on Monday and he took your valise and boots etc. to you. I am sorry that I could only find the orange hat, but men are so stupid when looking for things. Mother said you wanted a blue satin coat, and I could only find what appeared to be a dress –

Be sure and send me a line from time to time, at least postcards, and send them often – put enough postage on them.

Well Darling bon voyage and a great deal of love and many kisses from, Your Daddy.

Of course she did not go entirely alone. May had arranged for her daughter to travel with two artist friends, Daisy Smythe and Juliet Thompson, who had been unable to go to Haifa in 1921. Juliet, whose expenses May herself covered on this trip, was one of her oldest friends and had already painted the portrait of 'Abdul-Bahá. Both she and Daisy, who was a successful artist in her own right, now wanted to paint the Greatest Holy Leaf, and Mary travelled with them. They were her chaperones on the trip, although as a young Bahá'í, she was spiritually independent. On 17 April 1926, soon after she left, her mother wrote:

My darling Mary:

The first word of you came this morning, in the form of your brief, sweet cablegram, every word of which was so precious to Mother's heart. Of course, it is your sense of economy and desire to extend the money as far as possible that prevented you from cabling us before, but you must not do this, dear, because we must keep in touch with you, as it means everything in the world to Daddy and me while our little daughter is at such a terrific distance. However, you seem very near and close and last night on my return home here to Montreal I had a little prayer opposite your bed and felt your sweet and tender presence and the deep love and oneness of our hearts.

This letter will reach you when you are in that 'heaven on earth', the abode of divine love and peace, where you can hear each day the true voice of your Guardian, behold His blessed face and be in that Presence, dearer and nearer than all that is on earth. I beg of you to humbly touch his hand for me and give him my heart once more, my love, devotion and longing.

I know you will also give my deepest love and most humble homages to the Greatest Holy Leaf, in whose presence you are unfolding like a rose, the precious little rose of Canada. I hope she is well and I hope you will kiss Her dear hands for me and lay your head on the threshold of the three blessed Shrines, offering your prayer as coming from me. I mean that you should pray there in my stead for the cause of God, for all the near and dear ones, for the deepening of the spiritual lives, the love and oneness among all the believers.

I know you will have many wonderful prayers of your own, but these I ask you to say for me, because you know that the progress of the Cause is dearer to me than everything.

Please tell Juliet that I heard that Richard Meyer is beginning to turn a little toward the Cause again and I ask you both to pray for him, also that Yasha, Doreen, and others whom I have been teaching may become confirmed.

I had a talk with Robin on the telephone this morning and he was perfectly delighted to hear of you and is coming to supper tomorrow night, I suppose to talk about you. The dear boy is well and working hard, and I shall have so much to write you after I have seen him and Ginger. I hope you will ask Shoghi Effendi's advice regarding the Youth Movement because, if his blessing is on it, it will surely thrive.

Daddy is very well and busy and it is very hard to leave him so soon to go to California. However, I feel that we shall be entirely guided and that in whatever we do we shall do it together and both be very happy.

I do not know how much money you and Juliet will need in addition to what I already gave you in the form of Cook's cheques for your return trip, but you must talk it over with Juliet at once, find out what boats and rates and dates, and cable me how much more you need. Please tell this to Juliet at once.

Do you expect to come through on a boat direct, or return via France? The former way would be less expensive, I think, but you must decide to come with Mrs. Smythe and Juliet.

Will you also ask Shoghi Effendi if he considers it advisable for you to bring some Persian back with you to teach you Persian in Green Acre this summer, also if he approves of Rahim Yazdi, then cable me.

Oh my darling! you cannot think how wonderful it is for me to realize where you will be when this letter reaches you. I cannot speak of it, it overpowers my soul with love and longing and with unspeakable gratitude that God has permitted you to go. I know that you will pray that, if it is His Holy Will, I may entirely recover my health and serve Him in the way that he [sic] would wish to the end of my life.

Please give my love to the Holy Mother and each one of the true daughters of the Master, and I shall write to them in a few days, after I have finished my letter to the Guardian.

With love to Mrs. Smythe and dearest Juliet and my heart, too full for words to you, and love from Daddy, I am,

Yours,
Mother

Three days later, on 20 April, May wrote to Shoghi Effendi and mentioned her daughter's imminent arrival in the Holy Land, begging for his prayers and permission:

> I humbly supplicate on behalf of Mary, that her visit may be acceptable to you since the longing of her heart was irresistible at the hour when Juliet and Mrs. Smythe were going. The fact that so dependent a child, tender and young, would leave her father and mother and take this journey through the fire of love and longing in her heart I took to be an intimation from the Master who promised to overshadow her whole life, who ordained for her a great destiny in service to the Cause, and who told me that he would guide me with regard to Mary at every step. Therefore I humbly beg you to forgive me if I have taken too great a liberty and offer my earnest supplication in her behalf.

Mary's first letter to her mother was written on board the Cunard *R. M. S. Mauretania*, just after this historic voyage began.[9] It gives a delightful glimpse of the character of the 15-year-old, and those of her companions:

> Dearest,
> Well I am not a bit sea-sick! And I have not had any neuralgia.
> Mother you put it very mildly when you said that Juliet and Mrs. Smythe were not practical.
> Well, this is the way things are going, I'll have to put it down as a list.

---

9 This letter is undated but its receipt was acknowledged by May's cable of 9 April.

> After J's mother died she got some sort of a rash from the shock, and all she does is to scratch! We had the doctor last night for Mrs. Smythe has been taking injections for typhoid because she is going to the east the doctor said J. had better stay in bed today and Mrs. S. is also in bed as that injection knocked her out . . .
>
> Everything in the 2nd class is second class . . . it's alright though, and the music . . .
>
> Well I am eating enough and sleeping fairly well.
>
> I am the only body that does not take a sleeping potion as J. and Mrs. S. do.
>
> Well dearest I will write some more tomorrow.

Despite her scorn for her chaperones' ailments and idiosyncrasies, Mary herself fell ill with influenza just a few days later. May heard the news from her husband in Montreal, while she was in New York on her way to attend Convention, and so the parents were apart when they learned that their daughter had become sick in Port Said. Sutherland cabled Mary at the British Hospital on 28 April: MOTHER SENDS LOVE SYMPATHY DADDY, and one week later, May expressed her deep anxiety and concern in her letter dated 3 May: 'You can imagine dearest, how hard it was for me to continue my journey, going further and further away from you when you were ill. I talked it over with Daddy on Long Distance telephone and we both concluded that I should go on, that you would soon be better . . .' The mother's anguish over her daughter nevertheless provoked some deep thoughts. The theme of spiritual motherhood was sounded again and again in her letters at this time:

> It was at that great moment of crisis, Mary, when my mother's heart so wrung with love and anxiety for you that I realized as never before how the hopes of the dear Master have been realized and that I have learned to sacrifice my human motherhood for my spiritual motherhood to you . . .
>
> When I let you go to Haifa with Juliet and Marguerite, it was the supreme sacrifice but because I felt there was some deeper wisdom underlying your pilgrimage at this time you and I were both given strength and courage for this long wide separation.
>
> 'Abdu'l-Bahá said that the pilgrims coming to the shore of the 'City of [the] Tideless sea' coming to his Presence brought with

them the cup of their heart and filled it to overflowing from that vast ocean of truth, and then he added, 'My only sorrow is that the cups they bring are so small.'

Now you, Mary, have a larger cup, a fuller and greater capacity than I ever had and I feel that you are going to bring back to us all and to Canada and to all the youth movement, such a power of Divine love, sweetness, wisdom and understanding which shall profoundly affect us all . . .

Please darling, remind Marguerite Smythe to bring me a white stone for a ring, if it is possible, and if it is not asking too much, some Hetar [sic] of Rose.

Will you also buy some strings of beads and lay them in the Shrines so that we may give them away when you return, because there will be many new souls in Montreal and Toronto and this year is going to be one of the greatest years of growth the Cause has ever known.

The Convention has been wonderful and glorious, and in a few days I am starting on my homeward travelling trip with Elizabeth Greenleaf, after a short visit in Geyserville with Louise and John [Bosch], who like many others are very disappointed that you did not come.

Give my dearest devoted love once more to all of the members of the Beloved Family, kiss the hands of the Holy Leaf for me, give my love to Juliet and Marguerite and never forget that although you are my beautiful grownup daughter, you will always, always be mother's darling baby girl.

With tenderest love,
Mother

The above was typed by a stenographer, with the following added in May's handwriting:

Mary dearest, you are so much more mature that you will be able to pray with far deeper realization and faith in the Holy Shrines than when you were in Haifa three years ago, and for this reason I have a great favor, a most earnest request to make to you – which comes out of the depths of my heart – that you will supplicate for me that the spiritual may gain complete ascendancy over all physical tendencies and limitations in me – that the Power of 'Abdu'l-Bahá and His spirit may dominate all my life and existence. May He shower His Infinite Love on you and on us, my own precious . . .

While she was on pilgrimage, Mary wrote several letters to her mother. The following was written from the 'Persian Colony' in Haifa, and is dated 12 May:

> I started to write to you the other day but could not seem to keep my mind on it, you don't blame me do you? In such a place with its surroundings it is almost impossible to do anything.
>
> Shoghi Effendi was ill when we arrived and in much the same condition as we left him in two years ago, he had received news of twelve martyrs in Persia and then a few days later there were eight more. He wired to Persia for more information but we think they were not allowed to answer, however I think they got more news yesterday and Shoghi Effendi is alright again. We have seen him at lunch twice and Daisy and I went to the Shrine to pray and while I was praying in the tomb of the Master when I heard his voice I could no longer pray but had to go out to see him (I am in much the same state that you were in when you were here!) Oh Mother I wish and have spoken of it to the Holy Family and prayed that some day you and Daddy and perhaps Robin and I can come together to these Shrines and to our Guardian, wouldn't it be wonderful!
>
> Really I am having a fine time; I get at least two extra kisses from everyone just because I am your daughter and they are sending them back to you! Everyone loves you so much. Shoghi Effendi's first words were how you were and if you could walk and were well? And everyone else too, asks me first about you and your health.
>
> You know, Mother, that it is not necessary or possible for me to write you what I felt in the tomb of the Master. I can only say that my first prayer was prayed as though you prayed it. I cried very hard when I first entered the Master's tomb, but after a little while I was filled with such joy and happiness that it was almost sacrireligious [sic] to be so full of joy when everyone else was crying. I cannot help it but the only thought I had was 'how can we cheer our Guardian if we have nothing but tears and sighs, and why do we come to our lord weeping with sorrow for his passing when he is not passed but here with us more so than ever'.

The other day Shoghi Effendi sent me his copy of Thomas Harrison's letter and asked me to make a copy of it and send it to you, to send to Tommy! wasn't it wonderful that he would let me do it for him?

It is quite hot here now and very tiresome to write so I will have to stop soon.

Monera Khanum just came here and she says for me to send you her love and tell you that every time she looks at me she wishes more that you were here!

Everybody says I am the image of you when you first came to Acca and that they feel I am like you in every way this of course is the greatest compliment anyone can pay me!

Her guileless candour and characteristic frankness at this age stayed with Rúḥíyyih Khánum all her life. And as she later admitted, the person whose attention she most wanted apparently took no notice of her during the first days of her pilgrimage in 1926. Much to her discomfiture, Shoghi Effendi ignored her at the start. The turning point occurred after her visit to the Shrine of Bahá'u'lláh, where she wept bitterly and chastised herself for it, concluding that she must have done something terrible to merit his displeasure. Some time later, May received another letter from her daughter. The difference between this and the previous one was palpable. Something had evidently occurred to change Mary's spirit.

Haifa, May 24, 1926
Dearest Mother!

I am so – so happy! Really dear I wish you were here to let me tell it to you. Shoghi Effendi sent for me before dinner and told me what he wanted me to study and do, and everything!

It's no use I cant write, I cant speak, I cant do anything! But we will talk and talk when I get home . . .

Shoghi Effendi sends you his love and said he hoped you would not overdo too much in your work in the Cause but think of the future. Please do this dear.

Shoghi Effendi said he wanted me to get a good general education first and then (if my health permitted, that's just what he said!) to take some lectures in some good college on either Economics or sociology or literature. Wouldn't it be wonderful if I could do all these?

We are going to Tiberus [sic] this afternoon but we will be back in Haifa for the Ascension of Bahá'u'lláh.

Shoghi Effendi asked me to write you and ask you to write him of your attempts to get in touch with Mr. Hearst and all about it. He also assures you of his prayers.

O dearest! Its perfectly awful to be as happy and in love with everyone as I am! If I could be an insect and crawl around after Shoghi Effendi I would be a very happy being! And I love you and Daddy and Robin so much!

I spoke to Shoghi Effendi about my learning Persian and he said that if there were some young Bahá'ís who wanted to learn it we might have a class in Green Acre. He suggested Manucher Khan who we new [sic] in Montreal with Fazel, and the next day he told me he had received a letter from him saying he was finished with his education and was going back to Persia. Shoghi Effendi wrote to him that if he was asked to stay and teach it would be a good thing. Shoghi Effendi asked me to also write to you and ask you to write to Manucher about it. So you see dearest this is all my messages written and now, as I am writing this after Tiberias I will simply have to mail it. Missing you terribly . . .

Tiberias 27 May
Dearest,

Really I must tell you something before I forget it, it just [struck] my funny bone! There are a great many unmentionable insects in this country and sleep is a very ticklish sensation! Yesterday we were with Mirza Badi (Bushrui) who used to live in Haifa but is now Governor of Tiberias and he was sweet enough to point out a bee that was walking up my leg! did you ever?

Tiberias 28 May
O Mother! You are the only one that understands me . . .

Among her pilgrim notes, Mary recorded a dinner conversation with the Guardian:

. . . after dinner I said that I wished Daddy would work a little more for the Cause, he said that my father was a Bahá'í and I said yes but he might work a little more for this Cause. Shoghi Effendi then said that he hoped to see Mr. Maxwell – Smythe and French here in Haifa some day vying with their wives about the Cause. He said this may happen! This <u>will</u> happen!

Shoghi Effendi wrote a very touching letter to Mrs Maxwell about her daughter, one day after this conversation. This note to her was written on 17 May:

> The visit of your dear daughter, Mary, has reminded me of your sojourn in the Holy Land, the memory of which will ever linger in my mind. I am glad and grateful to learn from her of your good health for as I have already said I greatly value and prize your welfare and happiness realizing that every ounce of your energy and every minute of your time is consecrated to the service of our beloved Cause. Let not the difficulties and disappointments overpower you. Remember my prayers and love for you. My earnest hope is that Mary may follow in your footsteps and render memorable services to the Cause you love so well.

And indeed she did. This pilgrimage marked a shift in the heart and mind of Mary Maxwell. In a note written to Sutherland later that summer of 1926, May enthused:

> Everyone speaks of the extraordinary change in Mary since her trip to Haifa and the progress she has made and we must do everything in our power to cherish this exquisite flower of spirituality that is just blooming in her heart which is best done by showing her the utmost love at all times for that is the only all-conquering power.

And writing to her dearest friend Juliet, on 17 August 1926, May confirmed:

> You know the Master told me that I should become Mary's spiritual mother and that then I would find a great joy and the transition from my human motherhood to this new relationship has been going on ever since Mary and I were in Haifa and my human motherhood was so deep and strong that that transition was intense and painful

at times but in the past year it has been consummating very rapidly and now since her return we stand in a total and new, unique and profoundly mystical relation to one another. Of course I know and have realized that she is as the stars above me, nevertheless through the bounty of those inner ties I am privileged to be eternally related to her. I have always felt this way toward you and Lua and it is so wonderful, such a sacred happiness, to see this coming generation of Bahá'ís entering into these new spiritual relationships with us and with each other.

For the next decade, Mary Maxwell's correspondence with her mother is characterized first and foremost by their mutual desire to obey the wishes of Shoghi Effendi and to serve the Cause according to his instructions. The true spiritual collaboration between them, which was to blossom into such a fruitful tree in the years ahead, became visible and showed its fresh, green shoots from this time on.

1927–1930

1927 and 1928 were extraordinary years in the history of the Faith in Canada, and May's activities at this time surpassed what she achieved in the rest of that decade. But it is touching to note that the person she considered jointly responsible for all these achievements was the one behind the scenes. Writing to him from New York on 8 February 1927, she confessed to Sutherland:

> You know dearest, how deeply I appreciate your wonderful cooperation at all times. There are very few people who can look back over their lives and say to anyone 'that never once have they failed them', but I can truly and with all my heart say this of you, and it has given me, throughout my life a sense of refuge, peace and security which is identical in my consciousness with my spiritual life in the Cause of God.
>
> I know how hard it was for you, with all the work of the Ball, Mary's illness and need of you and everything else to attend to that Spiritual Assembly work regarding the coming Convention and the National Assembly, and I want to thank you, darling, with all my heart.
>
> I do not see what more you can want than to have such a success as this Ball, an artistic creation, a source of happiness and enjoyment to hundreds, lifting the social and artistic standards of Montreal out of the quagmire of past *banalité* and conventionalism, to the modern standard of artistic beauty, vitality and real meaning. How lovely the balloons must have been! What a scene of moving color and light! And how I realize that you bring to the external world that coordination, harmony and motion which I humbly strive to bring to the inner life and heart and mind. Just see what our cooperation over the new library and reading room has brought to Montreal!

> Did you see the article in the McGill Daily? How encouraging and how happy we shall be if this centre becomes of real and permanent value to the City!

May travelled constantly to New York and Chicago over this period. She also collaborated on a teaching project in Toronto, as will be seen, but two very significant events took place in Montreal itself in 1927. One was the first World Unity Conference in Canada, and the other, to which she refers in the letter above, was the 19th Annual Convention of the United States and Canada, which took place at the Windsor Hotel in Montreal. May helped to organize both events but Sutherland was also responsible for their success. His wife's letter of gratitude indicates how much she depended on him.

Early in February she advised Sutherland about the logistics to be covered in the consultations of the Local Spiritual Assembly of Montreal which had been given the responsibility for organizing the Convention. It is quite remarkable to see her managerial skills at work long distance in this letter of 8 February 1927 to Sutherland:

> I understand from Horace Holley that he has written your Spiritual Assembly in Montreal requesting them to appoint a Committee for the coming Convention, and as you should probably take action sometime this week, I would like to give you my thoughts on the subject.
>
> The work of getting up a Convention in a City is not arduous, but requires experience, and I do not know which of the friends there have ever taken part in the Committee work of Conventions and their preparation.
>
> For instance, you have to decide upon the most advisable place to hold the Convention from every standpoint . . .

She literally taught the infant Assembly how to go about its work:

> The Montreal Convention Committee will, in consultation with the Spiritual Assembly, decide on the place to hold the Convention, preferably in some hotel where they can have a quiet, comfortable hall, where delegates can stay, if they wish and where all can get meals at convenient times. I would say that for practical purposes

the Windsor Hotel would be the best, but the matter would have to be carefully looked into. The Convention Committee is usually composed of about three people who can work together intelligently and harmoniously without excitement or obstruction, appoint their sub-committees, such as Hospitality and Housing of Delegates, Reception of Delegates, Arrangements Committee for the general welfare, comfort and happiness of Delegates and all visiting Baháʼís. I have done this work, as you know, in the past and am very familiar with it so that should anyone on the Spiritual Assembly suggest me as a member of that Committee, please, darling, do not oppose it with the thought that it might be too much work for me. Of course, I may not be suggested but should I be, it would be very wrong to refuse it as this is our first Canadian Convention, is of supreme importance to the Cause and Canada, and should be carried out with a beauty, harmony and power worthy of its greatness.

Will you explain all this to the friends (of course, not what I said about myself) and all of you take into deep prayerful consideration, the capable experienced and high type of people to carry out this important work, then your Committee when appointed can meet, any time within the next month is ample time and appoint their sub-committees . . .

It is also the work of the Montreal Convention Committee, always of course in consultation with the Montreal Spiritual Assembly, to make arrangements for the feast of the Riḍván, and for which tickets are sold at so much per person. Usually in the hotels where we have held this banquet in past years, the hotel has allowed us our Convention hall free in consideration of our holding this large banquet. There is time enough to consider all these details when I return in a couple of weeks or so.

May was more experienced in administrative matters than many of the other Baháʼís. She had told Sutherland how busy she had been in organizing the previous Convention and Congress. And now, knowing her husband was aware that she often would work beyond her endurance, she tried to reassure him about the limits of the work involved in organizing this Convention for which the Local Spiritual Assembly of Montreal had been given the responsibility:

Remember it has nothing to do with the World Unity Conference which is carried out entirely by the N.S.A. who appoint their own Committees, and who will, no doubt, hold their Conferences in different churches and centres with which they will make contacts as they have done in other cities.

She tried to set his mind at rest and fix his sights higher regarding her involvement:

(S)hould I be on this Committee my experience will have taught me a much better and simpler way without strain or fatigue, and of course, the larger part of that work was the Public Congress which now does not exist at all and has been replaced by the World Unity Conferences which as I said before, are carried out by the N. S. A. . . . If the friends prefer to have you on the Committee instead of me, I can pass on all the information to you and act on a sub-committee, you know that it is not that I want to be appointed to anything but I want the Spiritual Assembly to be free to follow the Divine Guidance at this crucial time, unhampered by any fears or anxieties of yours on my behalf which in the end would make me more ill than any amount of work. I know you understand all that I mean.

The World Unity Conference took place in Moyse Hall, McGill University. It was chaired by Mr Maxwell himself, who introduced the two speakers, Agnes Macphail, member of the House of Commons in Ottawa and the first Canadian woman Member of Parliament, and the philosopher Professor John Randall from Columbia University, and it was widely publicized with an article in the *Montreal Gazette* on 30 April 1927 under the headline:

BAHA'I MOVEMENT DISCIPLES CONFERENCE

But although the gathering was being held under the auspices of the National Spiritual Assembly, May – as Sutherland had feared – assumed full responsibility for its preparation, despite her reassurances to the contrary. In addition to using this opportunity to acquaint distinguished personalities with the name and the aims of the Faith, she drew public and media attention to it by inviting local and regional authorities in

Montreal to speak at the event. In fact, she was a one-woman Office of Public Information and Relations for the Bahá'í Faith in North America for her time, and the tone, style and manner in which she performed this service was a model for the future. In a letter of invitation dated 12 April 1927, addressed to Agnes Macphail, she wrote:

> I want to say that we would deeply appreciate your cooperation in this World Unity Conference, the first to be held in Canada. We feel that your work and those splendid ideals for which you stand so courageously would find a true and far-reaching expression in our humble effort to bring to the thinking people of Montreal these Conferences for human brotherhood and peace.

The ease with which May made initial contacts and maintained links with influential figures was truly exemplary. Her warm personality brought her in touch and enabled her to make fast friends with all kinds of people. In addition to all her Bahá'í commitments, her membership on the National Spiritual Assembly, on the Publicity Committee and World Unity Conference Committee and her responsibilities as chairman of the National Teaching Committee, she was also active in various non-Bahá'í clubs and associations in Montreal. She was on the advisory Board of the Youth Group, and the Women's Canadian Club; she was also the Honorary President of the Negro Club in Montreal and a member of the League of Nations Society in Canada. The range of her acquaintances both inside and outside the Bahá'í community can only be guessed by such a wide gamut of commitments. As a result, she was able to make the Faith known to a wide spectrum of important people.

Her contacts, moreover, were based on real respect, sincere interest, and honest admiration. She was not merely 'cultivating' people with ulterior motives, but always maintained genuine relations with them. A few years later, for example, on 30 September 1931, she again wrote to Agnes Macphail, whose friendship she had cultivated since the Unity Conference in Montreal, to invite her to speak at an event that was not, at first glance, anything to do with the Bahá'í Faith:

> Mrs. H. E. Stewart, President of the League of Women Voters for the State of New York, has asked me whether you could be the guest speaker at their Armistice Luncheon to be held in Utica on Saturday,

November seventh. They are ardent workers for peace, and know of your great interest and influence in this connection. Last year, they had Sir Herbert Ames and they have an audience of from three to four hundred at these Annual luncheons.

Indeed, if so many prominent people respected May Maxwell, it was not only because her vision was all-encompassing but also because she affirmed that theirs was too. Several years later, she was still in correspondence with Agnes Macphail, with whom she had retained good relations. On 8 April 1935, she received a letter from her about penal reform. The Member of Parliament thanked Mrs Maxwell for her letter of 22 March 1935, in which she had evidently offered her assistance to this cause, saying:

> Yes, you can certainly help, by getting people who are prepared to deal with the question in a scientific way interested, and by organizing groups to petition their local M. P.s and the Minister of Justice for reform in our penal system.

Although there is no reference to the Faith in this correspondence, it is interesting to note the following remark of Miss Macphail's in the above mentioned letter: 'I have not received the book you say you are sending,' after which she adds: 'I shall be interested to read it when it arrives.' Whether May actually did organize any groups or petition any M. P.s on the subject of penal reform is unknown. But if she promised to send a book to Miss Macphail, she undoubtedly fulfilled her pledge. Thus it was that through the integrity and fidelity of her contacts she was able to present the Faith to leaders of society in a manner at once direct and dignified.

The hallmark of May's bond with others was always spiritual; the friendship she developed was invariably between souls. It did not matter how important or how socially insignificant the person was. It did not matter, either, whether that person ever became a Bahá'í. What mattered was that the name of the Faith be associated with integrity and truth, both in terms of high ideals and human relationships. Her sincerity can be glimpsed in a letter she wrote at the beginning of 1928, to Evelyn and Stanley Kemp regarding a new-found friendship:

Now my days are absorbed in the visit of a rare soul, a gifted pianist, Princesse de Broglie, the wife of Prince Jacques de Broglie, one of the oldest and noblest families in Europe. We found each other in this arduous journey towards God and clasped hands by the way, and the meeting has been one of the rare experiences in life; she has been in our home for some time and I must limit my correspondence for a time for her sake.

Later that same year, in the midst of a punishing schedule of conferences and travels, May wrote from Rye, New York, to Mrs Mansfield Ferry, who was giving a reception for Lord and Lady Allenby. Her courtesies were impeccable:

You will, I am sure, pardon my delay in sending the enclosed letter addressed to Lord Allenby for your signature. My doctor ordered me out of town for a few days' rest, otherwise he said I would not be able to meet the heavy demands upon me in the next few weeks. It is so good of you to give this reception in honor of the Allenbys and on behalf of the members of the National Spiritual Assembly I cannot find words to express my appreciation. I only hope that Lord and Lady Allenby will be able to spare the time in their great itinerary to give us all this opportunity to express our devotion and gratitude for the historic service which Lord Allenby rendered in the most crucial hour of our beloved Master.

May's work in public relations and her commitment to teaching the Faith in Canada was not only pursued in influential circles. As can be seen in the list she made, a few years later, of all the people who were attending meetings in her house on Pine Avenue, in Montreal, the doors of her heart and home were open to all. She wrote this list on Friday, 1 September 1933, but it gives some idea of the range and variety of her contacts in the late twenties. Many of them were simple, ordinary people and some would rise to great distinction in their services to the Cause:

Women	**Men**	
Janet French	Fred Schopflocher	Mr. Lagne
Ruth Lee	Emeric Sala	Frank Burnett
Marjorie McNeil	Gerard Sluter	Mr. Popliger
Dorothy Ward	Ronnie Hofman (David)	Mr. Leach
Rosemary Gillies	Eddie Elliot	Leach's friend
Elizabeth Cowles	Mr. Daird	Mr. Maxwell
Mary Maxwell	Mr. Prenidas	Thin man?
May Maxwell	Friend	Michel Ortenberg
Regina	Mr. Marshall	
Poppie Rickman	Mr. Jones	
Alberta Simms	Friend	
Nora Johnson	Audie Herran	
Liv de Livi	Mr. Robert	

* * *

May knew how much Sutherland suffered from her absences. She too missed her 'two darlings' and was forever hoping to be with them again. But as soon as she was back home, there would be a flood of meetings in the house and a flow of visitors passing through the doors of 1548 Pine Avenue. Sutherland, whose temperament inclined him to be somewhat reclusive, was swept up in a whirlwind of activity on May's return. It cannot have always been easy. The manner in which he coped with such strains on his sensibility was exemplary. The Guardian gave May the rare accolade of a martyr after her death but he called Sutherland 'saintly'.

Even saints sometimes reach their limits, however. Sutherland was not always happy when his wife placed her Bahá'í obligations before everything else in life. From time to time, this long-suffering and patient man protested. And in May 1927, after seeing May assume all the work of the Assembly in setting up the Convention in Montreal and then finding himself the sole parent at home when Mary was sick with tonsillitis,[1] Sutherland finally put his foot down. He refused to let

---

1 On 25 May Sutherland wrote to May that Mary's temperature was 102/5 at night: 'Dr. Quackenbush keeps in close touch with her – uses his electric lamp for inspecting and I had a talk with him – an hour ago . . .'

her go off on yet another teaching trip when it seemed to him that she had been away from home for long enough. She must have heard the warning bells for, on 28 May 1927, she confessed to Elizabeth Greenleaf that her husband had 'taken a stand':

> Jackie will have told you of our telephone conversation and my great disappointment in not coming. Sutherland was really upset; the Master told me I should appreciate his love and generosity in giving me so freely to the Cause and that he would obtain his everlasting reward, but when he takes the stand that he did last night, and feels so disturbed and resentful as though some great injustice were being done, I must yield or I would not be free to carry on the work of the National Assembly this year, which I must admit is of supreme importance. He said that although he did not want me to be on the NSA and that he felt it very keenly yet he accepted it as the will of the majority and would cheerfully let me go to the meetings each month provided they would hold at least one meeting this year in Montreal.

Sutherland had not only come to the end of his own tether but also knew May's propensity to over-stretch her physical limits. When she was not on the road travel-teaching or attending meetings, his dear wife was usually laid up in a hotel in some remote town half-way across the country recuperating from the strain or the Canadian winter. May must have done all she could to restrict her trips between Montreal and Toronto in 1927 therefore, in order to try to respect her husband's feelings, but there is no doubt that her most interesting services in Canada at this time were linked to her continued collaboration with Elizabeth Greenleaf.

They made an effective team. May was the planner, the organizer and the public speaker; Elizabeth was the steady functionary, the 'doer'. But they used a different strategy in Toronto from the one they had followed in Vancouver the previous year. This time, in order not to stray too far from home May travelled back and forth from 1548 Pine Avenue to Toronto while Elizabeth remained *in situ*, arranging meetings and making sure that May's punctual visits received the maximum publicity. The headline of one Toronto paper from June of 1927 announced two lectures which May was to give:

EXPONENT OF BAHÁ'Í CREED ARRIVES IN CITY
FROM EAST TO DIFFUSE IDEAL PRINCIPLES.

Mrs. Maxwell will speak in the New Thought church Sunday evening and on June 17th will address the Soroptimists' Club. Today her guests are members of the British Progressive League . . . Mrs. Maxwell is traveling through Canada with Elizabeth Greenleaf for the diffusion of the ideal principles of the Bahá'í movement.

Marion Jack also joined in this historic teaching campaign in Toronto. She had been one of May's spiritual children from the early days in Paris, and her love for May was nurtured by their collaboration in the teaching field all through the first decades of the twentieth century.[2] Writing to Marion in September 1919, for example, when she had gone to teach the Faith in Alaska, May described the unity amongst the Bahá'ís who were teaching the Cause together. Their letters, she said, were being passed round among the friends

> and read with tender joy because you blessed souls are in the front ranks, and the gaze of the Divine Commander is upon you, and the faithful hearts and prayers of His loved ones follow ever in your shining pathway . . . Since the Divine Convention we are all being drawn closer in the bonds of servitude and this servitude constitutes a flame of love and attraction which is uniting us all over the country, as one life, one soul, one body and one temple. The friends are no longer indifferent to the glowing and vital services of the dear ones far away but follow their activities with absorbed interest and joy. I have often realised that I am nearer to you and dearest Emogene than if we were in the same room . . .

While in Toronto in June 1927, May also wrote to Mountfort Mills to say that Leonora Holsapple had arrived to join the teaching work there, and on 22 June she wrote to Anne Savage, another soul to whom she had taught the Faith in Montreal, describing her joy in this partnership:

---

2   Writing to Rúḥíyyih Khánum in July 1949, Marion Jack, whom 'Abdu'l-Bahá called 'General Jack', said of May: 'There has never been anyone for me – outside the holy family – like May and I long to see her in the happy hunting ground bye & bye. Can I ever forget that day in Stuttgart when darling May told us of her early Paris service? Her writing about Thomas Breakwell is fine, but it lacks the first-hand account.'

We are having a wonderful time in Toronto. Marion Jack is unique in the pioneer field, she has a way of getting people together that is like a spiritual gift, and holding them together too, and Elizabeth is like a burning lamp amongst them and a fountain of living water. She has captivated the hearts and is confirming a number of souls.

She then asked Anne to make some compilations for her of the Writings. It was as though she wanted to involve her in the team too. 'I badly need these compilations in my work,' she told her, 'and the first one I would like to have is on immortality . . .' May had the art of recognizing the capacities of people. Some months later, upon learning of the financial plight of this dear soul, she wrote to Sutherland:

Just one important matter: a letter from Anne Savage written last month tells that they practically have nothing left to live on and will not be able to stay in Montreal. I suggest that the Spiritual Assembly appoint her as librarian in the new hall, with a salary of about $60 a month to keep it open in the afternoon and evenings, as a circulating library. This will keep one of the most precious members of our Assembly in Montreal and she will be very valuable in this capacity. See Anne about it as soon as possible and at the meeting let the suggestion come from you . . .

As had been the case in France, so in North America too, a great love connected these early Bahá'ís who collaborated with May during the late twenties. They had a tenderness of heart towards each other which frequently found expression in terms of unbounded affection, and they shared a spiritual bond that was surely immortal. May directed their gaze towards every opportunity to serve their beloved Faith in Canada and the United States and moved among them like a guiding star. She was also the one who bore witness to their sacrifices and their services; she was their spokesman and the guardian of their memories. Writing to Mary and Sutherland on 20 September 1927, she gave what amounted to a testimonial and tribute to a whole generation of Bahá'ís:

On Sunday the National Assembly all attended the funeral of Mrs. Dodge at St Marks in the Bowery. She and her family were the first to establish the Bahá'í Cause in New York City and their home was a haven of rest and hospitality for literally hundreds of thousands of people thru [sic] the years. Her funeral was impressive and deeply moving, the Episcopal service beautifully conducted by Dr. Guthrie; followed by the exquisite Bahá'í service conducted by Hooper Harris and Roy Wilhelm. Ned Kinney sang with an organ accompaniment and I can never describe all that I felt and lived through in that hour. All of the sacred past and deep associations in the Blessed Cause, of its early dawn when no one knew the Beloved was on earth except a little band of faithful ones who stood alone amongst the nations proclaiming the Blessed Name and laying in lives of service and sacrifice the Eternal Staff for His Cause. One by one those leaves of the Tree of Life are falling as the new young fruits of the new generation are appearing. What depths of God's love and Wisdom are revealed in the unfolding of His Plan and His Cause on the earth.

At the end of that same year, on 20 December, Keith Ransom-Kehler wrote to her in exquisite terms that showed how much the Bahá'ís depended on her example:

May – more than Mother – breath of the Master on my own soul, pray always that my deeds may be acceptable to Him and my action a praise to Him.

* * *

Despite her commitment to stay put that spring and the gratifying absence of correspondence during the summer, which bears witness to a family reunited at last, May was off again by the autumn of 1927, and the pressure on the accelerator was back on. After Sutherland's and Mary's return to Montreal by car, May issued a warning to them in her letter of 20 September from New York about the obligations ahead of them in 1928. They were responsibilities she could not avoid, and indeed welcomed:

I am happy to have both of your wires and I cannot imagine how you got home so quickly unless you flew, but I rather suspect a little driver that I know who certainly can get speed out of that car, more speed than anyone I ever saw. However, she must not speed in

Montreal because if she once gets caught up on it she cannot drive the car again for a whole year, and besides it is a great strain on the car . . .

Ruhi Effendi will probably come to our home for a couple of weeks to re-write his lecture course for the University as the National Assembly has highly approved this plan and has put the whole thing in my hands to carry out. You both know how happy and thankful I shall be to offer the hospitality of our home to a member of the Master's family and I know both will cooperate in that beautiful and loving way you always do and show Ruhi every kindness and consideration so that he may be happy and tranquil and inspired to write his lectures in the deepest and most wonderful way, because this is the most important undertaking since the visit of the Master to America, as Ruhi will lay the true Bahá'í foundation in the coming generation among the students in our centers of learning. And it is the power of God that has brought this about and I cannot be sufficiently thankful that we are privileged to help and cooperate in any humble way in our power in this great service.

Ruhi Afnan had requested permission to come to America, and though not sent officially by the Guardian, had been encouraged to meet the Bahá'ís while he was in the United States. The informal gatherings which had to be arranged for him involved a huge amount of effort and organization, most of which fell on May's shoulders. She was the one who had to prompt the invitations in the first place, adapt them to the needs of the believers as well as Ruhi's schedule, arrange for the logistics, and frequently pay for the transport herself. It was not easy. As she wrote to Lorol Schopflocher on 28 February 1928, she had to organize conferences in 'sixteen cities in a period of one month, calculating the necessary time in each place according to the needs and conditions of the group; not to mention the more arduous labour of stirring the Spiritual Assemblies and arousing their enthusiasm for the right type of public meetings in their cities . . .'. But it is highly indicative of her positive nature that she saw the challenge of doing all this work as 'a new and thrilling experience . . .' rather than an additional burden on her shoulders.

This conference tour was only one of the many she arranged for other quasi-permanent travel teachers such as Howard Colby Ives and

Louis Gregory. Whenever she wintered in New York, she also encouraged other Bahá'ís, like Orcella Rexford, to give public meetings and special courses. On Sunday, 5 January 1929, for example, Orcella wrote to her saying that she had given a lecture in the Pythian Temple on 'What is God?' – a basic introduction to the Bahá'í Faith, to about four hundred people. 'On Monday evening', she reported triumphantly to May, she had spoken 'to about eight hundred people . . . and Tuesday evening to about the same audience.' Five days later, on 10 January, she announced that 'A class of about one hundred and fifty . . . were turned over to Keith Ransom-Kehler to teach at the next meeting.' It was an example of the systematic method of teaching and deepening which May had begun to implement, with Shoghi Effendi's encouragement. It was also an example of the way May's vigour and intensity in the teaching field acted like a magnet to others. Her very movement caused others to stir.

On 20 February 1928, she wrote to Mrs Schopflocher: 'The measure of my silence is likewise the measure of my work for the past few weeks.' Typically, she never thought for a moment that the range of the activities she herself rendered in her administrative capacity was in any way a measure of her own commitment to the Cause. She interpreted these opportunities as proof of the grace of God and the goodness of her fellow Bahá'ís to her. It is salutary to discover the manner in which she literally interpreted work as worship. She continued, in the above letter, to thank Mrs Schopflocher for such wonderful chances to serve the Faith:

> . . . and I owe much of this happiness to you for having so generously given me the opportunity to be Secretary and I hope that the members of the National Teaching Committee will be pleased with the results.

During the Riḍván period that year, right up until 5 May 1928, May was in Chicago and in Evanston, Illinois. The 20th National Convention was, in her words: 'this very inspiring Convention, held for the first time in the Foundation Hall of the Temple'. To live history is something many do without being aware of it; to realize the privilege is something few do, except in retrospect. But May did both: she recognized the significance of the day in which she lived even as she experienced it. She was once again elected to the National Spiritual Assembly that year and one can only surmise what Sutherland thought of the fact.

He was busy applying for new architectural commissions as well as completing old ones during this period. Already, in the autumn of the previous year, with May marooned in New York and Mary skipping her studies in order to look after her mother, he had been under mounting pressure at work. Sending him encouragement and reassurance on 27 October 1927, May mentioned some of his projects at this time:

> I have been so delighted to hear the results of your work for Collins and I am sure the whole thing will be a finished work of art and will charm him as your work in his office did before. I love to hear all about your work and just what you are doing and keep as close to you in every way as possible, especially now that my strength is returning and I am less submerged and am becoming more conscious of my life and its vital connections.
>
> You need not worry over my taking up any work; I am coddling myself like a new born baby and turning over all my national teaching work to this new committee with a great sigh of relief. I feel that I need months of real rest and just the National Teaching work which will always give me supreme strength and inspiration.

She was, as her daughter later wrote, a very 'traditional' wife: she was sincerely concerned about her husband's professional commitments and gave her wholehearted attention to his work. A few days later, on 31 October, she wrote again, full of appreciation for his letters and reassurance regarding her health. She had evidently fallen sick again, exactly as her husband had predicted the previous year, and she was anxious to make amends:

> You have been writing me so often and I deeply appreciate it with all you have to do because your letters are such a joy and comfort. You know the Master said – 'a letter is half a meeting' and it seems to bring you so close to hear all the details of your work and how everything is going . . .
>
> Well, darling, you ought to be very proud of me because for your sake and Mary's I am giving up a very important meeting with the National Teaching Committee and letting them go it alone,

although I am supposed to be the Chairman. After all, we are none of us needed as much as we think we are and I know the work will go on splendidly with this strong committee.

Sutherland had his own deadlines to meet in the new year and early spring too. While May was busy in New York with public meetings and Mary was chauffeuring the cousin of the Guardian from New York to Montreal, 'little Bill' was 'on the jump' with architectural plans, as he wrote laconically to his wife on 4 April 1928:

Mary and Ruhi arrived this A. M. I came down to breakfast and they were calmly enjoying their meal.

It was a great satisfaction to personally greet fifty percent of my family and the balance will receive an equally cordial welcome on arrival . . .

Pitts is still confined to his home with a cold but will appear tomorrow, weather permitting.

I have just about finished plans for the conversion of an old residence facing Fletcher's Field, with an apartment house scheme. I have another to do for the same parties. I have to complete a perspective for the golf club by Monday so little Bill is on the jump.

I gather from Ruhi and Mary that your appearance is satisfying and that you look well – I know it will take some time to get yourself rested but it will take place.

Mary likes the china and two prints of Aberdeen where the MacBeans came from.

Well Gyp is feeling antique but showed signs of life at seeing Mary. Polly Junior is more agile.

I am well and send a great deal of love to my treasure.
    Love Sutherland

Mary says be sure and get the shoes you purchased at Hannan's in New York.

His wife must have laughed at the dryness of his humour but no doubt picked up on his anxieties. Sutherland had never been one to waste words, but May knew when he needed her affection and encouragement. In a letter written on 5 May 1928, she took great care to concentrate on his activities and interests, although she was writing about the teaching work with great excitement to Mary at this same time:

> Your letter came this morning and although it was brief, it contained all the good news I long to hear.
>
> I am so glad that you are going ahead with the golf club, and I feel that you will get Taits' and Dodd's house to do, although it is a pity that this work is coming just now when later you should have a summer vacation.
>
> However, you can probably arrange that and in either July or August we can all have some time together in some lovely cool place . . .
>
> It is splendid that you and Mary are bowling and getting exercise together, and that you are both so well, and now that the weather is becoming mild and settled, I hope you will soon take up your golf.
>
> You must have enjoyed your Pen and Pencil Club dinner, and I know of old, what artistic menus you make. I hope you will let me see them when I return. Are you still buying lovely books and what is the latest? My eyes are much stronger, and when I return, I am going to browse around and enjoy those fascinating pictures in your beautiful book collection.
>
> A couple of days ago I went to see Carl Scheffler's Art School which is just a block from my hotel; he is doing a portrait of a very attractive woman, and really paints very well, and the whole composition and background were good. He teaches in his Art School, pen and ink drawings, color posters, advertising, enamel box work with brilliant Art Nouveau colorings and flowers, dressmaking and designing, and various other forms of decorative work. You know he is our Treasurer on the N.S.A. and the most unartistic looking person you could imagine, not temperamental, nor does he suggest the Artist in any way, and yet he is able to carry on this very successful commercial art school.
>
> Of course I know, Darling, what you would think of it all, but then you are a rare being, with that fine type of discrimination and sense of beauty which so few have . . . I have just had a longing to write you this little letter to let you know that I am thinking of you all the time, that I am steadily improving in my health, and that I send you all my love.

Writing to her daughter two weeks later on the 19th, May confessed that she could not help herself from longing to return to her teaching work but promised:

> I shall not overwork, because we have decided to distribute the work over every member of the Committee, but I would lose the mainspring of my strength and inspiration if I had to give it up.

No wonder that, despite Sutherland's 'stand' the year before and May's own efforts to restrain her travels and activities, normal family life for the Maxwells became the exception rather than the rule. As May wrote to Harlan Ober on 11 September 1928:

> I suppose Grace is home again and your children with you, and you are all re-united, as we are; one of those rare spells of complete family life of the Maxwell family!

* * *

Although her daughter's well-being was of vital concern to May, she had always made it very obvious to Mary that her priorities lay elsewhere. Just as she had warned Sutherland before she married him that the Cause had precedence over every other commitment, so too she made it clear to her daughter from a very early age that the needs of the Faith came first in her life. As a result, Mrs Maxwell managed to remain her daughter's closest friend throughout her adolescent years. Her note written to Mary on 13 November 1924 from Chicago reflects her priorities clearly:

> You must have had a beautiful meeting at the house last night to celebrate the birthday of Bahá'u'lláh. I was with you all in thought and spirit and simply longed to be with you, but I attended the feast here and spoke to the friends again of the beloved Guardian. They cannot hear enough of him and I have felt it my duty to stay and water this parched land and help to establish his standards and ideals for this Spiritual Organization. I know how you and Daddy have missed me, but I also know that God will greatly bless you for the sacrifice you make for the Cause in letting me go.

Well darling today I had a reward beyond anything I could ever deserve, a message from Shoghi Effendi through Mirza Azizullah Khan, dated October 16th, 1924.

Shoghi Effendi says that his heart is happy, that he is pleased with my letter, that next time I write he will answer me with his own hand, that he hopes I am working vigorously to unite the hearts of the friends. He sent you his love ...

I know all this will make you very happy and you must let Daddy read every word of this letter as I am too tired to write him tonight but will do so tomorrow.

I expect to be home next week, in the meantime I am so glad you are getting on well with your studies and that you had such a lovely time at your cousin's.

With love and kisses to you and Daddy.

But by the late twenties a crisis was looming. May had tried to train her daughter in accordance with 'Abdu'l-Bahá's directives. She had kept her attention focused on service to the Cause in response to the Guardian's hopes. And she involved her more and more in the work of the Faith as she grew up. But by 1928 she was beginning to realize that although Mary had attained her spiritual maturity and gone on pilgrimage two years before, there was still much she had to learn. Although her resolution to apply herself more systematically to her studies on her return from pilgrimage had been sincere, it was hard to break old habits.

Mrs Maxwell always gave her daughter the benefit of the doubt. Her little notes of encouragement constantly echo and reaffirm Shoghi Effendi's wishes over this period. On 26 August 1926 she wrote to Mary from Portsmouth:

Mary darling, are you getting lots of sleep and taking the best conscientious care of yourself for the sake of your studies as Shoghi Effendi wishes? To live for Him, for His well-being and happiness and to serve Him in all that we do, nothing else can be compared with this can it dearest?

Four months later, on 10 December of that same year, May wrote to Mary again from Boston, where she was wintering:

> I really feel, Mary, that the great spiritual blessings which are coming to you in guiding so many souls to the Blessed Cause, is not only due to the power of spiritual attraction which 'Abdu'l-Bahá gave you, but also to your strict obedience to the instructions of Shoghi Effendi. In these last days of consultation we have traced every difficulty and problem in the Cause to some form of disobedience to his instructions, and wherever blessings and confirmations flow we have found it to be due to obedience. I cannot tell you how these conferences with these beautiful souls have strengthened me, and how happy and full of faith I am.

Whenever she saw signs of progress in her daughter's study habits, May was full of encouragement. Writing to her 17-year-old on 19 May 1928, she enthused:

> I am glad you are making such good headway with your Political Economy and your studies in general. I am also glad to see an improvement in your handwriting, for it is an outer sign of an inner thing...

By 1930 Mary had taken charge of her own education, and in her early twenties she applied for enrolment as a non-resident student at Sarah Lawrence College in Westchester County, New York. Her mother explained her plans to a correspondent, at the end of January that year:

> Mary was planning to enter Sarah Lawrence College next Tuesday, but we have a slight draw back as they are not sure about her scholarship on certain points. They want to give her a test of some kind and then we hope she can enter and if not she will spend the rest of the year in a preparatory school so as to enter this College in the fall. She has been extremely keen on going there ever since hearing Dr. McCracken, who is President of the Sarah Lawrence College as well as of Vassar, when he spoke at the People's Forum here last year, and in my absence Mary entertained him and his wife at a dinner here.

The initial results seemed promising when Mary visited the college on 6 February 1930 in the company of her uncle, Randolph Bolles. Writing to her daughter two days later, May expressed relief at the news of the interview:

The French liner S. S. Paris, on which May and Mary Maxwell crossed the Atlantic Ocean, leaving New York on 7 March 1923 en route to pilgrimage

Programme of the 'Concert Symphonique' of 11 March 1923 on board ship

Mary Maxwell, age 12, riding 'Petty' in front of the Western Bahá'í Pilgrim House, Haifa, 1923

May and Mary Maxwell at Ramleh, Egypt, 1923

May Maxwell with Dr Lotfullah Hakim at Ramleh, 1923

Mary Maxwell at about 13 or 14 years of age

The R. M. S. Mauretania, *from which Mary wrote to her parents 'on board the ship' to Haifa, with Juliet Thompson and Daisy Smith, 9 April 1926*

Sixteen-year-old Mary Maxwell, the year of her second pilgrimage

William Sutherland Maxwell at the Arts Club Ball, Montreal, February 1925

Princess Marie Antoinette de Broglie with May and Sutherland Maxwell, in the garden of the Maxwell home in Montreal, August 1927, and below, with Mary Maxwell

This is the only photograph found of the three Maxwells of Montreal together. It was taken in 1927 when Mary was 17 years old

Daddy and I are very happy over the encouraging news of your school and we still hope that you will be able to enter some time this month as a non-resident for special courses. I expect to be in New York on Monday to take you to the school Tuesday to interview some of the teachers and will let you know definitely when to expect me... Last night I received an Epistle from the Guardian in which he speaks of you most lovingly and his great hopes for your future as a Bahá'í teacher. I will bring the letter with me.

The letter from the College on 11 February 1930 also confirmed the possibility that Mary Maxwell could take a scholastic aptitude test some days later:

> ... In as much as Miss Maxwell has had no education experience in schools comparable to that of our students we felt that a different form of admission might be devised to fit her case...
>
> If Miss Maxwell can obtain a grade on this examination which the Committee feels is of such merit that it would prove her unusual training adequate and her equipment suitable for our work, they will be glad to set examinations in three fields chosen by her for which she might prepare, and take them in June.
>
> Our policy is to require fifteen units of secondary school work satisfactory for graduation. We are, however, interested in a girl with exceptional talent or ability and on this ground we offer this opportunity at this time for your daughter to ... give us proof of such ability.

But unfortunately, her unconventional educational background had not equipped Mary for such examinations. Had she been this motivated earlier in her adolescence, she would have easily acquired the basic skills for enrolment at Sarah Lawrence. However, later that year she became a part-time student at McGill University, where she studied Economics and History, receiving second class honours in a fourth-year Economics course.

Amatu'l-Bahá never blamed her mother for her lack of formal schooling in her early years. On the contrary, in later life she recognized the hand of providence in her educational peregrinations. Had she succeeded better in her own intellectual achievements, would she have been willing to forgo the honours and the opportunities they provided? Could she have identified so passionately with the illiterate and the deprived throughout her life or been so intrepid in her readiness to take on such extraordinary physical and psychological challenges?

The reality was that her mother had given her the greatest spiritual education in the world. Their unity, their kinship, their eternal bond was built on it. And as the years went by, it was this education on which she would have to rely when it came to the real spiritual tests she had to face; it was this training on which she was to depend. Her mother taught her to distinguish between the important and the most important from an early age, and by the time she was in her late teens, she had been groomed to be May's most trusted and effective partner in the teaching field – an honour greater than any college diploma, a distinction higher than any academic degree.

* * *

May trusted the spiritual bond she had with young Mary. She had sown the seeds of faith in her daughter from early childhood and had faith in their fruits. Besides, 'Abdu'l-Bahá had given her a promise regarding this harvest, a promise to which she had clung over the years. She never forgot it; she always reminded her daughter of it. On 23 February 1925, during her winter sojourn in New York, May had quoted the Master's words directly to Mary:

> It made me very happy to hear the clear tones of your dear voice on the telephone last night and after all the days of longing and loneliness, it brought me such sweet relief and comfort to speak to you, to find you so helpful, cheerful and selfless. I thought of the words of the beloved Master about you when he [sic] said: 'God gave her to you to be a comfort to you.'

The following year, on 10 December 1926, shortly after Mary's return from pilgrimage, Mrs Maxwell referred to the significance of this spiritual bond again:

> Last night your spirit came to me in the most sweet and lovely way – I felt that you had prayed for Mother and you just seemed to be

enfolded in my heart and soul in that way that has come to be so deep and precious to you and me.

When Mary was 16 or 17, her mother echoed this same promise in another undated letter:

> I feel your love and prayers always and your pleasant influence in my life, and you are not only my daughter but my dear spiritual companion and comfort and blessing as the beloved Master said you would be.

And soon afterwards, when the World Unity Movement held its conference in Montreal, May wrote a letter to Shoghi Effendi on 14 June 1928, enclosing the names of those who were working, as she put it, 'for the absolute union and close affiliation' of this association with the Faith, and included the names of at least two youth, both of whom had been among those chosen to unveil the Tablets of the Divine Plan eight years earlier: Elizabeth Coristine and her own daughter. It was a practical demonstration of her confidence in Mary's collaboration in the teaching work:

> Our very beloved Guardian,
> Nine of us have gathered and humbly supplicate for the absolute union and close affiliation of the World Unity Movement with the direct Bahá'í Teaching in this country.
> With yearning love and devotion we are thine:
>
> Harlen Ober
> Ella G. Cooper
> Juliet Thompson
> Marie L. Hopper
> May Maxwell
> Lena L. Lee
> Grace Ober
> Elizabeth Coristine
> Mary Shirin Maxwell[1]
>
> Our supplication is conditioned upon the Will of God and your wisdom and judgment.

---

[1] For a short period in her teens, Mary Maxwell called herself 'Shirin'.

May's ability to teach her daughter the true meaning of faith reached its apogee when they were able to collaborate in teaching the Faith. When Mary wrote to her about teaching one of her friends in May 1928, she wrote back exultant:

> Your precious letter came this morning and it breathed of such a selfless devotion to the Cause, such insight and understanding, such a mature grasp of your responsibility in dealing with souls that I was both amazed and overjoyed . . . How happy you must be, Mary, to be doing this work . . . I heard 'Abdu'l-Bahá say in New York, 'There is no happiness in life compared to the joy of teaching a soul.' . . . My whole heart and soul are with you in the work you are doing and my love and prayers surround you all the time, my own precious daughter and spiritual companion.

Later still, on 3 December 1930 when Mary was 20 years old, her mother wrote to her from Geneva, New York, once more recalling the Master's words:

> You know in the Bible it says, to him to whom much has been given, much shall be required, and because you have received so much of the very essence of 'Abdu'l-Bahá's love and life and spirit, so, much is required of you and that is why your life, although it is young and normal and full of natural spontaneous joy, is yet like a fruitful tree, 'bearing the most wonderful imperishable [fruits]'.

Three years later, on 5 May 1933, her mother was even more explicit regarding Mary's spiritual obligations when she addressed her as 'you blest and fortunate daughter of 'Abdu'l-Bahá!' at the end of a note written to her during her stay in Washington.

May also gave her daughter the tools with which to resolve the paradoxes in her life. Writing to her on 8 March 1929, she instructed her in prayer and meditation:

> You do not know what it meant to me to speak to you on the telephone this morning and in these days of hard work I have felt your spirit and your new-found strength in the Cause nearer than ever before and the greatest support to me in all my work . . .

What I meant about this mental tension that you suffer from when you are alone is, of course, as you know, due to the activity of the objective mind and the greatest calm and tranquility of mind and spirit lies just beyond this over-busy brain. Of course our brains are just as busy when we are with other people but their presence and companionship creates a mental equilibrium which brings a reaction of a certain mental poise and calm; when we are alone we are in our own atmosphere and thoughts and the strain can become very great.

Bahá'u'lláh, 'Abdu'l-Bahá and even within the last year Shoghi Effendi, have all shown us ways to pass into the deeper water of the inner spiritual mind, it is a delicate mental adjustment to which we can gradually become accustomed if we use their methods.

The objective mind is the driving mental faculty in relation to our surroundings and sustained all unquestionably by an effort of the will. I have not time now to give you all the references of the tablets and teachings on this subject . . . However, in the meantime Shoghi Effendi's instructions regarding prayer and meditation are found extraordinarily helpful when persevered in. I will just give you a summary of the teachings as I know them on this subject.

The first stage of prayer is petition or request; the second, is supplication, which is a step beyond the first, relating more to spiritual things; the third, is to enter into a conscious connection and this is the first stage of the deep waters of the calm inner mind. Shoghi Effendi said, first, turn to Bahá'u'lláh and pray, laying the matter before Him; secondly, become calm and receptive and attentive and <u>wait for the reply</u>. Third, when you receive the impression of guidance or the reply or the wave of Spirit, however it may be, inwardly and firmly decide to act in accordance with this guidance <u>without wavering</u>. (That is, he says, we must firmly accept and establish the attitude or guidance we have had and not become undecided or wavering); fourth, to have absolute <u>faith and conviction</u>; fifth, that this faith and conviction and this inner inflexible decision may become so united, so strong that we may move and act in a way to actually produce the desired results. In other words, we unite ourselves consciously with God in a cooperative effort to carry out what He has revealed and shown to us, and in this way we gradually enter into a relationship with God which is sustained, calm and tranquil.

The cause for so much mental activity is also the rational mind, we think and rationalize everything and this keeps the mind in continual action. According to the Divine Teachings we substituted reason for faith, which is not only a deeper realm within the soul, but a universal world of light which envelopes the soul and with which through Faith we come in contact.

The objective mind seeks to solve and think out everything itself, the spiritual mind is <u>receptive</u>; receptivity, reflection and meditation are the keys to that calm and relaxed attitude by which the images of God are thrown into this calm and tranquil mirror of the heart, mind and soul. A great help towards this is to relax the body.

One thing more, this receptive and meditative attitude must never be blank or negative; it must be that quiet, positive, inner assurance in our relation to the Infinite Being. And since we know Him, and are in the continual stream of the radiance and spirit pouring from Shoghi Effendi, it is not difficult to gradually establish this inner relation attitude and consciousness.

In another letter I will give you some references; in the meantime, darling, I feel the greatest growth in you at this time that you have ever attained, a new strength and responsibility, spiritually and humanly and you will find that gradually this influence emanating from your life and character and development and Faith will affect your environment and everyone in your environment, whether you know them or not, who are attuned to the subtle vibrations of the Spirit.

'Abdu'l-Bahá said that one sincere and faithful and spiritual Bahá'í in a city, even though unknown, will affect the whole life of the people.

I am glad you are so well and happy my precious, and keep young and happy and joyous and have a good time and do not ponder along serious things, but relax and pray when you are not studying and working, because one of the greatest secrets for development for ourselves and others, the Master said, is true, joyous happiness. We have everything in the world to make us happy and I am so much better and stronger, Daddy is having a wonderful time and you are surrounded with love and friends and the opportunity to serve in the home of the Master.

The way in which Mary was trained by her mother to value spiritual above material education makes fascinating reading. It was a training which was first and foremost based on moral values, demonstrated by deeds, through May's generosity towards her daughter, her encouragement, her trustworthiness. But this moral training was also expressed in words. May praised Mary's growing maturity whenever she could. She looked for every opportunity to point out improvements in her behaviour. Writing to her on 26 June 1928, she commended her thoughtfulness towards others:

> This is just to tell you, my darling, how much I love you, and appreciate your beautiful qualities. I know you went back to New York for my sake, so that I could be alone and rest and collect my thoughts for my work for a couple of days, and this is the sign of your growth and development, your deeper spiritual understanding of life and its true purpose. Also, you are much more selfless in little things, such as doing without things you want, helping me to economize (not my strong point), and in regulating your window at night to suit your guests rather than yourself.

In another letter written to her on 17 January 1929, she commented:

> This morning the manicurist from the Hotel Roosevelt was saying some very sweet things about you. She spoke of your considerateness in little things, little thoughtful acts of service which she has noticed and which she considered not only signs of a beautiful character but of good breeding. And I do feel this great growth and development in you, Mary darling, and I am sure you are remembering your promise to me to be very kind and considerate while you are with the Coristines; keep your room in order and altogether behave like a 'gentleman'.

The following month, on 6 February 1929, May sounded a note of warning. She also had to teach her daughter to distinguish between teaching the Cause and respecting the rights of others:

> You know that we cannot interfere radically with other people's lives, nor change their environment, because . . . Bahá'u'lláh says that

there are no accidents in life and it is not wise to unsettle people in relation to their home and family and their environment, although it is good to arouse in them new ambition, courage and intelligence. These two things are not the same – one is a right, spiritual and Bahá'í influence and the other is a disturbing, disrupting force.

Some time later, May wrote another letter to her daughter from Geneva, New York:

My darling Mary,
That was a lovely letter you wrote me, filled with such a potency of the spirit that it revived my whole being. I had been rather weary from this intensive Committee work but your letter affected me just as elixir, and I have noticed this quality in your letters in the past year which is a proof that the power of God's spirit is working through you.
. . . It is so sweet of you darling always to tell me about my 'spiritual children', those who you think were attracted to the Cause through your mother and it is this great love you have for me and your faith in me that often revives my hope and courage.
Do you realize Mary how greatly your spiritual life has deepened and how the spirit of selflessness is becoming so manifest in you that it even breathes through your words? I suppose I notice this particularly because in the past months I have reflected a great deal on the state of consciousness of the western world and it has been borne in upon me ever more clearly and forcibly that it is primarily the <u>mind</u> of the west that has matured, the power of the intellect as it relates to the external universe; and that the soul, the innate character, that which relates to the world of heart, ethics and of the spirit, is so undeveloped that it is like a tiny child. This great disparity in the individual and in the nation, is a startling realization and it is obvious that this real nature of man will not evolve from the embryo to the mature being save through the power of Bahá'u'lláh and His infinite spirit. I observed this first in the world and then I studied it in the Bahá'í Cause and I have realized that our growth has been stunted, the progress of the Cause retarded, its inner significance undeveloped and its depths unfathomed. Not so much because of the average level of development and consciousness of the believers

as because many people have been put in key positions of trust and influence in whom only the intellect was developed, while spiritually, morally and hence in their deeper and diviner relations, they were still infants.

'Abdu'l-Bahá said, 'Unless your entire life and character is changed by the power of this great Cause it is better never to hear of it.'

I am not now speaking of the fact that the mental and intellectual aspect of the believers without that moral and spiritual regeneration is overbalanced in the Cause. I mean that this mental aspect has actually been taken as a substitute for the reality and this is a very deep and serious thing. Undoubtedly the older believers and teachers have not deliberately and consciously directed the new believers coming into the Cause and the younger generation growing up in it, to the <u>true foundation</u>. They took it for granted and have not realized that a generation is growing up around us of new believers, whose roots are not firmly established in the spiritual soil of the divine teachings, but who have grasped the great generalities and fundamental truths of the Bahá'í revelation intellectually, who have felt a certain emotional reaction toward its great beauty and truth but in whom the moulding, creative, regenerating power of the spirit is not actively operative.

It is no wonder we have had to pass through such severe tests in New York and elsewhere in order to make us aware of the presence of the spirit and the direct power of God in our lives . . .

I have reflected much upon the words of Bahá'u'lláh, 'Until one has reached the station of sacrifice <u>he is deprived of all good</u>,' and I have realized that in the West through our lack of spiritual understanding and insight, sacrifice is regarded as something difficult and painful instead of the very joy of life itself; it is like a bird singing, giving out all the energy of its quivering little body in order to pour that melody into the air and this is its joy and ecstasy.

The whole Christian concept of religion, being a religion that found its expression in the West, is materialistic; a somewhat gloomy and severe God requiring prayers and propitiation; Who, having made the world so wicked, sacrificed His son on the cross as an act of propitiation against His angry and vengeful spirit toward mankind; a religion full of dogma, creed, form and ritual as alibis for a pure, devoted and sacrificial life; so much easier to offer prayers and candles, to go through forms and ceremonies, to adhere to some professed religious doctrine, than to live a daily radiant, beautiful life full of service to God and to our fellow men. Everything beautiful that God has given us we have twisted into a penance and a duty so that even our schools have been for centuries uninteresting and unattractive, our philanthropic institutions, places of discipline and depression, and our institutions of penance and reform centers of vengeance and cruelty. All these things have sprung from our dark concepts of the glorious God Who through the intensity and excess of His love created beings out of the substance of His love to live forever in the wonders of His love and to make this life a school for learning the secrets of His love.

We have taken the very signs and symbols of His love on this earth, marriage and the home and the child and submerged them in the darkness of our ignorant concepts of the divinity of sex and birth and we have so warped the fabric of human society that in our so-called advanced civilized state millions of human beings can find no work and must either be a charge upon the public or die and when we stop to think that in the midst of all this that the money that is being expended at this very hour on preparations for war and means for destroying the creation of God, if it were turned into the channels of human life and well-being would lift this entire crushing burden off the world, giving every human being their rightful place in society in relation of the ideal forces of mankind! What a spectacle! It is no wonder 'Abdu'l-Bahá tells us that it is only through the regeneration of the individual that the world can hope to be regenerated and in the words of Shoghi Effendi that only to the extent to which our private lives and personal characters conform to the divine teachings can we hope to impress the validity of our sacred Faith upon mankind.

. . . I shall wire you and daddy now telling you that I am still here and shall wire you when I leave and where I am going so that we can always keep in the closest touch and in the meantime it is the greatest support and inspiration for me to see how you are becoming an ever-increasing centre through which the bounty of 'Abdu'l-Bahá and the spirit of Shoghi Effendi are flowing to the group in Montreal and you can share any parts of this letter you may wish with the younger Bahá'ís ... how kind it was of them to write me and I shall be sending you all another communication ere long.

Give daddy a big hug and kiss for me and with tender love my own Mary.

It was typical of May to widen her embrace to include any of Mary's friends and other 'young Bahá'ís' with whom she might wish to share this letter. Her relationship with her daughter was intimate, personal, tender and unique, but never exclusive, and her bond with Mary's generation is a whole subject in itself.

* * *

In the fiery ordeals of the year 1929, the mettle of the three Maxwells of Montreal was tested and proved to be pure gold.

1929 has become synonymous for most people with the collapse of the world financial markets. It has been seen, in retrospect, as a critical turning point in Western democracies, a financial watershed that was to have an effect on generations to come. This economic catastrophe was not the single cause of the Great Depression of the 1930s, which led to the rise of fascism throughout Europe and another calamitous world war, but it played an important part in the birth of the first international institutions conceived to regulate wealth and poverty on the planet. Although these institutions, like the League of Nations before and the United Nations later, would prove embryonic in capacity and restricted in authority, and although the Bretton Woods Accord, which gave rise to the International Monetary Fund and the World Bank consequent to World War II, would need revising and re-evaluating as the world grew increasingly interdependent, the collapse of Wall Street must surely mark a milestone on the long road towards the Lesser Peace.

The storm did not break out of a blue sky. Shrewd analysts had already forecast a threatening economic future for Europe in the clouds gathering over the signing of the disastrous Treaty of Versailles, in 1919. After the horrors of World War I, the twenties were notorious for both frivolity and despair. This was a period of thoughtless wealth and post-war poverty, when the rich grew giddy on glamour and gauze while the poor were dangerously ignored. In some ways, this epoch, which produced Scott Fitzgerald's *The Great Gatsby* and was followed by John

Steinbeck's *The Grapes of Wrath,* was similar to the early years of the 21st century. For in the years leading up to the Wall Street crash there was a sense of unreality in the air, a mood of cynicism and speculation combined, a tendency towards decadence on the one hand and despotism on the other. And the financial irresponsibility of some, combined with the economic uncertainty of others, created instability in minds as well as markets. The period *'entre les deux guerres'* was one in which people lived on credit and looked for their salvation in stocks and shares.

The Maxwells were people of a certain social standing in Montreal, a certain heritage, and they lived much as other members of their class might do – with the same enjoyment of luxuries when they could afford them, the same concern to invest in the 'right' bonds to reap more interest, the same pleasure in buying new cars, new clothes, new art objects to adorn their home. Except that their home was inundated with a constant stream of visitors, many of whom would never have crossed the threshold of other houses in Westmount. Except that their priorities were on teaching the Bahá'í Faith and serving the cause of peace in ways most people thought irrelevant at that time. Except that they were willing to forgo their personal needs, their personal comfort and time, in order to sacrifice for that Cause.

It is interesting to read the words of Mrs Maxwell to her daughter at such a time, when everyone around them was accruing wealth and speculating on their assets. Writing to her on 19 May 1928, May encouraged her to place her trust in the far greater security of Bahá'u'lláh's mighty Covenant, and assured her:

> Mary darling, we have no need to be anxious about anything, for the affairs of all mankind are in the grasp of God and we are hastening toward that time when He Himself will put a quietus on all our human plans and everyone will come under the thrall of His power. . . . [I]n a recent message Shoghi Effendi has said that he will tell us all what to do in ample time. What a refuge and calm this gives me, because His people will be protected and they in turn will be a protection for others. The more I study human conditions and the awful state of humanity today, the low, unevolved types that people the earth, scarcely awakened even to the knowledge of their humanity, much less their spiritual destiny, the more I realize the inevitability of certain events.

May's personal attitude to finances was marked by the liberality of spirit that characterized all her actions. Her generosity towards others was boundless in adverse as well as prosperous times. Her acts of charity were legion throughout her life and there are many examples of how she treated the indigent and the needy. She was like a fountain to all who crossed her path, bubbling with generosity, ever-giving. And she was sometimes a little profligate too, by her own admission; her contributions and her gifts extended beyond the limits of responsibility. Like many who strive for spiritual detachment, she considered it a spiritual weakness to be preoccupied by money-matters. But paradoxically enough, beneath her unstinting magnanimity and frequent extravagance, May was also quite shrewd when it came to a knowledge of her investments. She very much liked to be in charge of her own money.

Amatu'l-Bahá often used to say that 'Abdu'l-Bahá had advised her mother to consult her father in all financial matters. Rúḥíyyih Khánum used to tell the story of how her father, during these years of financial upheaval, having reduced May's fortune to half its value by an unwise investment to which she herself had been opposed, phoned her when she was in Green Acre in order to give her the dreadful news and asked, sheepishly, if she wanted to divorce him.

'Of course not, you idiot!' was her furious reply.

Four years later, at the height of the Depression, when May was approached by a Bahá'í with a request for a loan, her cable of 19 February 1934 to Sutherland and Mary, asking for their joint advice, reveals the spirit of unity and consultation shared by the three Maxwells of Montreal in making major decisions:

> _____ NEEDS URGENTLY TWO THOUSAND CAN PAY BACK WITH INTEREST ONE HUNDRED WEEKLY MAY I PUT UP COLLATERAL FIFTH AVENUE BANK HE TO PAY THEM WEEKLY PLEASE ADVISE ME BY WIRE

Their reply was written at the foot of the cable by Sutherland:

> Advise not lending P . . . Stop If his business is in such shape that his bankers will not accommodate him it is reckless to step into the breach Stop Your capital has been reduced too much already.

This response caused May acute concern, as she wrote to Mary on 21 February:

> Many thanks for your wire which, however, distressed me terribly... I have an entirely different conception of Bahá'í solidarity in which I believe our lives are so interwoven and interdependent that a balance must be maintained at every point, some are in financial need, others in need of health, others in need of love and understanding, others in need of a job, and so on indefinitely, and wherever we fail at any one point we unbalance the whole structure of these collective needs.
>
> For instance, yesterday I had to wire P. that I was awaiting Sutherland's reply and advice in this matter, and from [that] time... I was completely physically disintegrated, I felt physically desperately ill for the first time since I came out here. It came on so suddenly that at first I did not understand the cause... but I firmly believe it is the operating of the underlying law of unity. In this because, 'No man liveth unto himself and no man dieth unto himself,' and when I see wealthy Bahá'ís create spiritual deprivations I realize the terrible operating of this law...
>
> Our conceptions of unity thus far are childish and puerile. Nevertheless you and I have tested out certain basic principles (and no doubt others have done the same) through the law of love and this very fact opens up new vistas, new knowledge of these mighty and mysterious laws... if I had considered this fact alone I would have loaned... the money without a word to anyone, but now our family's solidarity has to be considered, we owe that to each other and to combine these slightly divergent, although not opposite, phases of unity and solidarity is our supreme problem...
>
> I will keep you and Daddy posted and will do nothing without our united action. Please read him what I have written you.

The daughter of May Bolles and William Sutherland Maxwell was similar to each and different from both her parents. She was a perfect mingling of their weaknesses and strengths and naturally much influenced by their example. But she was also a product of her times, as well as being unique in her response to it. Given her privileges of class and of birth, she received a salutary education in economics from the Wall Street crash. Like many girls, Mary Maxwell loved pretty clothes and jewellery. She was also fascinated by automobiles.² But unlike most of her contemporaries, she interpreted Black Thursday in non-materialistic ways. She was encouraged to think about the spiritual impact of the financial crisis and make it a stepping stone instead of a stumbling block in her life.

The Guardian's advice to Mary Maxwell on her pilgrimage in 1926, to study economics, was to prove prophetic during the Depression. Economic reform became one of the critical needs of the age. Spiritual values, however, soon emerged as being as important as monetary ones in North America. It was clear to Mary Maxwell that Bahá'í ideals were valueless unless expressed in practical terms. The focus of her final paper and its motivation are clearly reflected in the letter she wrote to the Professor of Economics at McGill University to whom she submitted her essay, on 8 May 1931. It was entitled 'The Bahá'í System of Public Finance'.

Dear Dr. Hemmion,

This essay is illustrative of a few of the plans proposed by Bahá'u'lláh for remedying our present economic–social disorder. I have enjoyed ever so much writing it and I hope you will like it!

No one could have shown a greater love and sympathy for the poor than 'Abdu'l-Bahá, indeed in the prison city of Akka where he was a political prisoner because of his Religion – he was known as the 'father of the poor'. However there was one side of the question I could not very well put in a paper on Public Finance, and that is the inner or more spiritual reasons for things happening. So I am

---

2   In September 1930, when Mary saw a second-hand Stutz, she was smitten on the spot. She bought it, without a second thought, with money she had been given by her mother. The Sedan her father had bought in June 1927 three years before was called a 'Peerless', but the Stutz was 'more peerless' by far! May, ever the exponent of courtesy and always ready to approve her daughter's choices, wrote to thank the man who had helped them purchase it: 'Mary and I were most grateful for your kind helpfulness and you may be interested to know that we bought the Stutz, a very high-powered car, extremely comfortable and satisfactory in every way, at a very low figure . . .' Three years later, however, May confessed that the peerless Stutz was too expensive for them to run. Deploring her husband's decision not to accompany her to the Convention that year, she wrote to Mary on 23 May 1933 about her disappointment, saying: 'There would be a great deal of expense involved in taking the Stutz on account of paying the storage, getting it ready with plates etc, and it uses so much gas and oil that we figured it would cost more than $50.00 round trip, in short more than the train.' The demise of the Stutz occurred shortly before Mary's departure for Europe in 1935. Perhaps it even saved her life, for it came between her and an ongoing tram which failed to stop at the lights where she was crossing. She was flung out on the pavement as the tram destroyed the car. But even late in life, Rúhíyyih Khánum continued to defend her acquisition stoutly, and would recall in detail the tooled leather body, the elegant lines, the purring speed achieved by this peerless but petrol-guzzling marvel.

going to append a few extracts that may bring this out more clearly.
 I hope I haven't bothered you too much over all this!
 Sincerely,
 Mary Maxwell

The response of another of Mary's professors at McGill, on 20 November 1930, to a proposal she had made to ameliorate the problems of unemployment in the city, also illustrates her earnest desire to apply spiritual theory to practice:

Dear Miss Maxwell,
 I am much interested in what you proposed. This is what I would like to do. I will write a paper pamphlet called *Unemployment. What You and I can do about it* and will at my expense print several thousands for distribution.
 I will call attention to the personal features of your scheme – free shelter, plain free food, 'canteen' work by organized volunteers, and subscription or the *Feed a Family* slogan. Before I print it I will read it over to you and your committee, or band or group & see if it fits in.
 Then you must get:–
(a) Some people of high standing like General Currie to send us the names, so that people will know that there is no fraud or graft
(b) And or one or two hundred young people as workers without pay, who will be ordered & controlled like a little army
(c) Canvassers who will go . . . to the offices & get money
(d) Two or three, – but only two or three – paid workers who will work all the time at the organization.
 I wish I could take a heavy part in the committee work but I am not well enough. But I will write the pamphlet & pay for it and will pay for a family & do all else that my time & strength allows.
 I am going to the country on Friday night for a rest over the week-end & will not be back till Tuesday afternoon. But perhaps, then, you might care to talk further of your plan.
 Very sincerely
 Stephen Leacock[3]

---

3 Canadian professor, author, lecturer and humourist who will long be remembered for his best-selling book *Sunshine Sketches of a Little Town* (1912) as well as the numerous awards and honours he received during his illustrious lifetime.

Leacock even went so far as to write to the Mayor of Montreal about Mary's proposal:

> Mayor Houde
> Montreal
>
> Dear Mr. Mayor
>   The bearer of this, Miss Mary Maxwell, is anxious to see if she can be of use in the present situation of unemployment & depression. She proposes to organize a band of (unpaid) workers to help in carrying on a canteen service & free meals & to collect the money to pay for it.
> Very faithfully,
Stephen Leacock
Professor Political Economy

May had always been the first to encourage her daughter to act on her ideals, and frugality was the first lesson she tried to teach her. Without in the least encouraging a miserly attitude in Mary, her mother wanted her to restrain herself from overspending. As early as 10 December 1926, she cautioned her against waste:

> Now, darling, about yourself, you must do as you think best about the jewellery you want for Christmas, provided it is not going to be too expensive. You know that almost all the beauty in jewellery lies in its art and Birks is an absolutely inartistic jewellers . . . Would it not be better to wait a little longer and go to one of those wonderful men in New York, who can make you something unique and beautiful?

One week later, on 18 December 1926, Mrs Maxwell wrote to Mary again addressing the awkward subject of consumerism directly:

> How are you getting on with your Christmas shopping? I had hoped to have a line from you so that we might work in close co-operation, but I know you have so much to do that I am not expecting it.
>   First, <u>one thing of great importance</u>, I want to impress on you; do not do all your shopping at Henry Morgan's just because we

have an account there, as it is the most expensive store in the city. There are lots of small places where you can pick up charming little things at almost half the price, and if I get a great big bill from Henry Morgan at the end of the month, I shall feel very much disappointed, because, darling, you and I know that those demands in the Cause of God come first, for it is progress and development which is the only hope of the yearning heart of Shoghi Effendi.

There, please do not waste any money.

I am enclosing a check for $20, which you can cash at the bank and spend in reasonable ways, for things that would cost $40, if you get them at Morgan's. I hope you and Daddy are working closely together and consulting about it all.

Also remember that we can find the loveliest, cheapest things in New York for Daddy and each other, so do not get anything there for us . . .

It may be well to remember that during this time many of the Bahá'ís in the East as well as the West still maintained traditional habits in connection with their Jewish, Christian or Muslim backgrounds. As late as 13 December 1930, Mrs Maxwell was still giving her daughter instructions about Christmas shopping, in a manner, it must be noted, more indicative of her own magnanimity than anything else:

I am sending you this line to say that we really must begin to think a little about Christmas before it is too late, and this year I do not want on any account to neglect little JJ as we are the only friends he has who would really give him anything nice . . .

First I would write him a little French letter, just a few lines, daddy will help you, asking him to give you a list of what he would like for Christmas and how old he is now, and do this at once asking for an immediate reply, then you can get him what he would like.

I think you should get gifts for the Page children, Lorne and Bobby, a little remembrance for Sterling because he is alone (inexpensive), for Athala's baby and Eva's little boy, and Gloria French. These are all things that should be bought in Montreal and you are a very good and practical little shopper and have good judgment and sense.

Now about yourself, Mary darling, do give me an idea of what you would like. You have such quantities of jewelry, plenty of clothes, etc., but every girl needs some little things and I do not seem to have the vitality just now to think and plan. Would you like a white fox fur, or do you feel that you do not need it? Tell mother everything that is in your heart and also find out what daddy would like and let me know.

In fact, what she gave her daughter that year was a book, *The Garden of the Heart*, which contained a compilation of the writings of Bahá'u'lláh and 'Abdu'l-Bahá and was inscribed, without any sense of contradiction, with the following dedication:

> To my beloved Mary, in the eternal love and life of His Holiness Bahá'u'lláh from Mother. Christmas 1930.

It was not until the mid-1930s that Shoghi Effendi was able, with wisdom and with patience, to wean the friends from Christmas presents and to encourage them, gently and persuasively, to disassociate themselves from the customs of previous religions. It was not easy. Many years later, after her daughter's marriage to the Guardian, May wrote a most loving note to her on 22 December 1937, which touches on this and many other sacrifices she was being called upon to make. Once she became Rúḥíyyih Khánum, Mary Maxwell was obliged to give up far more than Christmas:

> I have a little note of some amusing words of yours, February 6th last in Haifa, after the Guardian had said what he did about Bahá'ís celebrating Christmas, you said: 'Well, we have no more Christmas; all we can do is to feel a tweeny ache down in our big toe and give it a private wiggle.' Do you still have a few private wiggles, my precious lamb, my own darling little girl?

As a result of her early training, Rúḥíyyih Khánum came to enjoy a 'good deal' almost as much as she loved shopping, and was as delighted as much by the bargain as the beauty of her finds. She was very pleased when she could save money. Writing to her mother on 20 May 1930, she proudly informed her:

> I'll have you know that though I may be a very bad housekeeper, I

am a cheap one! And you ask Daddy if our bills have not been much less . . .

Four years later, in May 1934, she reported:

> I have . . . three dollars . . . of the money you gave me in N.Y. I spend it from time to time on things that don't concern Daddy. I have some left too . . . the scotch daughter!

Even after she had reached her majority, Mary still depended financially on her mother. May covered her expenses with a continuous trickle of cheques, whenever the need arose. As late as 1934, when her mother was in San Francisco, her daughter added a wry little note in one of the letters she sent her:

> I hope the check is on its way because although it is nice to hear that there is a check in a letter, it is hard to capitalize on when the thing is there in spirit only!

The checks on which Mary depended were invariably for very small amounts – $10.00, or $20.00 or possibly $25.00 – and were intended to cover household expenses as well as to provide her with pocket money. It may perhaps have been because of this that Amatu'l-Bahá was a bargain-hunter all her life. She would often economize strictly in one area in order to spend more in another! But the result of this financial dependence was that Mary often depended on her mother for guidance regarding personal economy as well as for reimbursement of funds.

By her own admission, May could never say no to her daughter. From the time that she was still in her teens, whenever Mary asked her for anything her mother generally acquiesced. But having done so, she would always add a proviso. She would invariably remind her that the Temple Fund was their priority. Writing to Mary on 7 September 1931, she added a familiar postscript cautioning against waste:

> Please darling use this money only for expenses, & do not waste it. You know what I mean.

When the needs of the Fund came first she did not hesitate to urge self-abnegation on her daughter, as in a letter written in May 1933, when Mary was in Washington:

> [P]lease do not spend one unnecessary cent, you have plenty of clothes, and plenty of new and lovely materials at the house to make up when you come home . . .

* * *

Despite the troubles associated with these darkening times and the insecurities which they engendered, the priorities in the Maxwell household never wavered. The real meaning of money was that it was the 'life-blood of the Cause'. It was a lesson May had learned long before, from her teacher Lua. Writing to her on 16 September 1899, soon after returning to the United States, Lua told May about the Ḥuqúqu'lláh:

> But now let me tell you an <u>important</u> thing which I do not want you to tell to anyone <u>yet</u>, as it would not be understood. In the Katab-il-Akdas – the Book written by the Manifestation – is written: 'Let him who desires to serve in the Cause of God, give one <u>nineteenth</u> (1/19th) of all he possesses to God, that God may purify his possessions, and bless him.' Abdel-Karim told me this when I was in Cairo, and as soon as we arrived in America we sent 1/19th to the Master and He sent us the receipt for the same. This money from the different Believers goes to relieve the poor, and sick, also to help advance the Cause in the Orient. I was the first American to fulfill this command from the Manifestation, and now Darling I want you to send 1/19th of what you have to Abdel-Karim in care of Cook & Son, or send them the check, and they will see it is delivered to him – (i.e. send a check from Cook & Son in Paris, payable to Abdel-Karim, by Cook & Son in Cairo) he will send it to the Master – and the Master will send you the receipt. Please tell Abdel-Karim that I told you about it and that you desire to do <u>this</u> for the sake of the <u>word</u> of the Beloved. This will be a great blessing to you darling, and your possessions will increase instead of diminish after that.

Throughout the 1920s, especially in the years before as well as during the great financial crash in the United States, May contributed generously to the different Bahá'í Funds. She had always known how to proclaim the Faith and touch the hearts of those who showed an interest in it. But after being advised by the Guardian in the course of her third pilgrimage to ensure that such efforts were efficient and could be sustained, she helped the Assemblies set up teaching plans and the 'circuit' travel teachers involved in these had to be supported. By encouraging the friends to become systematic in their efforts to spread the Cause, the Guardian was training the community to rely less on individuals and more on institutions. He was teaching them to support the Bahá'í Fund. And May was in the vanguard of this activity.

She gave generously to the national as well as international Funds, contributing large sums of money for the purchase of land on Mount Carmel, for the building of the Western Pilgrim House in Haifa and, of course, for the Temple in Wilmette. She was exceedingly generous all through her life in supporting the needs of the Cause.

As early as 22 January 1926, Shoghi Effendi had written to May:

My dearest, most precious Bahá'í sister,

It is always a joy to hear from you and to read your letters which reveal most beautifully and powerfully the dynamic, all-pervading spirit of the Cause. I am touched by your magnificent donation and I assure you that your recent services to the Cause have served to heighten the already lofty position you deservedly occupy in our eyes and hearts. May Mary fulfil your fondest hopes and become in time a most radiant light in the firmament of the Cause. No need to assure you again of my earnest, loving and continued prayers, for yourself, your dear husband and daughter for whom I have the greatest admiration and affection.

On 21 June 1927, May had written to Romeyn Benjamin, to say, 'The $3,000.00, which I gladly contributed has brought no return satisfactory to me or to yourself.' She was referring to a contribution she had made to the Publicity Committee of the National Spiritual Assembly of the Bahá'ís of the United States and Canada and which she felt had not yet been effectively exploited. 'I naturally find it hard to leave this field of teaching in Toronto,' she continues, 'where we are holding large meetings every day, the people are attracted, the Word of God is penetrating the hearts and a great work will be consummated in a short time, and I am wondering if it would not be possible in the circumstances to make the date of our Committee meeting a little more elastic in order to enable me to finish this very important work.'

One day later, on 22 June, a receipt was sent to May Ellis Maxwell for a contribution of $1,000.00 to the Bahá'í Fund of the National Spiritual Assembly of the United States and Canada. She had written to the Treasurer of the National Assembly, Florence Morton, enclosing a cheque for the above amount, saying:

> The Montreal Assembly at this time is changing from one centre to another (and as I mentioned in the last meeting of the National Spiritual Assembly, entailing considerable expense) and my cheque of $1,000 to the National Spiritual Assembly, as pledged in the last meeting, represents practically all my surplus.

Although she was responsible, as the Secretary of the National Teaching Committee, for all the circuit trips of travel teachers that year, her duties went far beyond the mere logistics of these visits. Her letters as Secretary not only offered guidance from the Committee on which she served, but also contain illuminating educational materials, which were often quite personal. One to Keith Ransom-Kehler, dated 15 November 1929, exemplifies the remarkable degree to which her correspondence served an inspirational as well as administrative purpose:

> One reason we are giving the teachers more time on their circuits is to enable them to give to the same groups several talks, instead of one. The Master told Lua to give the message in three parts: first, a general preparation, signs of the times, past Divine dispensations etc. leading up to the revelation of today; then, to tell of the glorious appearance and message of Bahá'u'lláh, in the way that He Himself did in this country, and third, a follow-up meeting to strengthen the bond between the teacher and those who are sincerely receptive, so that they may enter into a new spiritual consciousness and their hearts receive the elixir of life.

May seized the crisis facing the markets in the West to raise the call for greater sacrifice in the Bahá'í community. And characteristically, the manner in which she did this was through the power of example. On 7

January 1930, she wrote to Leroy Ioas, the Chairman of the National Teaching Committee, about a particular teaching circuit that the Committee had organized which she felt illustrated perfectly the spirit of self-abnegation that was required at that difficult time.

> Keith Ransom-Kehler has been carrying on a remarkable teaching circuit through the middle west which will include between thirty to thirty-five Assemblies and Groups. The spirit in which she undertook this journey has reminded me of the travels of St Peter . . . During her entire trip Mrs. Ransom-Kehler has been self-financed, with the exception of a very small additional sum . . . We would appreciate an immediate air-mail reply, in order to plan her circuit . . . before she sails for Barbados late in March.

May was more than qualified to draw attention to the self-financing travels of Keith. It is not hard to imagine where the money was coming from to maintain all her own activities, or who was footing the bill for the hiring of halls and the advertising of meetings for her own ceaseless travels during these years. On 1 December 1927 Shoghi Effendi sent her these wonderful words of encouragement:

> Your notable achievements in the teaching field are graven upon my heart, and I cherish the brightest hopes for the extension and consolidation of your present activities. Kindly assure your dear husband and daughter of my best wishes and prayers for them, that they may in the days to come effectively reinforce your heroic endeavours for the spread and consolidation of the Bahá'í Faith.

There is no doubt that Sutherland's Scots-Canadian upbringing had not encouraged a natural expression of generosity in him. It is all the more touching to see how his faith nurtured the positive aspect of his traits and encouraged him to think of spiritual priorities in relation to the use of money. Soon after one Convention, Loulie Mathews wrote a letter to Sutherland enclosing a receipt:

> I am very happy to send you this receipt for the two thousand given in your name at the Convention that completes my indebtedness of three thousand to you. It was wonderful to have it. I knew how

happy it would make you to feel that when the crucial hour arrived your generous and beautiful gift was uncovered and that your three thousand went right to the Temple! I was so pleased! We had a most interesting convention and I hope you will offer your valuable advice as an architect well known, to the Temple because 'taste' is not among the qualities we have so far developed. I suppose we should not expect too much . . .

Such contributions were a godsend, for the strain on the little Bahá'í community of North America became intense during the Depression and the life-blood of the Faith was literally threatened. Individuals and families who had been in comfortable circumstances found themselves stripped of material means overnight. Contributions for the work of the Faith and funds for the completion of the Temple became a matter of personal deprivation for the friends. But May never wavered in her contributions or in her efforts to support the Bahá'í funds. She saw the economic crisis that was gripping the country and the social upheaval that was sweeping through the land as an added incentive to sacrifice for the Faith. And Sutherland was much influenced by her example.

On 11 December 1929, while she was wintering in New York, an 'overwhelming Epistle of our Guardian' was received, which, according to a letter she wrote to Keith Ransom-Kehler, 'moved New York as I have never seen it moved since the days of the Master'. This letter of the Guardian, written on 25 October 1929 and pleading for the 'resumption of building operations on our beloved Temple', was copied and sent to all the Bahá'ís in the North American community by May and a few others. '[L]ast night,' she says, 'the Kinneys, little Carrie Marsh and I sat up till three getting off the last of the flood to the whole country.' In a later letter, written after the response to the Guardian's appeal, she states that

> the penetration and potency of the Guardian's words had pierced every soul with a shaft of life, and the raising of $40,000 in three weeks after all the sacrifices of the past two years, is nothing short of a miracle.

Two years later, during the worst year of the Depression, May wrote an account for the Guardian 'of the most powerful, full and radiant

Convention we have had in years'. As a member of the National Spiritual Assembly she 'offered to travel and try to incite greater sacrifice & effort' at this time. This idea, however, did not initially meet with full support on the Assembly, as May recorded in the account:

> The members felt it unnecessary as they argued the friends all have the Unified Plan, but I said I felt it required an effort on our part and others to set the Plan in motion – and as a matter of fact it has been less thro steady flow of the Plan than those special intense efforts that it has been built. The N.S.A. graciously gave me a letter to the Assemblies and thro divine confirmation I was able to bring a deeper realization & almost 25 thousand dollars.

May, like many others, cut down on all personal and non-essential expenses in order to be able to continue the work of the Faith during this critical time. But she continued to be generous towards those more needy than herself and not only helped to alleviate their sufferings but also supported them in their contributions to the Fund. One of those whom she helped in this way was a friend from her Paris days, Lillian James. Despite working her fingers to the bone, Lillian had never been well off and found herself reduced to poverty in her old age. Rúḥíyyih Khánum recalled how this dear soul would walk from house to house in Chicago, to give piano lessons, in order to save the streetcar fare for the Temple Fund. Finally, with Mrs Maxwell's help, she was able to travel to Evanston and see for the first time the exquisite building to which she had been contributing her pennies. Her ecstasy at the sight of the Temple was so great that all she could say, as she gazed up at it against the sky, was, 'Oh, you darling!' When she became old and unwell during the Depression years, May watched over Lillian and showered her with innumerable gifts. She arranged for her to be looked after by another of her faithful friends, Agnes Kahlke, who wrote May a note on 18 January 1938, enclosing a receipt for just one of her many cheques to Lillian before she died:

> I want you to know what your check bought. The January sales made the values exceptionally good. A very nice warm black dress – with a fuscia colored scarf, three pairs of silk and wool hose and a pair of fabric gloves. When I told her they were from you, she said,

'Please thank her for me' – and then she clasped her hands together – her eyes filled with tears and she said, 'She is an angel!'

In the end, May even defrayed the expenses of Lillian's grave.

She had an extraordinary empathy for people and could not bear to see anyone suffering. During her daughter's absence on a writing retreat in the mountains in 1931, she wrote to Mary, on 16 July, telling her about those less fortunate than herself:

> A boy came here last night who worked his way, all the way, from New York, where he says thousands are starving; he stopped in every City – could find work nowhere – and has been unable to find any here. I gave him some work, his supper, allowed him to have a hot bath and change all his clothes, and shave; then I said, 'Where are you sleeping to-night' – he said, 'On Mount Royal, with three thousand others'!
>
> . . . As we pass deeper and deeper into the depths of human tragedy, we Bahá'ís inevitably turn more fully, more intelligently, more intensely to the Guardian – through which channel alone flows the mighty, all-protecting, all-sustaining power of Bahá'u'lláh. We inevitably turn more closely, intimately, and tenderly, to one another, to those deep spiritual ties which bind and unite us, making it possible for us to face the conditions for ourselves and the World, with immovable steadfast Faith, with the utmost courage and hope, with 'conscious knowledge' of the glorious end after the dark night has passed.

Six months later her financial circumstances were more restricted but her priorities were unchanged. In a letter to her brother dated 21 January 1932, she wrote:

> We are so hard up, that although I need to go away, I have to stick it out here, and Sutherland is photographing a number of pictures in the hope that you may dispose of some of them which may be of value, and give the money to the Temple . . .

* * *

May, Sutherland and Mary were united in their commitment to contribute to the Temple Fund. But from the moment the Guardian's heart-rending request in his message of 21 March 1932 came to the Bahá'ís,[4] May's attention would be fixed on this and nothing else. She had been closely involved in it before, of course, for she had already been a member of the Temple Committee while serving on the National Spiritual Assembly, and the construction of the Temple continued to be her priority until the end of her life. In February 1927, May had already organized meetings for Louis Bourgeois to speak on the Temple in 'Baltimore, Philadelphia, Boston, Montreal en route Chicago, also possibly Detroit'. His trip must have provided an opportunity not only to inform the wider public about the purpose and significance of the Bahá'í Faith, but just as importantly, to encourage the Bahá'ís in the community to seize their sacred right to contribute to the Temple Fund. It is salutary to consider that she had organized this trip barely nine months before so much money was to be rendered worthless. Writing to her daughter on 19 May 1928 she confidently affirmed: '[S]ince the raising of between $40,000 and $50,000 for the construction of the next unit of the Temple, a new and wonderful force has been set in motion and a new and deeper unity established.' In October and November of 1928, she took off time to travel 'to four or five different Centres, speaking day and night on the Temple' and what it meant to sacrifice to this vital Fund.

The Guardian's appeal was reinforced, as he wrote in that message of 21 March 1932, by 'the passionate, and perhaps, the last, entreaty, of the Greatest Holy Leaf, whose spirit, now hovering on the edge of the Great Beyond, longs to carry on its flight to the Abhá Kingdom'. But for the Maxwell family the appeal of the Guardian seemed even more personal, even more sacred somehow. May's correspondence with Bahíyyih Khánum over the years had been reciprocated as recently as 28 December 1930, by a cable from the Guardian which stated: 'KHANUM JOINS ME AFFECTIONATE GREETINGS PRAYERS SHOGHI'. His entreaty for a greater outpouring to the Temple Fund on her behalf was irresistible, therefore. It is clear from a letter written to May by Mary, on 20 May 1932, that all her mother's provisos had indeed had a profound effect:

---

4 'The Golden Age of the Cause of Bahá'u'lláh', in Shoghi Effendi, *The World Order of Bahá'u'lláh*, pp. 67–8.

> There is one other thing I want to ask you ... I feel desperate about this last plea for the Temple from Khanum and I <u>must</u> do something. I asked Daddy if he thought it would not be good for me to give up a servant and keep the house myself ... he does not like the idea at all. I am sure I could do it ...

Mary had another plan to raise money for the Temple Fund which was also inspired directly by her mother's influence. In 1932, she wrote to May about an idea she had to write a best-selling book or the script for a play or a popular movie, after her encounter with the great singer Paul Robeson:

> Now Mother I have been thinking a great deal about that book I wrote last year about the convent. I made a promise in my heart that I would give any money I made from it to the Temple. And I wrote it. I feel ... that the book would sell tremendously ... If I published [it] and no one knew I wrote it don't you think it would be justifiable? For the Temple? We MUST finish it for Khanum!

By the time she was travelling in Europe on her own in 1935, however, Mary Maxwell had become far more autonomous and her creativity was taking new forms. She was accustomed to sacrifice by then, as well as to economies, and far from asking for financial advice was now ready to give it. She was much more responsible about her finances, as her letter of 3 August to May from Munich indicates:

> Now Mother I insist on enclosing a rough account of what I have been doing with your money. I have spent more than I intended and it worries me. But then I could not have possibly gone in the States to 4 cities and done what I have on this amount. I have travelled 3rd class, eaten inexpensively but well, and bought only things I needed! ... Baggage is an expensive item to travel with, especially if it is heavy – which is wise to know ... Incidentally I am considering buying a bicycle here. You can get one for $10.00 or more and taxis are too expensive and going all about you get utterly exhausted on foot and in street cars, which anyway mount up.

It is also evident, from her report about her activities in Germany which she sent to Shoghi Effendi the following year, that Mary Maxwell, at the age of 25, had realized how pampered she had been in North America. Raised in an atmosphere of privilege, she was being readied for far more rigorous years of self-restraint ahead. But she had no idea of this, as she emphatically stated in later years, and her mother, despite her propensity to flashes of inspiration, never imagined it, even in her wildest dreams.

* * *

The late 1920s and early 1930s were not only a period of financial strain in the Bahá'í community but were a time of spiritual trial for the believers too, especially in the New York community and particularly among the older generation. These were days when the faith of many was put to the test and when the spiritual fate of several souls was determined. And it was during these years that May Maxwell served as midwife to the victories which were born at the height of the crisis caused by the attempts of some of the believers to break the Covenant of Bahá'u'lláh.

Ahmad Sohrab was a well-known believer who had for many years been one of the secretaries of 'Abdu'l-Bahá. He was an established figure in the Bahá'í community who had been sent by the Master to the United States and commissioned to write the history of the Faith in that country. He had also been instructed to continue translating the Tablets of 'Abdu'l-Bahá for the friends there, whenever they were received. After the passing of the Master, however, he gradually became disaffected and over the ensuing years grew increasingly ambitious for power.

For several years during this period, the correspondence between Shoghi Effendi and Mrs Maxwell had made more and more frequent reference to Ahmad Sohrab. In the course of the mid- to late twenties, it became clear that Sohrab was trying to mislead some of the believers regarding the instructions of Shoghi Effendi and was stirring up trouble in the community, creating grave doubts and profound misgivings regarding the station of the Guardian of the Cause. As his activities began to multiply, his attacks on the Covenant increased. The result was overt disharmony in the Bahá'í community and a final bid for power when Ahmad Sohrab established his 'New History Society'. Although the Guardian gave him every opportunity to change his ways and invited him time and again to be submissive to the laws and the ordinances of the Cause, his patience and forbearance was to no avail. As a result of this man's own insatiable ambitions, he finally drifted away from the believers and cut himself off from the Cause.

The first signs of his disaffection were evident when he failed to accept the Bahá'í administration, considering himself above the authority of the National Spiritual Assembly. After that, he gradually opposed the authority of the Head of the Bahá'í Faith, criticizing Shoghi Effendi openly and calling into question his directives regarding the establishment of the Administrative Order. He started his own private classes for the believers and offered them a sort of 'alternative' with his New History Society. All of this caused much distress and confusion among the friends.

May Maxwell was keenly aware of it. She was acutely conscious of any kind of criticism against the Guardian and well aware of how some old and well-established Bahá'ís might be seduced into limiting his rank and sphere of influence and even thinking themselves his equal, on the basis of his modesty. When she sensed the odour of intellectual arrogance, among the young Bahá'ís in particular, she was vigilant in her response. Writing to her daughter as late as July 1931, she confided:

> Everyone seems to feel the greatest affection and regard for E. while realizing that there is something wrong somewhere, and a few nights ago when they were all up here . . . he made the statement that Shoghi Effendi's power was limited and that the Hands of the Cause and the International House of Justice had some jurisdiction or restraining power over the Guardian's actions and decisions . . . These influences are very insidious; the World and the Cause are in a very grave condition. Europe has just averted a complete financial collapse, and the end is not yet – for the headlines on last night's 'Star' read, 'London moves to untangle Europe', and if the International Bankers had not come to the rescue a few days ago – Germany would have gone under completely . . . As we pass deeper and deeper into the depths of human tragedy, we Bahá'ís inevitably turn more fully, more intelligently, more intensely to the Guardian – through which channel alone flows the mighty, all-protecting, all-sustaining power of Bahá'u'lláh. We inevitably turn more closely, intimately, and tenderly, to one another – to those deep spiritual ties, which bind and unite us, making it possible for us to face the

conditions for ourselves and the World, with immovable steadfast Faith – with the utmost courage and hope, with 'conscious knowledge' of the glorious end after the dark night has passed.

During these darkening years May became a beacon of love in North America and cast light on many of these misconceptions. Shoghi Effendi instructed her, through numerous letters and cables, regarding the way she should respond to criticisms of the Administrative Order in general and to Ahmad Sohrab's attacks in particular. He directed her how to act in the ways that might lead back to the Cause some of the more disillusioned among the Bahá'ís at this time. On 31 May 1929 Shoghi Effendi wrote to his 'dear & precious co-worker', Mrs Maxwell, saying:

> Your most welcome letter has truly cheered my heart. I trust & pray that you may be instrumental in restoring perfect harmony & cooperation among the friends in New York. I have the utmost admiration for your deep sense of loyalty, your tact, your loving-kindness & high endeavours & I will pray that you may be given the strength to carry on & consolidate the noble work you have already achieved. Your true brother,
>
> Shoghi

Another letter written to May on 23 April 1930, on behalf of the Guardian, very clearly explained to her the errors implicit in Ahmad Sohrab's interpretation of the Cause. and elaborated on his mistaken attitude towards the purpose of Bahá'u'lláh's message which had so strongly influenced one of the wealthy society ladies of her own generation, Mrs Lewis Stuyvesant (Julie) Chanler. His letter demonstrated how necessary it was to establish the Bahá'í community on a sound administrative basis for the future world order:

> Every one who has studied the Cause deeply cannot but be certain that Bahá'u'lláh's purpose in His Mission was not merely to expound certain principles & renew the spirit that the previous prophets brought to the world, but also to establish a definite social fabric that would make those principles of practical value. In a word what Bahá'u'lláh has come to this world for is a World State – the Kingdom of God – the greatest institution that the world has yet seen.

> The administrative side of the Cause which is the embryonic stage of that world order, is therefore just as much an intrinsic & indispensable part of the teachings, as the principle of unity of mankind etc. To consider a person a Bahá'í, who does not believe in the administration, is just as if we were to consider him as such when he takes exception to those basic principles . . .
>
> Shoghi Effendi does not have anything to say against Mrs. Chanler for she is making all that sacrifice for a certain noble ideal of service. He only pities her to be so duped by Ahmad. All of Shoghi Effendi's grudge is against Ahmad who, appearing in the garb of a servant, is doing nothing more than to injure the Cause by sowing the seeds of dissension among the friends, & of securing his own means of livelihood . . .

At the end of this vitally important letter regarding the building up of the institutions of the Cause, Shoghi Effendi added, in his own handwriting, a directive of utmost significance to Mrs Maxwell herself, which he clearly wished her to share with the friends:

> Regarding Ahmad, I feel that if the friends individually & collectively are not watchful, a gradual departure from the spirit & form of the Faith on his part, aided by the resources placed at his disposal by Mrs. Chanler, may soon bring about a state of grave confusion among the believers, & create a split in their ranks. We should be both firm and conciliatory. I look to you as a powerful instrument for the preservation of the unity & of the integrity of our beloved Faith, & will continue to pray for your high endeavour from the depths of my heart.
>
> Shoghi

By October of 1930, however, the situation had deteriorated to such an extent that Shoghi Effendi had no alternative but to tell the National Spiritual Assembly that the friends should be advised to dissociate themselves entirely from the New History Society. His handwritten postscript at the end of his letter to May dated 19 October 1930 once again gives her specific instructions, of a particularly delicate nature:

> The situation in New York is certainly confused & critical. The

utmost firmness & vigilance are required at the present moment on the part of the old believers, who have already experienced such crises & know full well that the Cause has eventually surmounted them. Ahmad is the one who will precipitate this crisis. Mrs. Chanler is his dupe. He will through her do his utmost to bring about a division among the believers. I urge you to endeavour to save Mrs. Chanler from his grasp & to open her eyes to the truth. I will pray that the Beloved may guide your steps, cheer your heart & sustain your devoted efforts. Be not sad nor disheartened, the Cause will eventually triumph.

Shoghi

This may have been the letter that May was referring to when she wrote to her daughter from Geneva, New York, on 30 November that year, telling her that she had just received special instructions from the Guardian:

> Daddy forwarded all my mail and there is a most important letter from the Guardian, the contents of which I wish to share with you immediately, although you must not mention it to anyone.... Shoghi Effendi wants me to go immediately to New York and make a supreme effort to save Julie Chanler from Ahmad. He says that Ahmad's supreme effort is to disrupt the believers and that Julie is his dupe, and I think Shoghi Effendi either has made or is about to make some drastic pronouncement and he wants Julie extricated first, if possible. <u>This is just for you</u> because I need your prayers and support and I think by Saturday I shall be strong enough to travel and see Julie not later than Sunday. I shall see her alone at some Hotel in town and without letting anyone know I am there and the Guardian is praying for success of this plan and I want you to pray with all your heart.

May Maxwell longed to relieve Shoghi Effendi's distress. She not only burned with ardour and devotion for the Covenant and was anxious to do all in her power to protect its unity, but was also a lover of 'Abdu'l-Bahá and of the one He had appointed in His Will. She could not bear to think that the radiance of that dear countenance might be clouded by these events.

On 29 November she sent a cable to Mary informing her that the 'IMPORTANT INTERVIEW WITH JULIE IS TONIGHT' and asking her to share this news with her father. It is enlightening to consider how much she took her 20-year-old daughter into her confidence and how earnestly she relied on her husband's support.

May was particularly attuned to the spiritual health of those dearest to her because some of her oldest friends had come under the influence of the Covenant-breakers at this time. Their blindness was a cause of grieving to her. Writing to her daughter from New York on 3 December 1930, when she was still attempting to 'save' Julie Chanler, May mourned for those who could not see the spiritual dimensions of the Administrative Order. She used the opportunity to teach her daughter vital lessons in the power of the Covenant at the same time:

> When 'Abdu'l-Bahá left this country He gave us one little book as our charter of existence, it was the Hidden Words. That Hidden Words, from the first word to the last, is nothing but a revelation of the Inner Path of life. The Master told us that we should read and study these Hidden Words and meditate upon them <u>every day</u>, until the inner door, the sanctuary where God is standing <u>within us</u>, 'powerful, mighty and supreme', is open to us. The fact of the matter is that we seek for God, for truth, for happiness everywhere but in the <u>one place</u> where it is to be found. Christ said, 'seek and ye shall find', 'knock and it shall be open unto you', and the Hidden Words are the key to unlock the door of our own inner being where lie all the secrets and treasures of life.
>
> ... I realize that something very wonderful is happening in the Cause, that the souls are being called one by one as they have the capacity to hear to make the spiritual transition into the spiritual kingdom of Bahá'u'lláh which is a study of inner light, inner life, inner consciousness and being. I realize that the Administration had to be formed and perfected as a vehicle for this new collective spiritual life. That the essential unity which Bahá'u'lláh brought to the world, of which He said, 'it is an essence', that this Unity or Oneness is a pure and perfect centre of life waiting for souls to enter. Another new and very strange realization which has been coming to me is that Shoghi Effendi is standing in the centre, <u>and is the Centre</u>, of the world of the Spirit of Bahá'u'lláh, calling to each one

of us individually to enter and that this is the true explanation of the great divergence in His written statements to individuals.

The new history society, among other things, is but an instrument and means of testing the Bahá'ís on this point of their true spiritual understanding and immutable relationship to the Guardian, the centre of light, and that His apparently conflicting statements to different ones are due to the fact that they are all on the circumference where truth can never be reconciled. You remember the Guardian said to us in Haifa that the Master's teachings are a mass of contradictions and that His <u>apparently conflicting statements</u> can only be reconciled through wisdom, and wisdom is the inner light of understanding.

Despite all May's efforts, however, and her insights regarding the nature of spiritual tests, Ahmad Sohrab continued to exert his pernicious influence on older believers like Mrs Chanler. Finally, in order to put a stop to him, and in her naive eagerness to reach out and be of help to the Guardian, Mrs Maxwell even wrote and offered Shoghi Effendi her own means to ease the situation. She suggested that if she gave money to Ahmad, he would perhaps relinquish his hold on Mrs Chanler. For she had known the man for many years and was well aware of his greed. She knew he had duped Mrs Chanler in order to siphon off her money and hoped that if his avarice were satisfied, the poor lady might be free from his influence.

Shoghi Effendi answered her on 23 March 1931, in his own hand. His appreciation of her motives was warm and generous; his grasp of the situation lucid; and his advice brief and to the point:

My dear and valued co-worker:

Your letter so eloquently testifying to your immovable faith and abiding loyalty to the Cause, has greatly refreshed me. In these days of stress, of suffering and turmoil – out of which the Cause must needs emerge purer, stronger and nobler than ever – I look to you as a shining light, a pillar of faith and a tower of strength overshadowing all who falter and feel disheartened. I strongly feel that the best way to meet the situation is to ignore Ahmad entirely, neither to openly denounce him nor to financially assist him. Try however to win unreservedly to our beloved Cause that pure and tender hearted

Mrs. Chanler, for whom I feel a great love and sympathy. Much love to Mary and her father.

                        Shoghi

Writing to Mary from New York on 13 December 1930, May confided:

> I find here that the principal trouble with all the older believers is that they are trying to run the Cause; as I said to a group of them laughingly, the other night, they had buried Bahá'u'lláh and were doing it all themselves, whereas in reality He is the only Teacher, the only Educator, the one who is permeating everyone and everything, and without whose Power and Spirit we could not utter one word and I think that as soon as we realize this, all our humble efforts become much more effective.

She made only one more attempt to reach Ahmad Sohrab, when the Guardian told her to do so. Many years later, in 1938, Ahmad Sohrab asked to meet with Mrs Maxwell. She naturally asked for Shoghi Effendi's guidance and when he cabled back on 16 March, telling her that such a meeting would be 'INADVISABLE', May sat down and wrote a letter to Ahmad Sohrab, inviting him to correspond with her instead:

> I had thought that when you asked to see me you wished to discuss matters relative to our beloved Faith . . . Since the years of your devoted service to the Master the Faith has developed into a living organism from which you have separated yourself and started a movement of your own. For this reason, due to the explicit text of the Will and Testament, of which you said yourself 'only a fool would doubt its authenticity', I cabled the Guardian and he advised that you write me anything you may wish to say. I hope you will feel quite free to do this, and please give my loving greetings to Mrs. Chanler.

He did not respond.

                        * * *

May continued to nurture those who had fallen under the spell of the New History Society throughout the early 1930s. With a constancy that marked all her relationships, she helped such people distinguish between the ambitions of a charlatan and the life-giving teachings of Bahá'u'lláh. She often went out of her way to encourage them to visit the Holy Land and meet Shoghi Effendi. It is interesting to note that in 1931 she was also appointed to be the Secretary of the Religious Congress Committee. Her abilities of discernment were evidently recognized.

May Maxwell was not only a brilliant teacher of the Cause, but a shrewd psychologist. She knew how to transform the lethargy of a community into coordinated action and how to erase the scars of disunity among the believers without leaving a trace behind. Her advice was not only wise but often revealed a subtle knowledge of people's weaknesses, which she did not judge but knew instinctively how to mediate. Writing to Stanley and Evelyn Kemp in Vancouver on 18 April 1930, for example, she concluded her letter with the following significant advice:

> I have so much more to say, but have a large class this afternoon and will only add this suggestion regarding the activities in Vancouver . . . [T]each as many new people as possible without in any way bringing them in contact with the Bahá'í friends . . . form a separate group in a class, if possible . . . Help them to read and study . . . and to become firmly established, and when this is accomplished, bring them among the friends.

On 27 March 1931 she had occasion to advise her daughter about mediating in another relationship. A maid of the Maxwells, whom May had greatly helped in the past, had asked Mary to come to her deathbed and to assume responsibility for her young son, whose life Mrs Maxwell had saved when a baby. Writing to her daughter from New York, she counselled her about how to deal with this delicate situation:

> Since telephoning you, the following thought has come to me, if A. wants to make some disposition of J. J. she can dictate it to you and then sign it and have her signature witnessed by the doctor or nurse; in that way if the time should ever come that we wished to take J. J.

and he wanted to come to us, and the grandmother should object, we would have [these] last wishes properly attested. This would also set her mind at rest about the future without obligating you to promise to take him.

On the other hand, if she wishes to have him brought up in the Bahá'í religion she could make a similar statement and you could promise that in the future we would give J. J. the teachings and explain to him that it was his mother's last wish that he would give heed to this great message. A. [does not] understand that you do not join the Bahá'í Cause the way you join the Catholic religion . . . If [she] had chosen to keep her little boy near her through all these years and inculcate in him the love of 'Abdu'l-Bahá she could have done so, but she took the easiest way and now, on her death bed, she hopes in a measure to atone for the past, and that is right and God will accept her repentance and you must tell her to turn her heart in faith and prayer to 'Abdu'l-Bahá and that we shall pray for her and she has nothing to fear, because she has a real love for the Master in her heart. I feel, Mary, that this service you are rendering in going to her is an act of grace granted you by God as a reward for your having fasted, and I feel it will be a great blessing for you now and in the future. Some people's reactions to every opportunity in life are purely negative, but the reaction of a true Bahá'í is always positive, dynamic and active, and I was very happy at the spirit in which you have responded to this appeal. Strange, in a way, that she has not asked for me at all, it is you she wants and I believe I understand the mystery underlying this based on our essential oneness which deepens through the years . . . Give my love to A. and tell her that Mrs. Bolles and you and I will all pray for her and her little boy.

One of May Maxwell's outstanding qualities was her sense of loyalty towards old friends. She kept in touch with those to whom she had taught the Faith, despite the distances between them, and if she sensed any cooling or apathy in their attitude, she went out of her way to try and reactivate their commitment to the Covenant, to help solve their problems, and to draw them back to the circle of the Bahá'í community. Sometimes, when she found new friends, they confirmed the efforts she was making to revive the old. Writing to Mary from New Jersey on 26 February 1931, Mrs Maxwell described one such experience:

But there is one remarkable thing that I must tell you because these are the things you always deeply understand. After being so ill down here... I went to see some Bahá'ís, Dr. T. and his wife and her sister. Dr. T. told me that his wife had had a severe nervous break-down, she lost her mother about a month ago and her nerves were already shattered by many causes and I thought perhaps if I go to see this woman who is so ill and suffering, I can help her in some way, and then happened a wonderful thing. I went to the home of these people and found them a lovely, colored family, refined and educated and loving the Master, with that love which is divine and eternal, that love which is the whole life, that quality of love and faith which has transcended all their sorrows and made them that most precious thing, the dear human being to the heart of 'Abdu'l-Bahá, 'True Believers'. In the same hour, Mrs. T. and I both began to recover, my soul was nourished, my life forces renewed, and when I saw her the next day, she also felt like another human being. And this is the greatest proof that I have ever had, and I have had many, that the Believers of God are under an entirely different law, all the science and religion combined of this world, all the laws of nature, absolutely nothing suffices them, but the sustenance they draw from the Spirit, from the power of the Covenant which is now in the body of the Believers as a whole, this and this alone is their life. Your prayers and Daddy's darling, have calmed me and helped me to sleep and in that bond of Unity with you both, I also draw that same strength of the Spirit, but these Believers, so genuine, simple and sincere, Believers of the heart and soul and not of the intellect, have satisfied some deep inner hunger which I have felt for a long time. I do not find this in New York, but the one day I did find it and all my strength was renewed was the day I spent with Julie Chanler. Her love for the Master is so intense and sincere that in spite of all the foolish veils and blindness which soon will pass away, her spirit reaches mine.

Mary already knew of the mission entrusted to her mother by the Guardian regarding Mrs Chanler, and so she would have understood the underlying principle which May wanted her to understand in a story she told of the Master in Philadelphia:

'Abdu'l-Bahá, when in America, made a wonderful visit to Philadelphia and then went on to Washington; on his return from Washington to New York, He took the fast express train, the Flyer that only stops two minutes in the station at Philadelphia, because the type of American who takes the rapid trains will not tolerate delay. When the train stopped in the Philadelphia station there was a large crowd of Bahá'ís who had come from far and wide to see the Master as He passed through, and 'Abdu'l-Bahá got off the train, stood on the platform and addressed the crowd! The doctor said he never saw anything so thrilling and astonishing. There the train stood with hundreds of waiting passengers leaning out of windows and [on] platforms, looking and listening, the conductor standing respectfully silent, never even saying 'All Aboard'! – just holding up the train indefinitely for the glorious Master! It is thus that the world stood still wherever He went, all the dull machinery of this mortal existence ran down and was still while the world of [the] Kingdom of Beauty and Peace held complete sway over the souls and lives of men.

* * *

The most important area in which May helped in her daughter's development, just before and after Mary's pilgrimage in 1926, concerned the way in which she matured into a woman. It was a great challenge at every level: physical, psychological and spiritual. Even by the most objective standards, Mary Maxwell at the age of 15 was already a stunningly beautiful girl. Her mother clearly thought so in a letter, dated 26 February 1926:

> Dearest Mary:–
> I left you sleeping peacefully, but it is for such a short time that my heart was at rest. I hope you are having a lovely time with your friends and that you will have lots of air and exercise tomorrow, to put those lovely roses in your cheeks, as you look so much more beautiful when you are full of vitality . . .

Young Mary was also extraordinarily cared for, and her mother ensured that all her needs were provided:

If you want to dictate your poems, darling, look on my red leather telephone list in my room (but be careful not to scatter the papers that are in it) and you will find the name of Mrs. Welden. Call her up and see if she can give you some time Monday or Tuesday. It only takes a few moments to dictate those poems – and have her make several duplicate copies – then you can dictate a letter to Shoghi Effendi and send him your poems, and thank him for his wonderful messages of love and encouragement to you. And you can also send a nice little note to Professor Sandwell in mailing him your poems.

Be sure and give your Honey Bear water every few hours and plenty of food and play and exercise at night. Now, I am going to Worcester to the Hotel Bancroft, where you can reach me by wire or letter any time, and I send you all my devoted love and kisses.

Yours, Mother

I hope you & Daddy can go to the Unity Feast Tuesday night at Mrs. Sherman's.

The counsels she gave Mary were grounded in universal principles of respect and courtesy towards any human soul. They were not only words of maternal advice but a shining example of the Golden Mean in life. And she dealt with her own daughter according to the same standards. Far from treating Mary with suspicion or mistrust, she affirmed, she confirmed, she believed and breathed confidence in her all through these years. Some time later, on 7 September 1931, when Mary was struggling like any other young person with the difference between theory and practice, May assured her of her best self:

I have to laugh when you say you are not a good Bahá'í! because you are so close to the reality of that sacred essence that you can not even perceive it!

She also used praise to stir Mary to rise above her limitations:

It is all the more wonderful that you have developed will power, strength of character, and a selfless attitude toward others when you might have been so spoiled by your environment, as 'Abdu'l-Bahá says 'Tests reveal the nature of a man.'

When Mary was away on holiday, her mother kept in close touch with her. Although she had reached her majority, Mrs Maxwell insisted on knowing everything her daughter was doing: what she was eating, how long she was sleeping, whether she was exercising 'and whether your spirit is joyous and your soul at rest and neither restless nor depressed as you used to be sometimes after we had been separated too long'. Her every breath was of 'keen interest to [her] adoring mother':

> All this I want to know because it sustains and nourishes my inner life and this united action and mutual responsibility between us feeds the fire of our inner love and that sacred bond which lives beyond and above all the conditions of this finite world . . . for to say that I miss you is just a misnomer, it does not describe in any way how I feel.

May gave young Mary a great deal of freedom and at the same time maintained a strong emotional and moral bond with her. The result of this intense relationship bore some remarkable fruits, as history has shown. One or two selections from May's letters to Mary in 1931 may suffice to illustrate how it was maintained:

> I would like to make one suggestion, darling, which might help you, and that is – that if you do not at once get the inspiration to finish your book, that you go to work correcting your other book and your play, so that we can get them published. I am enclosing a copy of the New Unified Plan of Action, which calls for tremendous sacrifices on the part of us all. I feel you are entitled to know this and to take any part that you feel guided and prompted to do, between God and your own conscience, and I will gladly help you to finance the publishing of your books if you feel that this is what you wish. I am praying, as you asked me, my precious one, that you will be inspired to complete your work, and it was while I was praying that the thought flashed into my mind – that your inspiration will come as you get back into the field of writing – and by working on your other Book that part of your mind will open up and the Spirit will rush in . . .

And again, a message showering her daughter with love:

> Mary – Darling,
> You have no idea of the effect upon my entire being, of our little talk over the telephone last night. The very sound of your voice – so dear to my heart – seemed to restore all my life forces, because the power of divine unity flowing through us is the source of our life. I realize it more and more, that it is to the complete attainment of this absolute unity and oneness to which we are being called and which alone can bring the perfecting power of the Spirit to us – spiritually, mentally and physically.

* * *

A touching characteristic of Mary was her need to confide her weaknesses to May. Even as a young woman of 22, she still turned to her mother when she wanted to check whether or not her instincts were, spiritually-speaking, 'on track'. One day in late May 1932, in the middle of spring-cleaning her room, she wrote to her mother about something which, as she put it, she needed to get 'off my chest!':

> [A]s you know this winter I had had a tendency to get discouraged . . . I don't know how other Bahá'ís feel but I do know that unless most of the thoughts about me are positive and constructive I immediately get negative. It's like something waiting to jump on me, and with very little provocation it does . . . but I don't think it is a <u>real</u> thing, do you? If you feel any convictions about this, not just things to comfort me but your deep understanding of the Teachings, please write them to me and when I feel myself getting that way I'll read it and know that it is what you really think about it.

May encouraged her daughter to seek guidance from Shoghi Effendi in all matters of personal interest and concern, as she herself had done all through her Bahá'í life, first through 'Abdu'l-Bahá and then later through Shoghi Effendi. As early as 1926, upon her return from her second pilgrimage, Mary wrote to Shoghi Effendi. In her letter to him, dated 1 November 1926, she expressed her love for studying sciences and wished to know what he thought about this. She received the following acknowledgement, dated 2 December 1926, written on behalf of Shoghi Effendi, with a postscript in his handwriting:

> Dear Mary:
> Shoghi Effendi has given me the pleasure of acknowledging the receipt of your first letter to him dated November 1st, 1926. He was very glad to see that you have made the service to this beloved Cause the primary aim of your life & will pray that you should succeed in it. This is the goal for which every Bahá'í youth should mobilise his forces . . .

And in Shoghi Effendi's handwriting:

> My spiritual sister:
> Your first written message has touched me deeply & has served to reinforce the bonds that unite me with your dear family in the service of the Cause. I cherish great hopes for you, & I will continue to pray for you that you may grow to become a shining example of virtue, of zeal, & of capacity to every worker in the Divine Vineyard. Study profoundly the Teachings, deepen your knowledge of social subjects & practice the art of public speaking that you may mirror forth the glory & beauty of this wondrous Revelation.
>   Your true brother,
>   Shoghi

Again, in a letter on his behalf dated 14 December 1927, the following was written:

> Of course he quite well understands your interest in science and hopes that it will mature into a sound & enlightened outlook, and your study of social sciences will prepare you, he hopes, to [have] a better understanding of some of the greatest problems of the world to-day and the illuminating light that the teachings of the Cause throws upon their ultimate and justifiable solution. I am sure you will find both fields equally interesting and absorbing.

And in Shoghi Effendi's handwriting:

My dear Bahá'í Sister:

I feel that while acquiring the fundamental facts of science, you should concentrate your energy on social studies, that you may teach in future with knowledge & understanding, & thus be enabled to attract people of standing, of influence & learning. I will pray for you at the holy Shrines, that you may mirror forth in your life & activities the glory & power of this Divine Revelation.

Your well-wisher,
Shoghi

In 1928 one of Mary's close friends had committed suicide. In deep distress she wrote to Shoghi Effendi asking him for prayers for this friend. She received the following letter, dated 14 October 1928, written on his behalf by his secretary:

Dear Mary:

Shoghi Effendi wishes me to acknowledge the receipt of your letter dated September 6th. He was very sorry to hear of this act that your friend did in a moment of despair. Life is a divine gift with, undoubtedly, a purpose in it. It is not for us to check the working out of that purpose by putting an end to it. But at the same time we cannot blame such an individual. We do not know of his sufferings, nor of the reasons that led him to such an act.

Shoghi Effendi will, however, pray that God may treat him with His mercy & shower upon him His divine Blessings. Undoubtedly such prayers will help him, for the Master assures us that prayers for departed souls is the greatest help we can render them.

Shoghi Effendi will also remember you in his prayers & ask for you divine blessings, so that you may succeed to render inestimable services to our beloved Cause.

And in Shoghi Effendi's handwriting:

Dear Bahá'í Sister:

Rest assured that my fervent prayers will be offered at the holy Shrines for your friend as well as yourself, that you may both be graciously assisted, guided & blessed by Him. I trust that you may be enabled by His grace & power to render inestimable services to His

Cause in the days to come & thus fulfil your dear mother's dearest wish.
 Wishing you success & happiness from all my heart,
   Your true brother,
    Shoghi

Rúḥíyyih Khánum often mentioned the story of her wanting to learn to fly an aeroplane, at the age of 19, and having registered her name in a school, when her father, for the first time in her life, emphatically disagreed with her. So she wrote to Shoghi Effendi asking his guidance and advice. In a letter dated 29 May 1929, written on his behalf, she received the following:

> Concerning the profession you have chosen, namely flying, Shoghi Effendi does not consider himself in a position to give you any advice along that line. What he wishes you to do is to abide by what your parents, both your father & mother consent to. What they mutually agree upon is his wish.

And in Shoghi Effendi's handwriting:

> My dear co-worker:
> I am much pleased to learn of your growing activities in the Cause & I will supplicate from the depths of my heart in your behalf at the holy Shrines that the Beloved may graciously guide you & assist you to render inestimable services to His Cause in the days to come.
>   Your true brother,
>   Shoghi

Although Mary was an only child and uniquely loved by her mother, she had to share her with all her other spiritual children. She was only one of the many souls who were able to pour out their hearts to May Maxwell. There were moments when she even expressed a little frustration at not having her mother to herself. When May was in San Francisco, en route back to Canada through Vancouver in the spring of 1934, Mary wrote to her, saying:

> Now if you are going to Vancouver you know as well as I that two weeks will never be enough! They just won't let you go! And when if ever will I see you? Must I get married like Rosemary to entice you home to a Bahá'í wedding?

It is not rare to have a mother who dotes on her daughter, but in the case of May and Mary Maxwell, the daughter doted on the mother too. Quite apart from their spiritual bonds, they adored each other. They had immense fun together. They enjoyed each other's company and shared common interests. After writing five pages on the Bible and mysticism to her daughter on 3 December 1930, May added a little postscript:

> I hope you will not think this letter is too serious because if you were here we would laugh and talk and go to a show, and go shopping a little, as soon as my legs stop aching! Taking you in my arms for one big motherly embrace and many tender kisses to my darling lamb.

Mother and daughter made a formidable team. Already, as early as 1929 when she had returned to Montreal after the Convention that Riḍván, May had written to her brother Randolph Bolles about her first teaching trip with Mary:

> Your letter was awaiting me on my return to Montreal ten or twelve days ago as <u>Mary and I have been on a three weeks' teaching trip since the Convention</u>. . . . I have been entirely submerged in the field of teaching with Mary where we have done our first united work together with remarkable results . . . You have probably heard that I am not a member of the National Spiritual Assembly this year which has given me a new freedom for the teaching I so dearly love
> . . .

It was the beginning of that wonderful mother and daughter team, which they both cherished and enjoyed so immensely. It was the start of a spiritual partnership that was destined to enrich the natural bond between them and long outlast their physical relationship.

1930–1934

Whenever May Maxwell taught a soul about the Bahá'í Faith, she first loved that soul. She never imposed her ideas on anyone nor did she befriend a person primarily to 'teach' him or her. The sincerity of her love never failed to leave its trace on people and invariably attracted them to the Cause. Both 'Abdu'l-Bahá and the Guardian had recognized this liberality in her, and both encouraged her to develop it.

May encouraged her daughter to develop this same attitude. Writing to her on 12 November 1933 about a young man who had evidently been attracted to the Cause through her, May advised:

> He detects very quickly any effort – however subtle – to teach or preach at him – but he is most susceptible to those real & tender and loving influences in which we nurtured him in the beginning. I wrote him lovingly and sanely yesterday and had the dearest note from him today in which he said he felt my love & <u>nearness</u>. If you write him without effort to put him right in any way – just in that deep bond he has with you – taking an interest in him and his life and thoughts and studies – sharing your own – telling him how happy I was to see him again – and suggesting that he always helped me and did me good – and you might touch on the deep bond between the Bahá'ís of the time of the Master and the rising generation – as only you can do – in a few words . . .

Although she had her father's temperament, according to May, Mary grew to reflect the largeness and liberality of her mother's faith. She learned from her to avoid a fundamentalist attitude, which May thoroughly deplored. Writing to May during a time of rising fascism in the early 1930s, Mary echoed her dismay at the propensity in human nature towards dogmatism:

> I wish he could get that tendency to fundamentalism out of his system! He is a rock of firmness and devotion but he could also be more plastic. I may be wrong but I cannot be dogmatic. Life has become so vast and my own insignificance so patent that I don't feel in a position to tell people where to get off. Do you think I am wrong? I can tell them the teachings and know in my heart that this is what they and the whole world need, but I can't feel hope is barred to them just because they don't see it in the way at the time I do.

It was with this spirit that mother and daughter embarked on their team work as teachers of the Faith. Just one letter from May to Mary will suffice to illustrate how wide their vision was, and how all-embracing, how magnanimous, and how forgiving. Responding to her daughter's complaints about what she must have felt were the inadequacies of understanding among some members of the Bahá'í community of Montreal, Mrs Maxwell wrote, on 13 December 1930:

> I have taken up the matter you mentioned last night regarding the standard of belief of some of the younger Bahá'ís, with the National Teaching Committee, without mentioning any names, because this is a matter I discussed with them when in Geneva and I suggested that the older qualified teachers should publish a letter every month in the Bahá'í News on just such deeper spiritual teachings; it is wrong to let the Cause become shallow and externalized in this way, but darling, you must never forget that we can <u>only</u> teach through love and kindness and <u>never</u> with a tone of superiority. I know your intense sincerity, and you are so earnest that you can hardly bear these things, but you will have much more influence if you are just very quiet about it, giving the true teaching and trusting in the power of Bahá'u'lláh to make it penetrate the heart.

But while her spiritual vision was broad and her attitude to those she met infinitely generous, May gave her daughter precise techniques when it came to teaching the Faith. Writing from Geneva, New York, on 3 November 1930, Mrs Maxwell told Mary how to make contacts and invite friends to the house:

> If possible, I wish you and daddy would stay over Saturday and

Sunday and go and call on Mrs. Joseph Kilgore. You will find her in the telephone book and she would be charmed to meet you both as she was very sweet to me. Please do this dear without hesitation. We must be like Martha Root, when every door will be opened wide to our efforts, conscious only of the Divine Beloved and His Message and entirely unconscious of self. Helen Grand is a sister of Mrs. Kilgore and would be delighted to see you both. You will also find the Pattersons in the telephone book under Colonel or Lt. Colonel Patterson. I think on Aylmer Street or Aylwin St. Give them all my love.

In my telegram I also suggested that if you can possibly make the time, you invite all the Bahá'í ladies to a delightful tea at our house as you and I planned in New York and you and Rosemary and Dorothy wait on them and treat them with so much courtesy, deference and loving consideration that you will gradually cement the bonds between the older and younger members of our assembly.

Mary darling, it will be a wonderful strength and support to me to have you carry on this work of unifying and cementing the hearts and lives of the Believers and bring the sunshine of happiness to many of these faded lives and it will give me fresh strength and courage to go on with my work and to try to get well.

She even sent her daughter instructions, by mail, regarding what she should serve her guests – 'Cider to drink or Ginger Ale and a demi tasse of coffee' – and all the housewifely arts of how and with whom and in what manner she should serve it:

Now after you get your girls, you must go upstairs and count the doilies and napkins that go together and see what you can work out. I have great confidence in your ability in this direction and if I were you I would not have more than six girls or you may crowd the dining room table, and I know you will make the center piece of flowers look lovely.

The manner in which May combined spiritual ideals with practical advice sometimes produced comic results, as in a letter written a few years later in 1933, in which she offered her daughter deathless insights and new hairstyles simultaneously!

> Only those absolutely oriented to the Focal Centre of this Age can keep strong and serene – or even sane in the midst of forces which are rocking the world. I am enclosing matters of interest – the two ladies with braided hair suggest a very becoming coiffure for you . . .

Mary was a born hostess and knew instinctively how to make her home attractive. Many of her letters to her mother, written when May was travelling across Canada and the United States, describe the dinner parties, the tea parties, the invitations given and received, which served as a framework for making friends and teaching the Faith. Indeed, throughout her life Rúḥíyyih Khánum loved having guests at her table; she knew exactly how to create an elegant meal, how to make her visitors feel at ease, and how to lift as well as lighten the level of the conversation. She was even able to fill the house of the Master, which had seen so much sorrow over the years, with joy and laughter. But it was her mother who had trained her to achieve such miracles. May was her model, her example, and above all her best companion in the arts of reception and entertainment. Increasingly, during the thirties, Mary begged her mother to come home from her travels so that they could be hostesses together:

> I feel dear that the importance of these contacts at this time cannot be over-estimated and I cannot believe that so many doors are opening to me unless I am meant to seize the opportunities they afford. I can barely wait for you to come home and help me. There is only one way to do these things and that is through continuous social contact. As soon as I can I'm going to have another evening for Daddy to show his books, there are already a number of people who, having heard about them, are very anxious to see them. Perhaps this gives you some idea of how busy I've been. I have thought of cutting myself off and not doing anything but study and write and yet when I see all these new souls and new openings I feel as if it would be wrong to cease these contacts when they are just starting . . .

Having made initial contacts with people and attracted them to the Cause, Mary often passed her friends on to her mother. She felt that May was the one who would fill their hearts with love for Bahá'u'lláh and could confirm their souls with the spirit of true faith. In a letter to her mother dated May 1930, Mary wrote:

> Last night I gave another talk in the Hall . . . Mrs. Simms . . . remember her? That little slim woman? Well, she wants to come on the voting list and there is a lovely middle-aged woman who is deeply attracted to the Cause but I feel that she needs you. I got that impression clearly last night. Your mind and spirit would reach hers perfectly and somehow I feel maybe others will do the wrong thing. She will be here this summer. I am so happy over Ingabor and Therese. Everyone says Therese is not the same person . . . and to me she looks like a Bahá'í! And Ingabor said to Alberta she thought she was a Bahá'í! Now with just the right few talks both these girls will come into the Cause . . . but I feel I have done my part and that that last something they are not expecting from me. If you know what I mean? So dearest a week or two here would do no harm!

Increasingly too, she shared news about the contacts she was making and consulted with her mother about how best to respond to their questions about the Cause:

> One more thing I want to tell you about in this line is Mr. R . . . As I mentioned yesterday he keeps remarking that he would like a Bahá'í book to read. I feel that consciously at least his motive is purely curiosity in regard to what interests me so much, so I naturally want to give him a book that will stand on its own merits and will appeal to him and I don't feel I know him well enough yet to decide just which aspect of the teachings would not antagonize him in any way. Please give me your advice, or do you think it is alright for me to wait until I'm sure?

In a later letter, on 20 May 1932, Mary wrote to her mother again:

> I saw Mr. R . . . All he does now increasingly is to question me about the Cause . . . and it keeps me terribly busy trying to answer with wisdom! I gave him Bahá'u'lláh and the New Era to read . . . because I could not find the little book you mentioned and I don't think it is too strong for him. Really mother you must hustle and get well! I can't manage him much longer!

In addition to planning her personal teaching campaigns with her mother, she also shared her triumphs with May; she told her about the wonderful experiences she had when a soul drew close to the Faith because of her direct influence. Her longing to share these victories with May make them all the more poignant and memorable:

> And I have a jewel of my own! A wonderful Jew that has been coming to the meetings and we have become dear friends and he came and confided to me the other night that he was on the eve of a very serious decision that would mean his life going up or down and asked my advice. We had a wonderful talk and he said I would know which way he had decided if he came to the meeting last night. Because one decision would mean he would never come again. He came and brought his brother with him! Isn't that wonderful? And they came home with Alberta and me and he said 'we' had won a victory. I am so happy about it. He may be in Chicago at the time of the Convention . . . I am just dying to have him meet you.

The bond was reciprocal. May acknowledged repeatedly how much she had learned from her daughter when it came to teaching the Cause. Two years later, in a letter to her dated 6 March 1934, written during her Californian sojourn, May confessed:

> Oh, Mary, how we all need you! Everywhere I go, I meet young people who are attracted to me and to my way of teaching, most of which I have learned from you, and I cannot help realizing what you could do for them.

This 'way of teaching', according to the same letter, was what May called 'our new Montreal approach'.

> I am very much astonished that none of the Bahá'ís in the West have any modern approach to the public, but are speaking as much as they did 25 years ago, and they are often startled by my suggestions as to new ways to teach, but they like it and need it.

May was thrilled that her daughter was continuing her 'study group with the girls' and had accepted to give her course of lectures at Green Acre, because, she averred, 'there is the greatest need for your spiritual influence and deep insight all over this country'. It was an influence that belonged to the new generation.

One of the most remarkable characteristics of the relationship between this mother and this daughter was the way in which it widened to include that whole generation.

* * *

On a Wednesday afternoon, 22 October 1930, at the Friends' Meeting House in New York City, the speaker for the two o'clock programme of the Mysticism Congress was announced: 'Miss Mary Maxwell, Montreal, Canada'. Her subject was 'The Mysticism in the Bahá'í Religion' and she was barely 20 years old.

In fact, it was May herself who had been invited to be the speaker at this event. She had even written the paper for it but was unable to attend at the last minute. And so she sent her charming daughter to give the speech in her stead. The outstanding participants in the three-day Congress included such names as Prof. Henry A. Overstreet, Department of Philosophy, College of the City of New York; Rev. H. Adye Prichard, D.D., Canon, Cathedral of St John the Divine, New York City; Rev. Samuel Schulman, D.C., Rabbi, Congregation Emanu-El; The Right Reverend G. Ashton Oldham, D.D., Episcopalian Bishop of Albany; and Syud Hossain, Press Representative for India at the Washington Conference for the Limitation of Armaments, of whom the New York-based Foreign Policy Association said: 'Of the hundreds of speakers who have addressed our conferences during the past five years, none was more brilliant or authoritative than Mr Hossain.'

When this girl, so conspicuously beautiful among the much older speakers of international fame, stood up and spoke to that distinguished audience on the subject of Bahá'í mysticism, she received a standing ovation. Her mother's prayers surely sustained her, as did May's cable to her:

> MARY DARLING YOUR LOVING WIRE BROUGHT NEW STRENGTH AND COURAGE ALSO DADDYS TALK FEEL BOTH YOUR NEARNESS AND PRAYERS . . . SHALL BE WITH YOU IN LOVE AND SPIRIT WHEN YOU SPEAK . . . DO NOT WORRY ALL WILL BE WELL

Just two months after she found herself giving a lecture on mysticism, Mary received a letter from May written on 3 December 1930, from Geneva, New York, referring to an article Mary had subsequently written on the same subject. Mrs Maxwell wanted to make sure that her daughter had made the connection between theory and practice, between ideals and their daily reality:

> I think the article you wrote on mysticism, darling, has produced a more profound chemicalization of thought within me, and with these seeds sown of the inner significance of Bahá'u'lláh's power to change, which is after all the <u>reality</u> of this Cause, I went to Geneva and realized in the fire of suffering that I was only nominally a Bahá'í. If you will get your blue Prayer Book and read the tablet, To East and West, on page 181, you will see that 'Abdu'l-Bahá shows us that the religion of God is an intense inner spiritual life expressed in action, and on page 186, His tablet on Meditation shows us the <u>way to attain</u> this inner spiritual life. He tells us that the sign of the intellect is contemplation and that this power of contemplation, reflection and meditation causes man to become connected with his own spirit which becomes bathed in the inner Light of the Whole Spirit. In other words, prayer, aspiration, meditation, communion with God are all possessions within the temple of our own beings and that we must rely more and more upon that inner support and power and less on anyone or anything outside of ourselves.

Mrs Maxwell had already suggested an 'action' to her daughter that might express the 'intense inner spiritual life' she had written about in her article and spoken about in her talk. Ten days before, on 20 November, May had had what she called 'a wonderful thought' which she had immediately shared with Mary:

> What seemed to me a wonderful thought came to me this morning just before I received a letter from the Guardian. I felt a great joy and illumination and I thought you should draw up a little letter in your own exquisite, spontaneous language addressed to Shoghi Effendi and get the signatures of all the Bahá'í youth in America and send it to him for Christmas greeting, expressing deep devotion and loyalty of all the Bahá'í youth and the earnest wish to fulfil their

responsibility in the Will and Testament of 'Abdu'l-Bahá to bring joy to his radiant heart, the hope that through his prayers there may be the utmost unity and love and cooperation among all the Bahá'í youth, not only with each other, but with all the Bahá'ís, and their preparation to serve wisely the administration, et cetera . . .

Should you decide to do this wire me here and I will send you by return mail the address of all the Bahá'í groups to which a copy of this letter could be sent with blank papers to which all of the signatures should be affixed . . .

Two weeks later, she wrote to Mary again:

I am . . . wondering what step the Bahá'í Youth could take collectively which would bring them into a closer bond with each other, a deeper realization than my generation has ever had, of their essential oneness, a state of being and consciousness which will render them of infinitely greater service to mankind. Somehow I have the thought that you could perhaps write a letter, as you can write, my darling, addressed to all the Bahá'í Youth of America, and signed by the nine young Bahá'ís of Montreal which would start a mutual correspondence and association which would lead to wonderful results.

I am enclosing a copy of the word picture of the world the Master drew around the time of the last war, and which, if it were amplified and magnified a thousandfold, would portray the world as it is today. Surely there is a step for the Bahá'í youth to take. Perchance, God willing, it may be shown to you.

Ten days later, on 13 December, May wrote to her daughter again, about the young people who had gathered round her:

It is simply glorious the work you are doing in Montreal and I try not to be proud of you when I hear so many people here speak of my marvelous daughter! I am so happy that you have gathered all the young Bahá'ís in one group, that they are affiliating lovingly with the older Bahá'ís at informal teas and receptions, and that you are gradually attracting and quickening the spiritual life of all the young people you know. It is no wonder, Mary dear, that you are so happy because as the Master said, nothing really makes us radiantly happy in life today except to teach and serve this great Cause.

Thus was born the Youth Group[1] which was to prove so vital to the teaching work in Montreal during the 1930s, and through which May was to have such a profound influence over a new generation. It was her collaboration with her daughter which inspired and educated these young Bahá'ís, who would assume roles of leadership in the North American community during the critical years leading up to World War II. It was her encouragement and guidance of her daughter that served to encourage and to guide this new generation of Bahá'ís. Typically, she insisted that it was her daughter who was their leading light. She saw her Mary in the forefront of this dynamic cohort of youths, marching to achieve victories for the Guardian. In a letter sent to her from Pasadena on 17 April 1934, May wrote:

My blessed Mary:

Your precious little letter telling of your trials and difficulties just came today and pierced my heart with tender love and sympathy for you, my darling! . . . Perhaps this is what the Beloved of our hearts is trying to teach us now, to become firmly established in the world of reality, of abiding love and beauty above the transitory conditions of this life, to become fixed as the Pole Star in the divine Beloved, so that by our inner strength, steadfastness and firmness, our inner stability in Him, we may stabilize all around us, draw all to us like a magnet and drawing them lead them to Him. This is as I always see you, Mary, even as you yourself have mentioned, as a Winged Victory with a group behind your wings, moving forward so swiftly, so surely that by your very momentum all are drawn along with you.

If you knew all that I have heard about your lectures, from Anne,

---

1 The youthfulness of Shoghi Effendi himself was undoubtedly one of the most powerful inspirations behind the Youth Movement in Canada. In a pencilled note scribbled on the back of a cable written by her mother, after her second pilgrimage in 1926, Mary confessed: 'Shoghi Effendi is in truth the youth of today, so young yet with the wisdom and knowledge of the ages; with a courage scarcely comprehensible he turns, smiling, untiringly to the tremendous responsibility of a great movement in its infancy, growing day by day and each day bringing a new problem that only he is qualified to solve . . .' Although it is uncertain whether she wrote this note in 1926 or many years later, it contains thoughts which Amatu'l-Bahá later incorporated into her biography of Shoghi Effendi, *The Priceless Pearl*.

Emeric, Rosemary, Roland and others, how you have swept all before you, how you have held your audiences in the palm of your hand, how you have taken their breath away! Moreover, the heights you have reached have destroyed all envy and jealousy and drawn everyone within the sphere of your deep and tender love, so protective, so wise and maternal. Yes, the wistful ones come from His Home, finding refuge in peace, and I often think of you as Keeper of the Shrine and I am glad and grateful that you are making that Shrine clean and orderly and beautiful for His dear sake! Is it not wonderful how you have taken on these sacred responsibilities, making of each new service in your life a stepping stone to those great heights to which the Guardian says the Master is calling you? How I would have loved to share with you, my Mary, the Guardian's mighty message to this country, but I know it has sunk so deep in your pure soul where it will produce light upon light. Although as you say we are all so utterly unworthy, so impoverished and insignificant, yet this littleness is swallowed up in His greatness, our inability and weakness is a million-fold compensated by the wonders of His mercy and bounty, the inexhaustible treasures of His love, His wisdom which encompasses the whole world of mankind gathering His wayward children into His everlasting fold.

May must have felt it was a confirmation of the great heights to which her daughter was being called when Mary was encouraged by Shoghi Effendi to develop her ability to speak in public. On 5 December 1932, Mary herself wrote to her friend Elizabeth Coristine[2] about it:

> I got a letter from Shoghi Effendi a little while ago saying some very encouraging things and that he wanted me to concentrate on public speaking and studying Nabil's Narrative. Hard as it is to get up in public and spout I have no choice but to obey him and having read the 'Dawn-Breakers' one gets so filled with the spirit of those early days that it is comparatively easy to speak. Have you read this marvellous book Betty?

Just five days later, on Saturday, 10 December, a one-column article in the *Gazette* announced Miss Mary Maxwell's public talks on the subject:

---
2   She was by this time married to Bob Libby of Eliot, Maine, and called Betty Libby.

LECTURE SERIES ON BOOK BEING GIVEN
'The Dawn Breakers' Contains Account of Persia in 19th Century

But although Mary's career as a public speaker had been launched by the Guardian's encouragement, it would never have been sustained without her mother's support. May encouraged her daughter to travel, to speak, and to teach the Faith, just as she did.

Mary followed in her mother's footsteps in fundraising for the Temple too during 1933. And although May missed her acutely, she supported her all the way:

> I cannot help thinking, dearest, that there is a great wisdom in your thus having become so closely connected with Toronto this year, and I hope the next time you go to one of your committee meetings, that I can be in Toronto at the same time, and we can have a lovely time together.

The following year, when Mary was in Washington DC May wrote to her again:

> Darling – I miss you more than words can say – and I feel very close to you in the depth of our love – and in our wonderful spiritual nearness. Daddy and I are happy, but we both miss you – yet we know that your work in the Cause is of the utmost importance.

But above all May reminded her daughter repeatedly of Shoghi Effendi's words.

* * *

At the same time as she was doing her utmost to fulfil her pledge to Shoghi Effendi to strengthen and revive the faith of the older generation of Bahá'ís who had come under the influence of the New History Society, May was also urging her daughter to watch over the spiritual health and harmony of the younger ones. It was a classic example of their team work. The significance of May's relationship with the youth in Montreal and her nurturing of this generation would prove instrumental in the unfoldment of the Guardian's plans in the decades ahead.

Interestingly enough, the letter in which she first shared with her daughter 'what seemed . . . a wonderful thought' regarding the Youth Group was the very same one in which she first mentioned the mission given to her by Shoghi Effendi to 'save' Julie Chanler. The spiritual significance of those nine signatures that May had suggested be collected by Mary and sent to Shoghi Effendi can only be understood in their historical context. When May encouraged these Bahá'í youth in Montreal to express their devotion and their loyalty to Shoghi Effendi in those dark wintry days of 1930 she was not only fulfilling the injunctions of the Will and Testament of 'Abdu'l-Bahá to bring joy to the radiant heart of the Guardian. She was also trying to stimulate a new generation to commit themselves 'to serve wisely the administration, et cetera', as she put it, at the very moment when the older believers were falling under the influence of attacks against the Administrative Order.

May had already been worrying about the spiritual health of the Bahá'í youth in Montreal weeks before when she wrote to Mary, on 3 November 1930:

> I shall be interested to know what has happened about the young people's group, whether E. and E. have come to a mutual brotherly understanding and good feeling. I am sure you can bring this about and thru the Master's wonderful love breathe a new life and spirit into the young people's group.

A few months later, on 4 February 1931, she was still dwelling on this same theme, still anxiously inquiring about the harmony among the members of the youth group in Montreal.

> Tell me, dearest, about S. and R.? I hope you all will be able to take them right into your hearts and into your lives, so that perfect unity and solidarity may exist among the rising generation. It is my belief from observation that unity under all circumstances is our greatest safeguard and that where there is insincerity or lack of confidence, God Himself will eliminate those elements if we are faithful to His trust of absolute unity.

After several weeks, she made similar inquiries again. It was as though she wanted to ensure that this young generation would catch a glimpse of a sharper, clearer level of spiritual maturity than was visible to the older Bahá'ís.

> Are you still holding the Friday night meetings with the young Bahá'ís? I hope you will not allow this loving intimacy among you <u>all</u> to die out or become weakened because as we look back in the perspective of time, we see that it has taken years to establish this foundation of Unity in Montreal. We had it in the early days in the utmost perfection, then came disturbing forces as partisanship and the clear waters of Bahá'í love and unity were troubled; now in looking back, you will see that one by one all these disturbing factors have been removed . . .
>
> Now you have rallied the young Bahá'ís into a wonderful united group and you must never for a moment lose sight of the fact that this is a great trust and responsibility from the Master to you, and you must not allow any cross currents . . . to enter this clear stream. I feel sure that everything is all right but as I have not been closely in touch with you lately, I did not know just how things are going.

Later that summer, when she supported her daughter's plan to go to the mountains, it was not only because she wanted to encourage Mary to write. It was also because she wanted her to grow strong in spirit and be independent; she wanted her to become a shield and shelter for the faith of others. In May's letter, she explained why she was pleased about this trip despite the fact that she would miss her:

> Each day I see the trepidations, the ebb and flow of the constructive and destructive forces in the young people's group; even the Master said, 'First I shall test the believers with each other and then I shall test them with the World', and I think, Mary, that you had to get away, get out of it all, to find your own impregnable centre, to become ever more deeply and firmly rooted and established, so that in these times of testing, difficulty and stress, you will be a strength and a comfort and refuge to all. I find the young Bahá'ís do not pray enough, some of them do not pray at all, and they are therefore not spiritually <u>strong</u> with that Substance of the Spirit which alone comes from communion with God and reading the Creative Word.

May was determined to educate the new generation of Bahá'í youth to understand the spiritual nature of the Administrative Order. One of her highest priorities during the early 1930s was to teach the youth of her daughter's generation and deepen their faith. Many of them responded to the Message of Bahá'u'lláh and had the honour of becoming her spiritual children. A few remained in the periphery, but were still devoted to her till the end of her days. Whoever was fortunate enough to cross her path, to enter her home, and to bask in the sunshine of her loving personality, never lost touch with her.

The way she nurtured the spiritual life of those youth was extraordinary. She loved them; she encouraged them; she even indulged them. At times she also admonished them. On 1 September 1931, she described one such episode to her daughter:

> The conversation I had with H. was very frank and very revealing and I made him clearly understand that he was both a liar and dishonest, that the Bahá'ís do not tolerate such people on their voting list and unless he changed completely he would lose his entire community of friends and be <u>alone</u>. I also made him understand that this was his supreme opportunity, that I believed in him, that I knew that he had had a bad upbringing and his character had become weakened; in short he left me in a penitent mood and has since written me a splendid letter showing me a real awakening and manly resolve.

Above all, she provided them with a vivid example to follow. This woman, who had been called the 'Mother of France' in her own youth, was not only the mother of Mary Maxwell, but became, to all intents and purposes, the mother of a whole generation of Bahá'í youth in North America during the thirties. Writing to Mary on 13 July 1931, she described a crowd of young people who had gathered at Pine Avenue, at her own invitation, and had a party during her daughter's absence:

> The enclosed letter, if you can decipher it, was written here last night by a large number, about 20 or 22 of the young people's group, who came to the house and had a big party, and they all missed you so much that they wanted to send this letter. The newspapers had said that we would have a rainy week-end and so I suggested that if it

rained on Sunday and they could not go on their picnic they should come here in the afternoon and have music, discussion, supper and dancing. It turned out to be a good day after all, so some went to the picnic in the morning and others did not, and most of them came here between four and six, and the Ballustrari (Italian) boys brought their sister, who is a very fine pianist, and she played for a couple of hours, and E. sang divinely, and there was that radiant atmosphere of happiness peculiar to the Master's home. They had a good supper and danced for two or three hours in the Studio, which I had had thoroughly cleaned and put in order, and they did not go home until after twelve – tired – but happy. They all send their love over and over again to you, and E. E. missed you so much that he consoled himself by more or less taking charge of everything, looking after everybody, under the plea that he was your brother.

May also strengthened their characters through the moral lessons she taught her own daughter. She knew that if Mary stood firm, she could influence her contemporaries; if Mary was able to maintain Bahá'í standards, she could mark and re-mould a new generation of young Bahá'ís. In her letter to Mary of 10 September 1931, she expounded on the meaning of morality, transforming it from a narrow framework of do's and don't's to a wide circle revolving around the focal point of the Covenant:

> As we know, the world in general is unbalanced in every direction; all the vices of nature are exaggerated. As Bahá'u'lláh says, they are wandering in a wildness of nature without a shepherd or a guide and grazing in pastures of lust and desire . . . Certain environments bring out certain definite aspects of our nature and temperament, any one of which may be good and beautiful in itself, but no one part constitutes the whole of life; we are complex beings and this complexity must resolve itself, in a great simplicity at the <u>highest point of life</u>, where all our complexities and tendencies, our responses to varying environments are under one dominant note of truth and reality. This is what the Bahá'í revelation is to humanity, a unifying power, not only among all the elements of humanity, but unifying the <u>individual with himself</u>, at the high watermark of his being so that he is never partially motivated by divergent impulses

The Bahá'í community of Montreal, Canada, photo taken by W. S. Maxwell on 19 March 1932 in the Bahá'í Hall on Union Avenue. Left to right, front row: Winnie Page, Mrs Cunningham, Rachel Fink, Babiyyih Randall Lindstrom (later Ford, then Winckler), May Maxwell, Elizabeth Cole, Ruth Cunningham, Dorothy Ward. Second row: Jean Mosher, Mary Pomeroy, Elsa Lohse, Alberta Sims, Mary Maxwell, Janet French, Rosemary Gillies (later Sala), Mr Leach, Dorothy Ward Sr, Hanna ?. Back row: Grenville Wade, Amy Harrison, unidentified, Walter Lohse, Eddie Elliot, Monty Lee, Emeric Sala, Norman McGregor, Anne Savage (who had met 'Abdu'l-Bahá), Edward Lindstrom, Henry Burkeholz, Ernest Harrison

The Montreal Youth Group, 1932 or 1934. Left to right, front row: Unidentified, Mary Maxwell, Glen Wade, Louis Deer. Second row: Ruth Lee, Rosemary Gillies), Alberta Sims, Elsa Lohse, Bahíyyih Randall Lindstrom, Dorothy Ward. Back row: Eddie Elliot, Walter Lohse, Emerica Sala, Norman McGregor, Monty Lee, Edward Lindstrom

Agnes B. Alexander and May Maxwell, in Portland, Oregon, 3 July 1934

Mary Maxwell at Green Acre, 1934

In 1934 Mary Maxwell gave talks on The Dawn-Breakers *at the Bahá'í summer schools in Green Acre and Louhelen. In this picture she is taking part in the pageant* The Gate of Dawn, *presented by the newly-formed Green Acre Committee for Plays and Pageants; this is the last scene in which, dressed as an angel, she recites the farewell message of the Báb.*

but is always motivated from that unifying point which makes his life a perfect whole, a manifest sign of wisdom, virtue, strength and beauty to the whole world.

When she warned her daughter against what she called 'the old depletion of individuality', she was redefining, for Mary as well as for her contemporaries, what it truly meant to be a human being, what it really meant to be a Bahá'í:

> [O]nly those who, having come under the shadow of this great Cause, are <u>directly</u> connected with the Source and maintain that Spiritual bond, that close and intimate connection, that divine guidance, and sense of nearness through obedience, can hope to have any vitality . . . It is the strongest law in the universe, identified with that which holds all the firmament in place.

Indeed, when she wrote to her daughter from Boston, on 22 October 1931, she was reaching out through Mary Maxwell and touching the hearts of a whole generation of lost and nameless youths who were struggling to make sense of the world:

> It is the spirit that this young man (I forget his name) feels through you that will first influence him and steady him, but he will need stronger spiritual food to enable him to throw off such a habit and you should begin, with your usual depth of understanding, to give him the Teachings so that he will begin to understand that there is a superior force in the Universe which lifts the soul above its habitual reactions gradually imparting the strength to become free.
>
> This is a great test of your knowledge of the relationship between mind, soul and body. I am enclosing some words of 'Abdu'l-Bahá on this subject which will help you, because most people are groping desperately for a clue to their problems, some solvent that will release them from the talons of the eagle.
>
> I know you will be positive and strong with him and enable him to understand this law of duality that governs the human soul and I have implicit confidence in your wisdom and judgment and the power of Bahá'u'lláh to guide and confirm you . . .

It was with this extraordinary ability to convey to others a vision beyond the mundane that May transformed the young people who flocked to her home. She taught them about the meaning of inner beauty, about the power of a lively conscience, about the importance of moral standards in their lives. With her generous nature she swept aside the cobwebs in their minds and brought them into the wide embrace.

In addition to giving them moral guidance and inspiring their teaching work, May was instrumental in involving the youth of Montreal in the administrative work too and in widening their definitions of service to the Cause during the early 1930s. Writing to Mary in February 1930, she described the activities of a mutual friend in order to inspire her daughter to emulate the same zeal:

> Martha is here now and is helping me, addressing labels and doing other work. I think she is beginning to understand that work and activity in the Cause is an absolute necessity for a Bahá'í and the only thing which can serve as a safe-guard from all the dark and negative conditions of the world today.
>
> I want you to be active and busy, Darling; go to the Bahá'í meetings. Be lovely and courteous and considerate to every one, and as the Master says, 'a shining example to all'.

One year later, on 4 February 1931 she wrote an official letter, on behalf of the National Teaching Committee, to Mary and two other youth in Montreal:

> My dear Bahá'í Friends:
>
> On behalf of the National Teaching Committee, and as representative of the contacts work, I have been requested to ask you to render an important service to the Teaching Committee and the friends in general at this time. We wish to publish as soon as available a series of pamphlets, each one covering a certain branch of Bahá'í teaching, and in consultation, we decided that the progressive young Bahá'ís in Montreal might be willing to undertake the pamphlet on Economics.
>
> The pamphlet will be composed in the following manner: A brilliant introduction in which the source of the teachings will be given with a brief outline of the general teachings and a special

application of these teachings to the particular subject of the pamphlet; compilation of Utterances from the writings of Bahá'u'lláh and 'Abdu'l-Bahá on the most fundamental and salient points in Economics, especially in their application to present world needs and conditions. Each one of these references must be quoted as coming from a certain source, such as Bahá'í Scriptures, or Promulgation of Universal Peace, or Some Answered Questions, etc., also the page of the book. At the end of the pamphlet must be a glossary of references to modern books on Economics suitable for students of these subjects to read or study.

She then gives the purpose of the pamphlet, and continues:

We have appointed you three as a Committee to prepare this pamphlet as quickly as possible, and you have the privilege of associating any one you wish in Montreal in this work, which would develop your efficiency or speed . . .
With my love and greetings and earnest wishes for your success to each and every one of you, I am
Faithfully,
Your friend and co-worker

On 1 September that year she wrote a letter to her daughter about the importance of the work of the youth in the Administrative Order of Bahá'u'lláh:

Now an important question. Are you planning to go to the Young People's Conference on Sunday Sept. 13, or do you not think it sufficiently important? You know they are going to discuss plans for the coming year and give suggestions to the Youth Committee. Probably your more important work would come later on in relation to a bulletin of news and information on youth activities which I have suggested to them to first circulate in Montreal, gradually widening its sphere to include the country, and ultimately I hope it may become an international youth organ.
I am not discussing this with anyone as you know there is quite a reactionary element against the independent development of youth activities but I have already given the idea to the young people's

committee in Montreal this summer and it has been favorably received.

She was so attuned to the interests and perspectives of the youth, moreover, that she was frequently invited to speak to them. Even when there was initial resistance to her role, she was able to overcome it. Writing to her daughter, who was away in the country during the summer of 1931, May shared with her the city news on 29 July:

> It seems that the young people held a Committee Meeting and the majority wanted me to speak, opposed as usual by E., but since then he has come around in a lovely spirit and is eager to have me speak, and last night in the Meeting B. had read a very long and masterly Paper on the Dictatorship of Mussolini, on a sweltering hot night! The room was packed to the doors, and as I was saying, E. grabbed me by the arm and almost put me on to my feet, commanding me to speak, so my non-resistance is winning its way with him and he is even going to be my Chairman.

It is hardly surprising to find, therefore, that when her daughter was becoming one of the leading lights in the North American Bahá'í community, May herself was an active member of the Youth Committee. When the Local Spiritual Assembly of Montreal asked her to give a series of nine lectures in the Bahá'í Library on 1456 Union Avenue, between 4 October and 29 November 1932, the subjects she broached were all chosen with the interests of the younger generation in mind. They included such themes as 'From Doubt to Faith', 'Belief with Reason' and 'The Relative and the Absolute', all of which indicate how well she understood the psyche and spoke the language of the 'progressive' young. The challenge, for her, was to ensure that there were enough young spirits in the Cause who had sufficient skill to fulfil the hopes of the Guardian, and sufficient faith so that when they undertook a task, they would carry it through to the end. Naturally, she addressed herself first to her daughter, and challenged her, in a letter written to her on 18 April 1932, to assume her spiritual responsibilities as though she were alone in the world:

> What has happened about the Youth Conference? I hope that

nothing in the world will prevent your going through with it, because it is a great weakness to undertake something and not carry it through to a finish, and even if you did not have more support, you singly and alone could do it with the power that is back of you; especially when Agnes Macphail has given you her full and unqualified support.

Even if you can only have it in May, I think it should be undertaken because, after all, some very important conferences for peace or social economic subjects are often carried on in the month of May and there is a good deal of nonsense about this seasonal idea, anyway.

Shortly afterwards, May wrote to a young man in Montreal in a manner that was both empowering and exemplary:

I am delighted with the result of your Youth Conference and plans of your committee and I hope you will write me full particulars, as I am naturally eager to hear everything . . . As to my being chairman of the committee for the Young Peoples Letter or Bulletin, nothing could make me happier if it is really their wish; on the other hand, if they think it better to have the committee entirely composed of young people I shall be equally satisfied as I have great confidence in your united judgment. In any case I would suggest that the first letter you send out should be a brief, vital, clear report, written in a warm and cordial spirit of your recent conference and its outcome, and I would suggest sending this to the youth groups of the United States and Canada first, or if Mr. Lohse wishes to translate it into German, it would be wonderful for the youth groups of Germany . . . In my humble judgment the spirit of brotherly love and friendliness accompanied by a spirit of genuine modesty (so lacking in the Occident) will be the truest path to the success of any well planned brilliant undertaking.

On 19 November 1932 she received a letter from a young non-Bahá'í in Montreal which she answered on the same day. She always went straight to the heart of essential truths in such communications as these, revealing a generosity of spirit that is thrilling to the soul:

> Your letter came today and I was so overjoyed in reading it that I must seize this moment in the dead of night, with only a pencil, to reply! . . . As I said to a beautiful Catholic boy Mary and I have come to know well and with whom we have been having wonderful talks during the past year, I said, 'Do you really believe André that in the infinite world of light, of mind and spirit of absolute existence towards which we all are journeying that there are any confines or limitations, any group or names, any Catholics, Protestants, Jews, Mohammedans, Bahá'ís or anything else!' His beautiful young eyes looked into mine and after a moment or two he said, 'No, they are all paths, we are all one,' and at that point our paths seemed to converge . . . now he is seeing the true meaning of the symbols and sacraments, the inner depths of faith in which he was reared and their essential relation to the faiths of all mankind and the fresh new vigorous faith of today in the Bahá'í Cause.

May had already shared her thoughts on the importance of the youth to the future of the Cause with her friend Ella Goodall Cooper early that autumn, on 3 September, soon after returning from a visit to Green Acre with her daughter:

> I wrote an account of 'Abdu'l-Bahá's visit to Montreal for Shoghi Effendi and in the course of this winter I hope to write a history of the early days of the Cause in Canada in collaboration with some of the early believers here, and also of that radiant fresh dawn in Paris.[1] Oh God! Those unsullied days before all the pain and bitterness and travail through which our glorious Faith has passed had even begun, we were all fresh and untried, young and enthusiastic with the breeze of morning blowing on our pure brows. Now we are living through another dawning, the dayspring of the Guardian in which the glowing army of youth is being recruited, and in their lives and in our love for Shoghi Effendi all the forces of youth are renewed.

Through her efforts and encouragement, the youth who accepted the Faith of Bahá'u'lláh during these years, both in Canada and the United

---

3 Unfortunately, only short beginnings of drafts of the Canada and Paris histories have been found in the Estate papers.

States, were to become some of the most distinguished believers in the world. They included people such as David Hofman, George Spendlove, Rowland Estall, Emeric and Rosemary Sala, Eddie Elliot, Teddy Edwards Alizadeh, Norman McGregor, Julie Russell Blakely, Dorothy and Glen Wade, Edward Dewing, Gerrard Sluter, and Rena Gordon, to name but a few. Each of these souls was destined to become an outstanding Bahá'í and a potent instrument to teach the Cause. And each of them forged an intimate bond with May.

Indeed, there was a vigour and joy in May, which meant that she never seemed to age. To many of those who met her and loved her, she seemed the spirit of youth incarnate. She was young in heart, fresh and vital, utterly different from the staid and sometimes stolid members of her own generation. She was accepted by her daughter's friends and acquaintances as though she was their own age, and as a result she had a profound influence on their lives.

Rosemary Sala, neé Gillies, was one of the youth who was taught, confirmed and deeply loved by May. In the winter of 1932, when May was unwell in New York, Rosemary wrote her a letter on 28 December, which is very revealing both of the relationship that May had with youth and the model she was for them:

> I have been meaning to write you ever since I received the sweet note and sweeter cheque you left for me! The money has all been spent and full value received and many children, especially the Page boys, made happier because of your generosity. We fed and clothed about thirty children besides feeding and remembering their mothers with some little gift. It was remarkable the way contributions and gifts came pouring in. The children were adorable and said their little verses in the sweetest way . . . Darling, we were so sorry to learn that you have not been well. You do your share and we'll pray Bahá'u'lláh to do the rest.

Another of the innumerable young people who were first attracted by the daughter, and then confirmed in the Faith by the mother, was a young woman named Gladys Cotton, later Gladys Weeden. One summer's day in July 1932, Gladys and her husband had gone to the White Mountains in New Hampshire, with another couple, for the purpose of sightseeing. Among the other sightseers she met there were two young women from Montreal: Mary Maxwell and Rosemary Gillies. Gladys was immediately attracted to Mary, first because of her unusual beauty, and then through her personality and trusting nature. This meeting led to a deeper friendship and finally an invitation to Green Acre. There Gladys met Mary's mother, in the Rockingham Hotel in Portsmouth, New Hampshire. The description of the event written by this young clerk in a department store is very telling:

> So when we got into her hotel room – Mary was outside somewhere – Mrs. Maxwell was in bed, and she had on a beautiful robin's-egg-blue negligée. She had a boil on her neck from the extreme heat of New York City and that was why she was resting that day. I was seated over here, and totally in awe of meeting such an important person. Finally she threw back the covers of the bed and put her slippers on, and she pulled a chair up beside me, and put – my hand was on the arm of the chair – and she put her hand on mine, and looked into my eyes. I felt as if she were looking right down to my feet, and she said, 'Now I know why Mary likes you.' I did not know at that time what the Bahá'í Faith was.

This chance encounter led to a lasting friendship. Years later, in 1948, Gladys was invited to Haifa by Shoghi Effendi to help him and Rúḥíyyih Khánum in their work. Despite her simple background, she became a distinguished Bahá'í and was of tremendous service to the beloved Guardian during the very turbulent years after World War II, and the War of Independence in Israel.

The correspondence alone which May maintained with young Bahá'ís over the years was phenomenal. In these letters too one senses the vitality and youthfulness of her spirit pulsing through the lines, despite her physical weaknesses and frailties. Writing to David Hofman just two years before her passing, May described how the Montreal Bahá'ís had been divided into groups to attend study classes three times a week, and gleefully added that after these intensive courses

> We shall have a big dance upstairs in the studio for all the younger groups, the hope and promise of our glorious Faith in this formative period.

MIDDLE YEARS 1930–1934

In the last year of her life, when she was almost sixty-nine, she wrote to her daughter with a cry of mingled dismay and incredulity:

Four more days & I shall be oh! so old! & I feel so young!

Three months later, on 8 March 1939, David Hofman invited her to England:

> ... there is now so much to do that it is almost an impossibility to do justice to my job and to the National Spiritual Assembly. We need a few young spirits like yourself; why don't you come over this summer and attend our Summer School?

May had always felt that the future of the Faith, like its past, was intimately linked with the ardour and commitment of young people to the Cause. At the end of her life, barely three months before she died, she was still thrilled by the promise symbolized by the next generation. In a letter dated 26 November 1939 to the beloved Guardian, handwritten by May in New York City, but which may never have been sent, she said:

> My beloved – You alone can know the joy your recent powerful and heavenly messages, published in Bahá'í News, have brought to the hearts – so full of hope and promise of the future towards which we now dare to look! So happy and rejoiced in the wonderful achievements of your young pioneers! None knows as you do that they are a new-born generation – wholly imbued with your vision – your fire – your indomitable strength and – action!

* * *

As if to mark the turning of a page in Bahá'í history and indicate the beginning of a fresh chapter in the annals of the Cause, Shoghi Effendi decided in the early 1930s to gather together records related to the older generation of outstanding believers. On 3 February 1930, May received a letter written by his secretary containing a highly significant request:

> Shoghi Effendi is in these days busy collecting interesting material for the forthcoming number of the year-book. Among others he is

collecting the pictures of some of the old friends who have passed away and who have rendered distinguished services to the Cause. He has already gathered the pictures of nineteen distinguished figures among those who have rendered eminent services to the Cause in the East. He wishes now to gather an equal number from among the old Western Bahá'ís who have passed away and who have done great services to the Cause.

It was part of the Guardian's life-long concern with gathering together the records of present and past Bahá'í activity in the historic volumes known as *The Bahá'í World* which he painstakingly edited and published from 1926 onwards. May now threw herself wholeheartedly into the work of helping him gather these materials. She also involved Sutherland in the task. On 8 March 1930, she wrote to Shoghi Effendi, saying:

> On receipt of the letter . . . instructing me to send you the names and photographs of nineteen believers whose distinguished services to the Cause should be recorded in the Year Book, I dropped everything in order to fulfil your wishes promptly. I had no idea of the difficulties that would arise in obtaining photographs of many of these early believers who had died, and rendered such signal service to the Cause . . .
>
> Knowing your high standard for the Year Book, I undertook to obtain original photographs, and this is requiring an amount of research delaying forwarding them to you, because first I had to find the people who might possess such pictures, and then obtain them.

Then she gives the following names:

> Mrs. Phoebe Hearst, as you know, took the first group of Pilgrims to the presence of 'Abdu'l-Bahá, and He told her that while all her great philanthropies and noble service to humanity had been accepted by God, yet all this was as nothing compared with the one act of being the means of this first group of early believers attaining to His presence.
>
> Thomas Breakwell was such a flame of the Cause in Paris, such a source of illumination and unfoldment to that group, that his death evoked from the supreme pen of our Lord ['Abdu'l-Bahá] the

eulogy, of which the Master said, it was so powerful it would melt the solid rocks and cause the streams to run dry.

The home of Mr. and Mrs. A. P. Dodge was the early centre and foundation of the Cause in New York City, where for many years the friends congregated and great meetings and gatherings were held; their love and hospitality was as a beacon light in the Cause, and the Master revealed to them many of the most profound early Tablets.

Mrs. Helen Ellis Cole was the one who gave the Fellowship House and grounds to Greenacre,[2] which have been a spiritual centre of Bahá'í activities for many years.

Mr. Albert Hall devoted his life faithfully to the Temple in the early days of its inception and foundation . . .

Robert Turner, the first Negro to enter the Cause, the man-servant of Mrs. Hearst, taught by Lua, and among the first Pilgrims. 'Abdu'l-Bahá said to him that should he remain faithful, in the face of tests, to the hour of his death, he would be the door through which his race would enter the Cause. As you know, my dearest Guardian, Mrs. Hearst's faith suffered a period of eclipse and denial,[3] during which time, Robert, although devotedly attached to her, never wavered in his passionate loyalty and faith, and when I was with the beloved Master in Akka, some twenty years ago, and told Him that Robert was dying, in a hospital, He dictated a wonderful message through me, signifying His great pleasure and acceptance of his soul . . .

Mrs. Margaret Peeke, another devoted and early Pilgrim, was distinguished by the Master in that when He was in Cleveland, He gave a certain sum of money to the believers there, instructing them to erect a bronze Tablet in her memory.

A letter dated 23 April 1930, written on Shoghi Effendi's behalf, acknowledged receipt of the photographs:

---

4   *Star of the West*, vol. 15 (June 1924), p. 80. She was a cousin of May Ellis Bolles Maxwell, and in November 1900 had made the pilgrimage to 'Akká and Haifa in the company of Mrs Emogene Hoagg and Miss Alma Albertson.
3   Regarding Mrs Hearst, May Maxwell wrote a letter to Mrs Katherine Page on 9 September 1930: 'When 'Abdu'l-Bahá went to San Francisco she [Mrs Hearst] begged to see Him and became once more a loyal and devoted follower of this blessed Faith and died a firm believer. I knew Mrs. Hearst from my childhood and was a witness to her wonderful generosity and many philanthropies and the memory I love best to cherish is her having been accepted by 'Abdu'l-Bahá.' See also the account in Hogenson, *Lighting the Western Sky*.

I am directed by Shoghi Effendi to thank you so much for your letter of March 15th with the photograph of Mrs. Knobloch and her Tablet enclosed. Also for the photographs you sent him under separate cover which have already reached him and in good time, thanks to your endeavour & enterprise. Of course you know that they are intended for the forthcoming issue of the 'Bahá'í World'.

Then, in his own handwriting, Shoghi Effendi added his thanks for all her efforts on his behalf:

My dear and precious co-worker;
The photos you sent me have all reached safely, and I am deeply appreciative of your efforts.

In another letter he added:

I have already cabled my joyous satisfaction and appreciation of your prompt response to my request. I am greatly pleased with your choice and these will in due course appear in the 'Bahá'í World'.

During the years 1930 and 1931, over and above all her administrative services and her interest in the youth activities, May Maxwell not only worked on obtaining photographs of the distinguished early believers for Shoghi Effendi's year books, but also on gathering articles and reports on Bahá'í history and activities for him. She was in New York a great deal during this period and from there wrote to Mariam Haney telling her about her attempts to collect photographs of various people in the American Bahá'í community. Among these important historical figures were Sarah Farmer, Joseph Hannan, Thornton Chase, Harry Randall, and Jean Masson. 'I have been trying', she adds, 'in the midst of so much work, to get my article on the Administration into shape to submit to you and Stanwood.' She had clearly understood, instantly and instinctively, the significance of what Shoghi Effendi was trying to do. She had realized that his vision of the future of the Faith required that its history be carefully preserved and documented.

It was during this same period that she wrote to Jessie Revell also, asking for a brief and concise summary of the teaching activities which the Local Spiritual Assembly of Philadelphia wished to have on record in the annual report. It was evident that the administrative work of the institutions was of just as much importance, historically, as the individual lives of believers. In this letter she also asked Jessie for good photographs of Isabella Brittingham, Miss Stewart and Dr Clock. In other words, she used every opportunity provided by her administrative duties as the secretary of the National Teaching Committee to gather materials for the Guardian's year book.

On 13 April 1931 May wrote a revealing letter to Nellie French, which not only indicated her personal commitment to write for the year book but also beautifully exemplified what she believed should be the high standard for such writing. Nothing but the best would suffice for these records:

> Have just received a line from you, reminding me of your former request, as Chairman of the Year Book Committee, to write the article about 'Abdu'l-Bahá and Canada, and believe I have already told you I will be glad to undertake the work, but I shall be obliged to do it some time in May and June, as I have too much work now to undertake anything of so beautiful and delicate a nature, and I hope that through the confirmation of God, I may produce something which will bring real joy to the pure heart of Shoghi Effendi.

By aiming at nothing less than 'bringing real joy to the pure heart of Shoghi Effendi', May managed to establish a universal criterion of excellence that transcended culture and time. By emphasizing the intensely personal nature of such writing at the same time, she was able to encourage others to write too. In September of 1931, while in Portsmouth, New Hampshire, she wrote to Archie Eddington on this same subject:

> Dear Archie, Many thanks for your kind letter and splendid cooperation! . . . I am so glad that you remember everything so vividly; in fact, I have always felt that you bore a unique relation to 'Abdu'l-Bahá's visit to Canada and feel that you, better than any one, could record those events both with depth of realization and accuracy as to date of arrival, places of meeting, type of audience and subject, and date of departure as no one else could do. Whenever you have written it send it to my home address, 1548 Pine Avenue, Canada

and it will be forwarded to me. If you will put it in an envelope such as the last one marked Montreal Daily Star, I will ask Sutherland to give it his special attention.

There was sometimes a considerable delay. On 20 October 1931 she wrote to her daughter from Boston, asking for her help:

> My dearest Mary:
>
> I have just dictated a long letter to your father so can only write you a line to ask you to attend to a very urgent matter for me. Archie Eddington promised me five or six weeks ago to write an article, or give me a complete outline, of 'Abdu'l-Bahá's visit to Montreal, as he said it was all so vivid to him as though it were yesterday, and he has all the data concerning the Master's meetings, public addresses, etc. in his office.
>
> Archie was very responsive and glad to do it, but I have heard nothing since, although I have written him twice in the matter.
>
> Now, will you go to the Star office tomorrow without fail and see Archie personally (he likes you very much and I know you can impress him) and make him understand that this is an urgent matter, as Nellie French must have all the data in hand by November 1st and she is on the Pacific Coast. I have written a little myself about the Master's visit which could be woven into Archie's article unless his is complete without it, and the article could be signed by us both and will appear in the next issue of the Bahá'í World. If Archie's article is complete without anything from me, it can be signed by him alone. Heaven knows, I do not care as long as we get it . . . and probably the Master wants Archie to write it anyway, he was so wonderful to the Master during his visit giving Him the finest publicity He had on His Western trip.
>
> Please get Archie under way if he has not already written it and tell him to send it to me at the above address.

Nor did May flinch from approaching non-Bahá'ís in her efforts to acquire suitable material. Indeed, she was so keenly aware of the significance of what Shoghi Effendi was doing with this project that she had no qualms in approaching influential people in government and asking for their help for *The Bahá'í World*. For example, three weeks before writing to Mary about Archie Eddington, she wrote to Agnes Macphail, on 30 September 1931, from Portsmouth, New Hampshire:

> Some weeks ago I wrote you asking if you would advise me how I could obtain the necessary information regarding progress and reform of various kinds, especially of a legislative nature, that have taken place in Canada in the past ten or fifteen years. I require this data for an article I am writing and felt you would be kind enough to direct me as to the best means of obtaining the information.

On 2 December that same year, Mr Maxwell wrote to Shoghi Effendi, enclosing photographs and referring to this article again:

> Beloved Shoghi Effendi,
> I am sending you today under separate cover, for your consideration, four shiny photographic prints of the Church of the Messiah wherein 'Abdu'l-Bahá spoke, of our home where he honoured us with his presence, and of the City of Montreal as it was when He visited Canada.
> I have written on the back of each a condensed title and description.
> If any of the pictures are desired for the 'Year Book' I suggest that the prints I send be selected. If you wish copies of them I can arrange for others printed on a more agreeable paper than the present one – which are of a type suitable for the use of photo-engravers.
> I question if I can obtain another print of the City of Montreal as it was a matter of luck to find a view of the city taken at about the time of 'Abdu'l-Bahá's visit.
> The other prints are for you with love from May and me. I took them in 1909 when we made our visit to 'Abdu'l-Bahá and the Holy Family. I have a few negatives of groups of Persian and other Bahá'ís, also taken in 1909. I shall esteem it a privilege, if you allow me to send you copies – I am sure they will prove of interest as many of the older believers shown must have died since the pictures were taken.
> Of course you know that the four shiny prints are related to the article May is writing on 'Abdu'l-Bahá's visit to Montreal and are related to the Bahá'í Year Book.
> We are all at home and well and send you my devoted and

affectionate regards in which I know May and Mary wish to be associated.

Devotedly Yours
Sutherland Maxwell

The following March, Mr Maxwell sent another letter to Shoghi Effendi:

Dear Shoghi Effendi,

    The photograph enclosed is of the Youth Group, Montreal Bahá'ís. It was taken on Sunday morning in my studio and is one of two exposures made, the other being less satisfactory.

    After the pictures were taken all adjourned to the dining room and enjoyed Persian pilau. Several most enjoyable hours passed away quickly and I am sending the devoted love of all who were present. I am sure I interpret the wishes of the party.

    The other photograph of the group will be enclosed with the pictures taken last night at the Feast in the Bahá'í Hall.

    I am writing rather hurriedly, having held the letter back in the hope of being able to enclose the other picture.

    I send you the devoted love of Mrs. Maxwell, Mary and myself.

Devotedly Yours,
W. S. Maxwell

But the high standards of excellence which Shoghi Effendi required of those who assisted him also demanded an equal degree of detachment. Three weeks later, on 14 April 1932, Shoghi Effendi wrote to May regarding her article about 'Abdu'l-Bahá's visit to Montreal:

Dear and precious co-worker:

    Please thank Mr. Maxwell for the splendid photographs of the Montreal Youth Group which I was very pleased to receive. The report of their activities was highly encouraging, & I have forwarded it to Horace for incorporation in the Bahá'í World. I would have so wished to include your article in the forthcoming issue, but in view of my decision to reserve all the material I had received for the future publication, I felt it unfair to discriminate in favour of your splendid account. You will, I am sure, realize the delicacy & difficulty of my position. I trust & pray that you will continue in close

collaboration with Mary & her father your inestimable services to the Cause of Bahá'u'lláh.
>Your true brother & well-wisher,
>Shoghi

It is ironic that the man whom the Guardian wished to thank for having gathered so many photographs for his year book in 1931 and 1932, with such meticulous care, was the same one whose own photograph would be included in *The Globe* newspaper the following year, on 18 February 1933, along with the eleven other members of the Royal Architectural Institute of Canada, over the subtitle:

> The twenty-sixth general annual meeting of the Royal Architectural Institute of Canada is now in progress in Toronto, with headquarters at the King Edward Hotel.

W. S. Maxwell was the Honorary Treasurer of the Institute at this time and very active in his professional commitments as well as his services to the Faith. His photograph, as well as that of his daughter, was also taken standing behind their Excellencies the Earl and Countess of Bessborough at the opening of the Royal Canadian Academy Fifty-Fourth Exhibition in November that same year, where he was identified as 'prominent architect, contributor to the exhibition, and vice-president of the Academy', a function he filled every year between 1930 and 1938. It is salutary to consider that a person of such social prominence nevertheless responded to the minutiae of the Cause with such fastidious detachment.

Another example of the detachment that was required for Shoghi Effendi's year book concerned the article written about the Faith by the influential pianist whom May had befriended in the late 1920s in Montreal. In a letter that May wrote to Shoghi Effendi on 29 December 1933 we learn of her dismay that

> The enclosed article written by Princess De Broglie, which Mrs. French asked me to translate, may not reach you in time for the Bahá'í World which I shall deeply regret, but I found it most difficult to translate and had it not been for the help I have had from Mary, I could not have accomplished it.

In fact, although both she and Mary made great efforts over the translation of this article, they had to defer to Shoghi Effendi's far wider vision of the purpose of the *Bahá'í World* volumes. In 1934 May received the following letter dated 18 January written on behalf of the Guardian on this subject:

> The Guardian has directed me to inform you of the receipt of your much-appreciated letter of Dec. 29th, and to express his heartfelt thanks for your painstaking efforts in connection with the translation of Princess de Broglie's article on the Cause. Your rendering is, indeed, very faithful and fully expressive of the beauty & power of the original. But Shoghi Effendi feels that the publication of the French text would not only do more justice to the author but would greatly enhance the universality & effectiveness of the 'Bahá'í World' itself. At his request one of our German believers is also writing an article, the German text of which will be published in the year book, and thus will give an opportunity to the non-English-speaking Bahá'ís to better acquaint themselves with the contents of the Biennial.

In her 29 December letter to Shoghi Effendi, May also mentioned that her daughter had written a play entitled *The Persian Wife*. Shoghi Effendi added a handwritten postscript on the subject in his response of 18 January 1934:

> Dear & precious co-worker:
>
> I was delighted to read Mary's article for the forthcoming issue of the Bahá'í World – a welcome evidence of her initial international activities & services for which I cherish the brightest hopes. I have not yet answered her letter to me preferring to wait until I receive a copy of her play the perusal of which will no doubt deeply interest me & the early publication of which the Reviewing Committee I trust will sanction. I am praying ardently for the speedy & complete realization of the Master's hopes in, & promises to you, & wish you to take the utmost care of your precious health. You & your dear family are often in my thoughts & prayers, I assure you.
>
> Your true brother, Shoghi

By withholding judgement on Mary's play until he could read it for himself and by simultaneously identifying the administrative procedure that should be followed if such material were to be printed independently, Shoghi Effendi was clearly formulating the criteria necessary for Bahá'í publications at that time, and since.

* * *

May had heard news through pilgrims of the physical decline of the Greatest Holy Leaf almost a year before she died. Unlike the sudden shock of the Master's death, the early warnings of this second loss had been tolling in her ears for some time now, but the thought of it was still inconceivable. It made her cling the more ardently to Shoghi Effendi himself, the last and only intermediary between this nether world and the realms of the kingdom. Writing to her daughter on 10 September 1931, May told her of the recent return of a pilgrim, adding:

> W. H. is going to Montreal and I want you to see and hear him there or here without fail or you will be missing one of the most important things in life. He also told us that dearest Khanum is losing her memory, and I suppose this we must humbly accept as the first sign of her onward journey and her flight from this world. I wrote her about two weeks ago, feeling deeply moved to do so. Oh Mary, how I wish you might see her again, for it is hard indeed for us to reach and penetrate that realm of sanctity and holiness, of beauty and perfection without this blessed intermediary! It makes us realize once more with infinite gratitude the Bounty of Bahá'u'lláh of granting us His eternal presence in our blessed Guardian.

When she heard that this luminous being had left this world on 15 July 1932 and had winged her flight to the Abhá realms, May's heart surged with waves of sorrow that she had not felt since being drowned in grief over the passing of her beloved 'Abdu'l-Bahá. She had known the Greatest Holy Leaf from the time of her first pilgrimage in 1899 and had maintained a close bond with her on her subsequent visits and through their correspondence. She loved and revered this 'liege lady' of the Faith of Bahá and adored her, above all else, for the comfort she gave to the beloved Guardian. The thought that he would now be all alone broke her heart.

She was in New York and doing a radio broadcast when she heard the news. She wrote to the Guardian's secretary immediately, hoping to cheer Shoghi Effendi's grieving heart:

> I feel his anguish so acutely and I hope to bring him one atom of comfort through the knowledge that a new door has opened for our beloved Cause in the field of broadcasting and that through a very sincere, devoted woman whom I have met here, I have had the opportunity to broadcast four times a week for the past month.

Shoghi Effendi replied to her through his secretary in a manner that acknowledged the extent of her grief as well as his own:

> Your messages of condolence & sympathy dated July 22nd and 28th, 1932 were received and were greatly appreciated by the Guardian. His sorrow-laden heart was much relieved at the thought that you are so kindly sharing his grief, and the news of your unceasing efforts towards a greater spread of the Cause brightened his hopes for the future of your work . . .
>
> In your last communication you had enclosed a letter to you by Lily Armstrong which indicated how eager this devoted woman is to spread the teachings of the Faith. Shoghi Effendi trusts that through your devotion, care and wisdom she will soon embrace the Cause and will be able to render it as many services as she can. In his moments of meditation & prayer he will always remember her & ask the Almighty to strengthen her faith, deepen her spiritual insight & open before her new fields of service.

And in Shoghi Effendi's handwriting:

> Dear & valued sister:
> I greatly prize your message as it comes from one whose past, & particularly her present, services have to a great extent served to cheer the heart of Khánum, in the closing days of her earthly life. This thought should alleviate your sorrow & impart fresh strength to your heart in the many services you are so nobly & energetically

rendering to the Cause of God. I will continue to pray for you that the Beloved may sustain, bless & guide your high endeavours.

>Your true brother,
>Shoghi

One year later, May was grieving another loss: the death of Keith Ransom-Kehler. They had been intimate friends and united by bonds of the spirit, for Keith had been taught the Faith by May and was her spiritual child. When she wrote to May from Persia on 20 March 1933, telling her about the great difficulties she was experiencing in carrying out the mission Shoghi Effendi had given her in that country, she evoked that vivid moment when she had accepted the Cause so long ago. Her 'twelfth spiritual birthday', she told May, had come and gone. It was an event she would never forget. She recalled how she and her husband, Jim, had 'sat in your dear presence and, as you spoke, embraced His Blessed Faith'. It was, she avers, 'a recollection springing up into everlasting life'. Seven months later, in the city of Isfahan, Keith died of smallpox. It was a terrible blow for May.[4]

Shoghi Effendi hailed Keith as the first American Bahá'í martyr. It was a significant accolade, and one that had a special resonance for those remarkable women who had, with such ardour, accepted the Faith in the days of 'Abdu'l-Bahá. Some of them, like Lua, had begged for martyrdom, and she was already gone. Now Keith had joined her. May herself was to attain that same station seven years later but she had thought about what it meant for many years. She was all too keenly aware that martyrdom was far more than being killed for one's faith. On one of the preliminary pages of her 1918 copy of *Abdul Baha on Divine Philosophy*, she had written:

> 'Abdu'l-Bahá told me that 'Martyrdom is a station, strive to attain it!'

It must have done much to assuage May's sorrow when her husband was commissioned to design Keith's gravestone. She wrote to him about

---

4   It is touching and indicative of their spiritual bond that Keith left her rosary to May. In June of 1934 May received the following message from Keith's brother, W. Worth Bean, Jr: 'In accordance with the Last Will and Testament of Mrs Keith Ransom Kehler you are a legatee of her estate as follows: To my spiritual mother, May Maxwell, I leave my Buddhist rosary.'

her feelings on 9 February 1934 from Los Angeles, where she was travelling at the time:

> I know you will make a masterpiece for the monument of our beloved Keith, soaring, unique and significant like herself, and I am so grateful to the N.S.A. for giving you this opportunity because she was so close to us all, and I often feel her overshadowing influence.

Less than a week later, on 15 February, she sent another message to him about Keith's grave, through her daughter Mary:

> I was delighted with Daddy's design for the monument for Keith, it is very symbolic and beautiful and I can see that he has put his whole heart in it. Tell him what I say and how deeply I appreciate it, and give him my love. I will write him also tomorrow.

A letter which Sutherland wrote to Mason Remey on 9 April 1934, in response to an invitation from the latter to visit him in his home in Washington DC, makes reference to his plans for the monument:

> My scheme for the Keith memorial contemplates the stone being cut abroad and the nine-pointed star made by Early using the same aggregates as those used for the Temple, but finer in grain if necessary. I have ordered a print and will enclose it for you.

* * *

The only remedy May knew for grief was love and the work of the Cause. This was the only cure she knew for the relapse into self-doubt and ill-health that invariably accompanied any experience of sorrow. And so she rallied from her losses and applied herself to her teaching and administrative activities. All through 1932, in addition to her local duties in Montreal, she also served as an officer of the National Teaching Committee, as a member of the Green Acre Program Committee, and as a contributing editor for the *Bahá'í Magazine*. From 1933 to 1935 she was a member of the History of the Cause in America Committee, on which she had already served in 1925. She also launched, during these years, a series of meetings in Washington DC that were among the earliest attempts at racial amity in the Bahá'í community of North America. But above all, she was extremely active at this time in her efforts to broadcast the Faith on the radio.

Her interest in radio had begun early too, in fact as early as December 1928, when she had written to Mabel Ives full of excitement about the idea of broadcasting the message of the Faith through the radio. She was keenly aware of its potential for the rapid dissemination and proclamation of the Faith. Her enthusiasm, almost a century of technological advancement later, is still infectious:

> Although my little teaching trip through Geneva, Buffalo, Cleveland and Detroit brought me many precious experiences, the two outstanding forces were you and Mrs. Esty . . . Now I have no time to do more than say that the more I have thought of it, I am convinced about this broadcasting over WEAF and I am going to New York in a few days, and from there to Washington for the National Spiritual Assembly meeting on December 8th; I shall put every bit of influence I have in motion . . . until we tap the right wire to unlock this magic door.

Two years later, laid up in New York City during the winter of 1930, she wrote to her daughter about some radio programmes she had heard:

> Last night Evangeline Adams, the famous astrologer, who broadcasts over the radio every night around six o'clock, mentioned the date of your birthday, among other dates, and said that in this year, 1930, people born on that date would have excellent opportunities for contacts, new friendships and relationships in the month of December, so I thought I would tell you that as she only uses astrology, not as something which governs our lives, but as something suggestive of opportunities, if we have the sense to seize them, and of warnings for protection, if we have the sense to take them . . .
>
> I have learned a great deal from the radio, which is in my room, in the last few days, because I cannot read the newspapers and it has brought before me a vivid and very terrific picture of the state of the world and the condition of mankind and I do not see how any conscious soul could bear it without the knowledge of Bahá'u'lláh. One feels the increasing sadness of the rush toward destruction and

through it the sincere yearning for light, the earnest gropings for truth, for some answer to the awful human riddle of this age. We know that the answer lies only in the knowledge of Bahá'u'lláh but in the past few weeks I have suffered so much both mentally and physically that a new thought has awakened within me, an entirely new conception, as it were, of the whole meaning of life, its true purpose and how we should approach this most vital of all questions, how to awaken the inner consciousness of man. We are, as it were, all whirling around on the circumference of a wheel, all living in our <u>objective</u> consciousness, even the Bahá'ís are still in the external forms and teachings of this Cause which makes them purely a sectarian movement, and how to enter the inner sanctuary of our own hearts and souls where God abides is the supreme question of this age for the whole human race.

It was not until the historic visit of Martha Root to Montreal in 1932 that the 'magic box' was literally, as well as metaphorically, unlocked. It was through the waves of spirit transmitted by Martha that the inner consciousness of the radio listeners awakened! Her visit was to be a turning point in the proclamation of the Faith in Canada. Months after she left, May was still remembering her as the touchstone for being a true teacher and the perfect model for the service of the Faith. Writing to her daughter on 21 May 1932, she said:

This has been a wonderful year for this entire continent through the visit of Martha Root who has both inwardly and outwardly thrown wide open the doors for the reception of the Cause. Did you know that Shoghi Effendi said that she was the greatest teacher the Cause had ever produced, either in the East or the West!

Already, after her first meeting with her in Wilmette at the Convention of 1931, the previous year, May had written a glowing note about Martha to her daughter:

I want you to know Mary that the majesty and beauty of the Bahá'í House of Worship, the greatness and simplicity of Martha Root and the unfolding life and growth of our beloved Cause through the Convention have given me a new strength and inspiration and a new realization of what Shoghi Effendi expects of me in the future. I am sure that you and Daddy must have received these spiritual outpourings through that deep unity which binds us to each other, and which brings such joy and refreshment to the soul. Martha Root loves you very dearly, she sent you a heartful of love and is eagerly looking forward to seeing you a little later in the year.

In fact, Martha Root came to visit the Maxwells of Montreal the following year, and when she arrived, several public talks and press and radio interviews had already been arranged for her. Amatu'l-Bahá Rúḥíyyih Khánum would often relate the story of this famous visit, in her public talks and private conversations. She used to talk about how her mother had tried to find an opening into radio broadcasting in Montreal for years, and how this stronghold of Catholicism was firmly closed in the face of the Bahá'ís. When Martha Root was coming, she had once again contacted the authorities of the radio station and had once again been faced by the same negative attitude. She had been told by the head of the radio station that Miss Root could speak about her travels but could not mention the Bahá'í Faith.

When Martha Root finally arrived and heard about all this, she said nothing at first, but simply asked May to take her to meet with the general director of the radio station. The story continues in the words of Rúḥíyyih Khánum:

> I remember very clearly the day they went to meet this man. As my mother and Martha Root were leaving our house to go to the radio station for their appointment, they went out of the front door – which was wide open with the sunlight coming in – and on the left-hand side of the vestibule was a shelf over a radiator on which there was a vase full of tulips. Martha Root leaned over, took one of the tulips in her hand (without wrapping it up at all), walked out of the front door and they got into the car and drove away. I remember so clearly, as a young girl, thinking: what an extraordinary thing to do; nobody does anything like that! We were much more fussy in those days and if we were going to take anybody flowers, we wrapped them up.
>
> When my mother came back later on, she told me the story of what had happened: When they arrived at the radio station and

were ushered in to meet the Director, who was sitting behind his desk, my mother said, 'This is Miss Martha Root'. He of course got up to greet her, and she walked over and handed him this single tulip flower – not wrapped up in anything. The Director took the tulip in his hand and looked at it, and he looked at Martha Root, and his eyes filled with tears. He said, 'How did you know that this is my national flower? I am a Dutchman and in Holland tulips are the national flower.'

This one very peculiar gesture by Martha Root opened all the doors! The man was completely melted; he offered her 15 minutes on the radio program – a very good period of time – and although he had told my mother that she must not mention the word 'Bahá'í', she must not introduce the Bahá'í Faith as such, that one gesture had unlocked his heart, and he said she could give a talk on any topic she wished. And she did – for half an hour, on prime time!

Martha Root's sole desire was to proclaim the Message of Bahá'u'lláh to the people of the world in any way that she could, and this was the history of her whole life. She was, as Shoghi Effendi said, the 'Star Servant of Bahá'u'lláh'. This unusual occurrence taught me – when I was still myself a young girl, a young woman – that if you turn to Bahá'u'lláh and want to serve Him, focus your heart and your feelings, your intention on His power, forget about yourself, your insignificance, your lack of knowledge, your lack of experience, that you will receive inspiration and assistance from Him in serving His Cause; it is really extraordinary how much guidance and inspiration you can receive, and how much you can reflect.

In Amatu'l-Bahá's vivid account of this event, she recalled that it was the first time that the name of Bahá'u'lláh and the Bahá'í Faith were broadcast from a Canadian radio station.

On 21 January 1932 May wrote to Randolph Bolles, her brother, about Martha's visit, summing up the miracle and sharing the marvel of the whole experience:

> We have just had a wonderful visit from Martha Root; she was only here two days, but stirred up thousands of thinking people in this city . . . She broadcast over the radio for one half hour last Thursday, and it was widely advertised and widely heard, and she refreshed and

MIDDLE YEARS 1930–1934

renewed the lives of all the Bahá'ís by her marvelous spirit of detachment, dedication and profound realization of the state of the world.

May was thrilled with the potential of the radio. Another very interesting contact she pursued, in the course of 1932, was Mrs Lily Armstrong Perry in New York, who had her own radio programme. In July, May wrote to Glen Wade in Outremont, P. Q., Canada telling him about this opportunity which she had seized to teach the Faith 'on air', as it were, and to draw the attention of many people to it:

> You have no idea how terribly I miss you all and nothing would induce me to absent myself so long, were it not for this wonderful opportunity to broadcast which has come to me. A Southern woman, Lily Armstrong, who has been interested in the Cause for some time, has a Universal Sunshine Exchange period of her own, four times a week over radio, WCDA and WMSG, THE VOICE OF THE BRONX, and we have become great friends, and she has most kindly and generously given me part of her time to broadcast the words of Bahá'u'lláh and 'Abdu'l-Bahá, so here I am in the sweltering heat, like North Africa, nevertheless radiantly happy because I feel that these words can reach a vast invisible audience which I could not possibly reach by travelling around.

Lily Armstrong was greatly impressed by May. In her report written about her programmes between 1931 and 1934, she described the circumstances which led to these radio broadcasts:

> I invited the members of the New York and surrounding Assemblies and communities to be guest artists on my programs and read a prayer or an excerpt from some Bahá'í book. Saffa Kinney, dear May Maxwell, Mountfort Mills, and many others accepted my invitation – Dear Saffa played and chanted on the programs. Maud Gaudreaux sent me some of her pupils to sing. I met May Maxwell at the Kinneys. When I invited her to broadcast, she told me she had planned to leave for Canada that day or the next, but would postpone her departure if she could broadcast the Bahá'í words on the radio – and asked how long she could broadcast. I replied: 'You can broadcast just as long as you want to – until Gabriel blows his

trumpet, if you desire to.' She stayed over for two or three weeks, if I remember correctly – can't say exactly. I was delighted and honoured . . . On Mondays and Fridays, when we had two broadcasts daily, we'd spend the day together . . . Dear May Maxwell was such a beautiful, love-filled soul. Her face radiated the light, beauty and love of the Heavenly Kingdom . . . She loved justice and righteousness and walked the mystic way with practical feet. Her heart was very tender, but she had the X-ray eyes of the Spirit that searched the depths of one's mind and heart.

May's relationship with Lily Armstrong was to endure for a long time and was characterized, as were so many of her relationships, by faithfulness and courtesy. In a letter written to Mrs Armstrong Perry six years later, on 11 April 1938, she acknowledged the debt of gratitude she owed her for having made it possible to broadcast on her programme a few years before:

You will be interested to know that two weeks ago I gave a 12 minute broadcast on the Revelation over WBNX and I owe a great debt of gratitude to you, my dear sister, for the broadcast you permitted me to do on your program many times years ago, an experience which laid the foundation for any such work I may do now or in the future, and I am grateful to you.

Many years later, Lily Armstrong herself described the impact of May on her, in a letter she wrote to May's daughter on 27 March 1958:

She looked like a radiant angel as she spoke or read on these programs, and it was a blessed privilege and unspeakable joy for me to have the close, warm, heart association I had with her for the few weeks we were together daily and broadcasting.

May was involved in broadcasting these radio programmes in New York and in teaching through this medium in the spring and summer of 1932, from April through to August. She wrote to Horace Holley, who was the Secretary of the National Spiritual Assembly at the time, enclosing a report about the twelve radio broadcasts she had aired over two stations in New York.

But she was being pulled in several directions at once. Her daughter could not wait for her to come home and embark on a different kind of teaching:

> Mother I feel sure that the future of our teaching activities is going to be increasingly with 'people of importance' as Shoghi Effendi wishes. And now darling I am going to take you to task the minute you get home! We are going to start entertaining! There is <u>no other way</u> to make these contacts. I already know, combined with your acquaintances, enough people. And entertaining nowadays is simple to say the least. Everyone knows we are Bahá'ís, and so in the course of our social activities we will be questioned all the time! . . . Now prepare yourself to become a social bug! When I think of your capacity . . . well I don't think! Look what the Bolles have been doing! GRRRR . . . I'm getting all excited!

In August that year May joined Mary at the Green Acre Summer School from where they planned to go on a teaching trip together to Nova Scotia. These summer months were in the immediate wake of the passing of the Greatest Holy Leaf and May possibly wished to dedicate this trip to her memory. On 31 August she wrote to the Guardian about the project, and received the following reply written on his behalf, dated 5 October:

> Shoghi Effendi wishes me to acknowledge the receipt of your letter dated August 31st, 1932, telling him that you now feel strong enough to start on a teaching trip with Mary.
> When visiting the Shrines the Guardian will think of you two & ask God to guide your steps & make your words penetrate to the heart of those that hear you & change them. The spirit of love & service you carry with you & your power of conviction is bound to win for you many victories & make of you a perfect channel for the life-giving spirit of Bahá'u'lláh.

On 18 October Shoghi Effendi followed this up with a cable:

> EAGER RECEIVE REPORT TEACHING TRIP WITH MARY SHOGHI

But the plan had to be cancelled when Mary became ill. On 20 October May wrote to Edward Dewing about the last-minute change of plans: 'just as we were on the verge of a teaching trip to Nova Scotia', she told him, 'she came down with scarlet fever'. After weeks of illness, she added, her daughter was 'making a very good recovery' but she must have worried about disappointing the Guardian. He had expressed such interest in their teaching trip and eagerness to receive their reports. But though they could not go to Nova Scotia that year, the visits of mother and daughter to Washington DC continued through the following winter.

* * *

On 2 February 1933, May, Stanwood Cobb and Mason Remey were the featured speakers at a meeting that was held in the Hotel Hamilton, East Room, 14th and K Streets NW, Washington DC. The subject of their talks was 'The Solution of the World's Ills' and the Chairman for the event was Mr Allen B. McDaniel. At the bottom of the card announcing this public meeting was printed:

> Bahá'í Study Classes will be conducted by the Bahá'í Teaching Committee at 2440 Massachusetts Avenue on Tuesday evenings in February at 8 o'clock.

What may not immediately be apparent in this modest announcement and can only be read between the lines of the titles chosen for these talks is that the focus of this mother and daughter team at this time was racism in Washington DC. One of the worst of the world's ills was racial disharmony and May was determined to address this issue and encouraged her daughter in her efforts as well.

This encouragement had begun some years before. On 3 March 1931 she had written to Mary from the Hotel President in Atlantic City, New Jersey, about a novel Mary had written the previous year, called *Green Amber*:

> I have written a long letter to Shoghi Effendi, and I have been about two weeks in the preparation of it and have just finished it so my head is a little tired, darling, and I will only write you briefly, but

there is one important thing I want to say. I feel that the time has come when we should publish your book, 'Green Amber'; lately it has been pressing in on my consciousness day and night that you have been inspired to write this book at this extremely crucial time and that merely to write it is not sufficient; it should be published and given to the world where I feel assured it will have the most powerful effect.

No one better than you realizes how critical the race situation is in this country, and while such a book might create an adverse reaction, it is bound to produce a ferment in society through the power of its sincerity and naked truth, its spiritual depths and basic significance. I am sure I would not feel so strongly about this lately without a definite cause, and if you call Miss Graham who has a stenographic office on St James Street, she may be able to supply you with a good stenographer, not too expensive, to whom you can dictate right on to the machine and if you start working on it now doing a little each day I am sure you will be greatly helped and strengthened in your effort in which so much is at stake. I hope you can soon start on your wonderful book so that we may publish it this spring and leave the results with God for I believe they will be very great.

Mary did indeed get stenographic help and had the 619-page, handwritten manuscript typed. However, it was never published, but, in retrospect, the fact that her mother so enthusiastically supported this project is almost more important. When one considers the habits of racial segregation at the time and the prejudice which poisoned the community in the capital, it is truly wonderful to see the courage of Mrs Maxwell and Mary regarding this 'most challenging issue'. Their audacity was such that they started classes in the nation's capital on the Bahá'í Faith in the spring of 1933, where both races mixed, in stark contrast to the practices of the time. It created something of a storm in the Washington community, where unfortunately even the Bahá'ís maintained distinctions along racial lines. On 11 April 1933 May wrote a glowing report of their activities to Shoghi Effendi. She longed to bring joy to his sorrowing heart at the time of his grief:

After writing you from Atlantic City, Mary and I came here, and meeting with the dear friends and with the groups in Mason's home, we gradually were able to reach groups of both colored and white people, to break down among the younger element the barriers of racial prejudice, so that a number of group meetings have been held which manifested providential or potent influences of the divine teachings in the welding of people together with the bonds of love and brotherhood. We, who are a witness, and to the extent of our humble power cooperating in these two-fold activities, realize that at the close of these nine months of sacred commemoration, in love and sorrow and prayer, the spirit of the Greatest Holy Leaf is resuscitating the lifeless body of the Cause in America.

When Mary remained in Washington in order to continue this work after Mrs Maxwell left for New York, the consequences were not altogether favourable at first. In early May she was criticized for having acted without consulting with the Assembly, and was also reprimanded by some of the older believers for having been too 'radical'. As far as the former failure was concerned, her mother was the first to acknowledge the error, despite the rightness of the cause. But as for the latter, she was adamant in her support of her daughter's aims. Writing to Mary, she acknowledged that she had 'broken a law of God' in not having consulted with the Spiritual Assembly, and encouraged her to maintain the standards of 'Abdu'l-Bahá by crossing the racial divide. She also, as was her wont, gave her daughter detailed instructions about what to do about it:

Saturday
Mary darling –
My heart was filled with such love for you last night – such joy and gratitude for this young daughter of 'Abdu'l-Bahá – which is just what you are! I know that you did right, because He could not bear to see those whom He alluded to in Washington as, 'that oppressed race!' disillusioned and disappointed in a Bahá'í – nevertheless the fact remains that you have broken a law of God – a law of the Will & Testament.
You are a woman now and these are the decisions and experiences which alone can lead you to maturity. Of course there is no conflict in <u>law</u> on any plane – but owing to our not having strictly

Newspaper report, 18 February 1933, of the Sixth Annual Meeting of the Royal Architectural Institute of Canada. W. S. Maxwell, Honorary treasurer, is seated second from right

Newspaper report, 25 April 1939. 'Montreal Architects Honored by P. Q. A. A.: The above Montreal architects were honored for their outstanding contributions to the profession, with the presentation of bronze medals of the province of Quebec Association of Architects at the Association's Annual Banquet last evening at the Cercle Universitaire, Montreal.'
W. S. Maxwell is seen in the centre photograph

Prospectus for the Legislative and Executive Building, Regina, Saskatchewan, Edward and W. S. Maxwell, 1909. watercolour and pen and ink on paper (©National Gallery of Canada, Ottawa, Royal Canadian Academy of Arts diploma work, deposited by the architect, Montreal, 1911)

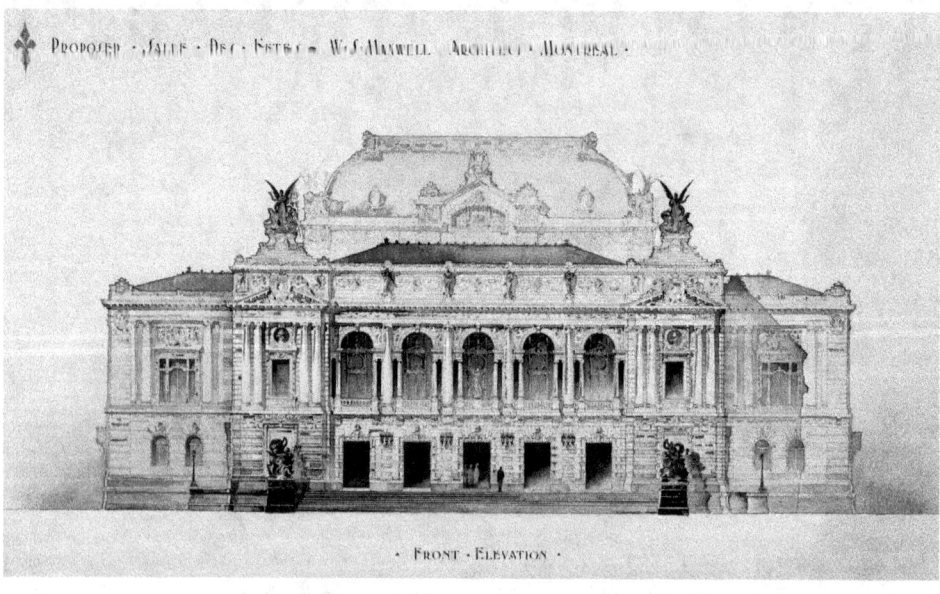

Front elevation for a proposed 'Salle des Fêtes', modelled on the Paris Opera, 'the quintessential Beaux-Arts building', and exhibited at the Academy of Arts Spring Exhibition in 1901 (Maxwell Archive, John Bland Canadian Architecture Collection, McGill University Library)

Château Frontenac Hotel, about 1923. The 17-storey central tower and tower block, a service wing, and the Saint-Louis wing were added by Edward & W.S. Maxwell, and Maxwell & Pitts, 1920–1924, bringing the number of guest rooms to 660 (McCord Museum, MP-0000.158.14)

BUCKINGHAM PALACE.

By Command

of

HIS MAJESTY THE KING

the accompanying Medal is forwarded

to

W. S. MAXWELL ESQ.

to be worn in commemoration of

Their Majesties' Silver Jubilee

6th May, 1935.

In May 1935 W. S. Maxwell was awarded a Medal 'by Command of His Majesty the King ... to be worn in commemoration of Their Majesties' Silver Jubilee. The engraved side of the medal reads: 'Presented to W. S. Maxwell F.R.A.I.C., F.R.I.B.A., R.C.A., P.P. P.Q.A.A.; P.P. R.A.I.C. in Recognition of Services Rendered to our Profession' and is dated April 24th 1939

OFFICE OF THE MAYOR

MONTREAL, Quebec
May first
1 9 3 5

Sir,

I am directed by His Worship the Mayor of Montreal to say to you that it has pleased His Majesty the King, on the recommendation of the Honourable the Secretary of State of Canada, to forward to you a Medal to be worn in commemoration of Their Majesties' Silver Jubilee.

You are accordingly requested to be good enough to attend in the Hall of Honour at the City Hall on Monday the sixth of this month at three o'clock in the afternoon, when the insignia and warrant of your decoration will be handed to you in His Majesty's name by His Worship.

If for any reason you cannot attend, will you be kind enough to let me know by return of mail?

I have the honour to be, Sir,

Respectfully yours,

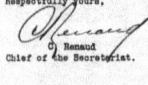

O. Renaud
Chief of the Secretariat.

W. S. Maxwell, Esq.,
1548 Pine Ave. West,
Montreal

followed the <u>law of consultation</u> with the Washington Assembly at the <u>right time</u> – we have had the punishment of breaking that law in the end thro force of circumstances. Shoghi Effendi says we must 'face facts' and do 'clear thinking' so let us admit that if you had gone to Mrs. H . . . and talked it all over with her – putting it in the <u>right light</u> – when you <u>first</u> had the possibility of giving this talk – all this serious trouble – and it <u>is</u> <u>serious</u> – would not have arisen.

Now there is just one thing for you to do – <u>at once</u> – go to [the] Chairman of the Amity Com. – and frankly, lovingly tell her everything – <u>acknowledge your mistake</u> – which will disarm her – and by the power of Bahá'u'lláh – and our <u>united prayers</u>, become once more <u>united with her</u>. Then go before the Assembly, explain everything and humbly ask them to forgive you. This is true Bahá'í love, and will prevent this whole matter getting much worse. As Mr. M. said last night, 'We know, May, that according to the law of Bahá'u'lláh a Bahá'í who carries on teaching activities in a city without the consultation and <u>collaboration</u> of the Assembly is not within the pale of the divine Administration.' You and I Mary believe this – we also believe that the attitude of the Washington Assembly & friends is getting them nowhere on the race question – nevertheless the Guardian told us that the whole progress of the Cause (no matter how long it is retarded!) is from now on based on obedience to the law – however imperfect the vision of those who administer it. If you go before them with a genuine realization that you have done wrong – with true humility – not in the spirit of setting them right – it may be that Bahá'u'lláh in His Mercy & Wisdom will bring <u>unique</u> results.

You have done one glorious thing last night – with great personal sacrifice – but you must make that still greater effort and sacrifice which will <u>perfect your action</u>. I am enclosing a statement to the Spiritual Assembly – read it – then present it to them when you go to them – because there must be the power & dignity of unity between you & me – no laying off any responsibility on each other . . . I know you will win by that mysterious power of [the] companions of the Báb – absolute courage and fearlessness combined with sweetness & humility . . . P. wrote you that the <u>radical group</u> – to whom the Assembly feared you were speaking – are <u>not the group</u> you addressed so the whole matter can be cleared up – but I hope &

pray that far <u>more</u> than this will be the result.

I am feeling <u>much better.</u> Will write & send money tomorrow. All my love & kisses to my darling girl,
                Mother

Mary's description of the 'unfavourable' aspects of her visit is recorded in an undated letter to May; but she had undoubtedly phoned May with the information it contained, as May's letter above indicates.

> I was invited by Mr. Booker to go to the home of some of his friends and meet a little group socially and quite informally. I asked Mason naturally if he would come and in the natural course of Bahá'í events he asked Stanwood if it was all right if he spoke at my meeting Saturday night. On the strength of this Mr. Cobb called me up in a state of trepidation, not to say wrath, and said I was disobeying the Spiritual Assembly and that I could not have the meeting until he had consulted with me, so although this was an entirely new aspect to me I met him at tea on Friday and he proceeded to limit the activities of the individual Believer to such an extent that I burst into tears and had to leave the table. I don't know whether it was my tears or prayers but when I returned we decided that either he or another member of the Amity Committee would go with me to the meeting . . .

The character of the young sensitive soul who 'burst into tears and had to leave the table' was to be immortalized in later years when Amatu'l-Bahá included a similar situation in her delightful satire *A Spiritual Assembly's Growing Pains*. But however melodramatic she might have later considered her behaviour, her sincerity is palpable, even long after the event, and was evidently felt at the time. In a letter written by May on 4 May 1933, and sent by Special Delivery from New York to Mary at the Hotel Burlington, Washington DC, where she was staying, Mrs Maxwell did everything to encourage her efforts:

> I hope you received my letter with enclosures (Guardian's letter!) and that you are planning to have <u>all</u> your friends who were kind to you at the party Friday night. I hope you asked them <u>in time</u> so that they could come – and that you are having very nice refreshments.
>
> I think it is a splendid plan to have the young Negro group you

addressed – those who are interested – come to a meeting at Mason's while you are there – and start this first class together.

I hope J. T. is now confirmed. I had a lovely letter from Elizabeth and am sending her the new Administration which she will study . . .

I shall be in <u>deep prayer for you tonight</u>. All my love,
Mother

Phone me tonight here when you get back from meeting.

On 5 May the Spiritual Assembly of Washington DC wrote the following letter to Mary:

> We were glad to have you with us at the meeting last night and appreciate your consulting with us.
>
> As to the meeting which you proposed for some of your friends who are interested in the Bahá'í Cause, the Spiritual Assembly last night took the following action:
>
>> Voted: That Miss Mary Maxwell be authorized to hold the group meeting suggested by her in consultation with the Local Spiritual Assembly at its meeting May 4, 1933, at the home of Mrs. Coralie Franklin Cook or at some other place to be chosen by the Inter-Racial Committee . . .
>
> The Mrs. Cook above referred to is a colored believer of rare quality, one who has high standing in the educational field here, and who has been for many years a member of the School Board of this City. She is and has been for quite some time a member of our Inter-Racial Committee.

Four days later, on 9 May, Mary cabled her mother:

> DEAREST GLAD YOU WITH DADDY AMITY COMMITTEE APPROACH TIRESOME BUT FEEL NEGRO CLASS IMPORTANT ALSO OTHER WORK SHOULD MOVE WYOMING AVE AND GO CHARLOTTESVILLE WEEKEND WHILE YOU REST AT HOME . . . LETTER FOLLOWING BUT WILL DO WHATEVER YOU SUGGEST LOVE BOTH – MARY

On the same day May penned her reply to her daughter:

Why do you not arrange with that Negro Forum Group to have a meeting in some home informally and you go and talk to them . . . Philip is going to Chicago at the end of the week to speak in the Foundation Hall of the Temple to five or six Bahá'í Communities in one great meeting . . . and if you want to arrange for him to meet the Negro Group, he will make a great impression . . . he is really inspired & a splendid example of Bahá'í youth.

Gradually, as a result of their purity of motive, their openness of spirit, and their love, May and Mary, between them, broke down the fear and prejudice by which they were initially surrounded in Washington. In the end, Mary was able to write to her mother:

However, it has all turned out very beautifully. Stanwood came to the meeting; also Doris Lohse. It was one of the loveliest ones I have gone to . . . Mason was not there and Stanwood took his place. After the meeting he seemed radiantly happy, paid me a lot of compliments, and is going to have me to tea again!

In the draft of her letter to the Guardian, written some time later that month, May sums up the episode:

Mary and I were in Washington for several months, and during the weeks we spent with Mason the mysterious beauty, joy and fragrance of the early days was recaptured! and we are so grateful to the National Spiritual Assembly for giving us the opportunity to work together on the History of the Bahá'í Faith in this country! (for which I humbly beg your guidance, inspiration and confirming power!) In Washington Mary became launched as a young and independent teacher in the Cause! For altho we worked together – held meetings – spoke to both colored and white groups – and at Howard University – side by side – yet Mary carried on an intensive teaching campaign among the cultured Negro population, besides her many social contacts through Mason and others – even for several weeks after I left for home. It is true she came in conflict with the Local Spiritual Assembly which we both sincerely and deeply regretted, and in the end the loving bond of unity, temporarily alienated, was cemented; yet without that temporary breach

– which we had not foreseen – <u>no work</u> would have been accomplished in the field of racial amity in Washington, as all the Baháʼís . . . in common with the rest of the population, live under that ghastly repression and restraint due to fear, public opinion and a peculiar obsessive force which ʻAbduʼl-Bahá described as ʻuncannyʼ. The atmosphere is charged with the darkness of this human prejudice . . .

May was much preoccupied during the last years of her life by the lack of spirituality in the embryonic institutions of the Baháʼí Administration. In a letter she wrote to her daughter a year later, on 9 June 1934 from San Francisco, she expressed her great distress over the news of a Baháʼí who had become alienated from the community and urged Mary to try and make him change his mind. She was certain that if the friends were able to glimpse for a moment the spiritual nature of the World Order of Baháʼuʼlláh, they would instantly sacrifice their all to establish it:

> I think you should see him and plead with him from your young pure heart and have the courage to warn him of his danger and beg him to write from his heart to the Guardian because our beloved Guardian is not responsible for the frailties and imperfections of the National Spiritual Assembly or the mistakes of that body in this nascent, immature period of the Cause. The time has come when we must do big and strong things like Mulla Hossein with his <u>Sword</u>!

It is at the end of this same letter that she interprets the dream that her daughter had had while on pilgrimage in 1926. Her interpretation, which may or may not have borne much relation to the original, nevertheless reveals a great deal about May herself and the yearning in her heart to raise up another generation of Baháʼí youth in North America who would understand the spiritual destiny of the institutions of the Cause and carry their faith to new heights of self-sacrifice:

> Mary dearest – there is something I want to say to you out of the depths of my heart. You remember the dream you had when you were in Haifa, of your deep love for Shoghi Effendi, and how you were with him & taking care of him when the carriage upset! This

dream has come to have a deep symbolic meaning to me – it is that he is the <u>Extension</u> of the Branch grown from the Pre-Existent Tree 'that shadoweth all mankind' that you – all the <u>Youth</u> – are growing <u>on that Extended Branch</u> – that the Guardian needs your love, the flame of your love and devotion in a new way . . . I realize that our lives – each one of us – must conform to a new standard of devotion! Let us – you & I – every day – at some hour in the 24 – turn unitedly – <u>one in</u> heart & spirit, Mary, and turning to him – send the living stream of our love – our divine love – pouring from the Master – to him!

May's love for Shoghi Effendi was so absolute that in February 1933 she even invited him to visit America; perhaps she felt that only he could resuscitate it from its lethargy. Shoghi Effendi's answer, written on 2 April 1933, was the essence of delicate diplomacy:

> I deeply value the sentiments & motive that have prompted you to extend an invitation to me to visit a land on which the Master has bestowed His manifold blessings. Not until, however, I feel the urge to undertake such a journey, will my presence in your midst prove of any value to our beloved Cause or promote those interests that are so near & dear to my heart. Your valued collaboration in so many fields of activity, above all the spirit that prompts you to render such inestimable services, bring immense joy & great relief to my heart. I feel so deeply grateful for them all.
> Shoghi

* * *

Next to the teaching of the Cause and the training of the friends in the spiritual nature of the Administrative Order, May's most passionate concern throughout the thirties was the fate of the Temple. During the grim years of the Depression in North America, when the economy had become stagnant and funds were increasingly difficult to find, she raised the rallying call for sacrifice. And when the Guardian's 'fervent plea' was made to all the Bahá'ís in North America on 21 March 1932, all the Maxwells of Montreal – mother, father, and daughter – rose gloriously to the challenge. They consulted together and decided to contribute their home on 1548 Pine Avenue to the Fund. May wrote a letter about it to Shoghi Effendi, on 11 April 1933:

> Dearest Shoghi Effendi, we felt moved from the depths of our heart to offer the dear home, hallowed by the presence of the Master, for the Temple. It was a great wrench for Mary particularly, but she came through with a gallant spirit and we offered it to Mr. and Mrs. Schopflocher with the understanding that the money, aside from a little that we would keep to buy a modest home in the country and raise what we are all going to need in the future, be put in the Temple fund.
>
> Mr. Schopflocher felt that he could not buy the house, he feels that he cannot contribute any more to the Temple either in this way or directly himself, and he told my dear husband, who cooperated in such a loving spirit in offering his home, that he felt that we have done enough and that we should not impoverish ourselves.

In early May, after returning from her teaching activities in Washington DC, she wrote again to the Guardian, referring to a contribution of twelve hundred dollars that she had secretly made:

> This morning I have awakened enveloped by the power and presence of the Holy Spirit, so rare, so sacred an experience that my whole being turns to you in love and longing! It may be that intensive teaching of a number of young souls, who have come, failing other opportunity even, in the dead of night! that incessant supplication, especially for the progress of the Dome and a recent contribution of twelve hundred dollars I secretly made through selling securities – the daily, hourly effort to conquer myself – these humble yearning strivings may have drawn to this poor one the compassionate glance of the Almighty.
>
> Nevertheless my heart's deepest most ardent love goes to you for every grace and favor, for the potency of your prayers which alone enables us to become receptive to that Holy Outpouring. Oh! My Beloved – if not to you, the visible, tangible Point of the Adored One, of His Beauty, Goodness and Perfection, the channel of His Grace and Will – to whom should we turn in the darkest hour of the world, with suffering mankind on all sides, for whom the only

hope of respite or relief is the passionate love and unity of His Community on earth – the speedy completion of the Dome! – the utter abandonment of self, the supreme loyalty, devotion and obedience, in conscious knowledge, to your every wish and behest. It is this nearness to the Heart of the Cause which gives it life, and the signs of life are on every side, and the good news of spiritual joy and activity of the consecrated effort for the Dome, of the ever devoted spirit in the Summer Schools, of every teacher who is able to travel a little, pours in on every side. I would love to recount in detail some of the events which have touched us most deeply, of the past months, but a brief word will suffice not to weary you or take your time.

Addressing the whole family, Shoghi Effendi sent the following cable to Montreal on 9 May 1933:

> YOUR ACTS SELF SACRIFICE FORGED FRESH LINKS UNITING YOUR HEARTS WITH MINE. SHOGHI

Apart from exerting her own efforts, May was unstinting in her praise of others who also sacrificed for the completion of the Dome. In her letter of 11 April to the Guardian she mentioned particular Bahá'ís who were labouring with her at this time:

> These are thrilling days in America when a new power has been set in motion through Ali Kuli Khan having come East and upraised the standard of the Cause with such flame-like utterances and such a spiritual potency under the shadow of your mighty confirmation, that nothing has been felt like this since 'Abdu'l-Bahá was on this continent. He arrived here twenty-one years ago today!
>
> Side by side with Mirza Khan has risen Philip Sprague with such a burning faith, conviction and divine enthusiasm for the Temple, that meetings are being arranged in all the Eastern cities, and Philip, neglecting his business, setting aside his affairs and sacrificing his life and his substance, is going from city to city appealing to the hearts of the friends with such a mysterious power that contributions have been flowing in by hundreds and thousands.

On 25 April, at the end of a long letter to Bishop Brown in which May described her historic trip to Washington with her daughter, she added:

> I . . . did not get to Baltimore, but Philip and Mason and Mary went on behalf of the Temple and met a very fine group of about 25, who made a contribution of several hundred dollars . . .

A few days later May received a letter from Roy Wilhelm saying: 'I am sure you will be made happy by this commendation of your work.' He quotes from a letter, dated 4 April 1933, which he had received from Shoghi Effendi:

> Dearest Roy: The cable I received yesterday from Mrs. Maxwell, informing me of her stupendous efforts in collaboration with Mason and Philip, on behalf of the Temple filled my heart with intense joy, hope and gratitude. It is my earnest hope and constant prayer, that at least a major section of the dome will be completed by the beginning of June, and that the work, which is involving so great a measure of self-sacrifice, will continue unabated until our supreme objective is attained. No words of mine can convey the gratitude and admiration I feel for those who in such times and circumstances, are displaying such magnificent efforts for a cause of such unique and eternal significance.
> Shoghi

On 9 May Philip Sprague wrote to May:

> I cabled the Guardian from the station, the following: WONDERFUL MEETING MAXWELLS HOUSE RESULT OVER FOURTEEN HUNDRED DOLLARS. A cable came just now: DEEPLY MOVED REPEATED EVIDENCES AMERICAN BELIEVERS HEROIC SELF-ABNEGATION SHOGHI.
> Darling this is all for you, for your sacrifices, vision and complete cooperation in this thing which we are doing for Him have been an inspiration. And I'm continuing to pray as I did when a little boy that He'll make me like you.

May referred to this cable in the letter she wrote that same day to her daughter, who was still in Washington at the time:

On the eve of our coming up here Saturday night Philip and I received a cablegram from the Guardian expressing the utmost gratitude for our united efforts and saying that he was spending the whole night in Bahjí, praying for Montreal! We raised $1400.00, which was nothing short of a miracle . . . [but] unless someone comes immediately to the rescue with $20,000 or $25,000 the dome will not even be half finished!

The following month, on 9 June, Shoghi Effendi sent another cable of gratitude, this time addressed to MAY MARY PHILIP CARE WILHELMITE NEWYORK; the text was conveyed to May by Philip Sprague while she was in Illinois:

> HEARTFELT GRATITUDE YOUR UNREMITTING EXERTIONS PERSE-
> VERE LOVE SHOGHI

Almost all May's correspondence during the late twenties and early thirties reflects the desire to respond befittingly to Shoghi Effendi's call for self-sacrifice, but this feverish drive to raise the money for the completion of the Dome of the Temple reached a peak during the year 1933. On 20 June, while still in Evanston, Illinois, she received another cable from Philip Sprague about the 'critical situation':

> THE FOLLOWING RECEIVED BY FRED SCHOPFLOCHER FROM
> THE GUARDIAN CRITICAL SITUATION TEMPLE CALLING FUR-
> THER SACRIFICE COMBINED RESOURCES AMERICAN BELIEVERS
> MY HEART YEARNS IMMEDIATE RESPONSE THINK IT IMPORTANT
> THAT YOU GO HOME THRU NY LOVE PHIL

Shortly afterwards, May received a letter dated 6 July 1933 from Sophie Loeding, Secretary of the Trustees for the National Spiritual Assembly of the United States and Canada, regarding the progress being made to arrange publicity for Bahá'í talks at the World's Fair. After writing about these talks which were to take place in the auditorium of the Hall of Religion, in the famed 'A Century of Progress Exposition' in Chicago, Miss Loeding adds:

> You will be happy to know that one result of the meeting we were

privileged to have with you on the Sunday afternoon in the Temple, is that the Temple meetings on the 9th of each month have been revived. We hope in this way to keep the great opportunities for service keenly awake in the minds of the friends . . . The draft of the proposed letter to the National Spiritual Assembly which you enclosed with your letter is splendid, the thought beautifully and clearly expressed. I could not have done it half so well. I hope you will send it to them, and that it may be the means of inspiration and guidance to them.

In August May was still in Montreal and wrote the following letter to Mason Remey, always encouraging him and reminding him of his past services: 'We are having the most extraordinary outpouring of bounty in the field of teaching,' she told him:

Thirty-five at our Friday night meeting, mostly eager, young people with openness and receptivity as we have not felt in years. Undoubtedly it is the new springtime of the youth filled with the joy and fragrance once more of that early dawn in the Cause in which you and I have so gloriously participated, dearest Mason. How thankful we shall be to share a second time in this rebirth due no doubt to the supreme sacrifices for the Dome!

Among Mrs Maxwell's papers is a receipt issued to her, dated 3 November 1933, from the Vice-President of Newhouse Galleries, New York for 'a pair of paintings attributed to Tiepolo at $15,000.00 net for the pair'. The receipt is in her name and she undoubtedly sold these paintings for the Temple Fund.

At a time of such a sacrificial outpouring on the part of the believers, the messages of the Guardian must have been balm to their hearts. Apparently Philip Sprague was so overwhelmed with his travels and fund-raising efforts that he became ill and May wrote to the Guardian asking for prayers on his behalf. The first part of Shoghi Effendi's answer, dated 24 November 1933 is written on his behalf by one of his secretaries:

I need not tell you how grateful Shoghi Effendi is to the entire body of our American brethren, and particularly to those who, like yourself, have had such a notable share in maintaining the uninterrupted construction of the Bahá'í Temple at Wilmette. Their spirit of cooperation & of self-sacrifice, and their strong & broad vision of the imperative needs & requirements of this struggling Faith of God in these days of unprecedented confusion in every department of life, have been responsible for the continued progress of the Temple work. Surely, in such a manifestation of exemplary loyalty & devotion to the Cause must inevitably be found the main key to the success which has attended the many & varied activities of our American believers. The laying of the corner-stone of this unique Edifice by the hands of the Master is itself full of significance, as it symbolizes the truth that the friends in America have been invested with that spiritual primacy which the early followers of the Faith in Persia did so fully possess. To faithfully keep this trust and to fully realize its special significance is the duty of every loyal & responsible believer.

Shoghi Effendi was grieved beyond words to learn of the severe illness of our precious Bahá'í co-worker & friend, Mr. Philip Sprague. His prayers on his behalf and on behalf of you all will continue to be offered to Bahá'u'lláh that He may remove all obstacles standing in your path, & that He may impart to you the guidance, help & blessing you need for the development & success of your work for the Cause.

But the postscript is in the Guardian's own hand:

Dearest Co-worker:

I am deeply touched by this further evidence of your continued self-sacrifice for so noble & sacred a cause. I grieve, however, to learn of your ill-health, & wish to reaffirm my request that you take all the rest you require for a full & speedy recovery. I will continue to pray for you from the depths of my heart. Your true & grateful brother,

Shoghi

May's reply to Shoghi Effendi on 29 December 1933 reflects the fullness of her heart:

We know well that it is your sublime influence and power that has utterly transformed Horace and brought out, among his many brilliant gifts those depths of love and sweetness which were latent with him. No doubt with the completion of the Dome, symbol of unity, that mysterious power has deepened in the Cause everywhere. No doubt the sublimity of Keith and her martyrdom has impregnated the friends with new celestial potency.

In closing, you will be happy to know that our dearest Philip is much better and that in another two or three weeks he will return safe and sound.

* * *

In 1934, May undertook a trip to the West Coast of the United States that was to prove a turning point for her in many ways. It was a turning point from a personal point of view because of its purpose and its outcome. She went for the ostensible purpose of her health, and not long after her return she left for another extended trip to Europe that was to change her life forever.

In the letter that she wrote to Shoghi Effendi on 29 December 1933, May spoke to him more frankly about herself than she had ever done before:

> Your precious message concerning Philip, the teaching work and especially your love and kindness concerning my health, reached me about a week ago and brought that wave of strength and inspiration needful to carry a plan which I had recently formulated into action. It came to me on the morning of the 28th of November that I should put myself under the care of a woman who lives in Pasadena [California] and who has a national reputation as a Psychologist and Psychoanalyst. Her books have been a great help to me in the last two years, but I am unable alone to go to the depths of those subconscious inhibitions which today are scientifically understood to lie at the root of my functional and nervous disorders. 'Abdu'l-Bahá told me that I was suffering from a nervous and functional disorder with which I had been born or which I had had from my childhood and he entirely cured me; nevertheless I had relapses. No doubt had I been <u>firmly</u> established in the soil of absolute faith I would never

have been ill again. You yourself know, Dearest Shoghi Effendi, how obdurate my condition was when I was in Haifa, nevertheless my health steadily improved through the years and I hope in my humble way that I rendered some service to the Cause. Now I have relapsed again! And I feel a kind of shame and sorrow in spite of the Master having told me that these conditions were not spiritual in origin and that I must never grieve over them. Therefore I am going to Dr. Josephine Jackson with great faith and hope that she will throw such light into the subconscious sources of my weakness that I myself can gain the self-mastery required for the balance of my powers and a permanent recovery. For this I humbly entreat and supplicate . . . I long with all my heart and soul to produce some acceptable fruits for our glorious Faith in times of such sorrow and darkness for the world and I am deeply grateful and touched by your loving words of appreciation for the very very little we have done . . .

May was away from home for over eight months and it seems that her consultations with Dr Jackson reaped positive results. Her physical and psychological well-being were both much improved by the doctor's counsel. In a letter written to her husband from Los Angeles on 9 February 1934, May wrote:

Dr. Jackson . . . is quite surprised at the progress I have made since my few talks with her in Chicago, and what will you and Mary say when I tell you that I walked almost a mile, felt decidedly cracked but am perfectly all right today! No pains around the heart and sleep like a top whenever I walk as much as I should.

I am convinced that 95% of all human ailments are due to fear and Dr. Jackson has put me so wise to myself that now when I have once or twice stayed awake practically all night, I feel none the worse for it, don't even notice it, and I hope the time will come through 're-education' that I shall no longer be the victim of my own hallucinations and self suggestions of a negative type.

But May had other motives for going to the West Coast than mere medical ones. It becomes apparent in her letters to family and friends in the course of 1934 that she was actually conducting a wonderfully invigorating teaching trip. She touched many souls profoundly during this time, and made life-long friendships; she participated in innumerable Baháʼí activities and taught the Faith continuously. Although she was in California for her own health, her priorities were, as usual, other people. In her letter to Sutherland of 9 February she confessed:

> . . . one last word to my honey boy. You want to know what is keeping me in Los Angeles when I came out here to go to Pasadena. Well, it is _____. You know _____, an elderly woman, strong character of the New York Assembly, who has been very ill, came out here to be with her brother for the rest of the winter. His wife became jealous of _____ and between them they put her out with very little money and wretched health. I have been going to see her practically every day and although the friends here are kind, I am the only one from 'home' and I have not the heart to leave here until she gets on her feet. A few days ago I moved her into a cheap boarding house where she has a lovely room and delicious food, and I am sure she is going to make steady improvement and I shall be able to leave her probably next week.

Three days later, on 12 February, she wrote an almost prophetic letter to Mary. In it she revealed a need for some space between them, for both their sakes.

> I know how hard it is, Mary, to live without me because I feel the same way, we balance and check each other but I feel that this period of separation is something we both need to deepen ourselves individually and, <u>above all</u> to take strong hold of our <u>direct</u>, <u>individual</u> and <u>independent</u> relation to Shoghi Effendi, the Focal Point of Baháʼu'lláh. For a long time I have needed to take stock of myself, to be alone with God, as it were, check up on the <u>direction</u> I am taking in life on every point. Baháʼu'lláh tells us in the Hidden Words 'to examine our deeds each day' and I am not only doing that once more, but I am taking a general examination of my whole life for the past few years, its weakness, its strength, its habits of thought and action, its tendencies, and, taking Shoghi Effendi's <u>direct instructions to me</u> (as well as his explicit instructions to us all in the Book of Administration), I am applying this standard daily and hourly to myself. I am trying to straighten out my whole life to

<u>His</u> standard and it is bringing me a new and wonderful strength inwardly and outwardly. It is just because the Bahá'ís lose track of this exact standard that they waste time, waste motion, lose energy, scatter and deflect their efforts, thus preventing them ever attaining what he desires.

You have always aspired to the highest, it is innate within you to be like that and I know, darling, that you unconsciously check your life continually to the Guardian.

There is no doubt that it was a relief to May also to escape the chill and cold of Canada. Two weeks before, on 24 January, she had written to Philip Sprague from the Hotel Mayfair, Los Angeles, telling him what it felt like for her to come to the West Coast:

> This coming to Los Angeles has been a very strange experience. From the moment I awakened on the train Monday morning and found myself in California . . . such a strange, thrilling happiness and ecstasy filled all my being as I have felt nowhere save in the Holy Land . . . Nothing has ever been harder for me in life than coming away out here and it was your great courage and fortitude that gave me strength and inspiration and I know there are heights still to be attained.

On 1 February she wrote another letter from Los Angeles to someone she called 'My dear Bahá'í brother'. Although she does not mention him by name, she does reveal a hope that seems closely linked to her recollection of the Holy Land, which she says she had on first arriving on the West Coast:

> Mary and I long to return to the East, and next time with my husband, but we have not been willing to leave this country until the Dome of the Divine Edifice in Chicago is completed. Now it stands white and gleaming in the sun with only the very peak waiting to be completed! What a victory the Guardian has won!

She was thousands of miles away from it, but May's thoughts and heart were still focused on the Temple. Once that white peak was conquered, it would be a victory for her too and perhaps she felt that if the Temple goals were filled, she might have the spiritual right to ask to see the beloved Guardian once again. As it was, she was determined to do her utmost to learn as well as teach while in California, and to raise the awareness of the friends about the importance of the Temple even as she acquired a new awareness about the links between her body and her mind.

It is interesting to catch a glimpse of her husband's occupation during her absence on the West Coast. The following excerpts from a letter of W. S. Maxwell to Mason Remey, dated 9 April 1934, offer a brief summary of his involvements and heavy schedules at this time. He was responding to Mason's invitation to visit him in his home in Washington DC:

> I am very appreciative of your invitation and want to accept it, but I am afraid I cannot go. I was elected president of the Royal Architectural Institute of Canada[1] and it means a great deal of work, the hardest part being related to starting filing the many letters etc.
>
> Another reason is our staff consists of one draughtsman and although we have one actual building underway, we have a development of a central property on the Boards, twenty-six houses, all a speculative promotion scheme. We have six weeks in which to 'put it over' . . .
>
> May's trip to California has proven a splendid thing for her in every way and her health is excellent.
>
> Mary is house painting. Quite a new inspiration on her part. She gave three of the series of nine Bahá'í talks in our new Hall. The place was filled and she spoke very well.
>
> I am disappointed about the trip to Washington. It would have been a very real pleasure.

May's own evaluation of her Californian sojourn is very interesting. On 7 January 1935, after her return, she wrote to her homeopathic doctor, Dr Martha Isabel Boger-Shattuck, saying, 'The eight months I spent on the Pacific Coast seemed to have done me a world of good, and I certainly had a much better grasp over my own condition, and

---

1 'W. S. Maxwell of Montreal, who has just been elected President of the Royal Architectural Institute of Canada at the 27th Annual Convention held in Montreal', article in *The Globe*, 28 February 1934.

my psychology . . .' But even during her 'cure' there, she had begun to have certain reservations. She had written to Philip Sprague the previous May, to say: '. . . whatever I learn from Doctor Jackson, and I am learning plenty, must pass through the scrutiny of reality which flows from one Source alone.'

Indeed, in the end she found that psychological and psychoanalytical theories were less enlightened than commonly supposed under that luminous Western sky. Doctor Jackson might have been a fine physician in her field but 'at times', May admitted to Philip Sprague on 2 March 1934, 'the very influence of her dead and un-illumined mind, spiritually casts a thin veil over my thought'. There were clearly things undreamed of in the good doctor's philosophy. Since 'Bahá'ís are highly susceptible to these things,' May continued, 'for this and other reasons I do not live in her house, but go to her as I am led and guided.'

And what she was led and guided to do, during her time in California, was not primarily to study psychology but to teach the Faith. Writing to Lucius Gilman from Pasadena, California, she confirmed that she was studying these new methods 'both for my own sake and the sake of others whom I can better teach and help if I have greater knowledge of the working of the human mind . . .'

She saw everything in relation to the Cause. At the same time as maintaining links with the Canadian youth 3,000 miles away, she was forging new bonds and teaching the Faith in California, as she informed Lucius in this same letter:

> There is a lovely girl here, Marion Holley, who already feels well acquainted with you through me. We are great friends and through her, as I did with you, I drink from the ever-loving, inescapable fountain of youth, of progress and of springtime.

Marion Holley was later to become Marion Hofman. A vibrant and brilliant young athlete, with a vigorous body and a dazzling mind, she had been acquainted with the Faith since her mother Grace Holley had become a Bahá'í in 1917, when Marion was 7 years old. Grace established the first Spiritual Assembly in Visalia, California, served as its Secretary, receiving several important letters from the Guardian, and was extremely active in Bahá'í activities in California including at Geyserville. But although Marion thus came in contact with Bahá'ís such as

Leroy Ioas, Martha Root, John and Louise Bosch, Helen Goodall and Ella Cooper, Isabella Brittingham, Nell French and others, by the age of 16, when following in her parents' footsteps she became a student at Stanford University, she had begun to think of herself as an agnostic. She often used to say that it was Keith Ransom-Kehler who convinced her intellectually but that when she met May Maxwell in 1934, during May's visit to California, she experienced a spiritual confirmation. Marion was set on fire by May and was to remain attached to her and profoundly influenced by her example and eloquence all her life. She not only married a man who had been taught the Faith by May but named her daughter after her too.

May's untrammelled spirit attracted spiritual giants to the Cause. And just as she enabled others to recognize true freedom in the teachings, so too she wanted to be 'free' as she put it, in her manner of teaching. But she had also learned from past experiences that it was important to maintain the correct relationship with the Bahá'í institutions. She obviously did not want to ruffle anyone's feathers, as was evident from another letter she sent to Philip on 1 February 1934:

> Last night I met with the Spiritual Assembly here, both through their courtesy and through my wish to obtain permission to teach freely as I have the opportunity, and not get into any such a jam as I did with the Washington Assembly.

On the same day that she wrote this letter to Philip Sprague, she wrote another to Miss Helen Campbell, from Hotel Constance, Pasadena, where she was staying:

> Last Saturday I spoke to ten or twelve women at Mrs. French's . . . Tomorrow we have another similar meeting, and on Sunday inter-Assembly meetings from Glendale, Los Angeles, Pasadena and other adjacent points, and a public meeting where Leroy Ioas and I will speak.

Old habits die hard, and May had arranged a punishing schedule for herself despite the fact that she was supposed to be recuperating. From Pasadena she travelled to San Francisco, and then on to Geyserville to be with her dear friends John and Louise Bosch. But she had hardly returned to San Francisco around 4 June before she turned round again and went to San Mateo between 13 and 15 June. She stayed in the Sir Francis Drake Hotel in San Francisco from 18 June until the end of the month before leaving for Portland, Oregon.

On 1 July she attended a public meeting in Portland which Agnes Alexander had arranged for a group of Japanese friends, and on the 4th she wrote to Shoghi Effendi about it. In a letter dated 8 August 1934, in answer to her message from Portland, Shoghi Effendi replied with the following letter written on his behalf:

> He wishes me, in particular, to express his feeling of profound gratification at the news of your recent meeting with Miss Agnes Alexander, during which you had been jointly studying the Will & Testament of the Master in the new light thrown upon it by the 'Dispensation of Bahá'u'lláh'. He is praying that your efforts to better understand, & to more befittingly present the contents of this important pamphlet to the friends & to the non-believers as well, may meet with continued and ever-increasing success.
>
> The Guardian is also praying on behalf of your daughter, that she may be effectively assisted and guided in preparing the lectures which she has been appointed to deliver at the Bahá'í Summer School at Lou Helen Ranch.

Shoghi Effendi added a postscript in his own hand:

> Those whom you have mentioned in your last letter to me dated Feb. 19 I have remembered & will continue to remember in my prayers at the holy Shrines. Those to whom you refer in your recent letter & particularly Miss Alexander & Mme Orlova will also be lovingly remembered. Your association & collaboration with Mme Orlova is most welcome & highly satisfactory, as you are eminently qualified to impart to her just those things she most vitally requires in her most promising work of service to our beloved Faith. I am so glad to learn that your precious health is restored & wish you to convey to Mary & to Mr. Maxwell my love & the assurance of my continued & fervent prayers. Your true & grateful brother,
>
> Shoghi

May returned from her long trip to the west coast of the United States through Seattle, Washington before crossing the border up to Canada. She passed through Vancouver, British Columbia and Calgary, Alberta on her way home to Montreal, where she arrived at last on 19 September 1934. In her absence Sutherland had joined his daughter Mary in Green Acre that August. From his little postcard to Mary, dated 2 August, it would appear that the pressure of his work might not have permitted him this respite had his wife not urged it:

> Heard from Mother. She is well – wants me to go to you and have a holiday. Making plans to do so and stay at least a week. Hope to get off Tuesday in Stutz when Pitts returns. Much love, hurriedly Daddy.

Sutherland not only attended the Summer School, but played a very active part in the proceedings. A pageant entitled 'The Gate of Dawn', in which Mary performed, was presented by the 'Green Acre Committee for Plays and Pageants', and in the report recorded in vol. VI of *The Bahá'í World*, we read: 'Great credit is due to the membership of the Committee as well as to Mr. Randolph Bolles, Mr. Sutherland Maxwell, Dr. Ambrose of Washington, DC, Mrs. E. N. Jones . . . and Mr. Max Miller . . .' (p. 436).

Once back, May immediately took up her responsibilities again, organizing meetings, giving talks, and travelling around Canada for the Faith. A few weeks after her return she wrote to Evelyn and Stanley Kemp in Vancouver, British Columbia: 'What do you think of our new program for October?' The list of the programme details is as follows:

THE HERALDS OF THE GOLDEN AGE

1 Early Prophets, Seers and Poets — by Mrs. M. Maxwell
2 The Eternal Christ — by Rosemary Sala
3 Islam – Power and Submission — by Mrs. M. Maxwell
4 The Báb and His Dawn — by Mary Maxwell

1935–1937

In the early winter of 1935 May was in Toronto, but the cold proved too much for her. She had been very excited over this trip, initially, and had mentioned it in several letters to her friends. In a letter to Mason, dated 16 January 1935, she wrote:

> Mary is . . . busy writing plays and stories and teaching, and I am leaving any day now for Toronto where I have six lectures scheduled as well as other group activities. I feel I cannot leave Canada if it is at all possible for me to stay.

In another letter to Louise Wright in Boston, Massachusetts, she said, 'Mary read your letter and then forwarded it to me here where I have come for a few weeks teaching, as there was urgent need for some work to be done in Toronto.' She also wrote to Ethel Edell in Pasadena, California, on 1 February, telling her, 'I am down town dictating this letter in Toronto where I have come for a few weeks to speak and teach.' But the demands on her time and energy, the cares and responsibilities on her shoulders, and above all the increasing cold had, as May put it, 'consumed away my forces'. She stayed at first in the King Edward Hotel. Soon afterwards, she changed to the Hotel Westminster on Jarvis Street for about three weeks. But the cold remained cold wherever she went.

May had suffered intensely from the cold since leaving France. She had repeatedly endured recurring bouts of what she called 'wretched health . . . due to the climate' in Canada. Although, as she had cheerfully assured Mason Remey in an earlier letter, the temperature in Toronto 'averages twenty degrees milder than Montreal', the fact was that she could no longer cope with another winter and was longing for a return to Europe that year.

There were additional factors that made such a trip timely. Her daughter had conceived a passionate desire to go to Spain and learn Spanish and Mr Maxwell wished to see the International Art Exhibition in Brussels which was due to open that summer. Moreover, since her sister-in-law, Mrs Bolles, was of German origin, she had determined that her children should spend some time in the 'old country' to learn their mother-tongue before her son went up to Cambridge. So it looked as though the European trip might become a family affair.

But the most important reason was the call of Shoghi Effendi himself. As Marion Holley later wrote,[1] Mrs Maxwell was 'arrested by his appeal to the American believers to turn toward Europe' at that time. It was a critical period in history. The rise of the National Socialist Party in Germany and the swing towards fascism in Italy and Spain made these decisive years for the development of the Faith on that continent. May sensed she should revisit the francophone countries and teach the Faith there before it was too late. Time was short and the challenges great.

And perhaps there was also another incentive. Now that the ornamentation of the dome of the Temple was finally complete, perhaps she also nurtured an unspoken longing, conceived in California, that there might be an opportunity for the Maxwell family to apply for pilgrimage all together, once they were in Europe. So she had written to Shoghi Effendi, on 11 December 1934, expressing her wish to travel to Belgium with her husband and her daughter and requesting his approval and blessing for the trip. Shoghi Effendi cabled his reply on 22 January 1935:

> APPROVE VISIT BELGIUM PRAYING FERVENTLY HEALTH SUCCESS LOVE SHOGHI

A fuller reply, written on his behalf, was dated 23 January 1935:

> With reference to your plan for teaching the Cause in Belgium, the Guardian has already informed you through cablegram that your wish in this matter meets with his complete & whole-hearted approval. There are, indeed, great possibilities for teaching the Message in this country. But so far we have had no one to spread the Cause there. So, the Guardian is fervently praying that your plans in

---

[1] In her *In Memoriam* article in *The Bahá'í World*, vol. VIII (1938–1940), p. 639.

this respect may fully materialize, and in this way give you a chance to enrich your national services by means of an added & glorious triumph in the teaching field.

And in the handwriting of Shoghi Effendi:

> Your suggestion to teach the Cause in Belgium meets with my wholehearted approval, & I trust that you will succeed in your efforts in this new & international sphere of Bahá'í activity. The cable I have sent you will I hope stimulate you to undertake this work which I hope & pray will enhance & further ennoble your past & historic services. Wishing you, Mary & Mr. Maxwell happiness & success,
> Your true brother,
> Shoghi

The time had come to turn east again. It was intended to be a brief visit.

On 18 August 1935 May wrote from Portsmouth, New Hampshire to Marion Holley: 'stopping en route to New York for Europe, for goodbyes . . . sailing with Sutherland in a few days on the *S. S. Columbus* for Bremen, then going to Brussels for the Art Exhibition'. Although she had already undertaken the Atlantic crossing with her husband on their historic pilgrimage in 1909, this journey was destined to be of even greater significance, both for them and for their daughter. It was characterized by radical changes in all their personal plans and would culminate in a manner none of them could have possibly imagined when they first set out.

Mary had already left for Europe one month earlier than her parents, on 11 July. She sailed less than a week before the Spanish Civil War broke out and by the time she arrived it was clear that her original plan to study Spanish had to be re-evaluated. Since she was travelling with her aunt and her cousins, she decided to remain in Germany with them until she could join her parents in Brussels and Randolph Bolles, Jr left for his studies that autumn.

All three Maxwells attended the Art Exhibition in the Belgian capital, which was held from 2 April to 6 November 1935. S. H. Abramson, a close friend of the family, wrote to May on 4 October, care of American Express in Brussels, saying,

I am so glad to hear that your travels have been enjoyable. Mr. Maxwell must be in his element at the exhibition. I hope it's lived up to his expectations.

But as it turned out, Mr Maxwell was only able to be 'in his element' for a few weeks. His plans too had been radically altered that summer. He and his partner, George Pitts, had been 'working hard on a big competition for some new McGill buildings' in Montreal, according to a note which May wrote to her friend Lysette earlier in February that year. He was, as she told her friend, 'very well . . . very hopeful and happy about everything', but busy, for he had also been commissioned to design some furniture for the Bromsgrove Guild at 456 Clarke Street, Montreal. Just before his trip to Europe, the McGill contract was approved. As a result, his departure date was not only delayed but his return date had to be fixed much sooner than expected. After a wonderful boat tour along the Rhine in the company of his wife and daughter during the late summer of 1935, Sutherland was obliged to return to Montreal because of work. Although May deplored his absence, as she wrote to the Guardian some months later, 'His journey to Europe last fall with us had a marvelous influence on his whole life!'

May's plans too had to be changed. Her health began to flag in the course of their Rhineland sojourn, and she had to remain behind in Stuttgart, on doctor's orders, from where she wrote a letter to her 'precious Sutherland and Mary':

Thursday
   Just a line, as the doctor has forbidden me to write – to say that my heart is better – the medicine is wonderful, but certainly not what we call homeopathy!
   You must be having a remarkable experience – and I share it with you with all my soul; do not hurry back. I must stay in bed until Saturday, then the doctor will come again & decide when I can travel.
   See all you can – and if you did not finish Nuremberg, you could return there. Do not worry over money . . . 'Abdu'l-Bahá promised me we should always have sufficient – and lately my faith has been greatly tested and strengthened – when your life force has gone as low as mine those hours before the doctor came – alone – in a

strange hotel – in a foreign land, you are faced with the stark reality of life – and death – and you find only Bahá'u'lláh, the One, the Single, the All-sufficient in all the worlds of God. I am moved & grateful beyond words to have found Him so near! So infinitely dear!

Please bring me several post-cards from Rotenberg.

After Mr Maxwell's departure for London, his wife and daughter stayed on at the Palais Hotel in Brussels before taking lodgings in the upper part of the city. It was from here that Mrs Maxwell wrote to Shoghi Effendi, on 9 October, 1935, informing him of Mr Maxwell's return and a worsening heart condition. Although she had committed herself to the teaching work in Belgium, she had to go south to Lyon:

> Mary has recently sent you a few lines, but I did not write having nothing special to report, except that in Germany and on the steamer we were enabled to interest a few people; especially my husband and I were happy that Captain Ahrens of the *S. S. Columbus* agreed to place some Bahá'í book or books in the ship's library.
>
> Yesterday a letter from Edith Horn brought the good news that a lovely young German woman of high culture, Edna Bley, whom I taught every day for two weeks in Stuttgart, is devoted and enthusiastic. This consoles me for the loss of time thru illness due to the cold weather. In her letter also Edith said you had mentioned that if we should travel to different centres you would wish Edith to help us in any way, and this, dearest Shoghi Effendi, gives me a different feeling about what you possibly expect from us. You had so lovingly and graciously supported our hope to teach here in Belgium that I had hesitated to go anywhere else without your permission, yet I could not trouble you on your vacation. May I therefore state briefly that Mr. Maxwell and I did not reach Europe until just in time to attend one session of the heavenly summer School at Esslingen – a never- to-be-forgotten experience! – due to some new and very important work which came to my husband just as we had hoped to leave in June.
>
> Now – oh! my Guardian – woe is me! and I hate to admit that I am sixty-five years old! and the doctor in Stuttgart, telling me of the unfavorable state of my heart (physically!) said that most of my

trouble is due to the fact that I am energetic and still imagine I am twenty! And these cold climates, especially at this season affect me very unfavorably.

We have been here nearly two weeks and I have tried my very best to rally my health and forces. Tomorrow my husband, who is now in London on business, starts for Canada and he has been anxious about leaving Mary and me here, but his spirit of faith and steadfast devotion, and his absolute assurance of your nearness and protection over us all, has touched me deeply . . . We are deeply grateful and full of hope and trust, and wish only to follow your least wish. In consultation, we thought that temporarily, and until we can definitely hear from you, Mary and I would go to Lyon, ten hours further south, where in a few weeks I might get built up, thru the warmer climate and being able to get out without getting more cold, and at the same time we might do some work in the Cause there, especially as Mr. Zabih had made the suggestion to us in Stuttgart.

By this time, her daughter's plans had changed too. Mary had fallen in love with Germany. It might be well to recall that her youthful ardour and naïve idealism were shared by many of her generation. Her tendency to romanticize German culture was not unusual at the time. Europe was divided into two camps by the mid-thirties: those harbouring anti-German sentiments and those inclined to defend the underdog. Since Mary Maxwell had been raised to believe that she should have no prejudice as a Bahá'í, it was hardly surprising that she should find herself, unwittingly, in the latter camp. Already, on 3 August 1935, before the Maxwells even set sail for Europe, she had written to her mother from Munich, expressing a flood of emotions:

My dearest one,
　I was so thrilled to get your letter – I mean your cable! last night. I had been longing for news but just could not hurry to Munich any faster – to go on where I left myself in my last letter!
　The Rhine was so beautiful it could never be described. All that has ever been said of it is little beside it. I am enclosing a few snapshots that give a poor impression of it, the rolling hills – the river where every quarter of a mile a new castle appears in ruins or

preservation on the top-most crag of a hill – or some village that faces the water and has stood since medieval times. And each castle has its own half-legend, half-history tale that goes with it and brings it to life – and over all, the lovely terraced green vineyards with here and there stretches of golden wheat. Just too beautiful to be real, almost.

I can truly say I nearly died of excitement. One just rushed from one side of the boat to the other to see things – and I felt utterly exhausted with emotion when we got to Frankfurt! In fact I have almost burnt up here with so much to feel and see and love! How I longed for you and Daddy to see it too . . .

On the train a nice German woman took me under her wing and when we arrived she had her son (in the Air Corp.) drive me (with her of course!) to the American Express and then home to my pension. I was overwhelmed by such kindness. I shall have them to tea when the Bolles get here.

Today I found a tutor and I have a lesson Monday – however I don't like her much and shall look for another one. I don't know yet if I will go alone and board with a German family or stay with the Bolles. I will see when they come . . .

Ah, there are so many things I long to tell you both. It has already in 3 weeks meant a lifetime to me in change of thought. I was too young to understand or think about all that I see so clearly now that I am back in Europe. We talk so easily in our America that is so free and far away from the rest of the world. We have no realization of what old war-worn Europe is up against. I can also understand why the Guardian holds so much hope for this Country. I love the Germans and Germany and I feel they are intensely like us, only with a definite youthfulness of spirit; they have the culture we lack . . . We have become power-sure and conceited by comparing ourselves with other countries – instead of being humble and grateful – and it is no wonder the Western spiritual torch will pass to Germany – who is chastened, grave, and gentle and strong all in one!

This is assuming the proportions of a book – yet I feel as if I were only beginning to say all I want to.

The change in her thought would evolve over the next eighteen months; there was much that she still had to learn. But like so many people in countries where human rights are being violated on a daily basis, Mary Maxwell was ignorant of the facts at this time. Unlike many, however, she was also innocent. Her thoughts were fixed on the spiritual susceptibility of the German people and it must have been the greatest confirmation in the world when the Guardian endorsed her plan to remain and teach in that country. After hearing of her wonderful experiences in Esslingen that first summer, his cable, dated 26 October 1935, was filled with praise:

> HEARTILY APPROVE CONCENTRATE PRECIOUS EFFORTS GERMANY DELIGHTED MARY'S PROGRESS LOVE

His subsequent letter to her mother, written on 3 November 1935, expressed concern for Mrs Maxwell's health and the hope that she should not overtire herself. He also applauded Mary's efforts, as well as those of her Aunt Jeanne, in infusing the message of Bahá'u'lláh throughout Germany. It must have thrilled May's heart.

> Dear and distinguished co-worker,
> I grieve to learn of the state of your heart, & hasten to urge you to take the utmost care of your dear self, to avoid physical exertions, & to rest assured that the unfailing protection of an ever-watchful Master will ever surround you & shield you in your devoted international labours for His Cause. The reports I received from Germany eloquently testify to the splendid impression which you, Mrs. Bolles & Mary have created in that land. This has impelled me to send you my latest cable. I am praying for the fulfilment of your dearest & highest hopes.
>
> Shoghi

* * *

Both Sutherland and May were very proud of their daughter when she first rushed into the fray of this 'fierce spiritual contest'[2] in Germany. '(M)y husband and I', May wrote to Shoghi Effendi, 'are unspeakably grateful for the strength and beauty she is finding – one of the many fruits of her most promising generation'. Writing about Mary

---

2   Shoghi Effendi, *God Passes By*, pp. 4–5.

to another friend she confirmed that Germany was the country 'where her heart is! among a people who seem so akin to her that – as I believe I wrote you – her whole nature has undergone a radical change under this new and profound influence.'

One can catch a glimpse of the 'radical change' which Mary was undergoing between the lines of a report she later wrote about her experiences in Germany between 1935 and 1936. Her mother decided to share her daughter's experiences with the Youth Committee of Montreal, no doubt feeling that her contemporaries would benefit from her daughter's insights. Although it may not have been this specific report which she sent to 'her home Assembly', the following sums up the 'change' in Mary Maxwell in the course of this European trip:

> The first contact that I made with the Bahá'ís of Germany was on the occasion of the Esslingen Summer School in August of 1935. Of all the many and varied impressions that flowed into my mind the deepest and most sacred was that of hearing the meeting opened by reading a Bahá'í prayer in German. Though I could scarcely understand it, the power and beauty of the Creative Word was distinct and a consciousness of the innate and glorious oneness of the followers of Bahá'u'lláh the world over streamed into me with a sense of joy and gratitude. How much we American visitors learned at that summer school session! Those of us who, like myself, know practically no German still took away at the end of the week a wealth of new concepts. It is almost a two-mile walk from the village of Esslingen to the top of the mountain where the 'Bahá'í Home' is; taxis being rare and expensive all excursions are on foot when one cares to go down for any reason, and as we would toil back up the steep hill on a hot August day we used to laugh and gasp and ask each other how many people would attend the American summer schools under the same circumstances? I must say we felt rather ashamed of our luxury-loving standards.

A letter dated 28 October 1935, written on behalf of Shoghi Effendi in response to Mary's 'message' of 3 October, reached her sometime in November:

> Shoghi Effendi feels very much encouraged & gratified to realize

that you are developing great interest in the Cause in Germany. Your visit to Esslingen, Stuttgart & various other Bahá'í centres seems to have left a strong impression upon you. Germany, indeed, stands to-day as the largest, most active & promising Bahá'í community in Europe. And the Guardian cherishes the highest hopes for its future, and feels convinced that, as clearly promised by the Master, it will gradually develop into one, if not the most, of the leading Bahá'í countries throughout the world.

In view of that, he would certainly encourage you to study German & to get in touch with the German believers, so that you may get well prepared for teaching the Cause in Germany in the near future. He would even advise you to make that country the main field of your teaching work in Europe. For although general conditions in Germany are, at present, not very favourable to the expansion of the Movement, yet the future of the Cause there seems to be very bright, & rich in all sorts of possibilities. Now, the main task facing the German friends is the consolidation of the Administration. The era of intensive teaching has not yet dawned upon them. But once their communities are fully organized internally, it will then be easy for them to effectively teach the Cause to the outside public.

And in Shoghi Effendi's handwriting:

Dear & valued co-worker:

I have, in my recent cable addressed to your dear & distinguished mother, expressed my delight in learning of the progress you have made in learning German & of the efforts you are exerting to teach the Cause in Germany. I have also expressed my full approval of the inclination you feel to work for our beloved Faith in that land, & I cannot but feel that your collaboration with the German believers will reinforce the foundation of your future international services & will serve to ennoble the work you are destined to achieve in the days to come. I will be soon writing to your mother, & I trust that the cable, assuring her of my prayers for her brother's family has reached her & relieved her anxieties.

Shoghi

MIDDLE YEARS 1935–1937

Writing on the first day of Riḍván, 21 April 1936, from the Hotel Nordland in Rostock, Mary submitted a lengthy report to the Guardian giving her 'impressions of the Bahá'í work here in general'. Included in this detailed letter were the following insights:

> My beloved Shoghi Effendi,
> One of the obvious problems here is that of the combinations of race prejudice, fearsomeness, intense championing of the Policy & Government, at present. When a Bahá'í with Jewish blood hears one without it rail against this part of his racial antecedents, it does not help the love or happiness of the community spirit . . . I must say truthfully I have found more fear of almost any kind of free action among the Bahá'ís as among the other many German friends I have contacted. They say their fear of really getting busy and doing something is so that they will not jeopardize the Cause in general and I can well understand this standpoint, but even so I feel they are much more timid than is warranted from the builders of a new and Divine Order with all the power that lies behind it to be drawn upon! In other words I have no sympathy with a scared Bahá'í . . . I mean in little ways such as teaching an individual or saying 'what would we do if a Jew became a Bahá'í?' (this in places where there are none!) . . .
> I am trying to write a book in German with the help of a wonderful boy I have met, only 19 years old. My bad German he puts into good German! Please, if it be within the Grace of God, pray I may succeed . . .
> I visited and read a speech in German on the Administration, in Dresden, Leipzig, Berlin, Rostock, Warnemünde and Hamburg (one night in each place) then was too tired to go on and stayed over a month in Hamburg to try and help them get going. I will stay a week or two here again in Rostock–Warnemünde.

On the left margin of the first page of this handwritten letter she wrote:

> I realize I have not thanked you for your letters or cordial invitation to visit Haifa! But Shoghi Effendi how can I thank you?

And on the left margin of page 10:

Alfons Grassle visited the Bahá'ís of Stuttgart and Heidelberg with Bertha Matthiesen! I am so inordinately proud of him! Bertha is a beautiful soul, devoted with real capacity but too modest to write to you!

Soon after, Mary Maxwell received a letter, written on behalf of the Guardian, dated 1 May 1936:

> But, as you rightly state, there is great need for suitable literature on the Cause that would appeal to the great public outside, & particularly to the modern youth.
>
> In this connection the Guardian feels he must express his deep gratification & also his grateful thanks & appreciation to you for your efforts for the preparation of an introductory book on the Cause in German . . .

And in Shoghi Effendi's handwriting:

> Dear & valued co-worker:
>
> I am delighted with your accomplishments. My heart is filled with hope & gratitude. I have sent you a cable of appreciation which I trust you have received. Your recent services will never be forgotten. Rest assured & be happy.
>
> Your true brother,
> Shoghi

The discovery of another culture, the learning of another language, and above all the unlocking in her heart of the treasures of certitude as she taught the Faith and helped to establish the Administrative Order in Germany had a profound effect on Mary Maxwell. She travelled up and down the land. She visited the most remote villages and towns. She met isolated believers. And she learned patience, persistence and perseverance from the Germans themselves. The sweetest fruit of 'Mary's devoted work' in Germany was first and foremost her own spiritual development as a Bahá'í.

But the year began with a tragic event, which was to mark Mary Maxwell profoundly. Early in the winter of 1936, around 15 January soon after she had arrived in Munich, Mary witnessed a terrible accident.

She had gone on a skiing visit to the mountains with a group of young people and had become briefly acquainted with a young man from Argentina, who was a medical student in the country at that time. The night before he disappeared in an avalanche at Zugspitze, he had told her all about his parents in the course of a conversation beside the dining-room fire. He had confided to her how much he loved them, how much he missed them. She had found herself, as she told her mother afterwards, drawn to him in a way that caused him to confide his most spiritual aspirations to her.

The next day Mary decided not to follow the party up into the mountains. She loved the snow but she had never been a serious climber, and as the young medical student set off for his climb, with a red cap on his head, she had a sudden, chilling premonition of disaster and urged him not to go. But he waved goodbye and disappeared, laughing. News of his death in the mountains arrived some hours later. His party had been engulfed in the snow and only one person had survived. Her young friend was lost forever. Mary was terribly upset. She wrote to his parents, telling them all that their son had said. She also wrote to Shoghi Effendi immediately, asking for prayers for the young man and his family, and even wired Leonora Holsapple in South America. And, in a state of great shock and distress, she phoned her mother, who was in Paris by then.

May, as might have been expected, was hypersensitive to her daughter's condition. Immediately after the news of the accident she wrote to her, on 16 January 1936:

> You know how absolutely I have been with you and with those who have passed thro this calamity . . . I can well imagine what it has meant to you. It has always seemed to me that you stand in some strange deep relation between the seen and unseen worlds in which you are destined to minister to the souls. Perhaps the wings of your spirit overshadow, as you once said, 'an unseen host' here and beyond, so that in reality your very presence in the hour of calamity is a bounty and blessing from Bahá'u'lláh!

More surprisingly, Sutherland too seemed to have been attuned to her brush with death. Writing to her on 5 February he expressed his thoughts on her presentiments of the disaster:

I received a letter from Mother last Monday in which she told me about the tragic accident. It must have been a terrible shock to you and I am so sorry it happened. I had for some period of time been uncomfortable about you and Mother – now this feeling has gone. You also had a premonition and as I understand . . . I am so thankful that providence spared you. Very strange how things work out. Take good care of yourself, and it's well to give consideration to guidance when it comes to one.

Two years later May Maxwell was to play her own important role in the affair. On 6 January 1938 she wrote to the bereaved parents of the young man herself. She showered them with sympathy and shared with them the deepest tokens of her love and, as she wrote to Mary, 'some beautiful writings of the Master on immortality'. It is remarkable to consider the closeness of the bond between the mother and the daughter that would have made such a communication possible:

> This is Mary Maxwell's mother writing you, for although I have never met you I have felt very close to you through the deep bond of friendship of my daughter for your dear son . . .
> You know I was in Paris at that time of the accident, and my daughter was so wrought up, so frantic with grief for the sudden extinction on this earth of that beautiful young life, that she called me from Zugspitze on the telephone, hoping that her mother might give her some peace and consolation. Although she grieved herself most keenly, her most intense sorrow was for you, those parents whom your son so dearly loved . . .
> I wanted to write you long before . . . When my husband and I were in Haifa with her we spoke so often of you both, and prayed that God would bring you that deep consolation and peace born only of His love, and we prayed for your son, for his glorious future in those invisible worlds of light that lie just beyond the veil of mortal eyes, where true and noble souls can find a freer, fuller expression, where they can reach us through their great love by the power of the Spirit, where they intimately share our sorrows, our aspirations and our yearning efforts to draw nearer to that Supreme Being whom they love and adore.
> All this I learned through the death of my (own) beloved

Mother, not through spiritualism, or seeking to communicate with her through artificial means, I loved her far too well for that, but by sharing her joy, her freedom, her heavenly happiness and progress into worlds so living and real that, beside them this external world in which we now live is but a shadow of a dream . . .

Whether due to the shock of this experience or the sheer hardship of her daily life in Germany, Mary Maxwell entered a new awareness during this time of the sufferings of others. Writing to her father almost a year after her arrival in the country, she mourned for the deprivation endured by its peoples and praised their fortitude:

One feels here how hard pressed Germany is yet in her economics; butter is limited, cream one cannot get, eggs are very dear, etc. She is really struggling harder than we in foreign countries know – harder than she lets us know. Often when I think of all she has gone through and still has to go through I cry. I can't help it. We don't realize Daddy what a wonder world we live in in the Americas – space – place for all, raw materials. The Europeans look at our continent as if it were fairy land and I'm beginning to think they're right! But we don't appreciate what we have.

But Germany was also being pulled inexorably towards war in the course of that year. Sutherland registered the shift of mood from afar and began to worry about the country in which his daughter was living and travelling. Several of his letters written during the spring of 1936 expressed increasing concern about the critical role that Germany seemed poised to play in world events.

That same spring, in the midst of his work in the aftermath of the Depression, his worries about the rumblings of war in Europe, and his concerns about his wife and daughter adrift between France and Germany, Sutherland found himself elected as a delegate for the American Bahá'í Convention. May pounced before he could scuttle away and hide, writing a mixture of political and personal advice to him from France on 16 March 1936:

Dearest:
Your perfectly delightful letter of March 4th has just arrived and

> I certainly find in you since we all came to Europe, a new fresh spirit, a new youthful enthusiasm, a positive creative energy which I love and adore! But dearest, if you wish to keep that fire of love burning in my heart you must positively not refuse to go to Chicago as delegate to the Convention. Let me explain how I feel about it and do not set up that awful Scotch resistance which is a mere ancestral trait and has no place at all in this new and modern world. For many years you have refused to go to Conventions, even although your Guardian requested you to go, but heretofore you were not a delegate and therefore you did not have a binding obligation. You must remember Sutherland that we build up certain things through the years and that when an opportunity presents itself it is an integral part of that up-building process and we cannot let it fall from our grasp. Today we see as clear as daylight as opportunities present themselves whether the nations measure up to these opportunities or whether they fall below them . . . It is not difficult darling with a little intelligence to apply the same test to ourselves, whether our reaction is positive or negative, whether it is as Thomas Carlyle says, 'The eternal yea' or the equally eternal 'nay'. It is a marvellous idea, and your own life has become much more positive, so much stronger in recent years, has deepened and widened in every way and you must not refuse to meet this divine obligation of representing the Montreal group fully as their delegate on the floor of the Convention, especially as they have paid you the honour again and again of making you their chairman, and this vote as delegate is a vote of confidence which you must honour.

Sutherland did not have much of a chance against May, especially when she went on, in this same letter, to appeal to his love of art. She attacked his Scottish reserve, while flattering and caressing his artistic soul. How could he resist her?

> I have just been to an exhibition of Corot and am sending you a couple of papers I picked up on the subject which I thought might interest you, but oh dearest in two beautiful oval rooms in the same gallery where they are exhibiting the Corot are the most ravishing mural paintings by Claude Monet! A transcendent riot of colour, streams and pools of water splashed with pond lilies but not like

anything you ever saw, each mural different, each thrilling, moving, vibrant, the very soul and essence of beauty, powerful and direct. You see I cannot describe it, I could only adore it and long for you. There was also a self-portrait of Monet, the essence of bonhomie, the true face of the artist, happy yet deep, smiling yet thoughtful and with a kindness, a universal kindness and warmth that baffles all description. I have seen you look like that and I know and love the look and I am so grateful to God that I married an artist, for the artists and the poets are the nearest to the Prophets.

At the end of this letter May added a reassuring note to try to dispel any anxiety he might have about the situation in Europe:

... don't worry over war, I seem to be unable to work up the slightest fear but I promise you that Mary and I will act promptly in case of any real danger.

Although Sutherland tried to maintain an upbeat tone in writing to his daughter on 9 March –

Well you are in Germany in an exciting period but I do not feel worried – Herr Hitler's offer to arrange for a 25-year peace pact with nations is about the finest offer that has been made – I do hope the other nations will co-operate.

– he expressed very different emotions to her mother two days later:

This is a time when living separated is a bit trying. The serious happenings in Europe as a result of the Germans' sending in their troops to the Rhine may lead to goodness knows what? I do not think the situation will lead to an immediate outbreak of hostilities and it may lead to some arrangements for greater stability and a period of peace. God grant this. Time of a letter to reach you precludes any specific advice being of value but I am definitely of the opinion that Mary should join you. Every few hours presents a new development so I am sure that you are in every way in touch with developments and will act with guidance, wisdom, and promptness. You said in your letter of Feby 19th 'that before long you and Mary should see each other' – this leads me to hope that she has joined you by now. I feel sure that as a family we are under Guidance and Protection.

Three days later, on 14 March, Sutherland was so concerned that he cabled May:

> RECOMMEND MARY JOIN YOU IMMEDIATELY AND CONSIDER GOING ENGLAND OR AMERICA PERHAPS DUTCH STEAMER LOVE REPLY SUTHERLAND

May finally registered that Sutherland was 'keyed to the highest pitch', as she wrote to Mary on 16 March. Writing to her again a few days later, on the 21st, she urged her to reassure her father and quell his anxieties:

> Daddy is very anxious; I sent you his cable and today I have a most uneasy letter from him so I am going to write Shoghi Effendi and tell him that you and I are going right ahead with our work as he instructed, and shall await any further instructions from him in the future and I shall beg him to pray for Daddy that he may be relieved of all anxiety and that he may join us. Your letters have a wonderful influence on Daddy so I hope you write him often, my precious.

However reassuring the letters from his 'chick', Sutherland's fears were not quelled and on 22 April, after telling May about the Riḍván meeting that had been held in their home in Montreal, he sounded another note of concern:

> I do think the European situation shows little improvement and think you and Mary would be well advised to return soon.

But May consulted a very different almanac from Sutherland's when it came to making plans. She was not worried about the Spanish War, nor listening to the rumblings of rising fascism in Italy and Germany. As she wrote to Shoghi Effendi from Paris in April 1936, 'the Master told me never to make plans!' She preferred to be ready to respond to whatever possibilities might occur. 'And in doing so,' she told him, 'my stay [in France] is being prolonged.' This, she continued, was because:

I have met some new people – not in the present group – and have been teaching – and I might easily stay until the end of May. Then Mme. de Hédérwary has offered to meet me in Brussels where she knows the finest group of people & wishes to have me meet them – which is the first real opening I have had. That would be June . . .

* * *

It had not taken long for May to return to France. Soon after her daughter left her in Brussels to go to Germany, she gathered up her affairs and made her way to Paris. As Rúḥíyyih Khánum frequently affirmed, her mother was much happier, both from a climatic as well as cultural point of view, in her adopted country of France than in Belgium. She felt more 'at home' in Paris than anywhere else. A letter that May wrote on an unknown date and to an unknown recipient at about this time shows why the atmosphere of Belgium was so difficult for her:

How often I long to write you – to share with you this rather awful life . . . awful because the higher forces of the people are at so low an ebb that for one so utterly dependent on love and unity as I there is nothing to take hold of – nothing to stand upon – except that which is invisible and intangible – and how often in anguish of spirit I cry out to Shoghi Effendi, the tangible 'Point' of the Infinite! It has of course been worse since Mary left to go to Germany . . .

In December of 1935 May was in Paris to attend the Sixth Annual Conference of Bahá'í Students. She had been invited by Laura Barney, and went initially because, as she wrote happily, 'they gave me the opportunity to speak on the activities of the young American Bahá'ís'. But she must have been more than eager to accept the invitation. Paris was her second home and she hardly needed her doctor's recommendation to cross the border. So while her daughter travelled around Germany, she remained in Paris from the Christmas of 1935 until April 1936.

On the 9th and 10th of January 1936, May wrote to Shoghi Effendi asking for prayers on behalf of a Polish lady, Madame Yagorski, who had recently accepted the Faith in the French capital. After saying that this lady was in some difficulty, she wrote, almost apologetically, to explain her continued stay in France:

The doctor in Brussels sent me here for a change, and my cough, which had lasted months, has gone – the believers here have been divinely kind and loving, are permitting me to teach the Administration – of which there is not a trace! – and enabling me to meet and interest new people! I am happy – and deeply grateful. I have been asked a little later to go to a group in Lyon & from there shall return to Brussels where the few seeds planted have begun to germinate!

Just before Christmas my dear sister Mrs. Bolles and her daughter joined me for a week, and her radiant spirit, her eager co-operation gave new strength and impetus to the work – everyone loved her. Mary did some very deep work in Munich, and her first German offspring! Alfons Grassle is now a true Bahá'í.

I must not take your time but just to thank you, from the depths of my heart for everything, especially for the wonderful love and sweetness of Laura Dreyfus after all the years!

May I beg your prayers for the health of Edith Sanderson – firm, loyal, devoted – but a great sufferer!

On the margin of an inside page of this letter she added:

I pray for Chevalier de Moranville – a man of great beauty & a nobleman who is reading the Teachings in Brussels.

She need not have apologized, for the Guardian was well pleased with her services in France. The importance of her second sojourn in that country as a Bahá'í is reflected in the many reports he received during this period; her own letters to him also showed him glimpses of the innumerable souls whose lives she had touched. Several of these letters, as she herself confessed, she did not actually send 'hoping rather to offer you some fruits of my sincere efforts'. But her return to Paris was very important for the development of the Faith. She found the Bahá'ís in a state of spiritual stagnation, under the domination of individuals, and far removed from both the form and spirit of Bahá'í administration. May could not contain herself, as she confessed to her daughter on 6 January 1936:

Many things are happening here, the worst being my very surprising conduct at a Spiritual Assembly (so called!) meeting . . . which was conducted like a social gathering. Not one prayer – <u>no</u> consultation [and] . . . the actual Chairman of the Assembly, the Secretary & all of the others sat by & 'took it'! I suffered tortures – no other word describes my sense of outrage. When I reached the boiling point . . . I do not know <u>what</u> I said – I was blinded by my feelings – but I remember I said that any united action of a Local Assembly – based on consultation acting as a body 'none of which had taken place thus far tonight'! – everyone was shocked – & as soon as the meeting was over I told Edith I would leave Paris the next day – I would not stay to see the Cause of God travestied! We went in to tea & cake (I was too choked to partake), then Edith asked me if I would explain what I meant – a few days before – by a Unity Feast! They had never had – nor heard of . . . these 19 day meetings – & I told just their character & significance . . . & the whole matter is coming up for <u>consultation</u> with the Assembly this week – so this is at <u>least one step</u>.

It must have done some good because later that same year, Sutherland wrote to May:

Say did I tell you that Laura Barney said a great many encouraging and flattering things about your work in Paris – she did so in New York – Gay Paree spiritually revived by your visit etc.

In April, May sent the Guardian a report about her meeting with A. L. M. Nicolas, who had translated the Persian Bayán over two decades before:

As you no doubt know, thro all the years, Edith Sanderson has maintained a very fine constructive friendship with Mons. Nicolas, and she arranged for me to see him, an unforgettable interview with which he seemed greatly pleased, because our hearts were united with the flame of love for the blessed Báb, and we were so united that I could speak to him with the utmost frankness of his false attitude toward Bahá'u'lláh! He was at first enraged – then he said he liked my frankness! Your sublime Chapter on the Báb, which again Edith had translated, wrought a miracle!

A few years later May received a letter from Edith Sanderson in Paris, which proved how much of a miracle that meeting had actually been. The letter concerned a request Edith had received some weeks before from Mrs French, who had wanted an article written by Mons. Nicolas and a copy of his photo for *The Bahá'í World*. She wrote:

> I was commissioned by the Spiritual Assembly to write to him and got a most charming answer in response, of accepting. The article will be on his early days in Persia and what led him to write his history on the Báb.

May was someone who was always ready for miracles. She was always open, as she put it, to 'the motion of the Spirit' and willing to summon it to her aid as well as interpret its meaning. But by the middle of 1936 it was clear that she would need the Guardian's intervention to assuage Sutherland's anxieties. He had already begun to register the possible length of her absence with dismay that April:

> [Y]ou are in fine spiritual fettle and your Lyons and Brussels trips will be very satisfactory I am sure – when you get under way with the assistance of springtime I get a little bit depressed – very slightly so – and only temporarily – at the thought that the time of your return and Mary's is going to be somewhat later than expected. However it's a rare opportunity for you both.

But on receiving May's reassurances regarding the imminence of war and her promise to consult with the Guardian about remaining longer in Europe he wrote:

> BOTH CONSULT AND IF RESTED AND INTERNATIONAL SITUATION SATISFACTORY HEARTILY AGREE TO DECISION AM WELL MUCH LOVE SUTHERLAND

Sutherland's submission to the Guardian's will was characteristic of his spirit of radiant acquiescence and extraordinary faith. His certitude was absolute in this regard. On 2 June he apologized to May for being unable to join her in Europe that summer, and agreed to accept whatever Shoghi Effendi advised her and Mary to do:

I am so sorry my cable was not clear and regret so much having disappointed you. In writing to Shoghi Effendi for his guidance and instruction you did the right thing. I would hesitate to be definite in any recommendation. The Arabs and the Jews are – even in Haifa – in a condition of strife. Quite a prevalent condition in Europe and elsewhere. Whatever Shoghi Effendi decides I accept without question.

That same month, while she was still in Lyon, May heard from her daughter about her teaching work in Hamburg. In addition to telling her in this letter, dated 19 April 1936, all about her activities and reporting with considerable pride her careful management of funds, Mary urged her mother to come and join her in Germany that summer:

Dearest Mother:

At last I uprooted myself from the Hamburgers who stuck to me like glue and begged me not to leave them. I hope to God that the month's work there really has helped the Cause! I have said things to them that afterwards in my room I had to laugh over, they were so awful! But they needed the stirring up. They were all sound asleep and the last few days I met, through one of the friends wanting to have a copy of this marvelous new letter of the Guardian's, a stenographer, a woman who jumped at the Cause like someone starving to death, is a Bahá'í already and wants to join them, and, I believe, will be the moving force there from now on. I hope so anyway.

Really they are a scream! A. and G. were both elected delegates to the Convention and I asked who was going? Or both? G. said she wouldn't so much enjoy being away from home on her <u>birthday</u> and A. said she never slept either on a train or the first night in a strange city! What I didn't say is not worth saying!!

Kitty[3] gave a superb talk, the finest I have ever heard her give and I and they will all go ahead now.

Darling I am, as you see, in a Hotel. I am rather tired from the 'Hamburgers'! Do you think I can stay here a week – it is a dollar a night? As usual when I have spent the money you send me I get discouraged and think I have been extravagant. But I paid half – over half – of the copying of the Guardian's letter. I am sending you one

---

3 Mrs Siegfried Schopflocher.

as I know it must be a sacrifice giving such a tremendously inspiring document out of your hands. Also I shall send Kitty one so it can help her in her further work in Austria, Sofia, etc. and will send one to Gladys and one to Charlie. There is <u>no</u> time to be lost and if this doesn't resurrect Charlie nothing will! However, the $6.00 (.50 of which I payed) will help the stenographer tremendously <u>financially</u> and she is going to work on the translation <u>free</u> with the Bahá'ís in <u>German</u> and when that is to be typed out I shall again chip in and we will present the German N. S. A. with a translated copy. Oh Boy! You've no idea how efficient I am! (compared to the Germans!) Also I have ordered books to the tune of $9.00 from America. They are <u>cheaper</u> if I pay here with registered marks than when I buy them in America. I am giving Alfons a 'Bahá'í World', a 'Bahá'u'lláh and the New Era', 'Wisdom of 'Abdu'l-Bahá', 'Peace talk' (or compilation) as he must have a good library for Munich and who knows when I can again have the opportunity? Also I feel Laurence Tombs will be a Bahá'í and sent him Vol. IV of 'Bahá'í World', also the excerpt from this latest letter from Shoghi Effendi regarding the League. He was <u>thrilled</u>. Also sent Jim Walsh 'Security for a Failing World'. All for $9.00! So if you want anything ordered it's the cheapest way. A $2.50 book costs me <u>$1.50</u>. I also ordered Vol. V 'Bahá'í World' to be sent to me here.

Darling I am trying not to worry <u>over you</u>. It seems to me I have existed this whole winter solely on <u>faith</u>. But please keep very closely connected with me!!

I have enough money for a week – so if you will send me more in American money to the <u>Hamburg</u> American Express Co., they will buy me Marks in Amsterdam at a good exchange and send them here. But this takes a few days so please, if convenient, do it at once. I thought I could go further on the last amount you sent but the books, Guardian's letter, etc. took it up.

I try not to think how desperately I miss you! Have you considered coming here to Germany within the next month or so? Just think of seeing each other! And the weather along the Rhine and in Munich will be beautiful. My darling, I hug you and kiss you. Your very own

Mary

You know I can come to you at any moment you need me! The only reason I didn't long ago is that the work is so terribly important.

P. S. my address here for letters is safest when you send it to the one on this envelope. (c/o Frau Walcker)

A few days later, on 23 April 1936, Mary wrote again from Rostock. The fogs in Germany were clearly more than merely meteorological at this time, and after sharing her dreams with her mother, as well as news of her administrative work among the German Baháʼís that Riḍván, which would be one of her last there for several years, she urged May to go south for her health.

My darling:

The news that you are feeling better is naturally the most important in my life and I was so grateful and happy to hear it. You know Mother sometimes I get in such a state of rush that one day becomes another without my even knowing it! So it was that last week when you heard nothing from me at all! I just did not realize so much time had passed. In fact Mother these last few months I can truly say I am living an entirely different life. First the teaching and talking in German. Then actually being called upon to give out what I have learned almost <u>exclusively through you!</u> to others! Then a somewhat mystical life seems to be growing. I mean I have dreams so often that guide and help me! It is astonishing. For instance before I got your wire saying you wanted to know where I was I dreamed you and Aunt Jeanne, Sister[4] and I, were going through some great underground caves, up and down very steep steps, through fire and Lord knows what! You said you wanted to go ahead and I said 'Can you?' and you did, then I came on alone, and then Sister and Aunt Jeanne. When you greeted me at the bottom you were exhausted and had a burn on your neck and I took you in my arms and kissed you and my heart ached and I said 'I should not have let you do it alone, it was too hard for you!' and I was bruised and sore all over and Sister and Aunt Jeanne had also suffered. You can well imagine this dream worried me terribly and when I got your letter saying how weak you had been and ill and could not go through so much alone! It was my dream! Darling forgive me! We are so close innerly [sic] that it is not necessary for me to say how deeply I feel the things that affect you!

---

4   In her youth Rúḥíyyih Khánum referred to her cousin Jeanne as 'Sister'.

Then night before last I said to God, sleepily, why don't you send me another dream? They help me so much! And the next morning I dreamt a man in this Hotel saw me from his window and came to my room because he said he had to know me! And to myself I said 'Pooh! I can have a youth group here in no time!' Then when I awoke I thought 'Yes, in your dreams its easy enough!!' As I left the Hotel a man came after me. He spoke to me – in fact in a nice way he just would not let me cut him off! I met him for lunch and his first question was, 'Do you believe in a life after death?' Then he insisted on seeing me again last night and told me a truly tragic story of the girl he loved committing suicide – showed me her pictures and her last letter! And when I at first told him why I was travelling and the teachings he was amazed. Later he said, 'You're a rare woman, I had no idea you knew so much.' We discussed science, religion and a life after death, etc.

What was stranger still was that he saw me only for a moment in the door of my room and waited downstairs for me, determined to know me. And I had already an appointment for yesterday that was broken suddenly! If it had not been for my dream I would not have let him pick me up! But, my dear, the Bahá'ís <u>all over</u> I find are Bahá'ís 'on-again – off-again – Finnegan'. They are cold and unfriendly and suspicious towards their fellow men. Now is this the time in the world for formality?

I had a very strong urge to be here for the Riḍván meeting on Tuesday. The Hamburgers literally with tears asked me to stay and advise their incoming Spiritual Assembly but I did not feel any guidance to do so. Well! here they were about to form a new Spiritual Assembly and this is how. There are 12 voting members, but 3 are not active but still claim their Bahá'í adherence. The 9 active ones had decided <u>they</u> would be the new Spiritual Assembly and 6 of them were present on Tuesday night to <u>elect its officers</u>! I told them it was invalid, that they must give <u>12</u> people the privilege of the vote! So the 6 present voted and mailed ballots to the 6 not present. Was I right?

Darling, always I overflow with news and leave the last part for what is most precious, your health. I don't know exactly where to advise you to go. How about Southern France? Spain? Or Italy? You must find out where there is SUN! We live in a fog up here! I cannot also recommend Germany at present as the weather is coocoo! It snows instead of having spring. I am staying here in this Hotel till the money comes as I am too tired and too broke to move! Lorol [Kitty Schopflocher] wrote me an adorable letter and I wrote the Guardian a ten page report! Keep in close touch with me my own beloved and I will do the same! Doesn't our Daddy sound like the sweetest old pie on earth? Your very own adoring,

Mary

P. S. Gladys wrote me a radiant 'love letter'. She begs our prayers as she is going to try and interest a group and she says Frank is not the same man! Also she wants <u>books</u>. Shall I order her a present from us? I <u>mean books</u>!

May still had every intention of going to Brussels as she had promised Shoghi Effendi she would. She expressed this hope in her letter to the Guardian, written from Lyon on 22 May. In it she also told him of the meetings she anticipated in that city, as well as asking for his advice and instructions about staying in Europe with Mary through the summer. She had already written to Sutherland about what she expected him to do that Riḍván and he had replied to her rather ruefully on 2 April, confessing that:

> Your letters are perfectly exquisite and a delight to me. Your last was quite inspired and touched high spots. One spot gave me a less enthusiastic reaction than I should have registered – you settled the matter of my going to Chicago and as you may divine it's a kind of a duty I shall undertake because the fates are against my natural capacity to absorb days with inspired souls . . .

Although she must have been disappointed that he would not join them that summer, May doubtless agreed with her daughter that Sutherland was 'the sweetest pie on earth' when she received his letter of 2 June. It was a classic example of his appreciation of her unique contributions to the Faith and his diffidence about his own:

> Your letter of May 23rd arrived this morning – quick work but you are a keen observer of steamship sailings. The petals of a rose enclosed are beautiful in colour and so in keeping with the mood

of your beautiful letter – yes, our life together has been a happy one and I needed the spiritual uplift you contributed. I am only modestly evolved on that plane and even today I feel like a martyr if three spiritual meetings have to be held in one week. I encourage you in your work because you are the kind of a plant that has to have that kind of water. In the hereafter we shall get along splendidly and maybe my wings will sprout and we shall love flying together.

The little note he wrote to his daughter the following day echoed his sentiment about overload:

Three Bahá'í meetings this week – enough says I.

May could never have enough of serving the Faith in France, however. Although her motives were surely sincere in wanting to fulfil her pledge to the Guardian to return to Belgium, as long as her daughter was performing her 'apostolic' services in Germany May's heart remained with her own 'apostolic' past in France. In June she sent Shoghi Effendi photographs from Princess de Broglie and M. Obouhow, to which he replied on 26 July 1936 in a letter written on his behalf:

Your welcome letter of June 30th with the enclosed photographs, as well as the accompanying messages from Princesse de Broglie & Mons. Obouhow, have all duly arrived & brought much cheer & comfort to our Guardian's heart. He cannot but feel rejoiced at the repeated evidences of the marvellous work which you are accomplishing for our beloved Faith in France. The Lyon group, & particularly Miss Zamenhof, are all filled with a new zeal, a renewed determination to work for the spread of the Message. Their hearts have been deeply stirred, & their energies fully galvanized through their contact with you. May this revival which your visit has brought to these dear friends in France long continue to reveal its beneficial influence . . .

By July 1936 May had finally returned to Brussels, and as may be indicated in a cable she received on 30 July, plans were already under way for her daughter to join her from Germany. After many months of absence, Mary was going to be with her again. She was travelling across Europe by train:

MIDDLE YEARS 1935–1937

BERNER HOF TRAVEL SECOND WIRE PLANS LOVE MARY

* * *

May anticipated her reunion with her darling Mary in characteristic fashion. On the back of the cable she had received from her on 30 July, May scribbled some disjointed notes in response to the questions her daughter had raised in her letter of 23 April. She was eager to see Mary, of course, but also longing to discuss with her the meaning, the function and the spirit of the Administrative Order of Bahá'u'lláh. Perhaps, too, she was preparing for a talk at Esslingen:

> Order – heaven's first law – day when heaven on earth – Adm. Order based on higher law – collectivism leading to unity Bahá'u'lláh gift to mankind consultation – will of majority kills will of ego – will of flesh – will of man – will of God. Today no individual salvation – explain – Bahá'u'lláh has given us certain principles which are for the good of society – for the moral & spiritual health & happiness of all mankind – but He has gone a step further – He has given us a system by which these great laws can be put into practice – a system by which the life & effort of every unit, every Bahá'í may be consecrated to the collective good & life of the entire Bahá'í community. This above all should appeal to German Bahá'ís because they live in a country based on law & order – a people in whom collectivism has reached a very high point. Verboten – gross – liberty: symbol animal – obedience to law strength & assurance

On 29 July 1936, May wrote to Sutherland from Brussels to tell him about their daughter, and about her own health, which was another reason why Mary had come to join her. Father and daughter knew all too well that when May was physically down, she could not make travel plans. But she wanted to consult Sutherland about Mary too:

> Dearest:
> Mary and I were so grateful for your cable and I began to feel better as soon as I knew you had taken me under your wing, so to speak. You know your prayers have always helped me more than anyone else's and that, combined with Dr. Schepens' wonderful

homeopathy, is getting me back to normal. I think Mary wrote you that he found my general condition greatly improved, but my blood pressure is still high and this he lowers by complete relaxation of my nerves. Also I have been having my teeth attended to here in Brussels and Mary and I expect to be able to leave to-morrow or Friday. We shall break the journey to Munich by one night at Frankfurt, and then go into the country somewhere near Munich where I can have the fresh air and rest which I promised you I would take.

You will be interested to know, dearest, that a couple of days ago I had a very deep talk with Mary. As I wrote you before, she has greatly developed, is much more of a woman and much more selfless than ever before, nevertheless she constantly gives me the impression of a person who has felt too much, suffered too much and whose nervous system, or sensitive brain, has suffered too great a shock. She has less power of concentration, that is, in the casual things of every-day life, although fully as much concentration when she writes or really converses, as she ever had before. Something of her girlish joyousness is overcast although she does not seem aware of it, and after our long conversation she said this, 'Mother, I think I shall never be myself again until I go to Haifa. I have lived through too much, especially that awful shock in the Zugspitze, and I simply cannot get back the zest of life, the spontaneity I once had.'

I feel, Daddy, that you as her father whom she so devotedly loves, and she speaks of you constantly with great longing, should know just Mary's state of mind. She does not want to return to America, but if she could visit Haifa in the fall such new creative energies would flow into her, such joyous enthusiasm, such peace and assurance as will wipe away all her sorrows and she will be ready to take up her life wherever her fate may be cast. She is making her own efforts in this direction and has already written to Paul Robeson and a London playwright about her Persian play, about which she has had some very good advice from people we have met, and she hopes to be able to sell this play at a good figure which would do wonders for her life and character because at her age she naturally longs to be economically independent. Time will show what will come of all this and in the meantime it is our united efforts that are more powerful than all else. We went to the Wiertz Museum where there is a picture of Napoleon Bonaparte burning in hell, a delightful revenge for the painter, and Mary kept saying, 'I wonder if Daddy saw this museum.' It is the same everywhere, your spirit, your love, your actual presence is with us all the time. I believe Mary has written the Soloways [sic] and we shall probably see them in Munich.

The Guardian had already been told of May's decision to spend the summer with her daughter in Germany and had given it his blessing in a letter to her of 26 July written on his behalf. He knew that anything she could contribute to the understanding of the German friends on the subject of Bahá'í administration was of vital importance during these critical months when their institutions might at any time be disbanded:

> In this country too, the Guardian feels confident, your visit will have an abiding & most beneficial effect on the Cause. Though the Faith is far more alive & promising in Germany than in any other part of Europe, yet there are many vital points on which the believers need much enlightenment which you are admirably qualified to give.
> The Guardian wishes me to stress two points in particular: first that you should arrange your program in such a way as to have ample time to visit all the centers in Germany; & also that you should make every effort to attend the Summer School at Esslingen where, he hopes, you will be given full opportunity to address the friends & to give them the great benefit of sharing your long & rich experiences in the Cause.

And in the handwriting of Shoghi Effendi:

> Dear & prized co-worker:
> Your welcome letter truly rejoiced my heart, & I cannot refrain from adding a few words in person & express my gratitude for what you have achieved in France & my hopes for what you will achieve in Germany. I am glad you will soon join Mary, about the progress of whose work I have received encouraging & most welcome reports. Wishing you both good health, happiness & success. Affectionately
> Shoghi

May Maxwell followed Shoghi Effendi's instructions faithfully and met with most of the Bahá'í communities in Germany in the months that followed. These visits began in the city of Munich, where she arrived from Paris with her daughter on 1 August 1936, and from which they proceeded to the Esslingen Bahá'í Summer School. How wonderful it must have been for the mother to accompany the daughter again, this time to meet the souls Mary had befriended, to see how warmly she was greeted, and above all to hear their enthusiastic reception of her services and her talk, delivered, as Mary wrote in a report of her work in Germany, in

> an incorrect but very sincere German, which all the friends accepted in the spirit in which it was given and overlooked the many mistakes. How happy [I was] to again see the faces of the Bahá'ís, grown so near and dear through a year's association, to know their problems, speak their language, love their beautiful country and respect their people.

And how thrilling, too, for her mother to see, as her daughter wrote in this report, how much she had 'gained through [her] close association with them, as Shoghi Effendi had said [she] would'. This historic session in Esslingen in which May and Mary Maxwell participated that summer of 1936 proved to be the final one before the Faith was banned in Germany the following year. Not until after the war would the German Bahá'í community be allowed to speak openly of the Faith again. Not until bodies had been pulverized to dust and cities flattened would they be able to raise up the standard of Bahá and begin the task of building a new world order on the ruins of the old. By urging Mrs Maxwell to participate in this thrilling final session at Esslingen, and encouraging her daughter to visit every single Bahá'í home and centre in Germany during the previous year, it was as though Shoghi Effendi were doing his utmost to ensure that the spiritual fires burning in the hearts of the friends in that country would be kept ablaze during the dreadful dark years that followed.

Mary continued her travels to Schwerin that summer where, as May informed Shoghi Effendi in her letter of 30 November 1936, 'there has been a spiritual revival'. She had met a group of youth there to whom she was teaching the Cause with great fervour and enthusiasm.

May too continued her travels by going on to Stuttgart, where she stayed at the Hotel Marquardt, the same hotel in which 'Abdu'l-Bahá Himself had stayed twenty-five years before. According to her letter of

30 November, she had spent a month in Frankfurt 'with Edith Horn and her very vital and strong group, part of the time in Wiesbaden where I had the joy of deeply interesting Professor Wilhelm K. – of philology – a scholarly & cultured man, who is studying the teachings, and attending Edith Horn's meetings'. She was delighted to report to Shoghi Effendi that this gentleman had introduced the Faith to his friends and had promised to give her introductions to more acquaintances in Berlin. She had plans to continue from there through Leipzig and Dresden, and via Prague and Belgrade, to Vienna. A letter from the National Spiritual Assembly of Germany and Austria, dated 10 September 1936, had warmly encouraged these plans:

> To our beloved lady-friend Mrs. E. Maxwell –
> All the members of the National Spiritual Council of Germany and Austria are very rejoiced of your wonderful letter of 23.8. They believe also, that every work in the Holy Cause in Germany will bring very good fruits.
> According to the desire of our beloved Guardian you and your kind daughter will work in our country. The desire of our Guardian is also always our desire. Wherever you both are working for the Holy Cause in Germany it will be good and according also to the desires of the National Spiritual Council.
> Our good wishes and our prayers will always be with you
> Your humble secretary, Friedrich Schweizer.

One of the friends Mary made during her travels in 1936 in Germany was a young man by the name of Hubert Matthias whom she and her cousin Jeanne had met together during their early travels. Since Mary had encouraged him to visit her family and herself in Montreal after their return home, May invited Hubert to the house on Pine Avenue in 1938. As a result, a deep bond of friendship was established between herself and this young man. The following touching letter he wrote her after their first meeting in Germany reveals the depth of Hubert's feelings for Mrs Maxwell:

> Dear Maman, You see, I am not going to cease calling you mother and I hope you still permit this expression . . . Having so true friends . . . really is a miracle.

May kept in touch with Hubert right up to the outbreak of war. On one occasion she wrote to him in Germany from New York, saying,

> I have missed so much our correspondence during these past weeks ... in the meantime I feel very close to you and I have the assurance in my heart that the day will come when we shall be reunited in the utmost happiness and joy.

After the war, in which he suffered greatly, Hubert lived in Portugal where he became an ardent Bahá'í and met and married Louise Baker who was pioneering in Portugal in 1948.[5] Louise was the daughter of another dear and much-loved friend of May's, Dorothy Baker, who was appointed a Hand of the Cause in December 1951.

* * *

The services rendered in Germany by Mary Maxwell during the critical years before the war deserve a special chapter in the annals of the Cause, but Mrs Maxwell will be most remembered for her extraordinary teaching work in France during this European sojourn. Izzatu'lláh Zabíh, a Persian Bahá'í who was studying in Lyon at the time, dedicated an essay entitled 'How Light Came to Lyon', to Mrs May Maxwell. In it he gives us a beautiful picture of her services in this city during the years 1936 and 1937.

He had originally met May at the Bahá'í Summer School in Esslingen, soon after her arrival in Europe in 1935 during her first summer in Germany:

> There I came to know a truly 'grande dame', Mrs. Maxwell, the first and foremost teacher in Europe and the founder of the Bahá'í group in Paris ... I became bold enough to ask that great lady to come to Lyon and help us in our teaching work. It is impossible to describe how happy I felt on hearing Mrs. Maxwell had accepted my invitation to come to Lyon. Late in March she came. The presence of Mrs. Maxwell bestowed upon us a new vigor and impetus.

---

5 See Hubert's charming account of their meeting in Freeman, *From Copper to Gold*, pp. 240–41.

Izzatullah Zabih observed that during her periodic stays between 1936 and the summer of 1937 in Lyon, Mrs Maxwell, 'that great and most remarkable Bahá'í teacher', met many persons from all over the region of the Rhône Valley, high and low alike, 'from the city proper and from the villages and the country'. To all of them she mentioned the name of Bahá'u'lláh. Through her they all heard of the Bahá'í Faith. 'She spread the seed far and wide', he wrote, 'in that central region of France'. But the most important person to whom she taught the Faith was a young woman by the name of Lucienne Migette. Mr Zabih continued in his report:

> Soon after her arrival, the first Bahá'í of Lyon declared herself and registered. She was Miss Lucienne Migette, a highly educated young woman and an industrial chemist in the City Water Department of Lyon. Two Iranians, then residing in Lyon, also embraced the Bahá'í Cause. The first Unity Feast was observed in the month of May, 1936, at the home of Mrs. Maxwell in the outskirt of the City . . . When our number exceeded nine, the first local assembly of the Bahá'ís of Lyon was formed under the direction and inspiration of Mrs. Maxwell.

May had already mentioned Lucienne in a letter written to Shoghi Effendi on 22 May 1936:

> I am teaching a lovely young girl here – doctor in Chemistry in the Government[6] – she loves the Faith! I am happy – grateful beyond words for the great privilege I have had – and yearn with all my heart & soul to serve to the end and fulfil your wish & will.

On 30 June May shared the good news with Shoghi Effendi of Lucienne's declaration of faith in Bahá'u'lláh:

> Mlle Lucienne Migette is the first young <u>French</u> person to accept the Faith, and I am so happy – so deeply grateful . . .

It was great news indeed for the Faith in France. The significance of Lucienne's recognition of Bahá'u'lláh was immense. The early Bahá'í community in Paris, all except for Hippolyte Dreyfus who had sadly

---

6 In a later report May gave her specific title: 'Chef de la Surveillance des Eaux de Lyon'.

passed away in 1928, were for the most part English-speaking expatriates from America, and in light of France's spiritual history Lucienne was, in effect, a new beginning for the Bahá'í community of that country.[7]

In a report on 'The work of Mrs Maxwell in Lyon' dated 8 April 1940, Lucienne herself described the impact that Mrs Maxwell had had on her. She wrote of May's meeting with 'Abdu'l-Bahá on her first pilgrimage as though that meeting somehow prefigured her own encounter with the Faith, and recounted how the Master had instructed Mrs Maxwell for six days on how to give the message to others. 'Those six days', May had confirmed for Lucienne in writing, 'remained for me as the six days of the creation of the world.' In her innate modesty, Lucienne preferred to quote those words of May to describe what she herself had felt in meeting Mrs Maxwell, but she further elaborated:

> A mere glance from May Maxwell would mirror forth her spirit in all its beauty, purity and love. From her first look, a new force poured out which awakened Lyon to the great Message. She had given it to France in 1899, when returning from her first pilgrimage in 'Akká, founding the group of Paris. She founded the second French group in Lyon in 1936 . . . She was an immaculate channel through which the knowledge of God flowed.
>
> As to her personal Bahá'í training, the words . . . from her mouth express, much better than any description, the soundness of her knowledge and her wisdom drawn from the Source: 'Work in the Cause of God brings joy such as nothing in the world except this experience can give . . . I am married; I adore my daughter. But nothing in my whole life has ever given an infinite joy such as that of having been the humble and unworthy instrument of guiding a single soul to God.'

An undated account by May of her work in Lyon, in turn, contains the following description of Lucienne:

> Her vivid beauty, her charm, her intelligence, were but the tangible signs of a soul of great capacity . . . The Master tells us there

---

7 For an account of her life see Pierre Spierckel's *In Memoriam* article in *The Bahá'í World*, vol. XIX (1983–1986), pp. 610–11.

are those who know of the Manifestation of God upon the earth without having been told, those who have instantaneous recognition when they hear the Glad Tidings, and those who believe and accept through proof and explanation. Lucienne needed no words. She instantly grasped . . .

May always kept close links with those to whom she taught the Faith, but her link with Lucienne proved to be something special. Their correspondence over the brief years that followed seems, in retrospect, to constitute far more than a mere exchange between individuals. It was as though May were addressing the future French Bahá'í community through this young woman. Her words to Lucienne have the quality of prophetic utterance and her bond with her endured the rest of her life. Long after she left the land of her own spiritual rebirth, she continued to pour out her love to this young woman who had accepted the Cause – as she had done – in France.

Her first letters to Lucienne after leaving France came from Haifa. Less than a year after she had declared her faith in Bahá'u'lláh, Lucienne received a letter from her spiritual mother, dated 11 February 1937, from the Holy Land:

> Shoghi Effendi is very happy about the progress of Lyon, especially your work, and he considers with more and more joy and confidence your future work for France. He said several times that Lyon is the heart of France, that this town will perhaps become the spiritual centre of France, that it could overtake Paris . . . He very much approved your attitude towards the priest who himself (the priest) said that you had not tried to attract him. Shoghi Effendi likes very much your way of teaching. He does not want me to return to France, at least for some time . . . but he wants that you and I through our great love and spirit of unity, work together.

Two weeks later she received another message from May conveying further thoughts and comments of Shoghi Effendi:

> Shoghi Effendi is very moved by the flame of your love, and he says that later you will travel to other towns to spread the Cause, and that the urgent thing to do now is to found a spiritual centre.

A month later, May wrote to Lucienne once more:

> Shoghi Effendi has not only given me permission to return to Lyon to see you, but he himself has also instructed me to do so. He has very well understood the beauty of your work, your dedication, and the great love between you and me.

During her brief passage through France in 1937 May saw Lucienne again, for the last time, and for a most historic reason. After Lucienne returned from her vacation, May arranged to join her in Lyon where, as she reported to Shoghi Effendi from Marseille on 19 July 1937, 'we shall work together to prepare the way for a Local Assembly'. Lucienne's work towards this goal continued after May left; the Assembly was formed only after May's passing but it included a certain Madame Borel, who, as she informed the Guardian in her 1937 letter,

> is recovering from a severe operation and has declared her faith (and) will take the place of young Yazdi who is leaving this week having become a doctor.

Since May was well aware of the vulnerable foundations on which the Faith of God was raised in France, it is hardly surprising that she maintained such close links with Lucienne over the next few years. On her return to Canada the correspondence was resumed between herself and this young French Bahá'í, and on 19 January 1938 May wrote to her:

> We are quite inspired by your work, my dear Lucienne, not only I but also other close friends with whom I shared important and interesting parts of your dear letters, and I assure you that we are feeling so close to you that the heat and the flame of your love for the Beloved penetrates our hearts. How moved I am by the message of our dear Guardian in which he tells you that now the future of the Bahá'í Cause in France rests upon you! What a wonder! . . . I thank God wholeheartedly that He has raised up you in France, like Joan of Arc to save a part that God must have chosen, as He promised to have a group of every country in the world, and in the Qu'ran, it is written that the names of those who will be saved are already written in the Book of Life . . .

The events that you describe to me which are taking place in Lyon, the work you are doing, this exact direction in your life, as if the Hand of God were moving you even in the slightest thing, all this is so well known by me, it is as if I were living again my youth, the first years of my work, in you and through you, and I feel linked to you in every aspect of life like one substance, one spirit.

In another soul-revealing letter sent to Lucienne at this time and written to her on 11 February 1938 from the room in which 'Abdu'l-Bahá had stayed in the Maxwell home during His visit to Montreal, May states:

Your letters are no longer letters, but rather spiritual documents, like Epistles to the Apostles of Jesus . . . I feel Lucienne that I have already told you that the Master called me the Joan of Arc of France, and the group that He founded through me at the beginning is a living cell . . . Throughout eternity, I would never know how to thank sufficiently the Beloved for having allowed me to resuscitate a young Joan of Arc to save France in this new epoch . . . He promised me in this room in which I am just now writing to you: 'Haven't I always answered your prayers? Have I ever refused something that you asked Me? Thus it will always be more and more, until all that you ask will be granted by Me.'

And on 21 May 1938, she poignantly responds to Lucienne:

I am very moved by your last letter, and the cry from your heart for France reminds me strongly of the words of Joan of Arc when exclaiming on the battlefield: 'I never saw the blood of France poured forth, without my hair standing up on my head.' . . . No doubt the influence of this beautiful and courageous soul of one who saved France in its hour of danger, casts her blessed shadow upon you, even as 'Abdu'l-Bahá said at the dawn of the Cause in France when speaking about me. He said that the spirit of Joan of Arc protected me for the spiritual awakening of France, and now it is you, my Lucienne, who is shielded by this inspired girl, and you suffer as she did. Blessed be this suffering, the drops of blood of your heart enkindled by love of God.

Another of May's letters to Lucienne, written on 9 August 1938 when the storm-clouds were beginning to lower ever closer and Europe was being drawn inexorably towards war, contains these heart-warming sentiments:

> Each word of your letter gives me strength, unparalleled inspiration, especially owing to the deep relationship between our souls, a spiritual relation that the Guardian said to me he likes very much. You are so humble and simple that you do not suspect the hope he has in you, and far from thinking that you could become weakened, I know that you are rooted like an oak that the strongest storms will never shake, that it is God Who has raised you to save the soul of France, even though this soul in general is no longer in existence, as in all the countries today; but this spiritual soul of our dear France exists only in a small number of individuals known only to God! It is He Who directs you towards them, and He Who resuscitates them through your burning heart, your dedicated soul.

And yet again, on 16 September 1938, a short year before war broke out, she addressed these words to her:

> I am surprised and pleased with the divine bounty given you and France, that He confirmed you, has sown the sacred seed – the spiritual seed <u>before</u> this terrible hour which is coming over the entire world. I am amazed by your work – your travels for the Cause of God – just like the Apostles of Jesus, the heroes of the early days of the Báb! Each sentence of your last letter spread an immense strength, an emanation of intense spirituality and if, through that letter, I felt such radiance, what strength – what creative impulse you have been able to release in your dear country, from which you will see an infinite harvest.

In April of the fatal year 1939, when the lights of civilization had begun to darken all over Europe, May wrote to Lucienne, saying:

> You suffer, my Lucienne; your sufferings, your tests increase as far as the entire world is preparing for destruction, the suicide of mankind. I sometimes suffer terribly for you – but I have faith, immense courage for you . . . We will be separated (during the war) without

possibility of communication with the Guardian. But as he wrote to you <u>so deeply, tenderly, we will be near him in the spiritual world.</u>

And in May she wrote again:

> You see how you are guided in everything, and it is precisely the scholarship of Bahá'ís which qualifies them more and more to teach at the highest level in the world.

On the eve of the outbreak of war May wrote the following to Lucienne:

> At the time of the world's peace hanging by a hair in the fingers of God, despite an unparalleled force which surrounds me during these terrible days, my heart felt a strange anguish, and I wanted to take you by force and remove you from the monstrous hell that I saw approaching. And now you are exhausted! My God, it is not enough that these Heads of State precipitate war in the world, but they take, as 'Abdu'l-Bahá said, the flower of mankind, the youth, the heart, the strength, the vitality of the future generation.

And a little later she urged her:

> I know that you will become one of the most perfect translators ... I advise you to translate as much as you want, and to have it duplicated ... as this Holy Word is the sustenance of the soul.

Then May penned these precious words of courage and love to Lucienne:

> You have received from the Guardian a perfectly wonderful message. I see many messages from Shoghi Effendi, but I have seldom seen one like the one he has just written to you. It is kind of a 'firman', a document that a king gives to his ambassador, which places you above any danger or attack whatever, like a divine promise, a shelter, an impenetrable shield ...
>
> I see that you have made great progress, as your tests are already more dangerous, and it is God Himself Who estimates the strength and quality of each test according to the state of the soul. When

comparing your tests with those that you had two or three years ago, it is like the difference between a woman and a child. You have passed through tests of your thought, intelligence, heart and love, and you overcame all of them! How can you doubt that you will always win? The love of Shoghi Effendi for you . . . you, quite new and young! And there is a poignant tenderness in his words to you that if you could understand them, Lucienne, you would never fear . . .

Shoghi Effendi wants me to stay <u>continually</u> beside you, in spirit, love and protection and correspondence. He wants that step by step we walk together, you and I, that I may impart the little wisdom I received from the Beloved during my long Bahá'í life, and that you, in turn, give me strength, courage, and joy that I could never explain to you. You and my dear daughter and Marion Holley in America are like three jewels in my heart, each one a divine pearl which radiates a celestial light through the spaces of visible and invisible worlds, that I cannot express to you . . .

I hold you to my heart, and thus united under the wing of the Guardian, we challenge the world.

Another letter from May to Lucienne states:

As you know, Bahá'u'lláh often speaks about 'satanic veils' (veils of selfishness) in which each soul is enveloped, and He says that nothing except the fire of love for God may consume these veils and make them vanish. This is the state of martyrdom, as 'Abdu'l-Bahá Himself told me, martyrdom is a state of the soul and not only the fact of being killed. One can be killed without being a martyr and one can also be a martyr without being killed, and this state of complete sacrifice to God gives life to mankind.

On 19 September 1939, just two weeks after Britain declared war on Germany, May wrote to Lucienne:

I feel that the real war has not yet begun. A spark will set the world on fire, and then you will be guided by a light, an unparalleled force.

The last time that she wrote to Lucienne – on 17 January 1940 while in New York City, just before leaving for South America – May stated:

May and Mary Maxwell at the Brussels Exposition, Belgium, 1935.
Photo taken by W. S. Maxwell

Sketch (originally in colour) by W. S. Maxwell, dated 12 May 1936 and entitled 'Cheerio'. It humorously depicts May and Mary leaving Lyon en route to Haifa, where they arrived in early 1937

Mary and W. S. Maxwell with Alfons Grassle in Munich, Germany, 1935

Mary Maxwell in Rothenburg, Germany, circa 1936

Conference of the North German Bahá'í centres, at Diedrichshagen, a village near Rostock, Spring of 1936. Mary Maxwell is standing 5th from left

Mary Maxwell in her skiing outfit on the Zugspitze, Bavaria, 1935–6

Bahá'ís at the Esslingen Summer School, Germany, 1936. May Maxwell and Marion Jack are standing on either side of the Greatest Name; seated on the ground in the front row are Mary Maxwell and her cousin Jeanne Bolles

Two cousins: Mary Maxwell and Jeanne Bolles wearing traditional German dress, the dirndl, Stuttgart, 1936

Bahá'ís of Lyon, France, 1937, with May and W. S. Maxwell. Lucienne Migette is standing next to May

May Maxwell in Lyon with some of the Persian Bahá'ís, 1937. Seated at the far right is Izzatu'llah Zabih; at the far left is Dr Roshan Yazdi. The other two are Mr and Mrs Modaber

May Maxwell with some of the Bahá'ís of Lyon, 1937. Madame Borel is holding the picture of 'Abdu'l-Bahá

Mary Maxwell in the garden of the Western Bahá'í Pilgrim House, shortly before her marriage to Shoghi Effendi, 1937

The more the tests are poured in torrents on the believers, the more the sacred Cause spreads, and you live, my dear Lucienne, almost always in suffering in one way or another, and it is thus that the divine light shines outward in an ever-increasing circle.

May's extraordinary bond with Lucienne, from the day she first taught her the Faith in Lyon to the end of her life, was not only due to the tenderness of her own heart and the instincts of her own soul but was also in response to Shoghi Effendi's specific instructions. As early as 28 July 1938, Rúḥíyyih Khánum had written to her on behalf of Shoghi Effendi, saying,

> He has deeply appreciated all the work you have done for him this Winter and has now certain advice to give you: Your spiritual child, Lucienne Migette, is doing wonderful work in France and the Guardian wants you to keep in closest touch with her and give her all the support and inspiration you can. She has recently taken the Cause to Orleans and a believer is now confirmed there through her efforts. Such wonderful development in the work in France has greatly cheered the Guardian, and he feels you are largely responsible for it, so you cannot do enough to guide and help Lucienne.

This mandate, among so many others, she fulfilled, till her last breath.

* * *

In January 1936, after reporting her activities to the Guardian and requesting him for prayers on behalf of all the souls she had been teaching in Paris, May had allowed herself to breathe the hope that she might have the privilege of returning once again to the Holy Land:

> I cannot bear to say good-bye and I dare not hope to see your blessed beloved face once more – I am humbly grateful that it is ever before me – as I turn my heart to Bahá'u'lláh! the only way – the only path I know – to Him.
>
> > Ever yours,
> > May M_____

When Shoghi Effendi's secretary responded on his behalf to this letter, on 21 January, he himself added a personal handwritten postscript at the end, answering the request which May had barely dared express. The delicacy with which she asked for the favour of seeing 'your blessed beloved face once more' is a testimony to her profound modesty. She knew she had already received so many bounties from his hand that to ask for more, except with bated breath, was utterly presumptuous. But even so, the Guardian's generosity of response must have overwhelmed her.

> He is so pleased to learn that you are keeping well, and that your trip to Paris has proved to be highly beneficial to your health, & that you have been accorded such a warm welcome by the friends. He sincerely hopes that your stay with them will have imparted to their hearts a fresh incentive to work for the firmer consolidation of the Cause in that centre.
>
> He also trusts that your journey to Lyon will be quite successful, & that the small group of new believers there will receive through your visit a new vision & inspiration. That group is very promising, indeed, but a competent teacher is needed to better ground them in the Cause, & particularly in the Administration.

And in the handwriting of Shoghi Effendi:

> Dearly-beloved co-worker:
> I wish to assure you in person of a most hearty welcome. Your distinguished services, so loyally, courageously & devotedly rendered, in both the European & American continents, fully entitle you to visit the Holy Shrines & to draw fresh inspiration from the Source of His inexhaustible grace. I am profoundly thankful for what you, Mary & Mrs. Bolles have achieved, & for the spirit which animates you in His service. The Beloved is well-pleased with the many evidences of your exemplary devotion to His Cause & of perseverance in the path of service. Affectionately
>
>   Shoghi

She could not immediately reciprocate, however, involved as she was in her teaching trips. On 21 April 1936 the following cable, addressed to her in care of Madame Borel, Lyon, was received from Shoghi Effendi in reply to a message of love and greetings sent to him and signed by all the believers there:

LOVING APPRECIATION REMEMBRANCE SHRINES SHOGHI

after which she wrote him another letter:

> Months have passed since the receipt of your most precious words of love and encouragement in Paris, and more recently of your cablegram...
>
> Your suggestion that I might again be in your presence and visit the Holy Shrines overwhelmed me with my utter unworthiness...
>
> In the meantime Mr. Maxwell wants us to come home but although I will go if necessary I cannot urge this on Mary. I feel she is doing valuable work, and her whole nature is at present against going back to America – it would – for deep reasons – crush her new-found life. This I have written my husband and urged him to join us, which he can easily do when he has finished certain present work. I long to have Mary go to the Holy Land since you have with such infinite bounty suggested it, but she is now spell-bound by her work in Germany – not nearly finished – besides your wish that she could go thro the Balkans.

On 22 May she wrote to Shoghi Effendi again from Lyon. One can sense her anguish between the lines, for though she was clearly longing to return to Haifa and indeed had been warmly welcomed by the Guardian to do so, she must have been torn by the knowledge that she and Mary would not, as she had so ardently hoped, be accompanied by her husband:

> Altho I am in the process of writing you a brief report of events – very small because I have done so little – yet a cable from my husband has precipitated the necessity for submitting our humble affairs for your judgment and decision.
>
> I had written you of the joy and gratitude your letters had brought to Mary & me! Of the overpowering influence upon all of your mighty Epistle to the West, of the great love and kindness of the Paris Bahá'ís, and more recently, of your dear cables to Mary &

to me, and of our hopes that Mr. Maxwell would join us and share all our happiness & blessings.

Now comes a cablegram in which he says he cannot come, and while I do not yet know the reasons, nor whether this decision is absolutely final, I know that I must submit the whole matter to you . . . Mary does not want to go home and I feel she should not – it would at the present time crush the spirit in her, because she is inspired by the thought that she is of some small service to you – she burns with the longing to help you – even in a small way!

On the other hand she dreads having me go home and leave her so far away – alone. This, I believe, however, can be entirely overcome, for she has found her true path to which all else will yield. Dearest Shoghi Effendi! I had never really dared to hope that we might visit you once more, yet your loving message gave us such hope, which I deeply long to have my husband share. He has so devotedly and loyally served the Cause for many years, both in our home and as chairman of our Assembly, that he, far more than I, deserves this incomparable blessing. You leave the Holy Land in June and the time now is short.

Either Mary and I should go to Haifa now, before you leave, without my dear husband, or we should wait and work in Europe in the hope of his joining us a little later when his immediate work at home is finished, and all go to you on your return in the fall, or – in case he cannot come, I think I should go home to be with him in the summer; he is very lonely, and the winter in Canada is impossible for me.

There is also the question of my health. My husband knows that at certain intervals – much longer intervals in recent years, I suffer a collapse of my vital forces, an exhaustion, such as I am having since I came to Lyon – and that, as you so lovingly state in your precious letter, the visit to the Holy Land 'renews my inspiration' and my strength. Therefore my dear husband is willing and happy to have Mary and me go to you, but what about him! I long to have him attain this great blessing! I am not sure that I am strong enough just now to go home alone – yet of one thing I am absolutely certain – that I am strong enough for anything you wish. I have no guidance – it all comes from you! . . . Only tell us what is best to do, and every problem of life will be resolved with a miraculous all-inclusive simplicity!

Shoghi Effendi's answer to the above letter was written on his behalf. It had been four months since the Guardian had extended a 'most hearty welcome' to May to come to Haifa, and the summer season was soon to begin. On 29 May his secretary wrote:

> Shoghi Effendi has asked me to thank you for your very kind & assuring message of the 22nd ins. just received. He is indeed glad to realize the wonderful work which you & Miss Maxwell are accomplishing for the Faith in Europe. Mrs. Bolles and her daughter have given him most encouraging reports about your activities & he sincerely hopes that as a result of all these strenuous efforts you have exerted during these months the Cause in Germany, & particularly in France, will make a fresh start. The inspiration which your visit brought to the friends in these countries will no doubt stimulate them to greater & more united effort, & enable them to accomplish more for our beloved Faith.
>
> Regarding your visit to the Holy Land; Shoghi Effendi would have very much liked to have you, & also Mr. Maxwell & Mary, come to Haifa & meet you all before his departure. But as summer is drawing near, & he feels so tired, & almost exhausted, after seven months of uninterrupted & strenuous work, he thinks it necessary to leave for his summer rest, & not to delay his going any longer.
>
> In the meantime he would advise you to stay in Europe & continue your teaching work together with Mary. He thinks it would be better for her to be with you, preferably in Germany where you can be of immense service to the Cause. He hopes that Mr. Maxwell will join you later on, & that you all three will lend all the help you can to the extension of teaching work not only in Germany but also in Central Europe.
>
> The Guardian thinks that the best time for you to undertake the pilgrimage & visit Haifa would be next fall. He hopes that you will arrange your program in such a way as to no longer delay your long-cherished pilgrimage to the Holy Land.

At the end of the letter Shoghi Effendi added a personal handwritten postscript:

Dearest co-worker:
   Were it not for the fact that I feel tired & exhausted, as a result of my exceptionally heavy responsibilities, cares and preoccupations in recent months, I would have gladly postponed my departure in order to welcome you & Mary. I am in urgent need of absolute rest, & I am looking forward to the time I can extend to you a hearty welcome in recognition of your many & notable services. I certainly advise you to be with Mary during the summer months & not to separate yourself from her under any circumstances. Affectionately
   Shoghi

It was not until late autumn that May Maxwell wrote the Guardian again about the trip to Haifa. On Tuesday, 30 November 1936, as a result of her deteriorating health, she had no alternative but to cut short her plans for extended travel through Germany, Austria and the Balkans.

Now I feel I should tell you, although I regret the length of this letter, that for a time my health was such that it seemed impossible to carry out your plans and our dearest hopes. On account of my heart & blood pressure (all so un-interesting! but my husband asked me to tell you!) my doctor advised against all this traveling, and Mr. Maxwell felt I should give it up. But with all the truth and sincerity of my longing heart I can assure you that my trust in Bahá'u'lláh far outweighed these natural human fears of my dear husband. I put my whole soul and life in the Hands of the Beloved, followed faithfully your instructions regarding a reasonable care of my health, took the doctor's good advice – and started on my way. Oh! My Guardian, every step of the way has strengthened my faith, every stage of my humble journey has been founded on reality, all causes for my dear husband's fears have been removed as tho by magic, and I am, inwardly and outwardly, stronger today than I have been in years. . . .
   We can come now if you wish; we can sail from Trieste at any point you wish, or we can complete the journey you so lovingly, so generously planned for us!

But even as the prospects of another pilgrimage became a reality, May struggled with her conscience. To her sorrow, Sutherland was still not able to join them. But how could she beg her Beloved to answer her prayers, if she had not done all she could for Him? How could she go to the Holy Land without having done her utmost to fulfil the Guardian's wishes? Four days later she wrote to Shoghi Effendi again, from Hamburg:

> After having sent my letter on Tuesday a strange deep feeling of disappointment and sorrow seemed to couch my heart which I could not explain . . . I feel that in my first letter I had not strictly obeyed you . . . Therefore I have consulted with Mary and we are going to Rostock and Berlin (I am speaking to the new group in Schwerin tomorrow night) and from there we shall go to the nearest point in order to sail from Trieste, and in that way we hope to fulfil your wish and inmost longing of our hearts to visit Haifa 'in the fall' . . . Nevertheless should you at this time have any other wish or plan for us we submit all to you . . . and you can always reach us at the above address.

On 8 December she received a cable from Shoghi Effendi, sent in care of the American Express office in Hamburg:

> HEARTILY APPROVE YOUR DECISION SAIL FROM TRIESTE LOVE BOTH

On Christmas Day, as recorded in Marion Holley's notes for her *In Memoriam* article on May Maxwell in *The Bahá'í World*, vol. VIII, they were on the train to Rome, and were due to sail for Haifa 'in a few days'. As it turned out, the few days were extended by more than a week, because of complications en route. Mary wrote a letter to the Guardian on 29 December informing him that they had been delayed in Naples. Although they had hoped to catch the boat two days before, they had lost some luggage at the frontier which they could not risk leaving in the hands of an agent and had therefore been obliged to wait for the next boat bound for Haifa that was not due to depart until the following Sunday. An added complication was Mrs Maxwell's health. Mary begged for Shoghi Effendi's prayers that her mother would recuperate her strength over the next few days so that they would not have to delay their departure still further. As it turned out, they were able to take the small Japanese liner on 3 January, rather than wait for the larger English liner bound for the port of Haifa, and sailed into the bay of Haifa on 12 January 1937.

Five days before, Randolph Bolles had written a letter to his sister telling her

> ... of the delightful visit I was having with Max ... my enjoyment lasted until the end of my stay at your home, and I regretted greatly to leave. Max gave me a great 'run' and I was kept busy with all the entertainment and engagements; it was certainly delightful to see so many old Montreal friends ... I have invited Max to come down as my guest, just as I did last winter ...

On the back of this letter May jotted down notes, as was her custom, in this case recording the various requests made by people who had asked to be remembered to Shoghi Effendi when she saw him in Haifa.

> MARION JACK, Stuttgart – Please mention me to our best beloved Guardian and all the members of the Holy Family. Please excuse me to your Beloved; tell him I am not here to enjoy life, but am trying to get braced up for another spurt in Sofia where my heart is.
> MR AND MRS COBB, Washington, DC – They report wonderful teaching activities and beg prayers in Shrines.
> EDITH HORN, Frankfurt – Please remember me to the beloved Guardian.
> PHILIP SPRAGUE, New York City – You already know his message of deep love and devotion.

Using whatever paper was at hand, she included her own dear brother in the list.

Mrs Maxwell and her daughter signed their names in the Pilgrims Book on 12 January 1937, as 'May Bolles Maxwell' and 'Mary Sutherland Maxwell'. This historic date marked Mrs Maxwell's final pilgrimage. She had gone to Haifa for the first time and met the Master as a young woman of twenty-nine. She had returned with her husband, for a second unforgettable pilgrimage in 1909, which proved to be her last pilgrimage in the presence of her beloved Master, although she was blessed to see Him again during His travels in the West. She had then come, prostrate with grief at the passing of 'Abdu'l-Bahá, to meet her

Guardian in 1923. This third pilgrimage, which was divided into two visits, might technically be considered as two separate pilgrimages, in fact, which extended before and after her sojourn in Egypt, from 23 April 1923 to the end of the following February 1924. Since that time, she had not been back to the Holy Land. Now, accompanied by her tall and queenly daughter of twenty-six, she was returning for the last time. And this pilgrimage, her fifth in effect, was to be a turning point in the life of all the Maxwells.

On 22 January, ten days after their arrival, May and her daughter spent a night in Bahjí, from where Mrs Maxwell wrote several letters to her family and her friends. To her husband she addressed these words:

> The Mansion, Bahjí – Acca
>
> My beloved Sutherland –
>
> This is the stationery used in the Mansion at Bahjí and it will be mailed in Acca, and when Mary & I came here yesterday to visit the Tomb of Bahá'u'lláh and to spend a day and night in this most Holy Place, Shoghi Effendi asked us to write from here to our near & dear ones as it would bring to them a great bounty. You, with Mary, hold that place in my heart, the nearest and dearest, and in these wondrous hours you are with me dearest, and I pray with you at the Holy Threshold, as we did together years ago. The Shrine, set here amidst a transcendent peace & beauty, on the shore of the blue sea, is indescribable in its majesty, so hallowed, so still, eternal and infinite, penetrated and pervaded by the Presence of the Great Being, the All-Mighty, under Whose Shadow every human being is protected, in Whom the most humble and abject creature finds hope. From the depths of my heart I am grateful, and send you a portion of that mighty, mysterious love which seeks to save and guide a dying world.
> P. S. It would be a joy to you the real artist to see the beauty, loveliness and simplicity with which Shoghi Effendi has restored the Mansion – it is a veritable dream of beauty and charm, which I will leave to the gifted pen of your true daughter to describe . . .

To Philip Sprague that same day, she wrote:

> Shoghi Effendi sent us here yesterday, and we have lived – Mary and I – an eternity of beauty, wonder and love. As I prayed for you

again in 'the Most Holy Shrine on earth' as the Guardian describes it, I had an overpowering realization of your great, your illustrious destiny.

And finally she also sent this letter to Lucienne Migette:

I want only to add that the Guardian is very happy about your enthusiasm and dedication, that he has much confidence and hope in you, that he prays for you and that he said <u>several</u> times: 'Who knows whether Lyon may become much more important than Paris, a selected centre, the heart of France'.

But the last two sentences of the postscript of her letter to her husband contain the most important of her insights during that precious night and day spent in the Mansion of Bahjí. Mrs Maxwell may not have realized, at that time, how prophetic were her words:

The more Shoghi Effendi becomes acquainted with Mary's talents, the more he asks about you – and never forget – he – the Guardian of the Cause of God, has invited you to come! Do you remember the new doors that were opened to you the last time you came – the great and beneficent changes that took place in our lives?

On 26 February 1937, a cable addressed to W. S. Maxwell was delivered to the house on Pine Avenue in Montreal. It came from his wife and must have given him quite a shock:

YOUR PRESENCE HERE BY MARCH TWENTY FIRST ESSENTIAL IN CONNECTION MARYS FUTURE HAPPINESS GREAT DESTINY COMPLETE SECRECY ABSOLUTELY ESSENTIAL MENTION TO NO ONE IF NECESSARY USE PRETEXT VISIT TO RANDOLPH YOU CAN SAIL BERENGARIA ON MARCH THIRD AND CATCH TRIESTINO MARCH TENTH TRIESTE ARRIVING HAIFA FIFTEENTH MAKE FLORIDA MONEY AVAILABLE CABLE REPLY OUR DEVOTED LOVE MAY

* * *

There is something wonderful about the fact that a pilgrimage is personal. No matter in whose company one turns one's face towards Bahá'u'lláh's resting-place, or walks towards that sacred spot, or circumambulates those hallowed surroundings, one is ultimately alone. No matter how hard one tries to convey the experience to others afterwards, or how well one puts the feelings into words, the experience remains a subjective, and ultimately private, affair. The notes which many Bahá'ís have written during their pilgrimages therefore reflect an intensely individual view of the Cause and of the Guardian. As Shoghi Effendi himself pointed out throughout his life, these personal and sometimes random or biased expressions cannot constitute an authentic standard of behaviour or interpretation of the teachings or be placed in the same category as the written texts of the Faith. But they remain a remarkable testimony of the pilgrims themselves and reflect the personalities of those who have undergone this precious experience.

The following notes taken during May's pilgrimage are included here because they reflect her immediate concerns and reveal the workings of her mind during this historic visit to the Holy Land. Although they are only her pilgrim's notes and should be treated as such, they nevertheless capture what she thought were the essentials as she listened spellbound to Shoghi Effendi's words and felt their power:

> Words of the Guardian, February 1937: We must always dissociate the human part of the Manifestation from His Spirit – it is the rule that the powers of the Manifestation are stronger, His sense of beauty, His memory, His power of endurance and strength – it is the spirit in Him that is more powerful – this does not mean that the body of the Manifestation is of a different stuff – so keen is the word – everything in Him is keener – this is due to His unique Spirit – not that His atoms are different – the body is not of a different order of that of the human beings – they are all the same, although the body is the same the soul is not the same – it is a more intense reality – it is of a different [order], quite different; unlike the body, if it is endued with a keener perception it is due to His soul. The saints, the Guardian, all else apart from the Master and Prophets belong to the human order. There is a tendency to introduce new mysteries into the Cause. We have a few mysteries in the Cause. We must not introduce any man-made ones. In order to satisfy our desires – our

emotions, we produce mysteries. Sometimes our emotions are bad, they can go too far. A desire is either corrupt or wholesome – but a wholesome desire, a love and devotion – a faith which is a wholesome thing, a good thing, even this must be restrained or it may lead to excess . . . Devotion to the Cause if carried to excess leads to fanaticism.

[Written on the side of the paper:] God's mercy overshadows all kinds of criminals even Covenant-breakers.

But the one mystery, man-made or not, which remains in connection with May's final pilgrimage and the summons of W. S. Maxwell to the Holy Land in March 1937, concerns the emotions which accompanied their learning the astounding fact that Shoghi Effendi wished to marry their daughter. As of this writing, only two records of the circumstances leading up to this momentous event have come to light in May's papers. The first was the cable she sent to her husband, instructing him to come to Haifa without delay. This message, with its clipped and practical emphasis, perhaps captures more intensely than any other record the private nature of the emotions as well as circumstances surrounding this historically important event. The second record was written over eighteen months later, on 28 September 1938, in a letter addressed to Leonora Holsapple (Armstrong). In this letter May recalls in great detail the days and weeks prior to her daughter's wedding:

> A few weeks after Rúḥíyyih Khánum and I arrived in Haifa . . . the Guardian with the utmost gentleness began to teach her Persian and to give special attention to her general training and education . . .
>
> Later, through conversations with his dear mother talking to me confidentially at his request (in the true oriental manner!), I was gradually informed, but at that time my daughter knew nothing about it, until the day, a week or two later, when the younger sister of the Guardian took her into his presence.
>
> Whatever happened at that time is known only to God, but He sustained and supported her in what was perhaps the most overwhelming shock of her life, with her deep reverence, almost worship of the Guardian as the sign of God on earth. It was almost too much for a human being to bear.

However, a third record of these events is contained in the exchange of telegrams between Mary and her father on 27 February 1937; Mary's handwritten message for her telegram reads:

> My dearest Daddy –
> Ask your consent for my marriage confirm my great happiness absolute secrecy required until after wedding and official announcement longing for your arrival bring originals Masters tablets please cable consent immediately
> Your devoted loving
> Mary

Mr. Maxwell's reply was sent on the very same day he received the telegram:

> SURPRISED AND OVERJOYED CONSENT GRANTED DEEPEST LOVE AND DEVOTION SHOGHI MOTHER YOU [.] LEAVE BERENGARIA WEDNESDAY GO VIA BRINDISI ARRIVE FIFTEENTH DADDY

Mr Maxwell boarded the *Santa Maria del Casale* in Brindisi on 11 March and arrived in the port of Haifa on 15 March, a day which coincided with the Birthday of Bahá'u'lláh according to the lunar calendar. That same day, May wrote the following touching note to Shoghi Effendi on the stationery of 'The Bahá'í Pilgrim House':

> Beloved Guardian,
> Today I realize more profoundly than ever in my life the deep meaning of the Master's Words to me in Montreal – 'God has perfected all His bounties in you' and this, despite my utter unworthiness. Now it is you, who take my dear husband to Bahji, and my thankfulness is overflowing. May I humbly beg, on this blessed day your prayers for all my near and dear ones in the seen and in the unseen worlds; for all those with whom my 'heart is vitally connected', for whom the Master made me such wonderful promises . . .
> With deepest love and humble devotion, I am yours, May M.

About the events of the wedding day itself, a few heart-warming fragments are available. In the same letter written by May in September

1938 to Leonora Holsapple, we are given a glimpse:

> As one might have expected, the Guardian's marriage was utterly simple, devoid of every earthly trapping, yet perfect in its beauty and simplicity . . .
> On March 24th [he] took Rúḥíyyih Khánum in his car to the tomb of Bahá'u'lláh where he chanted two prayers in the inner sanctuary and told her that that was the reality of the marriage. They were alone. When they returned, the Guardian's mother took them alone into the room of the Greatest Holy Leaf . . .
> Then all the families greeted and embraced them, the certificate of marriage was signed, and later Shoghi Effendi and his little western wife came to the Pilgrim House and it was our turn to embrace them and to feel all that it was possible to feel at such an overwhelming moment. There is no doubt that to us it was more like a dream than reality . . .

How different a marriage ceremony was this from a wedding to which a Western mother might have been accustomed to expect for her only daughter. But May dwelt on nothing but the spiritual honour and responsibility which this marriage had bestowed upon her family. All her prayers were for her daughter's strength of spirit to face and to surmount her spiritual tests. Her letter to Leonora said as much:

> The Guardian has shown her a love and kindness, an understanding and sympathy through which she is steadily developing, and although the tests are severe, Leonora, past all our comprehension, yet through the divine protection she is steadily attaining that station which God has ordained for her.

Many years later, May's daughter herself wrote of the event which so radically changed her life and which transformed her, once and for all, from Mary Maxwell to Amatu'l-Bahá Rúḥíyyih Khánum. Her manner of doing it serves as an example for future biographers. In *The Priceless Pearl,* she described her wedding day with the same simplicity and self-restraint with which she dressed herself for the occasion:

> I remember I was dressed, except for a white lace blouse, entirely in

black for this unique occasion, and was a typical example of the way oriental women dressed to go out into the streets in those days, the custom being to wear black.

May also recorded this historic event in her father's 'Daily Memorandum' book – a beautiful album made of red and black leather with letters tooled in gold. Her own words, however, are unadorned and simply relay the facts:

> Mary Sutherland Maxwell, daughter of William Sutherland and May Ellis Maxwell was married to Shoghi Effendi, the First Guardian of the Bahá'í Faith, on March 24th, 1937 at Haifa, Palestine.

On that day Mary wrote this moving short letter to her parents, addressed 'to Mother and Daddy' and written on letterhead stationery of

> The Bahá'í Pilgrim House
>
> My dearest, dearest ones,
> On this most glorious day of my life how can I ever thank you both enough and express my love to you – for the life you gave me? For all your devotion to me; the example of your own happy marriage that gave me an ideal in life; the beauty of our home which has enriched my very soul. From you both I have woven into me so many characteristics that I hope now will be of service to the Guardian and [the] Cause.
> Surely no child ever had two better, more loving parents than I! And as you have always been my pride and my dearests and my joy – so in my new life you will always continue to be!
> Your own
> Faithful Mary

LATE YEARS

1937–1952

1937–1940

The announcement of the marriage of Mary Maxwell to Shoghi Effendi Rabbani was first made to the family members. The Maxwell and Bolles families were both informed as soon as the wedding had taken place. A cable from Mr Maxwell went to his sister, Amelia Maxwell Hutchison, on that very day, 24 March 1937:

> SHOGHI EFFENDI MARRIED MARY WEDNESDAY NOTIFY FAMILY
> LOVE WILLIE

Two more cables were sent that day, signed by May, one to the Bolles family members in Washington, Connecticut and the other to those still in Budapest, both with the same wording:

> BELOVED GUARDIAN MARRIED MARY WEDNESDAY NEW NAME
> RUHIYYIH KHANUM ALL OUR LOVE

Four days later, 'Libbie' Maxwell, the widow of Sutherland's brother Edward, sent a cable back to the Maxwells on behalf of all the family:

> LOVING CONGRATULATIONS TO ALL
> LIBBIE AND FAMILY

But the Bahá'í world community only received the news three days after the wedding had taken place, on 27 March 1937. As Rúḥíyyih Khánum later wrote in *The Priceless Pearl*, the cable which conveyed the astounding information was addressed to the National Spiritual Assembly of the United States and Canada, over the signature of 'Ziaiyyih mother of the Guardian', but it had actually been drafted by him:

> ANNOUNCE ASSEMBLIES CELEBRATION MARRIAGE BELOVED GUARDIAN. INESTIMABLE HONOUR CONFERRED UPON HANDMAID OF BAHÁ'U'LLÁH RÚHÍYYIH KHÁNUM MISS MARY MAXWELL. UNION EAST AND WEST PROCLAIMED BY BAHÁ'Í FAITH CEMENTED

A similar cable was sent to the friends of Iran and acknowledgements were immediately received. To Ḍiyá'íyyih Khánum, care of Shoghi Effendi, the Secretary of the National Assembly of the United States and Canada addressed the following words:

> ASSEMBLIES WILL REJOICE YOUR HEART STIRRING ANNOUNCEMENT BESEECH DIVINE BLESSINGS

And to the beloved Guardian himself was sent this response:

> JOYOUSLY ACCLAIM HISTORIC EVENT SO AUSPICIOUSLY UNITING IN ETERNAL BOND DESTINY EAST AND WEST

The Guardian replied after another three days. On 30 March he wrote a second cable to the North American believers, which, together with the announcement of his marriage, was printed in the April 1937 issue of the American *Bahá'í News*:

> Deeply moved your message. Institution Guardianship head cornerstone Administrative Order Cause Bahá'u'lláh already ennobled through its organic connection with Persons of Twin Founders Bahá'í Faith is now further reinforced direct association with West and particularly with American believers whose spiritual destiny is to usher in World Order Bahá'u'lláh. For my part desire congratulate community American believers on acquisition tie vitally binding them to so weighty an organ their Faith.

Four days later, on 3 April, the National Assembly sent a further message to the Guardian:

> Hearts overflowing with gratitude we are sending $1349 being $19 each from seventy-one American Assemblies for immediate

strengthening new tie binding American Bahá'ís to institution Guardianship. Trust this modest contribution will be accepted as token ever-increasing devotion and unity American believers in service to World Order Bahá'u'lláh.

The following reply was received from the Guardian on 5 April:

> Accept deeply touched American believers spontaneous expression of ever-increasing devotion to crowning institution World Order Bahá'u'lláh. Noblest contribution individual believers can make at this juncture to consecrate newly-acquired tie is to promote with added fervor unique plan conceived for them by 'Abdu'l-Bahá.

A message from the National Convention was also sent to Shoghi Effendi on 29 April:

> American Convention gratefully celebrates dual gift, Master's historic visit and consummation unique union East West. Pledges undying loyalty renewed vigor extend World Order throughout Americas and all lands. Profound dedicated felicitations.

During the days immediately after the marriage, and in response to an inquiry from the National Assembly of the United States and Canada requesting to know the policy to be followed in making this momentous announcement to the rest of the world, Shoghi Effendi wrote:

> Approve public announcement emphasize significance institution Guardianship union East West and linking destinies Persia America allude honour conferred British peoples.

This last phrase, as Rúḥíyyih Khánum later confirmed in *The Priceless Pearl*, was a direct allusion to her Scots-Canadian father, but she also stated that Shoghi Effendi told her mother one night, over dinner in the Western Pilgrim House soon after their union, that 'one of the reasons I was chosen to be his wife was because I am the daughter of May Maxwell'.

* * *

Mr and Mrs Maxwell did not leave the Holy Land immediately after the wedding of their daughter. They remained in Haifa and in its vicinity for another two months. During this time Mr Maxwell took many photographs of the members of the Holy Family, which he used to illustrate an article entitled 'Recollections of Munírih Khánum' that was later published in Volume VIII of *The Bahá'í World*. When Agnes Alexander came on pilgrimage and 'reached the Land of Desire' on 20 April 1937, she recounted that she was thrilled to meet there 'my precious spiritual Mother' and learn of the momentous events that had just transpired.[1] And she added:

> How marvelous are the ways of the beloved Guardian!

But May was ill for much of these two months. The emotional upheaval must have been overwhelming – a combination of mixed feelings of exaltation over the marriage and sorrow over the imminent separation from her beloved daughter. She spent at least half of her remaining weeks recuperating from fevers, in Nazareth, from where she wrote a pathetic letter to the Guardian:

> I long so to see you! But the doctor said that only when I have no temperature could I get up, but you must feel the longing in my heart.

Her husband remained at her side, because it was obvious that she could not travel back to Canada alone. Her brother recognized the intense emotional impact on May of these life-changing events, as his letter to her, written from Washington, Connecticut on 9 April 1937 clearly indicates:

> Dearest May:
> I need not tell you how very happy I am to have your good letter from Haifa, written so soon after dear Mary's marriage to Shogi [sic] Effendi; nor to say how deeply I am touched by the many thoughts of beauty and feeling you express – which are indeed moving. I can well understand your feelings at a time when so momentous an event had just taken place; they must indeed have been overpowering – as you say. But, by this time you must have succeeded in adjusting yourself to the idea not easy to realize, I can well understand, that

---
[1] In her article: 'May Maxwell–A Tribute'.

Mary is actually wedded, and that your son-in-law is Shogi Effendi. I am glad that Max got to Haifa in time to help you to go through what must have been a very 'agitating' situation for you both. I hope that dear Mary has come thro the strain and excitement without anything other than great happiness. Please give her my dearest love and keep some of it for yourself and old Max; and convey my greetings and very best wishes for his happiness to my nephew-in-law; and say that I hope that he will come to this country for a visit with his bride at an early date. If I do not write further tonight, it is because this must go to the Post Office without delay – in order to go to Europe by the 'Europa' tomorrow. Good night, May: again my love; and I hope that you and Max will be homeward bound before long.

Ever affectionately,

BROTHER

Even Mr Maxwell's faithful secretary, Miss A. M. Parent (AMP), who added her congratulations with the rest, realized the toll these highly emotional events, and particularly the separation from Mary, might take on Mrs Maxwell's health. Writing to Mr Maxwell in early summer, she noted that while she was sure their daughter 'must be very happy in her new position', she could 'quite realize also' how hard it might have been at the same time for Mrs Maxwell. 'Life seems to be so strange at times,' she concluded, 'happiness must bring a shadow of pain also!'

Some time later, May wrote to her sister-in-law and her niece, who were on a teaching trip in Budapest, describing her condition at this time. Although she is referring to her own health, one can read the concerns of maternal heartache between the lines.

> You must by now have received the letter I wrote you from Haifa or Nazareth, telling you of my illness and my great disappointment in not being able to go to Budapest . . .
>
> If I had been able to get good medical help in Palestine I would have completely recovered, because to me there is no medicine outside homeopathy. No other medicine acts on my system, and there is not only no homeopathic physician in the whole of Palestine but no homeopathic remedies! Heaven help Rúḥíyyih Khánum if she gets ill, but with the care the Guardian gives her she probably will remain very well . . .

May's condition must still have been fragile when the Maxwells finally left Haifa on 30 May 1937. There is a very moving letter which she wrote to Shoghi Effendi on the midnight of their departure, from Azour's Ritz Hotel at 115 Hayarkon Street in Tel Aviv. Her words vividly reflect the turmoil of mind and upheaval of heart that she had experienced, and, in the end, refer to the Guardian's imminent plans of departure from Haifa too, for his usual summer sojourn in the Swiss mountains.

> My beloved Guardian,
> I have never left you for a moment, and in my waking moments in the night, my whole being was close to you, my yearning love and prayers watched over you, the most sacred, precious being on this earth! With every breath I thank Bahá'u'lláh that He gave me such a daughter whom He accepted for you, and chose to work beside you, to minister to you, and the centre of my heart and life is in you both, in this most blessed union, so profound and far reaching in its influence and in its significance.
> You know, as none can ever know, the depth thro which my frail soul has passed this winter; and that I have emerged tranquil and assured, filled with faith & courage for the future and for the work you have given me to do, is due to your sustaining grace!
> Never, Shoghi Effendi, in this world nor in eternity can I express the load of gratitude, the mighty inexhaustible thankfulness to Bahá'u'lláh, to you, for the bounties and mercies which have been showered upon us; had not His Mercy and Protection, 'thru him who shadoweth all mankind', utterly eclipsed His justice I would not have survived, and words sound empty and paltry beside what I feel as I write you, as I see your beloved face before me, <u>ever before me,</u> in the world of light, and in this tangible world, as a burning, guiding star, the rays of His Sun.
> May I ever walk in this path! The gifts, especially the ravishing Tablets of the Master, with which you have showered me are visible signs of what flows in a steady stream from your heart to mine, to each one of this most blessed family. This sea air would refresh & revive you. May you soon be 'away'!
> With deepest, ardent love and devotion,
> Forever yours, May M.

Beloved Guardian,

I forgot to say that Mr. Maxwell and I will soon be in a position, without in any way depleting our finances, to make certain contributions, both to National and International Funds, and in September we shall send you five hundred dollars which would make us happy to have you apply to your new home, or preferably to anything you wish and deem advisable.

Rest assured that we do this with ease and joy, & hope to have still greater privilege in the future.

Please forgive this very messy letter,
                                          Lovingly, M.M.

The next day, 31 May, Shoghi Effendi sent the following cable to Mr and Mrs Maxwell, addressed to: CAPTAIN SS NARKUNDA ALEXANDRIA-RADIO:

WITH YOU BOTH ALWAYS SHOGHI

A second cable to them followed the next day:

LOVING YOU BOTH TENDERLY VERY HAPPY OUR GREAT BLESSINGS
RUHIYYIH

They must have left Haifa shortly before the Guardian's own departure for Switzerland, for soon afterwards, on 29 June, Rúḥíyyih Khánum wrote from there the following letter to her mother, on behalf of Shoghi Effendi. It is in reply to the midnight letter May sent him from Tel Aviv, just before leaving for Europe, and is probably the first letter Rúḥíyyih Rabbani wrote to Mrs Maxwell on behalf of the Guardian.

Dearest Mother,

I am writing you on behalf of Shoghi Effendi to acknowledge the receipt of your letter of May 30th and to express how deeply satisfied he was to hear that you are feeling well and had such a good and restful crossing . . .

If you can, and your health permits, concentrate as much as possible on your work in Lyon, which Shoghi Effendi feels more important than Paris, and make a special effort, if possible, to have a local assembly established. Also to keep in close touch with them after you leave, through your correspondence.

He also reminds you to not neglect your history of the Cause in France! And when completed to send him a copy for his consideration. Do not hurry; the gathering of the material must be very thorough. Mrs. French has written him suggesting that you write an article on Thomas Breakwell for 'Bahá'í World' vol.VII. Shoghi Effendi approves of this and asks you to send the article, when ready, to Mrs. French.

Shoghi Effendi wishes to convey to Daddy his hope that he will be more active in the teaching work, not to neglect his administrative activities, but to collaborate with you. This is the best way you can both, unitedly, express your high appreciation of the honour conferred upon you through this marriage.

Assuring you of the Guardian's great love and prayers for you both, your loving daughter,

Rúḥíyyih Khánum

And in the handwriting of Shoghi Effendi:

Dearest co-worker:

It gives me great & genuine pleasure to append a few words to the letter which at my request & on my behalf Mary has addressed to you. I was deeply touched by your letter to me & and by the noble sentiments you have expressed in your recent letter to her – sentiments that I greatly value. The bond that has always united you to me has now been powerfully reinforced, & I feel sure that the services you will be enabled to render as a direct result of this new tie that binds us to each other will serve to draw me closer to you, & enable me to help you more effectively through my prayers. I wish you to concentrate your attention at present on the National Fund which stands in great need of continuous support by all the believers. Have no anxiety whatever. Concentrate your heart & soul & mind on the requirements of the Faith & of the Divine Plan which you have supported so splendidly in the past & which, I am sure, you will foster with increasing effectiveness in the future.

Shoghi

Kindly assure Mr. Maxwell of my great love & affection for him. I

have great hopes that he will in collaboration with you further the teaching work in Canada & thus pave the way for any international services he may be enabled to render in the future.
Shoghi

In a later letter written to him from Marseille, May rushed to assure him that she had already and would continue to do as he asked:

> I will follow your instructions with the utmost joy and have drawn a check – while I was in Nazareth – for Roy [Wilhelm] as I have always done, and I am now mailing these checks as I did not have sufficient funds before to cover them.

From Marseille, where she wrote to him on 19 July 1937, she made a special request. It is very touching to read it and heart-rending to consider the emotions she would have gone through to put such a request in writing at all. Her candour is breath-taking, as is her courage, her simplicity and her respect for the Guardian. Her maternal instincts were being tested to the utmost:

> My beloved Guardian,
> Before replying to your precious letter may I say that I hope I am not trespassing on the new and wondrous tie I have with you in asking you to buy some flowers for Rúḥíyyih Khánum on August 8th. I know you said that in the East you never celebrate birthdays, but she was born and nurtured in the West and it is just a little token of our love on her first birthday at your side, and as you said one day to me, 'I understand, she is your only child!' And now she is with you, always near you, surrounded by that love which burned into my heart during all the pain, the fear, the adjustment of those days in Haifa, when that which had befallen our daughter, far beyond our human ken to grasp, and knowing my nothingness I believed I had lost her – forever, your mighty love, your deep understanding sustained me as it ever has and always will, to the end.
> ... As to teaching it has always been the essence of life itself and my joy and faith are as a thousand-fold through this 'tie we now have with each other!' as you state in your wonderful letter. I have become so open, so susceptible to your most precious nearness that

when you pray for me I feel it through all my being...

Rúḥíyyih Khánum has written us several beautiful letters, deep and tender which nourishes our lifelong love and unity founded by the Master... we yearn and strive to follow in her blessed footsteps, to become day by day more worthy of the infinite bounty of God, to attain a measure of that boundless grace which has become the heritage of the child He gave us. You know all that my inmost heart is whispering to your infinitely loving, merciful and holy heart.

Before leaving Haifa, May had evidently asked the Guardian if she could make stopovers to see her sister-in-law and niece in Budapest, on her way back home through Europe. On 15 June she had written to Mrs Bolles and Jeanne, conveying the guidance she had received from Shoghi Effendi:

I can see the great wisdom of the Guardian's firm decision that we should come directly to Marseille, stay here until I felt more recuperated, then go to Lyon and stay as long as necessary and finally to Paris; this was his plan from the beginning, although he softened toward Budapest considerably on account of the wonderful work you both have done; of course, the state of my health made it impossible.

There was, besides, another reason for the longer stopover in France. The Paris World Exposition was taking place there that year, from 25 May to 25 November, and as Mr Maxwell's secretary, the redoubtable AMP, put it:

I am glad you are going to the Paris Exposition as you will there see the latest...

His wife, in her letter to the Guardian of 19 July from Marseille, confirmed his plans to attend:

We shall spend a short time in Paris while Sutherland sees the Exposition and I will gather data for the history you wish me to write, from Edith and Laura. Sutherland will write you. He is well and happy and when he received your message he smiled and said 'I wonder why Shoghi Effendi thinks I can teach', but, strangely enough, he is joining some friends in Paris, wealthy and influential, who are devoted to him and through the marriage of his daughter this is his opportunity!

It was soon after his arrival in France, on 21 June, that W.S. Maxwell wrote the following letter to the Guardian, his first since the marriage of his daughter:

Dear Shoghi Effendi,
    I have been dilatory in writing to thank you for the very wonderful experience of my visit and for the thousand and one courtesies extended to us when we had the honour of being your guests. I am sure that I have benefited spiritually and the evidence of it is the greater amount of reading and the increased comprehension and interest I am taking in the literature of the Bahá'í Faith.
    The honour of being the father of the wife of the Guardian and being related to the Holy Family is one I cannot talk about, but I am deeply sensible of. It gives me a very real happiness to know that Rúḥíyyih Khánum has been deemed worthy of the exalted position to which she has been called, and this is infinitely increased by the knowledge of the great love she has in her heart for you.
    Your Mother and all members of the Holy Family have endeared themselves to me by the many evidences of devotion, love and consecration to the Cause, and on the human plane they rendered our visit memorable for the countless kindnesses and services they showered upon us. I esteem and love them on the spiritual plane and equally so on the human side.
    Our path has presented difficulties which render progress slower than we contemplated. Mrs. Maxwell is still under the care of a fine and competent physician and will have to go, when able, to a suitable country place and regain normal health.
    Mlle Lucienne Migette and four Bahá'ís from Lyon arrived Saturday night. It was a joy to be with them and on Sunday afternoon they and Mrs. Soghomonian and her father and myself had a meeting in the reception room of the hotel. Mrs. Maxwell was not able to attend as the time spent with Lucienne had exhausted her forces for the time being.
    We have received letters from Rúḥíyyih Khánum and they

indicate that your vacation has already refreshed you both and will do so increasingly.

I am quite well and join with Mrs. Maxwell in sending our heartfelt appreciation and love to you. To Rúḥíyyih Khánum we send our deepest maternal and paternal love.

Ever yours, devotedly, Sutherland Maxwell.

A few days earlier, on 16 June, he had written to Rúḥíyyih Khánum from Marseille about May's condition:

Today she has rested and I went to Aix-en-Provence, 28 kilometres out of the city. Country air and the most fascinating, small hotel amid gardens of roses, alleés of trees planted in the times of Louis XVI. In my judgement, a veritable paradise. Dr. Tailhard recommended the place and his advice is that we go there for at least two weeks, then to Aix les Bains which is about the same distance as Lyons [sic] but at an altitude which will clear up all the conditions Mother has had. This in my judgement will mean that she may have to forgo the Lyons trip as the climate there would not be conducive to improving her health – in fact it would be otherwise.

On 24 June in a letter to her daughter, May referred to a meeting with Lucienne Migette:

Last Saturday, Lucienne, with her characteristic energy and enthusiasm, motored from Lyon with four Bahá'ís (the fifth, making six with Lucienne, was out of town) and although it was a wonderful joy to see them all, I proceeded to celebrate by having a violent chill and shaking all over with the cold for one hour and a half, followed by a terrific temperature! I do not just know why it produced this effect but the remarkable thing was that we arranged to get the old man Bahá'í here, and his daughter, Mrs. Soghomonian, and they held a Meeting downstairs and had a wonderful prayer for me and my temperature dropped to normal in less than two hours! Next day the doctor was very upset over what he called my relapse, but could not account for the rapid fall in my temperature and I have had <u>none</u> since. Please tell Shoghi Effendi that Lucienne was deeply touched and very happy to receive the attar of rose with his love and she continues to do splendid work, and although Yazdi is leaving for Port Said early next month there will still be five devoted Bahá'ís in Lyon and I hope and pray to get strong and well enough to join them all in about three weeks – when Lucienne returns.

In my present run-down condition, I greatly need that creative, dynamic energy that comes from associating with the believers, especially certain types of believers, like the Kinneys, Juliette and others who have strong positive faith, and it will do me a world of good to see Edith Sanderson when I get to Paris.

The slowness of the Maxwells' voyage home was no doubt of great benefit to the Bahá'ís in France but was a cause of considerable anxiety to AMP in Montreal. In her June letter she had already admitted her concern, for she knew very well that no one in their office could surpass Mr Maxwell in artistic design. Although she was happy to think he would be able to attend the World Exposition in Paris, she was afraid that several commissions might be in jeopardy if he was not back in time to oversee them:

> I . . . must say I am anxious for your return home also . . . In the conservatory for Miss Van Horn, there will be a fountain (an old Chinese bronze vase being used) and the tile work to surround this is a great worry to me and unless it is done right it will spoil the whole effect – GMP[2] tried his hand at it, but the success was poor and very expensive – Also Mr. Geddes phoned re small station for the Club at Kanawaki etc. I know they are small but one's reputation has to be protected – I am writing this taking a chance of its reaching you before you leave . . .

One month later, on 28 July, she wrote again, in some distress:

> I do wish you were here and interviewed some of the officers. It seems terrible to feel that some of our best building is slipping away from us when we have done so much to try and satisfy every one . . . I cannot write any more I am not myself and so disheartened.
> Sincerely, AMP

---

2 George Pitts, Mr Maxwell's partner in the company Maxwell and Pitts.

May's brother Randolph wrote a letter to her in Lyon on 7 July, highlighting reasons for avoiding the worsening conditions in Europe at that time:

> Where is your husband now? In Paris, I suppose. I hope he will find something to admire at the Exposition! It would be wonderful if my people could be with you and Max for a time 'over there', but rather difficult to arrange I should say – under present conditions. I deeply deplore the course of events in Germany which have led the Government to suppress the Bahá'í activities in that land. I can imagine what a grief and disappointment that must be to you. . . .

The suppression of the Faith in Germany was indeed a terrible blow. May mentioned it herself, in sorrowing tones, in her letter to Shoghi Effendi written on the day of her departure from the shores of Europe. Two months had passed since she had requested him to buy flowers for her only daughter's birthday. And during these two months, when May had done her utmost to fulfil the Guardian's wishes – to visit the centres where she had planted the early seeds of the Faith in France and to shower her love on the fragile communities of Lyon and Marseille, as well as on Paris one last time – the Faith had been banned in the land which had made that daughter bloom into a veritable rose. The mature and sober tone of that letter to Shoghi Effendi, dated 19 September 1937, reveals to what a degree she had struggled and had grown:

> Dearly beloved Guardian,
>
> My love and deepest sympathy are with you always in the sorrows you have to bear in the path of God.
>
> Although the past year has brought you the joy and mystery of love and union with a soul in the sacred bond of marriage, yet you have had the blow of the suppression of our Faith in Germany, and the almost irreparable loss of such devoted, trusted and pioneer believers as Zia [Baghdadi] and Fred [Lunt].
>
> We know the might of your faith, and the all-encompassing power of Bahá'u'lláh Who sustains and overshadows you beyond the world and all that is, yet you, who are the heart of the temple of man on earth, whose love passes all comprehension, you suffer that which no mere mortal can ever know.

I hope and pray, oh! my beloved! that the daughter the Master gave us for you is so close to your loving heart as to help to heal its wounds, through her feminine tenderness, intuition and wisdom, which you know well as your devoted wife. She writes always of your love, your sympathetic understanding in this most arduous period of transition and adaptation in her life, with what restraint and gentleness you have helped her to preserve her spontaneous youth and human happiness in so sublime an association! We can only hope on our part to win ever more deeply your trust and confidence by our own complete dedication, to so live as to bring new joy, inspiration and vision to our beloved co-workers, and to strive without a trace of self-consciousness or artificial effort, so stifling to normal spiritual development, but spontaneously from our hearts to maintain your pure and lofty standard, and bring the very flame of your spirit to all. I will send you a full report from home, and I send you now and always my deepest love and longing, and my prayer for your ever-increasing happiness in your blessed union and in your ardent work.

Ever your own,

May Maxwell

The rumblings of war were growing ominously closer, the clouds ever thicker over Europe, and the prospects of separation from the Centre of the Faith must have seemed increasingly inevitable to the Baháʼís in the course of 1937. When Mrs Maxwell embarked on the steamer back for North America on 19 September she probably wondered if she would ever see her daughter again. The Arab Revolt, under the leadership of the Grand Mufti of Jerusalem, had just resumed attacks on Jewish settlements in Palestine, and a three-year campaign of violence and civil strife was raging under the British Mandate. She may have wondered too, if the situation worsened, whether she would ever again experience what Marion Holley later described in her *In Memoriam*[3] as 'the Guardian's immediate, revitalizing force' on her life.

As she turned away from the darkening wake of the east towards the western path of the setting sun, May must have felt that she was leaving her heart behind her in the Holy Land. It was a bitter-sweet

---

3 Marion Holley (Hofman) was asked by Shoghi Effendi to write the article on May's life for *The Baháʼí World*, vol. VIII.

voyage, one which she had first undertaken in her husband's company as a young bride, some thirty-five years and four months before, and one that she would never make again. But as Marion Holley later surmised, so accurately in her *In Memoriam* article on May, although she was never to return, 'in a deeper sense . . . she lived there, hour by hour to her last day'.

* * *

After the announcement in the April issue of the *Bahá'í News* of the United States and Canada of the marriage of Shoghi Effendi,, another notice appeared three months later, on page 7 of the July issue. It acknowledged all the good wishes that had been sent to Mr and Mrs Maxwell since this announcement, and apologized for their delay in thanking their Bahá'í friends.

> MR. AND MRS. W. S. MAXWELL
> ACKNOWLEDGE LETTERS AND CABLEGRAMS
> Mr. and Mrs. Maxwell have been unable to make acknowledgment of the many letters and cablegrams they have received in connection with the marriage of their daughter. They have requested the National Spiritual Assembly to express their thanks, and explain that personal replies will be made as soon as possible.

There must certainly have been a great many of them. Ripples of excitement had spread throughout the Bahá'í community in the United States and Canada over the news of this union. From the numerous letters which the Maxwells received from family and friends, one can sense the joy, the thrill, the fascination, the curiosity even, and the pride that had been felt in learning this great news. Many of the well-wishers wrote enthusiastic letters of congratulation; many were eager to know more about the event. May was obliged to reply to all of these with graciousness, with dignity, and sometimes with a great deal of self-restraint.

For even as her heart throbbed with pride, she must have also been filled with anguish. Yes, she was overwhelmed by the honour; yes, she was thrilled by the blessings; yes, she was more than ever conscious of the bounties of her Lord. But she missed her daughter. And she was also acutely conscious of the extraordinary responsibilities which accompanied the distinctions that were implied by this union. Her brother,

Randolph Bolles, in the long letter he had written to her on 7 July before her return home, had astutely put into words what she was experiencing:

> I am overjoyed to hear from you again . . . although deeply sorry to learn of the serious illness from which you are only just recovering. I am so glad that you are gaining; and hope very heartily that you will be your old self again by the time this letter reaches you. Of course, May, you know that the events of the past few months, culminating in Mary's marriage were enough to make any Mother ill – not to say kill them – and you have done well to come thru' as you have, in spite of a frail constitution. Keep up your courage; and foster your strength – for we will have an enormous amount of talking to do when you arrive in New York.

From Lyon, W. S. Maxwell wrote to Rúḥíyyih Khánum, on 16 August 1937:

> Dearest Mary –
> Mother had yours of 31/7/37 and returned it to me.
> What Shoghi Effendi said about me touches me profoundly and if my character has appealed to him, I am very grateful. As to my future development and usefulness – I feel sure that the encouragement received will cause the old roots to become more fertile and some useful fruit to be borne by the old tree! You know it takes all kinds of persons to make a world, and I have a leaning in certain definite directions – perhaps the winds of art have caused the tree to lean over as happens in nature; but there is enough sap in me to hope for a better balance and activity in my future growth.
> Of course you know how much I love and appreciate Shoghi Effendi on all the planes of his character and I want to add that Zia Khanoum and all the members of the Holy Family command my deepest respect and affection. It was a rare and profound experience to have had the privilege of spending so much time with them, and to Shoghi Effendi, his Mother and all of the Family, I send through you, my most respectful greetings and love.
>   Lovingly and devotedly
>   Your Dad

A month later, while her parents were still homeward bound in the waning days of summer 1937, Rúḥíyyih Khánum wrote to her mother:

> Often I pray God to make us all three as Shoghi Effendi would have us. He is like a sea and although I know and understand now little things about his temperament, yet I feel it is only like standing on the shore and watching the nature of the waves; what lies within the oceanic depths no one can know. It is a fatal mistake to allow oneself to believe or conjecture that this or that is his 'human personality', also fatal to ever assume you know what his reaction to a given thing will be! No doubt that element is there but who shall say which is which! Indeed who shall presume to say that even the human personality, not perfect as the Master was, is not manipulated constantly by God? We know there are some people who have tried to catalogue this distinction and to their great detriment.
>
> I know my darling that each day your happiness is increasing and winning over all distance, all worry and excess of maternal solicitude!! And I too am feeling the wonderful sustaining power of learning (I hope) to give up my will to God, which for me is to merge my wish to Shoghi Effendi's. Don't think this is a process that renders one spineless, on the contrary I feel as I look forward into the future that all my failures will be those of when I have not completely identified my wish to his.

In a letter from May, written several months later to Frank Irwin, the cousin with whom she had long associations from childhood, both in England and in Englewood, New Jersey, she recounts the news of the marriage in a manner that seeks to explain its significance lucidly and simply to someone who was not a Bahá'í. The beauty of her explanation lies in its honesty and its sincerity. She had no intention of pretending that this marriage, which she considered the highest honour her family could receive, had been an easy one to adjust to, or to understand.

> Dearest Frank,
> I would have written you long ago, my dear Cousin, about the marriage of our beloved daughter last March in Haifa, so sudden and overwhelming that it took us many months to adjust ourselves to this great event. The two years that we spent in Europe were not

alone absorbing in interest but also in energy, and I am sure you and Mary [Frank's wife] will understand if we send you our loving though tardy congratulations [on the birth of their grandchild] . . .

Mary's marriage was to her and to her father and mother, as I said, a really overwhelming experience on account of our faith and devotion to the Bahá'í Religion, our great love and reverence for the youthful Guardian of the Cause, and that he should in his wisdom determine to marry this Western girl, thus deeply uniting the East and the West at the very centre and the heart of our Faith, that we should have had the privilege of being present at his marriage, and that it should be our own daughter who was thus honoured and blessed, is something which we shall no doubt be unable to fully grasp on this earth. Yet it is all very simple and natural really; he has the most beautiful character and brilliant mind, and Mary has thus been able to fulfil her destiny in giving her whole life and arduous service to that Faith to which she has always been so devoted.

In this same letter, dated 20 December, May stated that she and Sutherland had 'returned home in October'. The ship reached New York near the end of September; Mr Maxwell returned to Montreal almost immediately, but May stayed in New York for a few more weeks. Mrs Stella Dean Estall, of South Eliot, Maine, writing to May on 29 September and sending her 'sincerest love to yourself and Sutherland', confirmed their arrival date as the 26th. Mrs Bolles and her daughter, Jeanne, also told Shoghi Effendi that they had been able to welcome Mrs Maxwell in New York the morning after their arrival there.

By the time May and Sutherland stepped on the shores of her homeland again and met with the American Bahá'ís, six months had passed since their daughter's wedding. They were greeted with open arms. Saffa and Vaffa Kinney wrote to Shoghi Effendi on 11 October about the Maxwells' reception:

Tears of gladness showered from our eyes the day our beloved co-worker Mrs. Maxwell arrived in America. It was my privilege to be the first to greet her as she came off the steamer and I assure you that she seemed to me to be a veritable Angel of light bringing with her much of the vibrations of that Holy and Sacred Spot, from which she so recently departed. For some time she remained on the dock while the Custom officers looked over the luggage of both Mr. and Mrs. Maxwell. He – Mr. Maxwell – was so kind and attended so faithfully to that end of the matter, while those of us who came to greet her clung to her, a little band of semi-worshipers – basking in the amazing influence and joy she seemed to shed from every part of her. I immediately became aware too, of a new Power, a New Bond of which she seemed to be a visible and vital part – a Bond between those two opposites – the East and the West – the Orient and the Occident. This Power seemed to grow – to grow – until when she addressed the believers at the Feast the following Monday evening, they all arose to greet her, and afterward – when she finished, the effect of her words was truly overwhelming! . . .

Give our tenderest, as well as our most respectful greetings to Rúḥíyyih Khánum, for whom we have always had the deepest love – even from infancy – How blessed the Union – may I say, How needed!

Saffa and Vaffa Kinney 'The Kinneys'

A letter dated 12 November 1937, written to Mr and Mrs Kinney on behalf of Shoghi Effendi by his secretary, acknowledges the warmth of the welcome, expresses the Guardian's appreciation of it and his hopes for a renewed dedication of the believers in their work for the Cause:

> The Guardian has also been moved to know of the very warm reception which the friends in New York, and you in particular, have so cordially extended to Mr. and Mrs. Maxwell upon their arrival in America. It is his hope and prayer that the return of these dear friends will awaken a new consciousness among the believers, and stimulate them afresh to dedicate themselves, more whole-heartedly than ever, to the service of the Faith.

In New York May spoke to the believers about the marriage of her daughter. Years later Gertrude Blum,[4] who had been present at that meeting, wrote the following touching observation to Rúḥíyyih Khánum:

> One could see that her great mother heart was torn between two

---

4 Gertrude had known Mary Maxwell at Green Acre; she and her husband Alvin Blum became Knights of Bahá'u'lláh to the Solomon Islands.

emotions, one of the priceless privilege that was bestowed upon her that the child she had so lovingly reared was chosen to be the beloved wife of the Guardian, and another, that in her deep insight and spiritual awareness she knew of the sacrifice upon sacrifice that her child would be subjected to in the great role that was given to her. She spoke of how Mary, now Rúḥíyyih Khánum, had to take on a different identity and that all former things were a closed chapter.

* * *

Mrs Maxwell had always depended on letters from the Holy Land to nurture her soul. She had always been nourished by this connection and had relied for years on this life-giving stream of correspondence, first from the Centre of the Covenant, 'Abdu'l-Bahá, and then from His appointed Guardian. She had written her letters to her Beloved with a candid heart, entirely free of self-regard. And she had always shared the heart-warming replies and guidance she had received unrestrainedly with the Bahá'ís.

After the marriage of her daughter, May's correspondence with the Holy Land acquired a new resonance. It also increased dramatically in quantity because May wrote many more times than she used to do, and her daughter, who missed her mother greatly, responded regularly, writing as a general rule at least once a week, as she herself stated and the correspondence in her estate confirms. And in one of May's letters, written a year before she died, she confessed to her daughter:

I have never missed a week since I left you.

In other words, between 30 May 1937 and 24 January 1940 she wrote at least 150 letters to Haifa. Although some of these may have been lost in the course of the war, and many may have also been addressed to Shoghi Effendi and not just to her daughter, this constitutes a considerable legacy.

It might be well to distinguish here between the private correspondence that took place between Rúḥíyyih Khánum and her mother and father after the marriage of the Guardian, and the correspondence that took place between the Guardian and her parents. Rúḥíyyih Khánum naturally responded to her parents' personal communications with private letters that were the source of joy and life, of comfort and reassurance to them. But how strange it must have been, at the same time, for them to receive letters that she wrote on behalf of Shoghi Effendi, addressing her own mother and father in the detached tones of a formal correspondent. And even stranger, to see Mary's familiar handwriting signing the unfamiliar name of 'Rúḥíyyih'.

All the Bahá'ís and her personal friends, too, addressed her from that time on by the dignified title chosen for her by the Guardian, which distinguished her station after their marriage. Rúḥíyyih Khánum said that the Guardian had given permission for her close family members to address her as 'Mary' as they had always done, and she also retained this intimacy, exceptionally, with her friend Gladys Weeden. But it appears that May, on occasion, referred to her daughter with the Persian title 'Khánum' (lady). In a letter dated 28 January 1939, Rúḥíyyih Khánum wrote the following postscript to her mother:

> P. S. Please dearest, the Guardian said you could call me Mary – don't call me Khanum! I don't like it.

Following Rúḥíyyih Khánum's marriage her signature on all letters other than those mentioned above, whether written on behalf of the Guardian or not, was always 'Rúḥíyyih'.

In a statement among her papers, written and signed by her after the passing of Shoghi Effendi, she also attests:

> It should be well understood that in all my years with the beloved Guardian I never mailed a letter to anyone, least of all my parents, which he had not either read himself or I read aloud to him to save his time.

This statement has extraordinary implications. Rúḥíyyih Khánum always insisted that Shoghi Effendi was first and foremost her Guardian, and after his passing she often reiterated this point, both publicly and privately.

May could not resist begging, from time to time, for the intimate bond between mother and daughter to remain unbroken, for their confidentiality to remain intact. In her letter of 26 January 1939 to Rúḥíyyih Khánum, May most touchingly betrayed both a consciousness of having pushed too far and a desire to push further:

My darling –
   ... I have so much to write you – & to reply to your last dear letter – but that will go to next week – & in the meantime I only want to say that you must always write me in the old confiding spirit no matter if you are ill – or discouraged – or hurt <u>in any</u> way – I implore you to open your whole heart & soul to me – for God has given us the deepest most sacred bond – & I can bear <u>anything</u> – my faith is so much stronger! – but I cannot bear not to be in your full confidence. I know – I feel – I am going to see you soon! God is so Merciful.
   Rosemary is writing you. She sends her deep love.
               With my deepest tender love
                     Mother

In response, Rúḥíyyih Khánum reassured her mother repeatedly that she was not withholding any personal information, that she was not breaking the bond of confidentiality between them on issues that concerned herself. In doing so she helped her mother distinguish between those questions which touched upon the Guardian's private life and those which did not.

In a letter to her mother dated 14 January 1938, Rúḥíyyih Khánum wrote these deep thoughts:

Sometimes I feel worried lest you should think I don't feel as confiding as I used to be! But dearest you know this is due to the fact that though I have a very personal life, it happens to be linked to our beloved Guardian's and so of course cannot be written about as one could in ordinary circumstances.

And also on 2 July 1938:

My own Dearest:
   Your last letter – written from Montreal – was such a great comfort to me. It not only showed you were feeling better but also breathed that deep spiritual insight that you have and that nourishes my spirit. You see Mother, I cannot write freely about my particular problems because they are now largely all the same as the Guardian's problems and naturally I cannot confide those to paper anymore

now than you or I could have expected to read such things in the past! If I were with you no doubt our beloved Guardian would let me speak freely of the things in my own heart – not affecting others – but this way it can't be done. I know you understand this perfectly and that you put your faith and trust in the Master and do not worry.

As a wife in a traditional oriental household in the 1930s, and the consort of the Guardian of the Bahá'í Faith, Amatu'l-Bahá was under certain constraints. She was, for example, obliged to keep her head covered discreetly in public. She could not walk about Haifa without attendants. And she no longer had the time to maintain a correspondence with her old non-Bahá'í friends in Canada and the United States. These, among others, were the basic facts of her new life. She accepted them without question but although she no longer wrote to her old friends, she did all she could to maintain these bonds on a spiritual level. In several of her letters, she even delegated her mother to convey messages to this effect. Her wistful query imbedded in a private letter, dated 27 December 1937, reveals just how lonely she may have sometimes felt during those years:

> Why don't some of my friends write to me? I would love to hear from them. Soon Emeric will be here and I am so happy he is coming.

In response to this appeal, May assumed the role of '*porte-parole*' and begged old friends and young Bahá'ís to keep their links with her daughter, and encouraged them to keep writing to her. She even wrote to Seward Prosser, a friend from her own girlhood days, to ask him to please write to 'Mary'. When May had been so weak, in 1921 following the passing of 'Abdu'l-Bahá, that she could not bear the difficulties of travelling from New York to Montreal, this genial and very wealthy friend of the family had offered his own private train to transport her home slowly and comfortably. He must have been a wonderful person, for fifteen years later, in December of 1937, May turned to him again and asked him, too, to keep in touch with her daughter:

> But one thing I do beg of you is that you write her in your own inimitable way, for she has never forgotten your wonderful goodness

to me when I was so ill in New York, and both she and the Guardian will be happy to hear from you.

Eighteen months after her daughter's marriage and less than a year before the outbreak of the hostilities of World War II, May was still trying to provide Rúḥíyyih Khánum with a network of friends who would stand by her through thick and thin. In November 1938 she wrote to David Hofman making the same request:

> Did I ask you before whether you sometimes write to Rúḥíyyih Khánum? I wish you would, dear David, for despite her exalted position and high happiness, she reaches out to us all with a yearning heart, and her courage and strength are ever renewed to fulfil her mighty task and sacred trust.

Rúḥíyyih Khánum later confessed that she would not have been able to survive without her mother's correspondence during those early years. Within the bounds of discretion imposed upon her, she poured her heart out to Mrs Maxwell and several times, during the late 1930s, signed herself as 'your adoring child' in her private letters to her mother. In one heart-rending example written to her on 2 January 1939, barely a year before May died, she begged her mother to look after herself because she still needed and depended on her emotional and spiritual support so very much:

> I hope you have taken yourself truly to task in this respect – I try so hard to do what <u>you</u> would want me to for my own health that I feel you should do the same . . . So please Mother behave. You have given all your life to the Cause far beyond your means and I think now – in your maturity, ahem! – you should conserve your strength for what is vital and that is serving the Guardian and staying on this planet . . .

The following excerpts from Rúḥíyyih Khánum's letters to her mother and father clearly show the depth of her feelings and of her faith and spiritual advancement. She speaks of Shoghi Effendi, the Guardian of the Cause of Bahá'u'lláh, the focal point of the Covenant, with not only deep love and respect but extraordinary maturity.

In a letter dated 29 September 1937 she writes:

Among other things he is teaching me is to see justly. To see people as they are both good and bad; not to judge or condemn or criticize but not to be blinded by either 'hate' or 'love' as it says in the teachings. And I know that the seed of this great change in our lives must be growing also in you and Daddy. Oh Mother dearest, how fortunate we are, how blessed, how privileged, to learn and to go on climbing! And always together.

And again, on 25 October:

Mother Darling
 Now for our ordinary letter! I was so divinely happy when I gave your long letter to the Guardian to read with the details of your arrival in N.Y. and the meeting. He read it out loud to me (I had already read it twice!) and I could see in his dear face the happiness it brought to him. He said 'that is the Maxwell spirit! That is one reason why I married you because of what your Mother is!' And he said you were brave and working in the front ranks, that he fully sympathized with how difficult your position is. Anyway we were energized. So see my own precious Mother that with your work and your many sacrifices and heart-pangs, you can bring such _real_ happiness to our Guardian's heart. I underline the _real_ because although I feel I bring at least a little happiness to him (it would be for him to say how much!) it is the Cause and the progress of its work, the news that clears up things which he is worried over, or which tells him an exact happening, that brings that deepest joy to his heart. And after all, isn't that true of every Bahá'í? How much more so of our Guardian.
 ... Rest assured always that all letters and telegrams, as well as messages that come to you from Shoghi Effendi are solely at his inspiration. I never suggest them – how could I? His bond with everyone is a sacred one over which _no one_ could possibly exert the slightest influence. I wish the friends could realize that he is absolutely alone and indifferent to the influence of anyone. Maybe you can help bring this home to them. Your remarks in your talk were _superb_ and Shoghi Effendi said he wished he had them verbatim

because then he could tell how others would have felt on hearing them – did anyone take it down? You could ask.

In her letter of 6 January 1938 Rúḥíyyih Khánum wrote to both her mother and father:

The Western Baháʼís have a Cause affected by the Western defects and the Eastern Baháʼís a Cause affected by the Eastern defects – of course both give their virtues to the Cause too. But Shoghi Effendi not only has the Cause in its reality before his eyes as no one else, he also is identified with it. So to a naturally small and limited degree because of my own limitations, I find myself becoming imbued with more of his thought, interpretation, of the Cause itself, neither East nor West but the balance that he holds in his hands. How many times Shoghi Effendi says 'I am a lover of goodness'. It is very strange, as much as I can dare to make an observation about him, I would say that even his love partakes of justice – it is a reward.

To her mother, she wrote on 2 March 1938:

My own dearest,
   Your letter from New York I have just read and it came to me like a breeze of love and stimulating thoughts, and the thought uppermost in my mind is what you ask about Shoghi Effendi's love. If anyone asked me what my theme was in life I should say 'Shoghi Effendi': I not only feel absorbed in him (I don't mean for a moment as a wife in a husband) but feel that I want to be more absorbed in him and that in this way lies all my salvation. There is no doubt about it his love is a strange love and not like the Master's – even as his function in the Cause is not like the Master's. I feel sometimes (and after all it's only groping, I can never encompass the Guardian in anything for even one instant!) that his love even is a kind of justice. He is fair to a degree that is like a mathematical instrument, a scales. He never misjudges even an enemy – he is justice embodied. And when we don't <u>deserve</u> his love in some way, I sometimes think we just don't get it. Our actions can call forth the springs of his love to flow – and likewise to cause them to dry up instantly. He is the center of the Cause and the Cause is a Cause

not to be tampered with. The powers in this Cause, I believe, are perilous to those who venture too far in the wrong direction; like a gigantic dynamo which can supply in legitimate manner the needs of millions in electricity, and can also burn a person to a crisp if they get in the wrong way! It is this wonderful justice – so heavy on our heads when we need mercy, forgiveness and comforting love – that is the hope of life for all the ground down, poor, miserable wretches in this world ... I sometimes think that he administers his justice with a degree of patience, long-suffering and forbearance, that we don't dream of. If I can say it, I feel he endures anything that can only harm him and his feelings, but if it will harm the Cause, its honour or interests, then he won't tolerate it at all.... He is so golden-hearted, so pure hearted, that sometimes when I catch a glimpse of it I am stunned.

Soon after, on 15 May 1938, in her letter to her mother, Rúḥíyyih Khánum wrote:

My Dearest own Mother:
We have had many pilgrims from Persia – all wonderfully devoted believers – and one of them is the sweet young woman you met who had a little boy. The child is adorable and a regular little lion for the Cause at the age of 3! He told his Mother yesterday, 'I know his honour Shoghi Effendi, I know his honour Shoghi Rabbani and I know his honour the Guardian, and I like all three!' He is full of fun and very keen!

Writing from Switzerland many months later, on 2 March 1939, the first day of the Fast, she shared her impressions of this blessed day with her mother:

My best dearest
I must share the first morning of the Fast with you! ... Hundreds of birds sang at dawn and there seems to be some kind of nunnery opposite as I could hear the sweet voices of women chanting. Maybe they are praying for the next Pope – and just across the street is one greater than all the Popes! with a God-given power to all men. How incongruous it seems. He slips unnoticed among his fellow men, in

but not of their world. I always feel that those who show him any kindness or courtesy are so blessed for it and I shudder when someone is rude to him! The Master received an ample share of both from humanity, didn't He?

But at the end of the day, their roles were mysteriously reversed. It was the child who found herself comforting the mother, in the deepest sense; it was Rúḥíyyih Khánum who gave the most profound spiritual counsel to May during this period. Her personal letters to her parents during the first three years of her marriage are gems of wisdom and illumination, and marked by characteristic pragmatism, humour and humility. While reassuring May about the state of her sleep and her exercise and her health, she also shared with her some of the deepest considerations ever expressed regarding the station of the Guardian and the meaning of obedience to the Covenant. There is something, in retrospect, about this symbiosis between body and soul and this interaction between mother and daughter, that is profoundly symbolic.

Their personal correspondence preserved this confidentiality to the end. Not only did May feel free to beg forgiveness of Rúḥíyyih Khánum, but Mary had no compunctions whatsoever against scolding Mrs Maxwell. On 20 April 1938 she sent a worrying note to her mother, whose echoes must have made May smile:

> I am afraid you have not been eating enough. Are you, at the expense of your health, practicing any false economy? I could shake you if you are! Your health you must guard, and as I strongly suspect you are run down I advise you to take a good rest after the Convention, wherever you can best get it.

One of May's lasting gifts to her daughter was to beg her to maintain the bonds of confidentiality not only with herself but with her father too. Just one year before May's passing, dated 10 January 1939, she appeals to Rúḥíyyih Khánum to keep in close touch with Mr Maxwell:

> His deep devotion to the Guardian colours his whole life and has greatly deepened his character – but he still longs for your love, and that close bond and understanding between you which is based on your being a very part of him – the incarnation of his love of beauty

– art – charm & culture, which you embody to him. He is glad you love and adore the Guardian . . .

* * *

Although Amatu'l-Bahá did not become Shoghi Effendi's official secretary until 1941, from the earliest days of her marriage she wrote to her parents on the Guardian's behalf. All other letters to individuals and institutions in the Bahá'í world over his signature were written by the Guardian's secretaries, who were at one time one of his brothers and at another two of his male cousins. In the end, one by one all his family fell away and Rúḥíyyih Khánum was the only one left at his side to carry the weight of this vital work.

It is wonderful to read the correspondence and the reports received and sent between Rúḥíyyih Khánum, writing as Shoghi Effendi's secretary, and her mother. A brief excerpt from one letter is quoted below. Written to May in response to her letter to the Guardian of 25 October 1937, it expresses these words of high praise:

> Shoghi Effendi was immensely pleased with the report you sent in your letter to me of the meeting in New York. He wishes me to tell you that you are working in the forefront and as a brave soldier of the Cause. In fact he said it might be the best letter you ever had written! He was so heartened and pleased by it . . .
> I send you my deepest love, ever your own loving daughter,
> Rúḥíyyih

And in Shoghi Effendi's handwriting:

> Dear & prized co-worker:
> I feel proud of the initial success that has signalized the resumption of your activities in America. I was deeply moved by your graphic account of the meeting & I hastened to cable you & urge you to persevere. Do take good care of your precious health & be assured that your task is by no means completed. Persevere & be confident. You are valiantly promoting, defending and consolidating the manifold interests of the Faith & for so meritorious a work for which you are highly qualified & newly & fittingly equipped

you should feel grateful & happy. You are often in my thoughts & prayers I assure you. Affectionately & gratefully
        Shoghi

In another excerpt from a letter written to her mother on Shoghi Effendi's behalf, dated 13 November one year later, Rúḥíyyih Khánum conveys his guidance in reply to May's desire to contribute to the 'hospitality' offered to the pilgrims in Haifa. Many North American visitors had had this idea before her, and neither the Master nor the Guardian accepted contributions for this purpose.

> My dearest Mother:
>   . . . He was very touched by your desire to contribute to the upkeep of the hospitality offered pilgrims in Haifa, but felt he would prefer to use the sum in your and Daddy's name for the purchase of land about the Shrine of the Báb on Mount Carmel. He felt this would make you both happy to have it spent for such a purpose. . . .
>   With the Guardian's love to you and Daddy, as well as my own deepest love,
>   Your daughter,
>   Rúḥíyyih

And in Shoghi Effendi's handwriting:

Your prompt & exemplary response to the suggestions & requests I have felt urged to make in recent months has served to heighten my admiration for the spirit that has always so powerfully animated you in the service of the Cause. I wish you now to concentrate for a time your energies and attention on the immediate needs of the teaching work in whatever region you find it most agreeable and beneficent to your health. I trust that in this renewed effort dear Mr. Maxwell will be closely associated, & in conjunction with you win fresh laurels for the Faith. Mary, who continually shares with me the joy & anxieties which the evolution of the Cause must necessarily occasion is well, happy, & continually progressing. You should be quite assured & happy. Affectionately & gratefully
        Shoghi

May had taken up her teaching work on her return from Haifa and as a result of the Guardian's encouragement, her husband had become much more involved in Bahá'í activities too. On 25 October 1937, Rúḥíyyih Khánum had written her mother on Shoghi Effendi's behalf:

> In regard to your winter's work he would urge you not to attempt to remain in Montreal during the cold months . . . but to go somewhere warm – New York, if not too cold . . . or perhaps South or even to California if necessary . . . He urges Daddy to so arrange his affairs that he can spend at least a part of the time with you so that neither of you will be alone, at least for very long, this winter.

But the most important activity taken up that winter was the holding of regular devotional meetings in their home on Pine Avenue. The doors were opened to Bahá'ís and non-Bahá'ís alike for the purpose of reading prayers and sacred writings. The combination of their two extraordinary natures and talents must have made for an interesting mixture of people at 1548 Pine Avenue. The gatherings which took place there from that time on achieved considerable popularity, and Montreal, according to Agnes Alexander, became a hub of spiritual attraction for the friends:

> My last visit with May in her home in Montreal, was in December, 1937. She was then conducting a weekly study class which was open to the public. It was my privilege to be present at two of these gatherings. Such a spirit pervaded the meetings that the friends and strangers came early and were loath to leave when the hour was over. The lessons were taken from an outline and there were readings from the Holy Utterances which May interspersed with beautiful explanations. This class proved the hunger of people for the Word of God.

But several of the Bahá'ís did not realize the importance of spreading out from a mother Assembly and widening the circle of activity beyond Montreal itself. Despite the launching of the first Seven Year Plan for North America, which included among its goals not only the completion of the exterior of the Temple in Wilmette but also the formation of a Spiritual Assembly in every state of the United States and in every one of the nine provinces of Canada, there was a certain resistance to administrative growth on the part of some Bahá'ís. Although there were signs of great progress to report and heartening news of growth and activity in the region, May noted, in her letter to the Guardian of 14 December 1937, that there was a reluctance among the Bahá'ís to spread out and establish new centres, and a preference to stay close together. She wrote asking for his 'ruling in this matter':

> Your letters to me, your cable messages, all breathing of your love, have sustained me in a way I cannot describe. I only have to turn to you dearest, beloved Guardian! by day and by night, to behold you clearly before me, your dear eyes looking at me, as in Haifa, and to feel through all my being that all pervasive Spirit, that powerful, directing current which flows through you alone. It is this ever-increasing realization of the Focal Centre, this 'concentration on the turning Point' which we so greatly need in America, where the soul is drowned in the clamor, caught in the under-tow, and must make a conscious effort to abide under your shadow, to be moved by the living Stream. This cannot be forced, but arises as an urge from within, the innate spontaneous motion of the soul in its true orbit.
>
> It made me strong and happy to know that you were pleased with me, and with my contribution for the publication of the Book of Prayers which I feel will greatly deepen the spiritual life of all of us and mark another mile-stone in our progress, our knowledge of the Supreme Being and His Wondrous Message and Teaching, just as did the Dawn-Breakers . . .
>
> You will no doubt have heard of the astonishing work achieved in Moncton, New Brunswick by Mrs. Mabel Ives who was sent there by the National Teaching Committee and has met with a phenomenal response. Great groups of people listening eagerly to the Divine Teachings and 7 declared believers in about three months! Later I hope to follow her work by teaching the Administrative Order and in the meantime Mrs. Rosemary Sala has joined Mrs. Ives and is also achieving great results. Unless the new believers in Moncton are very exceptional people would it not be premature to attempt to form an Assembly there, that is on April 21st? Now on the other hand, Dearest Shoghi Effendi, there is a different situation at St. Lambert just across the river from Montreal, a different municipality and where we now have residing nine declared believers, seven of whom have been active in Bahá'í service for a number of years, and

among these Mr. and Mrs. Sala and Mr. Walter Lohse are members of our Montreal Spiritual Assembly.

As they now have two new believers, strong and intelligent, which make up the number required to fulfil your instruction regarding the forming of an Assembly wherever there are nine declared believers, may I beg you to discuss this matter with Emeric Sala when he is in your presence in Haifa, that is if it is in accordance with your wisdom.

Not one of the Bahá'ís living in St. Lambert wishes to form an Assembly, for obvious reasons; they love the Montreal Community where they are all active workers; the Montreal Community has an outstanding prestige and is the Mother Group of Canada, and they dread to disassociate themselves from the communal life and activities of Montreal. Some of the St. Lambert members frankly admit this, others make various excuses, but in as much as there is a definite ruling in this matter whatever alternative have they? We have always understood that every new Local Spiritual Assembly constituted a great step in progress and would greatly strengthen the Cause in Canada (where we now have only two Assemblies) leading us forward to the time when as you said, Canada would have her own National Spiritual Assembly.

May was not the only one to ask the Guardian for 'definite rulings'. On 26 January 1938, her husband wrote a letter to him requesting guidance on the question of political involvement in the Province of Quebec:

Beloved Guardian,

I am writing about a matter which is being widely discussed and is meeting with a considerable amount of discussion and opposition in our Province of Quebec and elsewhere in the Dominion.

The enclosed papers are copies made for your information. They consist of a letter to the Bahá'í Centre from the Canadian Civil Liberties Union (a body occupied with matters concerning Labour and their attorney Mr. Colder has defended Communists etc.); one may, justly, say they are politically occupied, but are not a political party.

Accompanying this letter was a copy of the 'Padlock Act' as in force in the Province of Quebec and a copy of a petition which we did not sign.

Also a letter to Canadian Civil Liberties Union which I drew up and signed on behalf of the Montreal Spiritual Assembly. Do you find my reply satisfactory? It is in our file as a useful document in case we are at any time investigated.

I send you my deepest love, Affectionately, Sutherland

To this query Mr Maxwell received the following reply, dated 25 February 1938, written on Shoghi Effendi's behalf with his handwritten note penned at the end:

The Guardian was exceedingly pleased to receive your letter of January 26th with enclosures regarding the invitation extended to the Bahá'ís of Montreal by the Canadian Civil Liberties Union to join in making representations to the Canadian Prime Minister concerning the 'Padlock Act'.

He has carefully read all the papers you have sent, and wishes me to assure you of his whole-hearted approval of the letter you have written in answer to the above Union's communication addressed to Mr. Schopflocher. The tone of your reply, he thinks, is indeed splendid, and he has every reason to hope that it will be received in a good spirit by the persons concerned.

The attitude which the believers should adopt whenever such requests are made to them is to strictly uphold the Teachings, without however displeasing unnecessarily, through lack of wisdom and tact in their negotiations, their non-Bahá'í fellows.

The Guardian wishes you also to express to the Montreal Assembly the assurances of his appreciation of the action they have taken in this matter. He is well-pleased with the care and loyalty with which they have considered the whole issue, and is confident that the result of their deliberations will serve to considerably safeguard and strengthen the basis of their Assembly and work.

Before closing I wish to express to you in particular Shoghi Effendi's gratitude for the share you are so ably contributing towards the progress of the Faith in Montreal. He is praying for you and for dear Mrs. Maxwell, that you may both be given increasing strength and capacity to fulfil your new duties and obligations, and thus attain your highest destiny in His service.

Loving remembrances and heartiest greetings to you both from the family.

And in Shoghi Effendi's handwriting:

> Dear and valued co-worker:
> I wish to express to you and to your devoted fellow-members, my keen appreciation of your vigilance, your determination, your zeal and devotion to the Cause and its manifold interests. The manner in which you watch over and safeguard the institutions of God's nascent Faith is truly splendid and highly gratifying. I will pray for you all from the depth of my heart. Persevere in your noble endeavours.
> Your true brother,
> Shoghi

May had asked for 'definite rulings', and, in turn, was asked for precise details by the Guardian when her own letters to him had not been 'definite' enough. In retrospect, one can see how vital was the role she played in North America at this time. At the beginning of the first Seven Year Plan, which was to prepare the ground for the Guardian's second Seven Year Plan and subsequent Ten Year Crusade, the administration of the Cause was barely visible in the Americas. Most of the National Assemblies had not yet been born. The pillars upon which the Universal House of Justice was largely to depend were still nascent. And that vital and complementary institution of the Hands of the Cause and their Auxiliary Board members, later to be transformed into the Continental Boards of Counsellors and the International Teaching Centre under the auspices of the Universal House of Justice, did not yet exist. In order to have as full a picture as possible of the Bahá'í community, Shoghi Effendi had to balance the information he received through the minutes of these Assemblies with the insights that he garnered from trusted individuals scattered across the globe. With the tools at hand and the means available, he was building up the twin arms of the Administrative Order.

Soon after the launching of the Seven Year Plan, Rúḥíyyih Khánum wrote to her mother on 11 July 1939 on behalf of Shoghi Effendi, asking for news of the Bahá'ís' response to his messages. Approximations were inadequate; the Guardian needed concrete facts:

> My dearly loved Mother:
> On behalf of Shoghi Effendi I want to acknowledge your letters

to him of June 9th and May 15th, 1939. He is always pleased to hear from you and interested in receiving the news of the friends and the Cause and progress of the work in general. Indeed so much so that he wants you to tell him in greater detail the expressions of interest, satisfaction, etc. that you may hear about his last general letter or the Seven Year Plan, or things in general. If you had ever been questioned in detail by the Guardian about something that interests him keenly, you would know what I mean! He is so extremely eager for news and naturally the more he hears of the exact reaction of the individual Bahá'ís to different things, the more he can better gauge the work and help them to progress . . .

He feels your greatest service to the Cause can be rendered by helping the friends to deepen their own understanding of the great institutions of the Faith, its laws and teachings, as well as by teaching new souls – a function he feels you have a great gift for – and confirming them. . . .

In another letter written on his behalf by Rúḥíyyih Khánum on 15 January 1938, the Guardian was also obliged to ask May for more detailed information. This time, it was not the propagation of the Faith but its protection about which he was concerned. It was a delicate task and could easily have been mishandled; he could depend only on deepened Bahá'ís such as Mrs Maxwell to provide him with confidential information regarding those who had been alienated from the Faith through their association with Ahmad Sohrab. Rúḥíyyih Khánum had to ask her mother to be more specific:

> Again I have the pleasure and privilege of writing you on behalf of Shoghi Effendi to acknowledge your reports of your activities, dated Dec. 2nd and the 14th.
>
> He is very pleased with your interest in and fidelity to the mission he has given you but feels your task in this line is by no means completed. As he said in his recent cable to you he wants to have lengthy and detailed reports.

Shoghi Effendi added the following postscript to emphasize as well as temper the request:

Dear & prized co-worker:

    Your illuminating report is quite satisfactory, & I would deeply appreciate even more detailed reports whenever you find it convenient to send them to me.

Sometimes, as in a letter written on 9 February 1939, May could not fulfil the mission she had been set, for reasons of health as well as pressure of other work. When she wrote to apologize for the delay in her response her honesty was touching and her humility absolute:

. . . in spite of my eagerness to fulfil this sacred obligation I realize that I am not yet strong or steady enough to be careful, wise and tactful for which I realize the imperative necessity . . .

Whenever Shoghi Effendi set Rúḥíyyih Khánum the task of writing letters to May on his behalf, he invariably added a postscript in his own hand, not only to convey words of personal encouragement to May but also to tell her how her darling daughter was doing. In the letter she wrote on 15 January 1938, for example, after reiterating how much he would appreciate more detailed reports from her, the Guardian adds:

I wish to assure you that Mary is in very good health & is making real progress in her spiritual life & is cultivating those virtues & traits of character that will be of immense value to her in her highly responsible & exalted task which she is strenuously striving to perform. Rest assured, & confidently & happily persevere in your own meritorious & historic services to the Cause. For you & for dear Mr. Maxwell I am continually praying.
                Shoghi

The Guardian's reference to 'Mary' in this postscript, and to the 'real progress' she was making, is also a tender reminder of the private side of their lives and a tacit affirmation that her parents had their share in it. In a handwritten 'P.S.' to a subsequent letter to May, dated 28 July 1938, he further stated: 'Mary's progress is being maintained I assure you, & your mind should be at rest in this respect.' His sense of justice was impeccable.

The recurring reference to 'Mary's progress' in his letters is also touchingly reminiscent of the earlier days when Shoghi Effendi had written to May Maxwell about her daughter's education. In the past, the Guardian had given instructions to May about the priorities which he felt should play a part in her daughter's training. In the postscript of his letter to her dated 28 May 1926, written during the time of Mary's pilgrimage, he had stated:

> In my conversations with Mary I have strongly urged her to take up seriously her studies on her return to Canada & thus lay a broad & secure foundation for her future services to the Cause. A sound education is absolutely essential for her. I trust that her health will so improve as to enable her to deepen & extend her knowledge of those things that are essential for a successful career of service to the Cause. I cherish great hopes for her. Your affectionate brother
> Shoghi

Now, the mother's role as educator had been taken over by the Guardian himself. In the postscript of his letter to May of 25 February 1939 he wrote: 'Mary is quite well, & exceedingly busy in her study of the Bible at present which I regard as a necessary foundation for her future work.' And again, on 11 July 1939, he once more referred to 'Mary's progress' in his postscript, and reaffirmed the association of May's work with her daughter's. After expressing relief over the health of her husband and encouraging her continued teaching efforts during the second year of the first Seven Year Plan, he added:

> Mary is steadily quietly & surely progressing & developing in every way, & I am truly pleased & satisfied. You should with increasing joy, thanksgiving, assurance & ardour persevere in your work which is complementary to hers in your servitude to the threshold of Bahá'u'lláh.

It must have greatly comforted Mrs Maxwell to imagine that her efforts in the field of service were in some way 'complementary' to those of her daughter, working at Shoghi Effendi's side. And how gratifying to be given such assurances by the beloved Guardian himself.

On 24 March 1938, on the first anniversary of her marriage, Rúḥíyyih Khánum wrote to her parents these moving words:

My two dearest ones:

Today, a year ago, I was greatly blessed by our beloved Guardian and my thoughts have been so with you both all day! Remembering our wonderful memories – and feeling how deep our unity, strength and happiness is a year after we were so blessed – because this was much more than just poor little me becoming related to our beloved Guardian – it has been something we all shared – a union of us all to the heart of the Cause . . .

This has been a year of infinitely new experience for us all three; of great and abiding happiness, of sacrifice and sometimes I guess of pain too – but how much closer to each other, to the Guardian, to reality, it has brought us. I kiss you both with an overflowing heart and feel as close as if we stood in the same room together. This is the Mercy of God.

* * *

The first three years of Rúḥíyyih Khánum's marriage, which coincided with the last three years of May's life, were not only critical from a political point of view but also personally testing for the Maxwell family. Quite apart from the news of rising tensions and daily violence in Palestine during the last decade of the British Mandate, which increased in intensity with the Arab Revolt between 1936 and 1939, May must have been greatly concerned about her daughter's adjustment to a Persian household. It does not take great imagination to guess how hard it was to be a Western bride in an Oriental family in the 1930s.

As late as 1952, when Samiheh Banani went on pilgrimage to Haifa, she witnessed the impact of those years on Rúḥíyyih Khánum and, on returning, spoke about her loneliness. Being a Persian herself, she could well imagine how difficult it must have been for this young Canadian in those early years in the Master's House, unable to speak the language and surrounded by unfamiliar circumstances and the increasingly difficult family relationships. If a total stranger felt for her plight, long after the family had proven themselves faithless, how much more so would her own mother, even from the distance of a thousand leagues away?

The British Mandate not only witnessed rising tension between Arabs and Jews but also coincided with a period of growing disaffection in the Holy Land. There was great turmoil in the Master's house.

During the late 1930s Shoghi Effendi's relatives were drifting away from the Covenant, one by one. Even as the Guardian, who was keenly aware of the volatile political situation, sought to disperse the local Bahá'í community and send them out of Palestine to neighbouring countries and to Iran, members of his own family began to associate more and more closely with the Arab community and, in defiance of all wisdom as well as his expressed wish, to ally themselves by marriage to those overtly opposed to the Bahá'í Faith. Although he tried to contain their acts of flagrant disobedience for as long as possible, their own actions finally exposed their faithlessness to the Covenant and drove them from the Cause during the decade that followed. When the importance of family superseded the priorities of faith, it was crucial to distinguish between a husband and the Head of the Cause; it was vital to differentiate between a brother and the divinely-appointed Guardian. And this, the family of Shoghi Effendi, like the family of 'Abdu'l-Bahá and Bahá'u'lláh before them, tragically failed to do.

In one of Rúḥíyyih Khánum's regular letters to her parents, in mid-October 1939, she acknowledged the news of Martha Root's passing but she also wrote about the critical issues related to the protection of the Faith:

> The news of dear Martha Root's death was not unexpected as the Guardian had been sent the doctor's reports which were pretty hopeless. These are not the things which burden him. He knew she could not live forever! Like the Master, a breath of violation or the thought that anyone may be even a potential violator is, one might say, death to him! I often think it profoundly organic, the sense that the Center of the Cause has for this most venomous disease. Hence the importance he attaches to your vigilance in protecting the Faith and being on the look out – the duty indeed of every Bahá'í. Disobedience, an incorrect attitude towards the fundamentals of the Cause, failure to push on the teaching and temple work, these are the things he suffers from and not all the things the friends <u>think</u> he suffers from. He does not suffer over the deaths of others the way the Master did. He is here to judge and not to pity. You remember the Master said one bad apple would decay a whole barrel of good ones? The protection of the Faith is what burns into him!
>
> Everyone from the center outwards to the furthest point, has

failed befittingly to heed 'Abdu'l-Bahá's injunction 'that no dust of despondency may stain his radiant nature . . .'. I sometimes feel desperate. I feel if I could only bring to him the living sense of the love of the friends – why don't they pour their love on him? Don't they realize how alone he is! How isolated, how <u>heavily</u> burdened?

It is truly telling to see the contrast between the implicit obedience of the Maxwell family in their relations to the Head of their Faith, and the disastrous failure of Shoghi Effendi's own family to separate his personality from his authority as Guardian. In writing to her mother in general terms on the subject Rúḥíyyih <u>Kh</u>ánum was, in effect, sharing invaluable lessons in the Covenant with her own contemporaries. She was also sounding a warning bell to the whole North American community. For Shoghi Effendi had also educated her to distinguish between personality and spiritual authority in relation to the Guardian.

Such lessons, which were proving to be devastatingly relevant in the context of the imminent war, were also to be Rúḥíyyih <u>Kh</u>ánum's saving. She learned from the Guardian how easy it was to fall into the trap of personality worship, and counselled her mother about the dangers this posed to the American community in particular, whose naïve tendencies in this regard put them at risk.

As the darkness of that dangerous decade drew to its deadly close, May struggled heroically against her maternal instincts. In a letter to Ethel Edell dated 1 February 1938, she revealed something of the pain which her separation from her daughter caused her, and something too of the profound lessons in detachment and obedience she had learned from it:

Dearest Ethel,

. . . During the many months I spent last year with the Guardian, I not only suffered through the profound change which came about in all our lives in the marriage of the Guardian to our daughter with all that it involved for us, for a time an irreparable sense of loss, for I felt that I could never follow into that exalted world to which she had been lifted by the hand of God, but I also learned more of the mercy and bounty of God, of spiritual states of the soul, of how to progress, than in all my previous life. The Guardian was kind and loving, but very strict and stern where it came to absolute obedience to the highest laws of life, and to walking in the path of God's will.

I learned, dearest Ethel, that even the heart can become a danger to us through the emotional nature, and that only when the soul, with all its surging tendencies, its great quality, is controlled by the will and comes under the sway of the mind, will it be released from the subtle temptations of the self.

My very love for my daughter, perhaps the purest and noblest love of my life, became my greatest stumbling block, my supreme test; I had to learn true detachment and utter surrender, the giving of my will entirely to God and the building up of that mighty power of faith which alone lifts us into those higher realms of conscious union with the Beloved.

Rúḥíyyih Khánum's touching and sustaining outpouring of love for her parents is evident in excerpts from even a few letters written by her in 1938 and 1939:

February 6th, 1938

Your love for me dearest has warmed me all my life, like a divine kind of fire – but Mother my own, do please let me try and tell you what I feel the friends should have their attention called to. The Americans are already swamped in personalities, as a nation, and the Bahá'ís are also terribly personality conscious. Now please don't in any way let them follow their natural inclination and fasten themselves on my personality. It would be a great, great pity. (And if you share any of my thoughts with them, let this one be it!) We Americans are adolescent and I assure you in my short year's experience near the Guardian I have come to realize that this is no time for people to go wandering around in a set of lovely and pleasant dreams. They should take to heart, Bahá'ís and not only humanity, that an unforeseen calamity is following them. I don't mean that they should be frightened but we, all of us, should be preparing our souls for the tests which are bound to come to us as well as to mankind. This is something I feel too deeply for words. For the American friends to let themselves go in a lot of foolish, over-exaggerated ideas about me, is just wasting their precious time, and no one could better bring this to their attention than my own mother. I don't mean you should belittle me or criticise me because, darling, I know you not only could not (!) but should not. On the other hand I feel very keenly that instead of people saying (maybe they don't I'm just guessing!) that I was destined from birth to become the Guardian's wife – <u>he</u> has not said so, why should they? – and that I am so fitted, so good, so this, so that!! They should be praying I fulfil my task as a representative from the West. They should ask what my life is like, and is its discipline a symbol of the discipline they need and will get? They should be turning their thoughts to the Guardian – and to no one else on earth, nor associating anyone in thought with him – and studying him and asking themselves what their faults are, as American Bahá'ís, and where our weaknesses lie, and what in our personality or in the body of us as believers are vulnerable points which when attacked and tested may not be strong enough to withstand and protect us. I am very serious about this. I assure you my time is not spent in trying to enjoy life and skimming along as a young married woman usually does – on the contrary I am realizing just how serious one lifetime spent in the Faith should be. The greatest fallacy in America is this 'life, liberty and the pursuit of happiness'; it's bad medicine for people to go on thinking that either liberty or happiness or even life itself is a thing to be pursued, especially at this time. Steadfastness, character, devotion, loyalty and Faith are what I am now pursuing hot footed! And I am not a bit unhappy!! On the contrary I like it! I think you yourself laid the bedrock of my faith when you told me I should have such a belief in this Cause, that if you – my spiritual and physical Mother – left it, I would remain firm. It marked a turning point in my life when you said that to me! And all this type of thing, Mother dearest, is what I feel you should be teaching the Bahá'ís. If I sacrifice for the Cause – the Guardian is drawn and quartered for it. So it seems to me the friends should 'stiffen their characters'. That is what Shoghi Effendi says he is doing to me. And I feel <u>much</u> improved by it, I assure you!

I would not have you for the whole world feel different about me from the way you do! It helps and strengthens me. But I don't think others should feel that way – or at least be encouraged to – because of course what a person feels in their heart is their own business. Anyway you know what I mean. I can be an instrument, perhaps, to help the friends realize more about the Guardian if they see things as they in reality are, never if they just let themselves go the way of our national habit which is to eulogize some personality and get no further. I was thinking today in the Shrine, we may surround the Guardian, and through our human relation feel close to him – but in reality we are like earth around a lily – is there any close kinship between the wonderful flower and the earth at its feet?

... But I want to say something before I forget it and the time passes – strange one can think so much more clearly at night. You know dear a strange thought came to me the other night as I read your letter – you and Daddy, I know perfectly well, are concerned that my home should be beautiful and a surrounding such as I have always loved, and I was thinking that all my life, through you two, I have been spoiled (not in the bad sense, but in the sense of having a fullness of something) by all the beauty of our lives, both external and internal. Charm, culture, quiet, and – German is the best to describe it all – 'Gemütlichkeit'. Everything that is homey and charming! I have had such an extraordinary life of abundance and – well you know! And now I sometimes feel that a very extraordinary thing has happened. God has taken away in one sweep all that kind of being spoiled and given me an entirely new, strange and wonderful way of being spoiled – it is taken from the external plane to the inner plane. Gone are my friends, freedom, calm, charm of my home, everything of the past and in contrast to it I have a much harder external life – but look at how I am being spiritually spoiled by being the Guardian's wife! Is there any greater honour for me than being the wife of the Guardian? We'll just let it go at the word 'honour' and not mention all the other exquisite, wonderful things that go with it! I don't have to elaborate, you know what I mean. And so dearest I feel you and Daddy must just 'relax over it' as Bobbie used to say! I love all the things you send me, they do make a difference – a big one to me, they are a touch of my own home with you – but I don't think life here in Haifa can be as ours was! The Cause of God is like a kettle boiling all the time!!! And by this I don't mean the Guardian, he and all of us are enmeshed in something whose power is irresistible. Of course it manifests itself through his decisions – but the atmosphere is like that. At first I felt like something under pressure but now I am getting so used to it that I am astounded at myself! Shoghi Effendi says I have no right to call him a mystery! But I can say at least that to me he is and the result of my observations is that a Guardian is a touchstone applied to us all the time, he is bigger than he himself realizes – I believe this. There is no more dangerous maze for people to begin to wander in than the subject of the 'personality' of either the Guardian, or the Master or even the Manifestation.

April 16th, 1938
My beloved Mother:
I am reforming! I wrote Daddy yesterday and am going to try and write you each once a week. So let's hope for the best – you know I am never a wonderful correspondent! But love and thoughts are always crossing the Atlantic day and night to you both . . .

And referring specifically to the station of the Guardian, she wrote:

This is a Cause wide enough to embrace any soul, to chastise and yet harbour any sinner, but not wide enough for anyone whose belief in the burning point of the Faith is not sound, to remain in it . . . [for] no other Faith ever said categorically 'he who opposes him opposes God, he who denies him, denies God, he [who] turns away from him turns away from God – etc'.

April 11th, 1939
My own precious Mother & Daddy
I think of you so constantly . . . Somehow I realize now many things about you, and Daddy too, that I never realized before. How much you have suffered physically, how patient and self-sacrificing you have been to Daddy and me in a thousand little ways! And I see how sweet and good Daddy is, how he so unassumingly economized and gave up many little pleasures when he could no longer afford them. Such realization enriches love and makes it deeper and realler [sic]! . . .

I assure you I get the maximum happiness out of life! I refuse to borrow tomorrow's troubles and I think that is the way to live. To not suffer before the time comes is a wonderful saving. So many people go through a thing twice – once in anticipation and then in actuality, no sir! not for me! And besides I realize now as never before that the Plans, compensations, schemes of Bahá'u'lláh are capable of such infinite variety it is useless to waste time thinking what comes next.

* * *

The challenges of that period were not only inner ones. May Maxwell's role as the mother of Rúḥíyyih Rabbani raised administrative dilemmas too, which taught both May and the Bahá'í community to distinguish between principle and personality. It also placed her in the firing line, as it were, when Shoghi Effendi himself was attacked as a result of misunderstandings and misrepresentations of the Guardianship among older Bahá'ís who were still under the influence of Ahmad Sohrab during these years.

One such dilemma developed regarding the 'Notes' compiled by Mary Maxwell during her last visit to Haifa just before her marriage. The controversy began in 1938 and continued till the outbreak of World War II in 1939. During this period hundreds of letters were received from individuals requesting copies of these notes, and the flurry of paper that was raised over this issue as well as the manner in which it was curbed and controlled enables one to better appreciate the capacities of the Maxwells. Not only was May's relationship with her daughter involved in this controversy but Sutherland's also, and his commitment to the Cause was strengthened by it.

On 20 April 1938, just before May left for Chicago to attend the National Convention, she received the following important letter from Rúḥíyyih Khánum:

> It thrills me to know you and Daddy will both be at the Convention! It will certainly be a very momentous one! I shall be longing for news of it.
>
> Now darling I want to tell you something on behalf of the Guardian. He says you should be very careful in regard to two things – one your use of your pilgrims notes and the other your reference to me. He, as only he can, sees what certain tendencies may eventually give rise to and as you are in a position not devoid of difficulties because of your relation to him and to me, and also as you may have people who would be only too willing to cause trouble for you, you cannot be too cautious. Because you are my Mother you must not stress

either me or my thoughts too much – it could be bad for me and in that way not good for the relation of the friends to me – not that it matters, I only mean I must not cause any trouble! And regarding the notes, of course share them, as all pilgrims do, with the friends – but don't push them forward or give them unasked for because people might get the impression you thought or considered them better and more authoritative than others because they are <u>ours.</u> Of course I know you don't think for a moment anything of the sort! But be wise. You yourself know how fraught with possible complications the situation is and you can be of the greatest help to the Guardian by keeping clear of anyone having an issue with you! About me, your notes, or anything. Soft peddle me! And I shall nestle close in your heart and our love be just as wonderful as ever!

...

These are very tremendous and terrible days in the whole world and we who truly love this Cause, in spite of our pettiness and unworthiness, more than anything else, are certainly called upon to sacrifice and endure to the bitter end. But I take a savage pleasure in my share of suffering because it is for the Guardian – and yours is too my own beloved Mother!

Rúḥíyyih Khánum's warnings, however, did not immediately produce the necessary degree of caution which she may have intended them to do. Her mother was doubtless in a flurry of preparation for departure. And it was clear, even before it began, that the 1938 National Convention of the Bahá'ís of the United States and Canada was going to be a very special gathering that year. On 26 April May wrote a quick note to her daughter, which captures the excitement in the air at the time:

> I just arrived off the train from New York and am in a downtown hotel in Chicago. As I must send this letter air mail – special delivery to catch the Queen Mary tomorrow, then I shall go out to the Hotel Orrington in Evanston. Daddy will arrive in the morning and the momentous Convention will open at about 9.15 or 9.30.

The Hand of the Cause Agnes Alexander, recalling how many 'precious teachings' she gleaned from May in Evanston during this Convention, states:

The day before the Convention opened, an informal meeting was held to discuss teaching methods. As it was progressing May entered and was asked to speak. Her words were like light penetrating darkness.

In a report written about this Convention one can vividly see the influence of May's presence on the atmosphere and on the friends:

> The Convention received great inspiration from May's reading of the 'Notes' taken by Rúḥíyyih Khánum, her daughter, in Shoghi Effendi's presence ... Then May said, 'He is the quickening life in the body of the friends. He is the tangible Point on this earth. The law of the Focal Point exists in every atom of the universe. The Guardian is that focal point.' She told us how the Guardian asked her, 'How do you pray?' She replied, 'I first turn to you because you are in the body and so am I, you are the tangible point, and when I have made that connection, then I pray to Bahá'u'lláh and through Him I reach the Almighty Being.' He replied, 'This is exactly correct.' On another occasion when speaking informally, May said, 'We have to transcend, first our ego as inherited from our ancestors, then our national ego – transcend a thousand veils! We grow through struggles. The butterfly if liberated with help is weak. Its strength is in liberating itself.'

This was the first time the 'Notes' were shared in public. Two months later, on 25 June 1938, Mrs Maxwell mentioned them herself in a letter to Marion Holley:

> I stayed two or three weeks in Evanston because the believers of Chicago and the Lake Shore have the most intense thirst for every word of the Guardian, and the notes that Rúḥíyyih Khánum took so carefully a year ago last winter were in constant demand; in fact I read them aloud to groups, often of almost two hundred people both at the Temple and in Chicago ...

However, amid these positive reactions to the 'Notes' there were some negative ones to their distribution. There were objections of principle raised to the spreading of what were essentially 'pilgrims' notes', no matter who had compiled them; and murmurs were doubtless heard about democratic principles and the abuse of privilege! In order to curb the misgivings or the uneasiness of the friends, the matter was taken up by the institutions of the Faith and on 14 July 1938 May wrote to Shoghi Effendi saying:

> Sutherland and I have been invited by the National Spiritual Assembly to meet with them some time in Green Acre during their summer session, August 12th, 13th, and 14th . . . [We] are very happy to meet with them in the most loving spirit.

It is clear from a letter drafted by May to Shoghi Effendi some time in early August that May had decided to send these 'Notes' to him for his approval, in order to curtail any further damage that might be caused by their distribution:

> [T]herefore, asking you to overlook all the imperfections, I am forwarding a copy herewith, and humbly beg that, unless it is contrary to your supreme wisdom – you will pass upon the accuracy of these notes.
> In a few days we are meeting with the National Spiritual Assembly at their request, and we shall report the outcome to you.
> I love to think of your having a brief respite from your most mighty burden – although I well know that you can never, even for a moment, lay it down nor be free from such cares and sorrows as no man, not sustained by the All-mighty mysterious power of the beloved could for one moment endure. My heart's most deep, yearning love and passionate loyalty are forever with you, and daily I thank Bahá'u'lláh Who gave me such a daughter for you . . . Humbly yours – May

What happened in the course of the Maxwells' meeting with the Assembly was communicated in an interesting letter that May subsequently wrote to her spiritual child, Agnes Alexander, in September of 1938. She sent a copy of the 1937 'Notes' to Agnes at the same time, accompanied by the proviso that 'whatever you do, Agnes, do not quote me'. If portions of this letter have been included below it is only to illustrate how much we owe to Mrs Maxwell, over seventy years later, for our understanding of the distinction between pilgrims' notes and the Guardian's official statements. The difficulty she had in speaking to the Assembly in her 'new position', the concern she felt about limiting gossip and conjecture, as well as her honest appraisal of the value of the 'Notes', prove as salutary today as they were challenging in her own times. If our understanding of the issues has been modified since then, it is largely due to her courage and her ardent longing to share her experiences:

> ... for you alone, because, Agnes, to whomsoever we confide there is always another to whom they confide and our efforts will assuredly be handicapped if such ideas are spread about. What we must do is not to <u>talk about it</u> but to go ahead and do it with each individual we meet. Now when I was told in Green Acre that these notes are not officially recognized, I said, 'Of course they are not and that is quite all right, for this reason I will read them privately to groups.' Thus I frustrated any effort to suppress the words of the Guardian, and I suppose due to my new position as being related to him they dare not oppose me. Above all, whatever you do, Agnes, do not quote me. Each one is an independent entity and must stand in his place alone ... independent of all save God.

May's statement – 'Above all, whatever you do, Agnes, do not quote me' – is an ironical echo of her own daughter's advice to her, earlier that spring, to 'soft-peddle me'. Rúḥíyyih Khánum's warnings could not have been more relevant.

During the early months of 1939, May and Sutherland worked together to polish and reproduce the 'Notes'. They had evidently 'passed review' with the Guardian on condition that they were identified as personal. Shoghi Effendi had also permitted the Maxwells to mail the compilation out to any Baháʼís who specifically asked for it. May hired a stenographer to mimeograph the 'Notes', and on 10 January 1939 she informed her daughter of this in a handwritten letter – something of a novelty, as she was accustomed to dictating to a secretary:

> My darling –
> How do you like my own handwriting again. I so love every line you write that I thought I would send you just this line as I am too busy to write at length with a stenographer; the 'Nemesis' is still

these 'Notes' and many obstacles. Now I have a much better stenographer to mimeograph them and Daddy has worked faithfully to correct each stencil and add all the Persian accents – and he has loved doing it . . .

The task was arduous and full of setbacks. In another letter written to her daughter on 9 February May refers to some of the difficulties they had encountered in completing this quite large project of printing and distributing the 82-page, two-volume compilation:

As I wrote you in all my recent letters, I was working much too hard on the notes and I so longed to finish them and to be able to distribute those copies for which I had had appeals from all over the country. We met with one obstacle after another . . . The last obstacle was the loss of five or six stencils which set back the work at least a week . . .

In addition to making clean copies of the 'Notes', and correcting every detail in them with her husband's help, May wrote a cover letter to accompany their distribution and explain their context, so that no confusion might arise regarding their authority. She had sent this to the Guardian for his approval too, and had evidently taken the opportunity, at the same time, of extending to him an invitation to visit their home in Montreal, should the circumstances necessitate his leaving the Holy Land.

It was not the first time May had extended an invitation to the Guardian to visit North America. He had declined the offer before, but she probably hoped he might reconsider it this time in the light of the political situation, which in Europe had by that time become one of great concern and anxiety. It was unthinkable to imagine being cut off from the Guardian of the Bahá'í Faith if a war broke out in Europe. It was also unthinkable to be cut off from her beloved daughter at such a time. She must have hoped that there was every reason for Shoghi Effendi to respond positively this time, especially in light of her 'new position' as being related to him.

In Rúḥíyyih Khánum's letter written on behalf of the Guardian to her mother, dated 25 February 1939, she conveyed his approval of May's explanatory note and commended its appropriateness. And then she told her of Shoghi Effendi's response to her invitation:

The Guardian wants me to tell you he approves of your little note of explanation enclosed with the notes you intend sharing with the friends. He does not want to have any misunderstanding arise regarding them and so feels your note was quite appropriate.

He was very touched by your offer of our home to him if at any time he should be forced to go to that continent, but he feels such a thing is very unlikely indeed! However the spirit of your offer he accepts and the love that inspired it.

And in Shoghi Effendi's handwriting:

Dear & valued co-worker:
I deeply appreciate & feel much touched by your spontaneous and generous offer to place the house you live in at my disposal if ever I visit the States. This is another evidence of your passionate devotion to the Faith which I regard as an inestimable asset to the Cause. What you are achieving for the Cause in these days of stress & trial, through personal contact with the believers only serves to enhance the rich record of your past & outstanding services. Mary is quite well, & exceedingly busy in her study of the Bible at present which I regard as a necessary foundation for her future work. You should feel assured, happy & redouble your efforts in the teaching field. With much love to dear Mr. Maxwell whom I trust will be able to help increasingly in the magnificent work you are performing for the Cause. Your true & grateful brother,
Shoghi

May's 'little note of explanation' about the 'Notes' referred to above was distributed to the friends as a mimeographed circular letter. It was an apologia, in effect, and established once and for all, the clear distinction between pilgrims' notes and authentic texts. It also bore witness to the humility and the dignity of the Maxwells, as well as their deep faith:

Mr. Maxwell and I greatly appreciate your prompt and loving co-operation in sending us the names and addresses of those members of your community who wish to have a set of the Notes taken by Rúḥíyyih Khánum in the presence of our beloved Guardian, and which are now being forwarded.

> May we take this opportunity, however, to state that our revered National Spiritual Assembly most kindly brought to our attention a ruling of the Guardian published in 'Proceedings of the 1938 Convention' as follows: 'It was moved, seconded and voted to record the view in the light of the Guardian's general instruction, as quoted below, the National Assembly cannot sanction the publication and distribution through official Bahá'í channels of notes and records of pilgrims . . .'
>
> In our eagerness to reach all those who might desire to possess his priceless words, we have most unfortunately overlooked one of his binding instructions, and we wish to express our sincere regret.
>
> Only as we stand united in the strength, the beauty and symmetry of the divine Order, under the mighty Shadow of the Guardian, can we hope to attain the heights and depths revealed in 'The Advent of Divine Justice'.
>
> Will you please inform all the friends of the contents of this letter, including our deep appreciation of their many letters of grateful acknowledgment. These Notes are a free and loving gift from Rúḥíyyih Khánum to the believers of America.

This letter, written on 13 April 1939, was sent out to all local Spiritual Assemblies. They were informed that 'Vol. I and Vol. II of the Guardian's words, taken in his presence by Rúḥíyyih Khánum, have been sent to you . . . so that any of the Bahá'ís in your Community may have access to them.' The letter continued:

> Moreover, if among your group there are those who express a wish to possess a copy, will you kindly send their names and addresses to us as we do not wish anyone who sincerely wants them to be deprived of the words of the blessed Guardian.

An undated letter from Amatu'l-Bahá, over the signature of 'Mary Maxwell', accompanied the distribution of these 'Notes' and has, ironically enough, much enhanced their value from a historical point of view, without in any way changing their significance. The distinction this letter makes between the original compiler 'Miss Mary Maxwell', and Rúḥíyyih Khánum, is the same as the difference it highlights between pilgrims' notes and the official statements of the Guardian:

Beloved Friends,

It is a great privilege to share the notes with those Baháʼís who have asked for them both for themselves and to share with other Baháʼí friends. It will greatly simplify our understanding of their status if we bear in mind that they are not the official statements of our blessed Guardian, that he has not sent them through the Administrative, official channel, but that inasmuch as he sanctions both their recording in his presence and subsequent sharing with fellow Baháʼís, they are of priceless value being his free and spontaneous utterances to those Baháʼís who were actually in his beloved presence. These notes taken by Rúḥíyyih Khánum (then Miss Mary Maxwell) have the same status, in a vast field of subjects, as the notes of all others. Lovingly yours,

Mary Maxwell

On 12 April while in New York, Mrs Maxwell wrote to Sutherland to express her gratitude and appreciation for his work on the 'Notes':

> I cannot tell you how much I appreciate all the work and trouble you have had to get these notes off – & I am so grateful that you checked up on the lists – I know I had duplicated some addresses – but did not have the energy to check them up.
>
> I am enclosing a new, small list – and as soon as I feel stronger, shall go to the Holley's and look over all the names of American Baháʼís – & make a new, selected list.

Mr Maxwell kept a detailed account of every Assembly and individual to whom he sent the 'Notes'. He even made a cover for the material, adding a clipping on the back page from the *Saturday Evening Post* of an advertisement for Oneida silverware! It was an example of the challenge which the Maxwells faced in distinguishing between the private and the public in the story of these 'Notes'. They had to draw a fine line between sharing the Guardian's words with the friends, with dignity and accuracy, and giving the impression that their daughter had privileged access to him. Although May bore the brunt of the psychological pressure this must have involved, the arduous task of completing the project once it had been begun was carried out solely by Mr Maxwell. He was the one who had to check the 'Notes' for accuracy and handle the myriad requests for them, just at a time when he was also heavily engaged in his professional work. He was the one who had to arrange for their distribution during the very summer he was awarded a bronze replica of the Seal of the Province of Quebec Association of Architects.

Indeed, Mr Maxwell's participation in May's activities and his contribution to the 'Notes' seem to have marked a turning point in his relations to the Cause. And indeed, however hard the work involved, it must have been highly gratifying to have it so appreciated. The numerous letters of thanks which May received from individuals and from institutions for the Haifa 'Notes' exceeded all expectations. Most of these responses were written between March and December of 1939, just as World War II broke out. From Honolulu, for example, Helen H. Jones wrote to May saying:

> Words can't express how delighted I was today, in receiving the copy of the notes which you and your daughter took in Haifa. It was so sweet of you to want us to share in your fortune, and I certainly consider it a great privilege. Thank you so much! . . . I have heard so much about you through my cousin, Katherine Baldwin, and hope the time will come some day when I can really meet you . . .

Johanna Schubarth wrote from Norway in the course of this same year:

> I am reading and rereading your notes from Haifa, they are so instructing . . .

Another acknowledgement came from Omaha, Nebraska:

> I am a young man of 25 years here in the Omaha Bahá'í group and . . . I have just finished reading two volumes of your Haifa Notes of Shoghi Effendi's words of 1937. I am thrilled with the wonderful information it offers the sincere seeker in the Bahá'í Faith . . . I should like to own a copy of each volume for myself, please be so kind as to write me letting me know how I may secure these notes.

And finally, there was the response of the Spiritual Assembly of the Bahá'ís of Milwaukee, Wisconsin:

We were overjoyed to receive this priceless gift and when we read your letter (of April 13th) to the friends at the April 26th Feast all hands went up for copies. That would mean about 75 sets. We were embarrassed and hesitate to present the list of names before we inquire if you are prepared for such a request.

The embarrassment and hesitation expressed in the above letter can be explained by the fact that the Maxwells were personally paying for the production and distribution of the 'Notes'.

* * *

As 1938 drew to a close, it must have been clear to most people that another conflagration was imminent in Europe. The thirties had proven to be a brutal decade but many feared the forties would be worse.

Only the Bahá'ís could afford to look ahead with hope, and even they did not always realize at the time what they were seeing. Shoghi Effendi had changed the meaning of history and it would take hindsight to understand the full import of his messages to the world. When the financial markets had collapsed ten years earlier, and the Great Depression had paralysed Western society, he had unrolled a vision of a future civilization before the eyes of the believers in his *World Order* letters. When Hitler rose to power in 1933 and seized the role of Chancellor, the Guardian had summoned the Bahá'ís of the United States in soul-stirring words to assume their role of spiritual leadership in the world. By the time the Spanish Civil War broke out in 1936, he had already written his immortal *Dispensation of Bahá'u'lláh*, which was to all intents and purposes his will and testament. And in December 1938, one month after the looting and burning and pillaging and murder during the notorious 'Kristallnacht' which marked the beginning of the Holocaust, he had completed *The Advent of Divine Justice*, which called on the friends to exploit the very crises of the times for the purpose of 'spreading far and wide the knowledge of the redemptive power of the Faith of Bahá'u'lláh'. By the end of 1938, with the world poised on the brink of war and the Führer's tanks flooding into the Rhine valley, the Guardian of the Bahá'í Faith had enlisted an army of light to resist the forces of darkness.

1939 was a particularly anxious year for the Maxwells of Montreal for personal reasons too. As the countdown to World War II began, they did not know from one day to the next when they would be permanently cut off from their loved ones in the Holy Land. The deteriorating situation caused by the Arab Revolt had finally culminated in the deployment of fresh troops to try to contain the violence and a battalion of British soldiers had landed in Haifa the previous September. The situation was highly volatile and pilgrimages to the Holy Land were either cancelled or uncertain. Any hope that they might see each other soon would have been dwindling.

May celebrated her sixty-ninth birthday that January. Her health had deteriorated badly the previous year and she was suffering from heart problems as well as diabetes by then. No doubt her worries about her daughter's safety and her fears over their permanent separation also contributed to her weakened condition. As usual, she attributed her physical indisposition to spiritual weakness and chastised herself for having failed to serve the Faith. Rúḥíyyih Khánum did all she could to reassure her mother in a letter written on Shoghi Effendi's behalf on 20 May 1939:

> He was very sad to learn from your recent cablegram sent to me, that you have a diabetic condition. He hastens to assure you he will pray for your complete recovery and he wants you not only to continue treating this condition but to have complete rest <u>of body and mind</u> in order to entirely recover. He assures you that you have no need to worry on any score and that when the time comes you will return to him, and to my open arms, in Haifa. You must never have any doubt about this for a moment!
>
> He wants you at present to devote yourself entirely to recovering from this condition and only after you are recovered, to go on with your teaching work . . .
>
> Also he feels whenever you need his prayers, or wish to, you should cable him directly at once. This will greatly help you and you should never hesitate, for any consideration, to do so.
>
> In your last letter to me you asked me a question that I felt only our beloved could answer so I took the liberty of mentioning it to him, knowing his answer would be the true one. He says your illness has not the slightest connection with any spiritual state or failure. There is every reason for you to feel happy and proud because he is

pleased with you and you are doing your duty in every way. This illness is purely a physical condition and he is praying you will overcome it. He wants you not to worry over anything or think any dark thoughts . . .

You must always feel that he is not only happy to hear from you but eager to get your views as one so devoted to the Cause and so close to him!

And in Shoghi Effendi's handwriting:

It is a long time since I have written you but you have been often in my thoughts and prayers, particularly since I have heard about your illness which I trust will be soon completely cured. To be fully restored physically should be your first consideration. Everything for the present should be subordinated to it. Anytime you feel the urge to write me do not hesitate for one moment. Rest assured, and have no anxiety whatever either regarding Mary who is well, happy and protected, or in connection with the international situation & its repercussions. You and your dear family have in the past & under all circumstances been consistently & sometimes miraculously preserved, guided & blessed & will in the coming days be vouchsafed similar if not still greater & more abundant bounties & blessings. Be happy, confident, & thankful. Affectionately
        Shoghi

Five days later, on 25 May 1939, May's brother Randolph completed his translation of the French footnotes in *The Dawn-Breakers* and sent the manuscript to Shoghi Effendi. This gesture meant all the world to his sister. She must have praised him to the skies for his work. He wrote the following cover letter to the Guardian:

My dear Shoghi Effendi,
 I am forwarding to you a copy of my translation of the French footnotes in the 'Dawn-Breakers', which I have recently completed . . .
 I send this first transcript of my rendition of these notes to you with sincere regards . . . hoping that you will not find my work over-faulty.

In closing, let me add that I hope that, at no distant date, it may be my privilege to meet you.
Faithfully yours,
Randolph Bolles

Although May always felt that he had understood and accepted the Truth of the Faith in his heart, Randolph had never actually registered as a Bahá'í. On 9 July, in addition to conveying to her some of the family news, he attempted to explain his position to his sister. One can sense in his words how much he respected and admired her, but how hard it must have been to live up to her expectations:

> You are certainly very thoughtful of your 'Bro' and I wish it were possible for him to – somehow – prove to you his appreciation of your ever ready attention to him & <u>his</u> . . . but this is orally not a necessity, only a feeling. For, dearest May, even tho I may not be able to always act in accordance with your loving suggestions – you do really understand – as in the present case; know that I (am) ever grateful to you. Moreover, you know that I have my own inner light to guide me – that I cannot disregard; so you do not deem me careless . . .
>
> Well, May, I have written this in haste & will leave it to you to fill up the lapses . . . This hastily penned letter is a very poor 'return' for your two lengthy and wonderfully expressed epistles.

Ten days later, on 19 July, Randolph Bolles died of a heart attack in his hotel room in New York. May was grief-stricken. It was the first of many personal shocks that she sustained during a year that was to become notorious for the shocks it inflicted on millions. That same day she sent a cable to Shoghi Effendi:

> BELOVED IN LIFE AND DEATH WE ARE ALL IN YOUR BLESSED HANDS. MY BELOVED BROTHER DIED HEART ATTACK TONIGHT FERVENTLY SUPPLICATE PRAYERS HIS SOUL ON BEHALF JEANNE AND CHILDREN ASSURED PROTECTION RUHIYYIH KHANUM FROM SHOCK. DEEPEST LOVE SORROW LONGING.
> MAY SUTHERLAND

LATE YEARS 1937–1940

Due to a delay in communications, Shoghi Effendi did not cable back until 25 July:

> CABLE REGARDING BELOVED BROTHER DELAYED HEART FULL SORROW SYMPATHY PRAYING ARDENTLY SPIRITUAL ILLUMINATION EVERLASTING FELICITY SHOGHI

Amatu'l-Bahá Rúḥíyyih Khánum cabled her mother that same day:

> HEARTBROKEN MY UNCLES PASSING MUST ALL BE COURAGEOUS SUPPLICATING BELOVED ACCEPTANCE SOUL COMFORT BOLLES LOVE RUHIYYIH

Despite her bereavement, May Maxwell took the time to send a letter to the manager of the Hotel Barbizon Plaza on 29 July, thanking him for his kindness and expressing her appreciation for all that he had done for the family:

> I wish to express to you and to the personnel of your Hotel on behalf of all my family, our deep appreciation of the extreme kindness, courtesy and sympathy shown to us in the time of our great sorrow. Whether through the young ladies at the desk, the telephone operators or the bell-boys, they have conveyed to us a quiet sympathy and understanding rare in this modern world, and I for my part wish to thank them all, and to say that I am happy/thankful that my dear Brother Mr. Bolles spent so many happy months in a Hotel which has a human atmosphere.
> Faithfully yours, May Maxwell

It is extraordinary that she had the presence of mind, just at this time, to even remember such courtesies.

Some five weeks before her brother's death, May had had another cause for anxiety. She had returned from her own travels to find her husband ill in hospital with a severe case of gall stones. Accustomed as she was to being the patient in their marriage, she may have been a bit disconcerted to find herself the nurse. She wrote about the circumstances to Louise Bosch on 16 June:

> Here I am at home again after many weeks wandering and teaching, in a modest way, with a sick husband in the hospital. Sutherland developed gall stones in my absence, that is, the last week or ten days of my absence, and thought he had merely an upset stomach, but he was later rushed to the hospital with a severe pain and I came home to find him in this condition. The mighty power of the Guardian's prayers, combined with good, scientific treatment, is bringing him through and he is making a rapid recovery . . .

When Sutherland fell sick, the project of preparing, correcting, binding and distributing the 'Notes' stalled completely. May was obliged to send out another mimeographed circular letter on 27 June to the friends who had ordered copies and not received them due to his indisposition. In it she apologized for the interruption in deliveries:

> The delay in sending you the Notes which you have requested is due to the sudden illness of Mr. Maxwell. He alone had made the distribution, and any interference would cause confusion, which might deprive some of the friends from receiving some of their copies.
> Mr. Maxwell is returning from the hospital in a few days, and will soon be able to complete the work . . .

As soon as the news of Sutherland's illness reached Haifa, the Guardian immediately sent a cable of concern to the Maxwell household, dated 18 June:

> DEEPLY SADDENED SUTHERLANDS OPERATION PRAYING COMPLETE RECOVERY DEEPEST LOVE SHOGHI

Sutherland's little note scribbled on the back on this cable may have been intended as a reply:

> You misunderstand no operation appears necessary Sutherland making splendid progress.

On the same day as Shoghi Effendi's cable, Sutherland's daughter wrote to him:

Dearest Daddy Mine,

When Shoghi Effendi read me Mother's cable saying you were ill with a gall stone operation I was frightfully upset ... but the Guardian reassured me, and after reading and re-reading your cable he came to the conclusion that you were only ill with an attack of gall stones and had not had an operation (that is what I deduced). Tomorrow I expect to get another cable and then I will know for sure ...

About a month later, May received the following in a letter written on behalf of the Guardian by Rúḥíyyih Khánum, dated 11 July 1939:

He was very pleased to hear from you in your cable to him that Daddy was so much better, and he trusts you will both devote yourselves to becoming quite re-established physically and then go out and teach.

I know you will be happy to hear that Shoghi Effendi himself is well and feeling encouraged by the good news of the progress of the work in America and southward.

Your deep love for him touches and pleases him very much! He is well aware of your great devotion to the Cause and its Center.

He has permitted me to send this air mail to you, so excuse the paper, which is some I bought just for my air mail letters to you and Daddy.

With my heart's deepest love to you and Daddy and assuring you that the Guardian prays for you both and watches over you and me!
Your Rúḥíyyih

And in the handwriting of Shoghi Effendi:

Dear & prized co-worker:

The news of dear Mr. Maxwell's illness has greatly saddened me. What a relief to learn that he is well again & that no operation is required! The welfare & happiness of such a noble, such a pure & dear soul are ever near to my heart, & I pray that he may be graciously assisted & led to associate himself closer than before with the truly magnificent & historic work you are achieving, in these days of stress & trial, for the Cause of Bahá'u'lláh & its institutions. Mary is steadily quietly & surely progressing & developing in every way, & I am truly pleased & satisfied. You should with increasing joy, thanksgiving, assurance & ardour persevere in your work which is complementary to hers in your servitude to the threshold of Bahá'u'lláh. Be happy & take good care of yourself & of dear Mr. Maxwell.

   Shoghi

A few months later in a letter dated 5 November 1939, with a complementary paragraph added by May, Sutherland wrote that he had returned to work on the 'Notes'. He excused the delay in their distribution in his characteristic manner, without mentioning his indisposition:

> Delays in sending out the notes have been largely due to the requests having exceeded the available supply. It is expected that all requests will eventually be attended to in the future.

On 16 July Sutherland sent to Rúḥíyyih Khánum a delightful description of his experience in hospital, written in the course of his convalescence, which captures the atmosphere in the ward and gives a glimpse of the personnel in the Royal Victoria Hospital where he was a patient during June 1939.

> Extracts from a letter to Jeanne Bolles transcribed at request of human-dynamo No. 1 of M.E.B. and W.S.M. Pine Ave. Hook up station 1548 –
>
> Well I had a twenty-five day sojourn in the Royal Victoria. I rather liked the experience – nurses almost all Blue noses – which means they are from Nova Scotia. They were cheerful smiling good scouts: capable and desirous of rendering every possible service.
>
> I shall hold back that well-known urge of all who have spent some time as an inmate, to give detailed descriptions of their wonderful experiences; and as I had no operation my remarks would be lacking in thrills and no Hollywood Producer would care to have his scenario writer get in touch with me.
>
> Now I have good square meals daily and sleep splendidly – also go to the office for about four hours daily. Doctors prohibit my playing golf, becoming a prize fighter, driving a buggy in Bermuda or doing any horseback riding – that's all.
> NEWS FLASHES –
> — Bahá'í Exhibition to be held at Can Nat. Ex. Toronto, this year.

— Auntie – Taking rest-cure – Limiting her activities to marketing, making preserves, supervising new wardrobe for me, and limiting her telephone calls to 135 per day.

— Artie Hutchinson and sister Millie have owned a fine open Packard for 8 years – If sun is out and Montreal Star weather forecast says fine weather for next six days they take me for a grand drive – Car kept polished and spotless by Art. Total mileage in 8 years – 15,000.

— END OF BULLETIN —

Special broadcast for Rúḥíyyih Khánum
16 July

This afternoon Mother goes to Lohse's to speak to Tic Toc? Group or part of them. She spoke to the group last fall. Elsa very peppy and active does not want to fall behind the speed and activity of the Rosemary Centre on Riverside Drive –

Went to Salas last week to Feast had cold plate supper – thorough test-out of my digestive system – Rode the bumps fairly well.

Drove to Ruth's – Friday – nice apartment – had tea, nice visit – baby due in one month – Ruth resigned from S.A. – Monte drove us home –

Well that's all the news that's fit to print, so cheerio –
All love hug kiss, Dad

Three weeks later, on 9 August 1939, Amatu'l-Bahá wrote in greater detail to both her father and mother on Shoghi Effendi's behalf, expressing relief at the recovery of the former and condolences over the death of the brother of the latter:

Dearest Daddy:

Shoghi Effendi was very pleased indeed to get your letter dated July 25th, and to know that your health has so quickly recovered and that you realize the mercies and bounties of God to us, so frequently shown!

As he has already written you indirectly in his letters to Mother, he feels it is only right that you should not only sustain Mother in her teaching work, but that you yourself should take an active part in it. As much as your affairs permit, you should concentrate your talents and efforts in this direction.

The Guardian feels very sad that Uncle Randolph should have passed away so prematurely and he is praying for him most ardently.

Shoghi Effendi tells me to add, that in connection with your good health, the thing that he feels certain will most strengthen and assure it, is for you to strive in every way to serve the Cause increasingly. Therein lies your greatest protection and happiness and he feels you are well qualified for such service.

I send you my devoted and tenderest love and assure you that both the Guardian and I are well. Ever your most devoted daughter,
Rúḥíyyih

I forgot to say how proud and happy I am to be able to answer you on behalf of our beloved Shoghi Effendi!

And in the handwriting of Shoghi Effendi:

Dear and precious co-worker:
Your letter reflecting so clearly the beauty & serenity of your spirit, which I have come to admire during your visit to Haifa, has deeply touched me. I deeply sympathize with you in your great loss, & I feel that any service you & dear Mrs. Maxwell will be able to render the Faith will directly & effectively contribute to the progress & happiness of the soul of Mr. Bolles. I long to hear of fresh evidences of your renewed efforts in the service of so precious a Cause, & will continue to pray for your guidance, good health & spiritual advancement.
Your true brother, Shoghi

Rúḥíyyih Khánum's letter of condolence to her mother followed:

Shoghi Effendi was deeply touched by the depths of your love for and devotion to him as shown in your letter to him of July 25th.

He realizes how much the loss of your only and dear brother means to you, as well as to his family, and he has felt very badly that Uncle Randolph should have passed away so prematurely and under such tragic and sad circumstances, all the details of which he read in your long letter to me.

He wants me to assure you again of his prayers for my uncle's eternal felicity, as conveyed to you in his cablegram, and he feels sure that the work that Unkie did for the Cause, in such a good spirit and so painstakingly, in translating the footnotes of Nabil's narrative, will have a powerful effect on the progress of his soul in the next world.

The Guardian very much regrets the fact he did not meet Uncle Randolph, and he says he is sure he would have liked him very much! . . .

You should be greatly consoled by the Master's words to you and the knowledge that Shoghi Effendi is offering his ardent and potent prayers for your brother . . . The goodness of my Uncle, his many kind deeds, as I have already written Aunt Jeanne in reply to his letter to the Guardian, will prove a powerful factor in his spiritual unfoldment.

And in the handwriting of Shoghi Effendi:

> I deeply sympathize with you in your severe & sudden loss, & am truly touched by the sentiments so nobly conveyed & so tenderly expressed in both your cable & letter to me. I have felt the spirit of your dear brother draw closer to the mighty spirit of our Beloved, & feel certain that he is now basking in the sunshine of His love & care . . . Mary was deeply moved, but shows a radiant spirit, so indicative of the depth & purity of her faith. You should therefore feel assured, thankful & happy. My prayers for you, for him & for her will continue to be offered to the Threshold of Bahá'u'lláh. Take good care of your health & whenever you feel strong enough, redouble your efforts in the teaching field for which you are eminently suited.
> Your true & grateful brother, Shoghi

That was the last exchange before the outbreak of World War II. Three weeks later, on 11 September soon after Hitler's troops marched over the Polish border, Amatu'l-Bahá sent the following cable to her father:

> RETURNED HAIFA WELL RECEIVED CABLE GREATLY RELIEVED ADDRESS ALL CABLES CARE SHOGHI EFFENDI CLOSE CONSTANT LOVE RUHIYYIH RABBANI

* * *

During the first unreal weeks of war, May's thoughts and prayers were doubtless trained night and day on those nearest and dearest to her heart. She must have been immensely relieved when she received Rúḥíyyih Khánum's letter dated 24 September 1939, written on behalf of the Guardian:

> My dearest Mother:
> I am so happy that Shoghi Effendi has given me the pleasure of answering your letters to him dated the 1st and the 5th of September.
> He not only was pleased to receive the news you sent him . . . and to notice how vigilant you are in the service of our beloved Bahá'í Faith, but above all to see the wonderful spirit both you and Daddy are showing at this time of unforeseen separation and strain. Indeed he told me he is proud of you both and feels you are demonstrating your worthiness to be now so closely bound to the Guardian of our Faith.
> He was also happy to learn – from my letters – that you are both well and that you have met with such a true Bahá'í faith and spirit the shock and sorrow of your brother's sudden death. All these things show how you are progressing and growing ever closer to the beloved Master's presence.
> There is nothing you could do at this time that would be of greater service than to teach this Cause and also help deepen the faith of the Bahá'ís themselves. He is very happy that Daddy has taken his place at your side in this work.

And in Shoghi Effendi's handwriting:

> Dear and valued co-worker:
> The spirit you have manifested since the present conflict has begun, your confidence, your spirit, serenity & courage are indeed highly praiseworthy, & reveal the quality of your devotion to the Cause you adore & serve so well. I wish to assure you that Mary is in the stronghold of God's protection, is markedly progressing every day, is pursuing happily & serenely her work, & will I trust become increasingly capable of fulfilling her great tasks in the service of the Faith. These thoughts should cheer, strengthen & reassure you as well as her dear father, whose spirit of sacrifice in these days of

physical yet temporary separation I truly & increasingly admire. May He enable you both to render such services in these days of world turmoil as to enhance the position you have acquired through your relationship to His holy Household.

Your true & grateful brother, Shoghi

As the nations of the world found themselves increasingly embroiled in the horrors of the war, May experienced another personal loss: the death of her incomparable friend, Martha Root. Her love and admiration for Martha had lasted all through the thirties but its depth and sincerity was particularly evident from their correspondence during Martha's last weeks and days of illness, in Honolulu. On 22 August Katherine Baldwin, the faithful and radiant soul who took care of Martha Root at the end of her life, wrote to May after receiving news of her brother's death:

> What a comforting message from our beloved Guardian in speaking of your dear Brother: 'he is with the Master'. Your letter impressed me particularly because I realize how deeply torn is your human heart just now, but yet you hardly mentioned the fact. A true example, dearest, of your faith in Bahá'u'lláh! . . . Dear Martha is slowly losing ground. Her pain is kept pretty much under control I am happy to report.

On 7 September she wrote to May again:

> This morning I read your article in 'The Bahá'í World' on: 'A Brief Account of Thomas Breakwell' – it is so gloriously written that I have to tell you immediately. You have a rare quality of expression, which your beloved Daughter has inherited . . . Tonight I go to Honolulu so until the end will now be with our precious Martha. How I rejoice that I can be with her again so soon!

Three weeks later Martha Root winged her flight to the Abhá realm and joined her beloved Master. On 3 October Katherine wrote May:

> Flowers, roses, I ordered for Martha as soon as your letter came (jasmine I could not get) and she enjoyed them although she was

very ill. Two days afterwards a very beautiful letter I received from Rúḥíyyih Khánum asked me also to place flowers in Martha's room. I think Martha understood when I told her during a short conscious moment that the roses were from her because she smiled faintly, and then muttered something I could not understand. This was the day before she passed away ... Anyway your flowers and Rúḥíyyih Khánum's were the last she received, and hers were still fresh in Martha's room when she passed on. I thought this very significant ... I am enclosing a dainty handkerchief which your beloved daughter sent to our precious Martha on her birthday – it is right you should have this handkerchief ... Also Rúḥíyyih Khánum's letter to Martha I am enclosing – this, too, is your right.

When Helen Jones wrote to May in December of that same year, she described Martha Root's resting-place:

I am sure others have told you what a beautiful spot this shrine is in – flowering trees all around as well as other big trees, and the quiet and peace of Holy Ground. We all feel that it's a <u>wonderful</u> privilege to have her shrine here!

After the passing of May's brother and of Martha, Johanna Schubarth wrote to May from Norway:

My dear little spiritual mother – First my warmest sympathy with the passing of your dear brother; Mrs. Bolles wrote me about it; I felt so sorry for her and all of you. She wrote how glorious you are and getting ever more so. You were always perfect to me ... And now being the mother-in-law of our beloved Guardian I almost feel I am much too humble to approach you. But you were always so kind to everybody I do not think you could become proud about anything. ... Please do give my tender love to Rúḥíyyih Khánum, she has a big place in my heart. What a loss that dear self-sacrificing Martha has left us. I can hardly believe it, hoped always she would come to Norway again. I am enclosing the translation of my little article about her.

Perhaps the most painful of May's losses that year was a disappearance rather than a death. She had done all she could to keep in touch with her European friends during the relentless slide to chaos after the notorious Munich Agreement in March 1938, but once World War II imposed its terrible barrier between them, connections were tragically lost. One of the precious souls engulfed in the holocaust that followed was Lidia Zamenhof. The daughter of the Jewish founder of the Esperanto Movement and an ardent Bahá'í, she had first met May in France and had been privileged to do so again at the 1938 Convention in Wilmette, Illinois. This was where Mrs Maxwell shared her 'Haifa Notes' in public for the first time, and this was where she quoted one of the 'free and spontaneous utterances' of Shoghi Effendi to the effect that the Bahá'ís should adopt Esperanto at the present time as a universal language, even if only a temporary one. In the silence that ensued in the Convention hall at that moment, Lidia's heart must have been welded to May's forever. As she wrote to a friend some time later:

> I am very glad that you had the great spiritual joy which being with May Maxwell always gives . . . One feels closer to the Master when one is with her.

When Lidia was refused a visa extension and forced to leave the United States in the fall of 1938, May offered her refuge in Montreal if only she might be allowed by the Immigration Authorities to enter Canada. But the doors were closed against her there as well. So her last hope was Haifa. She wrote to the Guardian, asking if she might pass through Palestine on her way back to Poland, but by a strange twist of fate, her request had coincided with fresh outbreaks of violence in Palestine, when every Jew entering the country had become an excuse for another attack by the Arabs. The 1st Battalion Worcestershire Regiment had arrived at the port of Haifa on 26 September to try to stop the further influx of Jews, and the Guardian was obliged to dissuade her from coming. His cable, 'DANGEROUS SITUATION IN PALESTINE NECESSITATES POSTPONEMENT', meant that the doors of pilgrimage were closed to her too.

Lidia had no choice but to go on. There cannot have been many passengers travelling back to Poland that ominous winter before the outbreak of World War II, and her letter to May, dated 26 April 1939, was probably the last she wrote to Mrs Maxwell, or was able to send to her from Warsaw, for when the German army invaded that September, her fate was sealed:

> My dearly beloved May!
>
> A few weeks ago your letter came and today I received the precious Notes, for which I can never thank you enough, those Notes loaded with dynamic power. I have these days very much to do, but I feel that I shall put other things aside for awhile and plunge into these Notes!
>
> I have finished the Polish translation of Dr. Esslemont's book which is ready for printing. I wrote to the Guardian asking him what I should translate next and into which language. Meantime I felt moved to translate the 'Hidden Words' into Polish and as I knew that the Guardian's answer could not reach me soon I began this work hoping it would be done and I would be ready for another work when the Guardian's letter comes. I was really finishing the typing when I received the Guardian's letter. Now, imagine how surprised and happy I was when I read that what Shoghi Effendi wished me to do next was exactly to translate the 'Hidden Words' into Polish! It is done . . .
>
> I do not expect to go abroad soon – probably not before the War. I am so happy I could spend those precious months in America; it gave me so much inspiration! I long to see you again – at this moment I see you again as I saw you for the last time – on the platform of Portsmouth station – but really there is a bond between us which no distance and time can break. And I shall for ever consider this bond as one of my greatest treasures.
>
>   Yours ever affectionately, Lidia

Six months later, on 11 November 1939, Della Quinlan sent an urgent letter to May by special delivery, informing her of an article that had appeared about Lidia Zamenhof in a Detroit edition of the *Chicago Jewish Forward* dated 5 November:

> Vilna, Nov. 5th (ITA) Lidia Zamenhof the daughter of the famous Bialystok Hebrew scholar, Dr. Ludovik Zamenhof, who was the father of Esperanto, has been arrested by the Nazis in Warsaw.

After giving her the dreaded news, Della asked May whether she should cable Shoghi Effendi about it, or leave the National Spiritual Assembly to do this: 'in case it is not done', she adds, 'I feel confident that you really know if he would wish to know this as soon as possible.' We do not know what May did with this distressing news. But she would have known what it implied.

Ironically enough, Lidia was to outlive May by two years, in the trapped horrors of the Warsaw Ghetto; she somehow lived on in those appalling conditions, still managing to teach the Faith, until the orders came to evacuate the place in the summer of 1942. At that point, this brilliant woman who had immortalized the Polish language with the words of Bahá'u'lláh, was herded, together with thousands of other Polish Jews, into the death camp of Treblinka. Although Shoghi Effendi did not designate her a martyr after her death, he ordered memorial services for her, described her as 'dauntless', and praised her 'tenacity, modesty and unwavering devotion'. May was no longer alive to hear his accolades, but she had already grieved her loss.

* * *

On 3 October 1939 May Maxwell wrote to her daughter the following letter, which fortunately did reach her despite the dire circumstances:

My dearest one –

I am going to experiment – no words from you now in 4 weeks and by the same token you may have also no words from me – although your cable of some ten or 12 days ago says that you received the medicine & my letter. I have written you regularly – twice a week – so now I have an idea – I am mailing this today from Montreal – & shall send a similar letter by the next clipper from New York, through Philip – because it may be that Canadian mails are harder to get through.

Now for news – oh! God – how I long for a breath of news from you, my own dear Mary! Yet strangely I feel your beloved spirit & presence as never before – by day & night you are unspeakably near – & Daddy feels it too – & you must find us in the same incomparable bond – my darling – because God is so Merciful!

The death of Martha Root was a profound experience for me. I loved her. I adored her as a Saint – & I believe that her rising to that infinite world will gradually affect all our lives – for she is – in this human world – the peak of our teaching powers and aspirations – & she will no doubt have great powers of intercession . . .

Yesterday Rev. Este came to see me. Mrs. Roddick has awakened him spiritually once more & he wants me to work with him in his church – to speak & to supply him with certain Bahá'í Utterances & teachings which he can both quote & also incorporate as ideas in his sermons. Of course as usual he spoke with deep devotion & reverence of you – and he told me of a Mr. Douglas who said to him: 'If you wish to meet a group of very cultured – modern – liberal & inspiring people go to the Bahá'ís at the home of Mr. & Mrs. Maxwell on Pine Ave! Years ago I met their most beautiful and gifted daughter. I asked her a question about Christianity – & she raised her lovely hands in protest & said, "Oh you must ask my Mother – she is a wonderful teacher, she can answer your question!" What a bond there is between that daughter & her mother – I felt it at once – they are wonderful people these Bahá'ís!'

I always find the reassuring traces of your dear and beautiful self – of your worth & your spirit. What a joy & comfort you are to me, the very light of my life & in this new class I have started last Sunday – about 25 people! – I felt your influence so powerfully as I spoke – & remembered the beloved Guardian's words in a recent letter to me that my 'work is complementary to yours'! & ever since I grasped such a wonderful bounty my teaching work has greatly increased & also deepened. Everyone feels that I answer questions well – & this is so encouraging. I took for my first class the great universal Proofs of the Prophets & of Divine Revelation, which the Master told me always to preserve & teach – there was a great spiritual power – & at the next class I shall take a deeper, wider step in relation to the power & effect of the Word of God thro the Ages, also the great veils & superstitions which prevent people from recognizing the Messengers of God. I am dealing with it scientifically & historically as well as spiritually . . .

In closing I hold you – as I do every night & morning – close to my yearning heart. Give my adoring love to our beloved & my heart & soul & kisses to you my very own.

Mother

Barely three weeks later, on 24 October, May wrote to the beloved Guardian again:

> My beloved – my adored Guardian!
> Of all the merciful and heavenly Epistles you have addressed to me, the one which came yesterday has brought the deepest joy, the most vital spirit and greatest detachment to my soul. You have brought a burning hope and reassurance of the possibility of ultimate attainment for which I can find no words of humble gratitude and thankfulness. I have pressed your sacred message to my lips and to my heart, fervently praying that you will burn away all impurity of self and make me clean and sanctified – a white flame – a bright light to guide the wayfarers, a deep spiritual leaven to the souls, to gather the jewels for which you are so patiently – so longingly – waiting! You have already endued me with a new potency and penetrative utterance through my divine relationship to you! And I yearn and pray for an ever-widening field of effort, service & sacrifice!
> Sutherland also is under your sway – a new mellowness and peace – an absence of financial care and anxiety even under unfavorable present conditions – a new trust and deep faith, make his influence felt by all – and he is so dearly loved in this community!
> I humbly trust that we may draw ever closer to one another in heart and spirit, and be a strength and refuge for the believers at all times.
> . . . I know one on this earth who can forever banish these shadows – it is Shoghi Effendi!

Proximity in the realm of the spirit became May's goal in the last year of her life. It was the only way of enduring physical separation, the only means of achieving true reunion with her daughter. Besides, she was keenly aware, during the first months of the war, of the millions of people in the world who were being ripped from their homes, stripped of their dignities, shorn of their rights, and sent to their deaths. What right had she to complain of being separated from her daughter when separation in its most violent form had become the veritable scourge of the age. No one was spared and May did not ask to be. What she prayed for was to achieve detachment from the person dearest to her in the world, after the Guardian. And world events conspired to help her achieve it. With the outbreak of World War II, she could depend on no other means of communication but that which existed in the realm of the spirit.

And she refined it to an art. After her passing, Rúḥíyyih Khánum wrote to the Baha'ís in Philadelphia about this ability she had acquired, to let go:

> Mother always used to quote to me that poem . . .: 'what we grasp is ours never, what we lose we gain forever . . .' She believed this profoundly and acted upon it. She always gave up in the path of God and surely she received a reward undreamed of! It seems to me this is a great spiritual law which we all can and must learn. Not an artificial thing of practicing a kind of self-righteous asceticism, but being sincerely willing to give up anything we have, comfort, home, family, even life, to the Will of God, <u>if necessary</u>! Mother enjoyed everything in life a hundred per cent! Her friends, her family, nature, beauty – everything. But she was not attached to any of them!

On 31 October 1939 May wrote the following beautiful words to Rúḥíyyih Khánum. What they make clear is that when she did let go, and was not anguished by separation, the rewards were infinite, and measured in waves of gratitude which overwhelmed her:

> . . . it is beyond belief the goodness and bounty of God to our family – our marriage (Daddy's and mine), our lovely home from which the Cause has flowed in a steady stream for years, then our adored and most gifted child, the Master's perfect gift – and the consummation of all His Infinite Bounties in your lovely sacred union – the most blessed of all women of your generation. It is in His Room where I am resting (and I trust it will make you happy to have me rest whenever I need it, for I am <u>very</u> well, only tired) that 'Abdu'l-Bahá said to me: 'God has perfected all His Bounties in you!' You are that supreme bounty whom I love and adore – only He and the Guardian know.

There is something remarkably intimate in this scene: this glimpse of May – resting in the room of 'Abdu'l-Bahá in Montreal, with her heart overflowing with thankfulness for her lovely home, her happy marriage, and above all her daughter.

Her ability to transcend physical contingency was remarkable. May was profoundly conscious of things mystic. The membrane between the rational and the spiritual worlds was permeable to her; it did not need translation. From her early youth when she had dreamed dreams and seen visions of light; from her first encounter with 'Abdu'l-Bahá when she had felt His power wash over her like a wave of searing light; from the moment He had told her to sit further off from Him, so that she would not be too overwhelmed by this intense world of light, May Maxwell was conscious that she was moving on the frontiers of other realms.

Years before, in a letter she had written to her husband on 9 February 1934 from California, she spoke of her absolute certitude in the power of communication that could *'rise above words and letters and transcend the murmur of syllables and sounds'*:[5]

> We thought air mail was such a wonder but with a Continent between us, it seems like slow freight and I suppose in the future the only rapid transit will be through the ether when we can have full and complete communication with each other in heart and thought and spirit. You know the Master wrote me after the war that this kind of communication, independent of pen and paper had been established by me with Him during the last years of separation and more and more I am finding this bond with you and Mary, something that makes us independent of this crazy world and which we may need to put into full operation in the future.

In this same letter she also expressed her sadness and her disappointment that so few Bahá'ís seemed conscious of the laws governing the world of the spirit:

> I am more and more surprised to find how few Bahá'ís 'catch on' to these highly spiritual laws, and night before last we had a Memorial Meeting at the Unity Feast for dear Agnes Parsons and they very graciously asked me, as her personal friend, to read the Prayer for the Departed and pay her a tribute, which I did from the bottom

---

5 'Abdu'l-Bahá, *Bahá'í Prayers*, pp. 70–71.

of my heart. In the course of my brief statement I closed with the little story of her praying in the Temple two years ago at night all alone, and hearing light footsteps approaching her she turned and saw a little Negro boy 12 or 13 standing looking at her, and she said, 'Why, little boy, where did you come from?' and he replied, 'Why, lady, I wanted to climb to the very top and I went higher and higher but it was too high for me all alone and I got dizzy, so I <u>came to you</u>!' All the beauty, all the mysticism of her relationship to the Negro race, the imperishable foundation she has laid in this country through her amity conferences, which the Master inaugurated through her, was summed up in that little story, and <u>it went right over their heads</u>.

May Maxwell had very early on recognized that the exquisite Order which Shoghi Effendi was building, stone by individual stone, and arch by institutional arch, had been bequeathed to the Bahá'ís by none other than 'Abdu'l-Bahá Himself in His Will and Testament, and was intended to house the very spirit of the Revelation of Bahá'u'lláh. She knew that for this mighty edifice to be effective, it would have to enshrine the verities that the Master so palpably manifested in His life. In this same letter of 9 February 1934 written ten years after she had returned from her third pilgrimage, during which time she had imbibed with such ardour the lessons that Shoghi Effendi had taught her at his table, she deplored the absence of spirituality in the administrative affairs of the Bahá'í community:

> It is a pity that the technical details of administration, all of which are only a <u>means to an end</u> have absorbed the attention of the Bahá'ís almost to the exclusion of the deeper spiritual significance of a movement teeming with beauty, poetry and reality. It takes artists like you to appreciate these deeper values . . .

In her late years, she did her utmost to emphasize the link between the Administrative Order and the Master Himself. Writing to Juliet Thompson on 2 August 1938 from Montreal, for example, she suggested that there was a great need in the Bahá'í community to study the Will and Testament of 'Abdu'l-Bahá in order to grasp the rank of Shoghi Effendi. Her letter seems to be hinting to Juliet that there was as much ignorance about the Guardian in their own times as there had been about the station of 'Abdu'l-Bahá in earlier days.

> The way Bahá'u'lláh works is so profoundly mysterious as you and I of the early days know so well. How the Master knew that there were only a few in America who 'knew Him' as He told Jenabe Fazel, He could count them on His fingers and those who did not realize His Station (as they used to call it) lowered Him to the rank of an Apostle! Then He wrote Himself to America, uniting all shades of faith and opinion into one, at the lowest point. 'I am 'Abdu'l-Bahá, nothing more!' . . . We, many of us, became veiled to the holy mystic and exalted Centre of the Covenant manifest in the adored 'Abdu'l-Bahá. So in New York He martyred Himself for the sake of the Faith, for the believers by declaring who He was! and by circulating the Tablet of the Branch.

To have recognized the significance of the Faith for mankind but have missed its fundamentally spiritual message and its 'deeper values', was one kind of tragedy. But to have seen the ink of light on the tablet of the spirit and not fully grasped the name that was inscribed there, was another, in May's opinion. In later years, when writing about one of her dearest friends, 'a brilliant scientific woman, Dr. Isabel Boger-Shattuck', who had been her homeopathic doctor for many years, she confided to Leah Graham that she felt the reason for her friend's recent 'breakdown' was that

> . . . she came too close to the light without fully embracing it . . . it has grieved me very much and I feel that she needs more than anything in life to be awakened, stirred and resuscitated by the power of the Guardianship . . .

The Guardian's emphasis on the need for a deep study of the Writings and 'the extreme importance of penetrating the surface, of absorbing the inner significances and attaining a greater knowledge of the deeper teachings', as she wrote David Hofman on 5 September 1938, had attuned May to the proximity of the spiritual world. She saw beyond the surface of things. Eight years before, when she was writing to her daughter from New York, on 3 December 1930, May had evoked the importance of the Hidden Words as a means, as a key to unlock the door of 'the spiritual kingdom of Bahá'u'lláh'.

This year, as a delegate at what was to be her last National Convention, in Evanston in April 1939, at the gathering that was held in the Temple to celebrate the Declaration of the Báb, she read a prayer which seemed to hark from that very kingdom. It was, as Agnes Alexander averred in her 'Tribute to May Maxwell', as if she were already in another world:

> In the spring of 1939 I spent several weeks with May in Evanston where we enjoyed sunlit hours of companionship. In Inter-racial work she had supreme courage. Not only did she adhere to the Master's words regarding the complete union of the colored and white race but in her life and actions she lived His behests. One morning I was present when she said, 'Consciousness of race is a sign of absence of culture. Bahá'u'lláh has ushered us into a new world. He has inoculated us with a new virus. The Master never said we must be careful and cautious. He said if we didn't unite, the Negro race would rise up. The world is sunk in ignorance. We are sunk in the sea of imagination.' When I said to May afterwards that it had been a wonderful morning, she asked, 'What did I say?' She was a pure channel used by God's hands.
>
> During those weeks in Evanston, though physically unable to attend meetings, May took deepest interest in the racial work which she called 'the most essential work'. Several times I was privileged to accompany her to the House of Worship to pray; how joyous she was when she found she could climb the stairway! When she was absorbed in prayer I felt the invisible connection between her heart and the Center of the Faith, as though space was obliterated and the ideal nearness attained . . .
>
> The last noon with May in Evanston in June 1939, a little boy sitting near us came and threw his arms around her neck and kissed her several times. Then a second time he came and repeated it. May said to me, 'This is something mystic.' She did not reciprocate his caresses as she did not wish his mother to feel jealous. May then told me that the day before she had heard the mother nagging the boy and suggested that children did not like always to be with grown people, and that sometimes we should play with them. The little boy had felt May's mother love without words . . .

Rúḥíyyih Khánum was well aware of her mother's susceptibilities in this regard. She knew how May was able to send and to receive messages of love, not only without words but also across space and time. She had been receiving letters from her for years in which her mother spoke of seeing her standing visibly, before her, of dreaming of her palpably close, of hearing her voice clear as a bell in her ears. She was accustomed to her mother's receptiveness to the world of the spirit. Nine years before, when her mother had been in New York struggling with the crisis of Covenant-breaking caused by Ahmad Sohrab, Mrs Maxwell had written to her, saying:

> A few days ago, Mary dear, I had a strange experience, certain new, profound and basic truths and thoughts took possession of my brain and they were so out of proportion to my actual condition and state of health that for almost 24 hours my head felt like a pulp, but since then I have felt like a new being, and I realize the brain also is just a tool which the majority of us use perhaps twenty or thirty percent, especially using only certain parts and lobes but not allowing the thought forces to rush in and make the whole brain alive and active.
>
> Now we will leave these subjects for awhile, but it is a joy to share them with you, and the last time we spoke over the telephone (was it last night?), I felt and saw your very soul, your clarity and purity, a certain new simplicity and absence of self-consciousness you have attained, an unveiled and lovely study. Mary, I cannot tell you what I saw and felt because spiritual things cannot be described in words and are illusive and ineffable but so potent and penetrating that they pierce every barrier of time and space, all of the grades of the gross materials of the outer universe.

A few years later, when she was travelling in California in January 1934, May had written an undated note to her daughter, expressing the most intense empathy:

> Mary my own beloved –
> I have just had the deepest most sacred and intimate prayer for you, who are a part of my being, who are the finer essence of me, yet my own little girl! . . . You must know – you must feel, my precious, that this love of mine for you is His love, the mystery and fire of the

> Beloved shining thro the veil of your Mother! I have known and felt all that you have suffered – the pangs of your separation – of your life-long ardent love and devotion . . .! I have been with you day and night, my own. I have prayed your prayers with you, wept your tears! and I have felt and known much more than this which cannot be written or spoken but which you know – you, the mystery of whose life and destiny lies enshrined in your purest soul – in that heart of fire and dew. I had to write this . . .
>
> Let nothing weigh on your tender heart my darling – you are a pure channel for the living creative forces of Bahá'u'lláh – so you must be <u>very happy</u>, even when you suffer! . . . Mary – I long with all my heart & soul to clasp you in my arms, to rest your dear lovely head on my heart & bring you the deep comfort & peace you have always brought me!

During the same period, barely one week after writing to her daughter about her desire for her 'cloudless joy' on Naw-Rúz, May wrote again, on 27 March, to say:

> The day you wrote me this letter I received today . . . I had a strange experience. I was lying on my bed in a relaxed and receptive mood, feeling very close to the Beloved of our hearts, when I suddenly saw you in the inner world in such dazzling radiance and beauty, yet such girlish purity and sweetness as I cannot describe, and you just laid your lovely face for a moment against my heart and it was like an embrace from God, the most divine and mystical experience that I have ever had . . .

A few months later, on 15 June 1934, she wrote her another letter expressing the same certitude of communion with her:

> I long unspeakably to spend hours and days with you and catch up on everything, but perhaps we shall find that we have been journeying deeper [in] divine ways and shall meet on a plane of vision and understanding in which words play so small a part.

In early February 1939, Rúḥíyyih <u>Kh</u>ánum sent a cable to her mother inquiring about her well-being. From May's reply dated 9 February she learned that her cable had itself been the source of that well-being:

> At last I am in New York and nothing could have moved me out of Montreal except your cablegram. Of course the Guardian is the overshadowing power in all my life, but you are my direct guiding influence, almost like an emanation of his sacred influence flowing through you to me, and in a strange way I believe to all the West... You must have had some deep intuition in cabling me as you did because it was literally a life rope thrown out at that time... Please thank the Guardian from the depths of my heart for his message of love which quickens, strengthens and subdues my whole being to his sacred will, and give him my love and longing. With deepest tender love to you, & 1000 kisses! Ever your own,
>
> Mother

The intuitions shared by mother and daughter were clearly not of this world. At the end of that year, on 19 December, Rúḥíyyih Khánum felt moved to tell her mother about a conversation she had had with the Guardian. He had been speaking to her about a text of the Master related to the Old Testament prophets and to Zoroaster, which describes the communion of minds in the realm of the spirit. She knew that her mother would be fascinated by the 'mystic' faculty he had described:

> In an untranslated Tablet the Master says that Zoroaster came to Palestine and conversed with the Hebrew Prophets! Isn't that extraordinary? The Guardian told me. Shoghi Effendi sends you his dearest love, always, he says! And I hug and kiss you tenderly – ever your adoring Mary (Rúḥíyyih Rabbani)

One has the impression that Mrs Maxwell conversed not only with her daughter but above all with her Beloved in this way. In the following letter which Jessie Revell wrote to Rúḥíyyih Khánum in 1949 about her last encounters with May Maxwell ten years before, we seem to see the portrait of a soul poised for flight:

> In December 1939 a Teaching conference was held at the Bahá'í Centre in New York City. I attended it and Marzieh Khan was to close the evening session with a chant. In order not to miss my train

back to Philadelphia, I decided not to wait for the closing prayer and was on my way down the aisle of the Centre when at the end of the room, your Mother said as I neared her, 'Jessie Revell, where are you going?' I said, 'I am getting a train back to Philadelphia and I can't wait for the closing Chant or I will miss it.' Your Mother said: 'You are going to stay with me tonight; sit down.' I sat down and told your Mother that if I did that I would have to call Mother on the phone because I promised to return. She said, that will be alright, there is a phone at the Hotel. So I waited until the end of the meeting and then your Mother took me to a phone and after talking with my Mother, we went to your Mother's room . . .

We had a never-to-be-forgotten visit, talking about mostly spiritual things, and she telling me about her precious Rúḥíyyih and the Beloved Guardian – time seemed to be erased that night – I seemed to be in Heaven. Among other things, I said to her, 'Why don't you come to Philadelphia sometime, I am sure the friends would love to have you come and speak'; she said: 'I will if you will invite me'; I replied: 'You are invited' – then she said Shoghi Effendi had told her that Mr. Maxwell should travel around and speak for the Faith also, and I answered by telling her that he surely was invited too. That was in December 1939.

Your Mother surely was an <u>American</u> Dawn-Breaker and I cannot help but feel that at the time of her visit to us [in Philadelphia], Jan. 5, 1940, she knew she was soon to sacrifice her life and win all those prizes which our Beloved Guardian named in His cablegram.

Around the first of January 1940, your dear Mother telephoned from Washington, DC. She said that she was celebrating the birthday of Mason Remey in Washington and could come to Philadelphia the following, I think Friday, could I arrange a meeting, and I of course said, 'Yes'. There was very little time to notify the friends, but about 19 came out and that was a night never to be forgotten. She spoke so beautifully and so did Mr. Maxwell and after the meeting the friends gathered around her and she told of your holy wedding. Again it seemed like we were in Heaven. She was just all spirit, so ethereal and beautiful . . . She and your father stayed at the Benjamin Franklin Hotel, and before we parted that night your mother invited me to have lunch with her the next day at the Hotel. It was a cold snowy day and she suggested that I take a taxi; we had another heavenly visit, during which she seemed to want to shower me with gifts, putting a string of baubles around my neck, and as she did it, she said, 'Rúhíyyih Khánum would love these' – it seemed almost as if she were putting them around your neck instead of mine. She gave me American Beauty Roses to take to my Mother and a pin for Ethel – she did not seem at all to be in this world . . .

After she returned to New York, we three [Jessie, Ethel and their mother] wrote her a letter of appreciation of the visit and then I had that most beautiful letter of Jan. 7, 1940 where she speaks of the co-mingling of that holy essence with which the Beloved had imbued those who know and adore Him – and of this celestial potency emanating from the believers being the first and greatest teaching medium by which hearts and lives are changed, by which the seeker is led to the Ocean of the Word of God, and then she said: 'We know only too well that this potency is obtained at a great price – the sacrifice of all else save God.' Your beloved Mother truly made this sacrifice and I felt that so much during that last visit with her . . .

During that last visit she seemed to sense and be very conscious of a separation from the world and nearness to God, it seemed to be like a fragrance from her that I could almost inhale. I can hardly write about it, because it was such a spiritual perception that I had at that time.

* * *

On 12 December 1939 May wrote a delightful letter to David Hofman, which starts with praise for his achievements and ends with a joke at her own expense:

> I have just been reading the book of which you wrote me many months ago, Townshend's 'Heart of the Gospel', and I agree with you that it will have a profound influence in many Christian circles. It is so absolutely real, so denuded of all pretense, artifice and dogma that have grown up like a thick wall around the very heart of Christianity. It is sublime in its penetrative depths and utter simplicity. Speaking of 'sublime', it reminds me of an adorable little story Rúhíyyih Khánum wrote me about the Guardian, so revealing of his humanness and delightful sense of humour. He was at his desk one

day and remarked, 'Everyone has some word which is, as it were, the key to their temperament or aspirations. Your Mother's word is "sublime", sublime, sublime! On this word she rises higher and higher until she evaporates, and – then returns to earth!'

Towards the end of 1939, May's heart was aflame with the desire to do some special service to the Cause. It is extraordinary to consider what she felt was expected of her, not to mention what she expected of herself. When one reads about the travel-teaching trips that the National Teaching Committee alone hoped she would undertake across Canada, at the age of sixty-nine, it is difficult to overestimate how much she gave of herself. On 24 October she received a letter from Leroy Ioas, the Chairman of that Committee:

> Stanley and Mariette Bolton were quite enthusiastic when they left here for Australia, about their visit in Montreal, and were very happy to have been able to have made your acquaintance. Mariette was very happy when I told her you planned to do some teaching work in Quebec this Fall and Winter if possible, as her sister displayed some interest . . . The Teaching Committee has been wondering likewise, if your plans could permit you to do this teaching work in Quebec, as we discussed at the Convention, and subsequent correspondence seemed to indicate might be possible. Word coming from other parts of Canada indicates the public is attracted and responding as never before. This seems particularly true of Toronto, Winnipeg, and the territory around Vancouver.

But even this seemed not enough to May. As her daughter had stated, she longed to do more, give more of herself, expend even more of her material means and physical energies for the Cause; she wanted to express in some special way her love and gratitude to the beloved Guardian for the honour he had bestowed on their family. It was at the height of the Seven Year Plan, and the American community was being taxed to the utmost to fulfil the goals, particularly in South America. At this time May wrote to Rúḥíyyih Khánum and asked if Shoghi Effendi would approve of her going to Argentina for a period of some months. The following cable from Rúḥíyyih Khánum, dated 13 December 1939, contained his answer:

LATE YEARS 1937–1940

GUARDIAN HEARTILY APPROVES WINTER VISIT BUENOSAIRES
PROVIDING DADDY AND PHYSICIAN CONSENT DEAREST LOVE
BOTH RUHIYYIH RABBANI

For the rest of the month of December and during the holidays in early January, May worked to obtain the consent of both her husband and her physician, as Shoghi Effendi had instructed. She had been joined by Sutherland on her travels in New York, in Englewood, New Jersey, in Washington DC, and finally in Philadelphia. By the end of this long trip she had succeeded in fulfilling Shoghi Effendi's wishes, albeit with some resistance, and was finally ready to go. On the 15th and the 17th of January, she wrote two very touching letters from the Barbizon Plaza Hotel in New York City to her dear husband, who had by then returned to Montreal. She told him that she was going down to 'Cooks to make the final arrangements for Cabin 130 in the First Class' and asked him to send her the papers to help her acquire visas for certain countries in South America. Then, in spite of herself, she made a curious confession:

> You cannot imagine how hard it is for me to take this trip to South America; no wonder the French philosopher and scientist Bergson described the resistance of the atoms, of the whole natural world, to the penetration of a higher force, and I sometimes feel the very atoms of my body, like some dead opaque substance, resisting the penetration of the spirit, and the struggle lays me low.

She also added:

> I am returning herewith this heavenly letter from our child, one of her truly beautiful letters and which she was inspired to write to her Daddy. I often think that living together in one home (of which she speaks so tenderly) in lives like ours, so mutually congenial, so devoted to each other in the common Cause of Bahá'u'lláh, of art, of beauty, and higher human relationships, has laid such a strong and deep foundation in our lives that separation only serves to weld us closer together. What a blessed comfort that she has had this to cling to and has grown closer to us both, each in our individual relationship to her, through whatever she has had to endure the past

few years. Thank you so much, darling, for sharing this letter with me, which brought me a new strength just when I needed it most.

In that 'heavenly letter', dated 22 December 1939, Rúḥíyyih Khánum had written to her father:

> Mother wrote she wanted to go to Buenos Aires . . . I don't know if she was seriously considering it or not. But I cabled her the Guardian approves if you and the doctor consented. I know Daddy that this advice was very rough on you! To such an extent that I have written Mother she should not leave you if you would be too lonesome and neglect your health. But this is the way I feel about it. There is no use our doing things half way. I know very well how much you suffer, in spite of the realization of how blessed beyond our least deserving we have been, but you do miss me awfully as I do you. On the other hand we all only live on this earth once and we might as well while we are about it do the very best job we can. I feel I never want to be selfish about you and Mother attaining to your own highest good and so I am willing to have Mother go so infernally far away from me because it would be such a good service for her to render the Cause. You are both none too young as I realize only too well and I feel God will let us be together again after this beastly war is over. So whatever services you both can render to our beloved Faith while the opportunity is there I feel you both should. Do you understand what I mean? Now is the time for such things. Not only for you two but for every Bahá'í, then how much more for you to whom so much has been given? After all we were nothing so extraordinary and now God has raised us up and blessed us so richly that we really must try and prove a little worthy of it!
>
> The Guardian has written a beautiful letter in English about the transference of the remains of the Mother and brother of the Master to Mount Carmel and he is now writing one in Persian. As I am typing in the room next to him every now and then I hear his dear voice raised in chanting as he reads some quotation or composes! He is so sweet Daddy and he has such a hard life and so many blows to bear! He always tells me to send you his love but sometimes in my haste I forget. But you know it is there.

On 21 January May cabled Shoghi Effendi:

> BELOVED ALTHOUGH EXHAUSTED SEVERE WEATHER ASSURED YOUR HEALING MIGHT SUPPORT SAILING WEDNESDAY WITH NIECE CABLING DAUGHTER YEARNING LOVE GRATITUDE MAY MAXWELL

The next day, 22 January, she received an answer:

> PROUD NOBLE RESOLVE PRAYERS ACCOMPANY YOU BOTH SAFEGUARD HEALTH SHOGHI

That same day the Guardian sent a separate cable to Mr Maxwell; he well knew that Sutherland would be carrying the emotional cost of this journey:

> PROFOUNDLY APPRECIATE NOBLE SACRIFICE DEAREST LOVE SHOGHI

Two days later, on 24 January 1940, May Maxwell, accompanied by her niece, Jeanne Negar Bolles, sailed for Buenos Aires, Argentina, on the *S. S. Brazil*. On 29 January Rúḥíyyih Khánum wrote to her, on behalf of the Guardian:

> He wants me to tell you how very happy and pleased he is over your trip to South America. I remember one day about a year ago in speaking of the teaching work the Baháʼís were doing there, the Guardian said it would be very good for you to do work there – and now of your own accord you are doing this! He wants me to tell you not to stay too long away from home. He has no desire that you should make a prolonged visit there, but feels that during the winter the climate there is better for your health and at the same time you are rendering the Cause a wonderful service. Above all Shoghi Effendi wants you to be careful of your health and have that as your first consideration.
>
> Another thing Shoghi Effendi wants me to tell you is that you should concentrate your teaching work in one spot and devote your effort to consolidating it, not dissipate your time and energies over

different places. Also when you leave for home you are to go <u>straight</u> home to America and not stop off at different places! . . .

And in the handwriting of Shoghi Effendi:

> Your spontaneous response to the call of teaching in distant fields, despite the condition of your health, is indeed a further & still more striking evidence of your marvelous devotion to the Cause & your unquenchable enthusiasm for whatever may promote its truest & best interests. My special prayers will accompany & surround you & Jeanne in your highly meritorious enterprise. For your success, your good health & protection, as well as for the welfare of Mr. Maxwell I will supplicate our beloved Master while you are rendering Him such splendid services. Mary is so happy & proud of the spirit you are so powerfully manifesting. She is progressing in every way & speaking Persian fluently. You should be happy, thankful & assured. Affectionately
>
>   Shoghi

On 5 February May sent a cable to her husband from Rio de Janeiro:

> RIO WELL LOVE WRITE COOKS ALSO MARY AIRMAIL MAY MAXWELL

Three days later, on 8 February, she wrote to Mr Maxwell more fully from the Hotel Gloria in Rio de Janeiro, describing her experiences on her arrival there:

> I am so happy that the beloved Guardian cabled you in loving recognition of your great sacrifice in letting me go so far away. I had a strange experience the second night I was here. I was on the terrace with a beautiful stone balustrade overlooking the wide avenue and the palm trees, myriads of stars above, when suddenly I felt and almost saw Mary, she was right beside me, with me in an ethereal world, so real and palpable, and I know she was actually there and I also know it was the very day the Guardian received my cable, because I cabled him the same day I cabled you, and I hope my cable reached you dearest and made you happy . . . if we hear from one another often through the airmail, it will help to make it much easier for us all . . .

Now it is next day. I am at Cooks but the letters you sent me from Mary have not yet come ... Please pray often and in your powerful way for my teaching work – that I may teach some souls here!

It is very interesting to read some of the many notes May wrote to herself at this time. Her practice was to write notes to herself and then meditate on them, so these brief lists served as a ladder for her prayers. The following one was written on the stationery of the Hotel Gloria, Avenida Beira Mar, Rio de Janeiro:

February 15, after being ill in Rio
  Remember at <u>all times</u> Guardian's words to you,
  'Mrs. Maxwell – <u>remember</u> your <u>dignity</u>.' Consider all that this implies.
  First – you are the 'daughter of 'Abdu'l-Bahá'. He told you so.
  Second: The Guardian married your daughter –
  You are his Mother-in-Law – you are now a member of the Holy Family – the Family of God on earth. You must strive day and night to be of His Family in Heaven! by living that way <u>now</u> – there is <u>very little</u> time!
  Meditate on '<u>dignity</u>' every day – then <u>act</u>.
  Do not react to J. or anyone <u>personally</u> – <u>control</u> your speech.
  Do not make flippant, shallow, critical remarks about anyone or anything.
  Be <u>calm</u> – quiet – simple – <u>real</u> and deep.
  Hold to this until you attain it. Cease to be irritable or cross with <u>anyone.</u>
  Do not suddenly exert your will over people – be so quiet and non-resistant that they will <u>feel</u> your will.
  'Safeguard your health'.
  Safeguard your health. [This is written twice.]
  Devote yourself to Leonora.

On another sheet of paper she began a letter to her niece Jeanne which she left unfinished:

My precious Jeanne – I must just tell you how proud I was of you as a Bahá'í this morning, when I saw you subdue and conquer ...

On 18 February 1940 May wrote a report of 'our first meeting in Rio de Janeiro'. It took place at the home of Mr & Mrs Lee Worley on the occasion of Leonora Holsapple's arrival from Bahia, a few days before. With the help of Leonora, May arranged two teas at her hotel, the Gloria, in Rio de Janeiro. In the course of one of these, she extended hospitality to nineteen guests. A fourth meeting was held at the home of Mr and Mrs Lee Worley at this time. May also spoke to the President of the Homeopathic College in Rio.

The last letter which Rúḥíyyih Khánum wrote to May on behalf of the Guardian was dated 23 February 1940 and included, as usual, a postscript from Shoghi Effendi himself. It was addressed c/o Thomas Cook, Buenos Aires, Argentina, South America and arrived after May's passing. It was not opened until long afterwards:

My dearest Mother:

Your letter of February 5th has just been received by our beloved Guardian and he wanted me to answer you at once. He is so pleased over your trip and I might add is proud of you too! Which, of course, makes me supremely happy.

The main thing which he wants you to do I have already written you in my last letter on his behalf, and that is to conserve your health and not overdo while at the same time, of course, devoting yourself to teaching, also to think about not staying too long and come home direct.

If you find the time and it does not tire you at all, the Guardian says it would be good to keep in touch with those pioneers who are in the field near you, by mail.

You may be sure Shoghi Effendi is watching over you and praying for you and takes the keenest interest in your wonderful work.

He has written Jeanne to devote herself completely to this unique and priceless opportunity she has of serving the Cause, and also to take care of you at the same time.

I myself, dearest, am unspeakably grateful to you for arising to serve in this way, and it has given me courage and happiness in my own work.

With tenderest and undying love, your own daughter, Rúḥíyyih

And in the handwriting of Shoghi Effendi:

Dearest & precious co-worker:

I feel truly & deeply that you are such a co-worker, now that you have so spontaneously arisen, despite the difficulties in your way, to promote the Cause & lend a fresh impetus to its progress in such a distant field. You are adding yet another laurel to the crown you have deservedly won in its service. Mary is overjoyed & proud of the decision you have taken & of the work you are accomplishing. She is making excellent progress in her Persian & is in the best of health. You should have no anxiety whatever, & should concentrate your energies & attention on the glorious work you are achieving for our beloved Master. Much love to Jeanne & to your own dear self.

Shoghi

On 26 February 1940 Mr Maxwell also wrote to May about the work he was doing for Shoghi Effendi. At the end of it he mentions the historic re-interment of the bodies of the wife of Bahá'u'lláh, Navváb, and the youngest son, Mírzá Mihdí (the Purest Branch), whose remains were now placed on the flanks of Mt Carmel beside the grave of the Greatest Holy Leaf in what would later be described as the Monument Gardens:

I forwarded to you – via airmail – to Buenos Aires, Mary's 5-page, remarkable description of the re-interment. It's so fine and will mean a great deal to you and Jeanne.

May and Jeanne reached Buenos Aires, after a one-day stop in Santos and Montevideo, on 27 February 1940. It was the end of a long journey.

* * *

There are several notes and letters by May describing her thoughts, her feelings of joy and her anticipation about this trip and about the city of Buenos Aires. The first example below was apparently addressed to Emogene Hoagg, in February 1940:

Dearest Emogene:

Here I am way down in South America – I might as well be on the moon! . . . I came here with my niece, Jeanne Bolles, because I had written my daughter that I had become so keenly interested in the Bahá'í work in South America, through Mrs. Frances Stewart, that if I were not so old and heavy etc. I might go to Buenos Aires myself – whereupon our dynamic young Guardian <u>cabled</u> his 'hearty approval winter visit Buenos Aires'! I was thunder struck and incidentally – so was Sutherland!! And it took me some time to obtain his <u>willing</u> consent! I did so love and admire you for being a pioneer, dearest Emogene – and now I am walking in your dear footsteps! If we have a few ohs! and ouches! what of it! Someday – perchance, all our (<u>my</u>) sins <u>forgiven</u> – we shall live in a climate as heavenly as this one – joyous and blest forever in the adored Presence.

The second, dated 29 February, was written to Sutherland confirming their arrival in Buenos Aires. It was a letter replete with life, and conveyed the joyous reception of his mail. However, it was a letter that he would receive only after her death:

Jeanne and I arrived from Montevideo day before yesterday and it was such a joy to receive your two dear letters, so satisfying in every way, as well as Mary's letters and the sublime document of the Guardian . . . Yes darling, I am glad you read Mary's letters and then send them on to me, it is a comfort and happiness to us both, and somehow you both seem so very near to me all the time on this long trip. By the way, you seem to know more about Rio than I do. I had a beautiful view from my window and took a few drives and wrote several letters, and did no sight-seeing, and bought a new dress! I also had two lovely teas at the Gloria Hotel for friends of Leonora Holsapple's, all of whom are interested in the Faith, and although I love the Brazilians and Rio, yet I am thrilled to be here in Buenos Aires, a strong, beautiful modern city, and an interesting combination of North and South America, with an enchanting climate and delightful people.

However, the most detailed description of their arrival and of the events which took place during the forty-eight hours which followed is to be found in the letter written by Jeanne Bolles to Mrs Frances Stewart, dated 27 June 1940. It is inscribed on letterhead stationery of the Alvear Palace Hotel, Buenos Aires:

Dear Mrs. Stewart,

Ah, it was a strange Divine Decree that awaited our arrival here. Beloved May Maxwell was so delighted to be here that she was like a young girl of 16 in her joyous enthusiasm. She leaned out of the taxi as we rode through the streets, saying, 'Oh, Jeanne, look at the lovely people' and 'Oh, Jeanne, look at the pretty shops', and still again, 'Look, look at the cute, little omnibuses!'

From the moment she left New York, she talked of nothing but Buenos Aires, Buenos Aires, Even in Rio, where we stopped for 2 weeks, her thoughts were bent here, and she said more than once she regretted not going directly to Argentina, even though teaching opportunities in Rio were profuse, and dearest Mrs. Maxwell spoke twice there to groups of people interested. Dear Leonora Holsapple came to meet us there, and it was thru her we were able to meet so many people. (Later she flew down for beloved Mrs. Maxwell's funeral on March 13th, for which trip Wilfred Barton so generously defrayed the expenses).

The day of our arrival in Buenos Aires (Feb. 27th) we had a difficult time getting thru the customs – it took several hours and the afternoon was extremely hot – even I was exhausted after it. Then precious Mrs. Maxwell, tired as she was, forgot her pocket book in a taxi, just as we were about to take some tea to refresh ourselves. Thereby, she lost about $250 and a beautiful ivory rosary dear Rúhíyyih Khánum had given her! We did what we could; we went to the police. The purse was returned, but without the money! Then, that first night we spent in the Hotel Jousten, which had been recommended. There we spent a sleepless night, it was so noisy. Even she said that since arrival no one could deny that we had been beset by afflictions. The next day we moved over to City Hotel. That night dearest Mrs. Maxwell had a wonderful rest – she was so refreshed the next morning, and was full of energy and vitality. That night we had dinner in her room (she couldn't stand the air-conditioned dining room) and there on the 9th floor in room 920 we ate together 'the last supper' – strange, even the spoons and forks and knives were marked with a 9! Precious Mrs. Maxwell was so happy that night, for she had not only received Shoghi Effendi's marvelous account of the interment on Mt. Carmel of the remains of the Purest Branch and mother of 'Abdu'l-Bahá, but also a beautiful description of the same by Rúḥíyyih Khánum. The beloved Guardian's words opened worlds of new horizons to her, precious Mrs. Maxwell said.

That night, too, she spoke at length of those days when she taught in Paris, long ago, and of the early believers there. As you may know, dear Mrs. Stewart, dearest Shoghi Effendi said that Mrs. Maxwell was the first believer to take the Faith to the Latins – because of her teaching work in France. How strange indeed, as my own dear mother remarked, that she should speak of those first days of pioneering – at the end of the trail – her last days! That same evening Haig Kevorkian, the young Armenian Bahá'í, phoned. He told us how happy he was to know we were here; and dear Mrs. Maxwell held an animated conversation with him with all the enthusiasm of the beginning of her teaching work, which she anticipated so keenly. (Dear Mr. Tormo, I later learned, had gone to meet us at the boat, but had missed us completely – so dearest May Maxwell never met him or any other members of the group. However they attended her funeral on March 13th, and all seemed profoundly affected by her passing. They were dear to me in my great sorrow too).

The next morning, March 1st, precious May Maxwell awoke early, at 6 o'clock, with an intense pain deep, deep in her bosom. We had a doctor, who did not find her condition serious, although she was icy cold, and who said her pulse was slow but regular! After taking the remedy he prescribed, she was relieved, and slept an hour and three-quarters. Then once again that pain, the intensity of which was greater than any she had ever before experienced, returned. Oh, dearest Mrs. Stewart, it was terrible to hear her suffering and not be able to do anything!

Then at 2:15 just after eating a little soup, a heart attack came. My precious Aunt fell unconscious, and, before the doctor arrived, she had passed to the World beyond and was once again with her beloved Master –

Jeanne's letter continues with words of her deep and heartfelt appreciation to Mrs Stewart for the thoughts of sympathy and solace she had conveyed in her letter of 14 March:

Your precious letter of March 14th was forwarded to me here by Simon [Rosenzweig], and I cannot tell you how much consolation your dear, comforting words brought to my sorrow-laden heart. It meant so much to hear from you, not only because you loved my precious Aunt so much, but also because you have a connection (a very deep one) with Buenos Aires and therefore you could understand a thousand-fold more than many others.

Dearest May Maxwell spoke so often of you on the way down from New York – it was you, dear Mrs. Stewart, who inspired her to come to South America, and here she received that glorious crown of Martyrdom, for which she had prayed at the Holy Threshold of Bahjí. Beloved May Maxwell loved you very much, and admired you too, admired the marvelous work you had done and were doing in the Latin American countries as well as in North America; she, too, was looking forward to meeting you here if it was possible for you to come quickly.

The first indication Mr Maxwell received that all was not well was a cable he received from his wife on 1 March stating: SEVERE NEURITIS BEG PRAYERS. 'It was evident to me', Mr Maxwell affirmed afterwards, 'that it was her heart and not neuritis and May did not want to alarm me.' On receiving this cable he did not wait for further news, but sensing the seriousness of the situation, contacted Shoghi Effendi immediately:

> JEANNE BOLLES CABLED MAY DESPERATELY ILL BUENOS AIRES PLEASE PRAY FOR HER PREPARE MARY – SUTHERLAND MAXWELL

May had cabled Shoghi Effendi herself that same day, supplicating prayers, and so by the time the Guardian received Jeanne's second cable, sent at 3.37 p.m. that day, he, too, would have been prepared for the following message:

> BELOVED ONE IMPLORING YOUR GUIDING HELP PRAYERS OUR SACRED MAY MAXWELL HAS LEFT OUR MIDST FOR ABHA KINGDOM ALL LOVE TO YOU BELOVED RUHIYYIH KHANUM. JEANNE BOLLES

She had to keep a long vigil over the body of her aunt, from Friday to Sunday – a long wait without replies to her cables. Years later, when she and Rúḥíyyih Khánum visited May's resting-place together on 24 December 1967, she described the difficult circumstances:

> May was taken to a funeral salon here. It was night when these things had to be arranged. There were two other funerals at the same time, and these were taking up the nice rooms, so there was no place to lay the remains of May Maxwell. A man said that we would have to take her to the back of the establishment. As you know, we don't allow embalming. It was necessary to wash and prepare the body . . . As there were no Bahá'í women at that time, the first Uruguayan believer, Mr. Simon Rosenzweig, who was married and had several children, helped to prepare the remains of May Maxwell. When we asked for water, there was none. They finally said that we could bring water in the buckets used for the feed of the horses which drew the coaches. In these we brought water to wash May Maxwell's body. Her remains lay literally in the stables, in the courtyard, and there we washed her. She was finally enclosed in a beautiful casket. It had a glass top; she had flowers in her hands, and you could see her there in beautiful repose . . .

Sutherland had at first thought of having his wife's body shipped to the States, as May had expressed a wish to be buried next to her mother in Englewood. But when he received Shoghi Effendi's instructions 'INTERMENT BUENOS AIRES ESSENTIAL', he immediately cabled Jeanne to arrange for the burial there. The search for a grave proved difficult, however, as Jeanne wrote in her memoirs. The cemetery in Buenos Aires was not beautiful and a temporary burial had to take place until Quilmes was found. On 18 March Shoghi Effendi cabled Jeanne again, saying: 'UNDUE DELAY INTERMENT INADVISABLE PRAYING SUCCESS'. The following day, he cabled: 'APPROVE QUILMES MAIL PHOTOGRAPHS GRAVE CEREMONY DEEPEST APPRECIATION SHOGHI'.

Rúḥíyyih Khánum had written to her mother one month earlier on 29 January, and had sent her and Jeanne flowers from the Shrine of the Báb. The letter had brought May great joy, and the violets, as Jeanne afterwards wrote to Mrs Stewart, were 'laid within beloved Aunt May's coffin'. But there was not much of a community in Argentina to take charge of the funeral arrangements:

Up to this time there were only three real, firm Bahá'ís in Buenos Aires. These were the only Bahá'ís in Argentina at the time. There was a large group of other people, mostly Argentines, who were interested in the Faith but were not Bahá'ís. The Kevorkians and Boigharians had not yet met this group. At the funeral they all came together, and together carried her casket . . . A month after this the three original believers and the other group who had joined the ranks at the funeral gathered and decided to form the first Assembly in Argentina.

The day after her death, which coincided with the beginning of the Bahá'í Fast, 2 March 1940, Shoghi Effendi sent a cable to the National Spiritual Assembly of the United States and Canada announcing her passing and calling for memorial gatherings to be held in 'both Americas' in her name. It was a befitting summary of the life, the death, and the enduring legacy of this immortal apostle of 'Abdu'l-Bahá, and it contained a confirmation of her rank as a martyr of the Cause:

> ABDULBAHAS BELOVED HANDMAID DISTINGUISHED DISCIPLE MAY MAXWELL GATHERED GLORY ABHA KINGDOM STOP HER EARTHLY LIFE SO RICH EVENTFUL INCOMPARABLY BLESSED WORTHILY ENDED STOP TO SACRED TIE HER SIGNAL SERVICES HAD FORGED PRICELESS HONOUR MARTYRS DEATH NOW ADDED STOP DOUBLE CROWN DESERVEDLY WON STOP SEVEN YEAR PLAN PARTICULARLY SOUTH AMERICAN CAMPAIGN DERIVE FRESH IMPETUS EXAMPLE HER GLORIOUS SACRIFICE STOP SOUTHERN OUTPOST FAITH GREATLY ENRICHED THROUGH ASSOCIATION HER HISTORIC RESTING PLACE DESTINED REMAIN POIGNANT REMINDER RESISTLESS MARCH TRIUMPHANT ARMY BAHAULLAH STOP ADVISE BELIEVERS BOTH AMERICAS HOLD BEFITTING MEMORIAL GATHERINGS SHOGHI

On the very same day, the beloved Guardian also sent a cable to Mr Maxwell in Montreal. It is deeply moving to see how his immense sorrow at the loss of this heroine of the Cause coincides with his pride in her achievements and his tender sympathy for her husband. His empathy with Sutherland in his grief is followed by an immediate invitation to his father-in-law to come to Haifa. Who but Shoghi Effendi could combine such extremes of sensibility within a single message?

> GRIEVED PROFOUNDLY YET COMFORTED ABIDING REALIZATION BEFITTING ONE SO NOBLE SUCH VALIANT EXEMPLARY SERVICE CAUSE BAHAULLAH STOP RUHIYYIH THOUGH ACUTELY CONSCIOUS IRREPARABLE LOSS REJOICES REVERENTLY GRATEFUL IMMORTAL CROWN DESERVEDLY WON HER ILLUSTRIOUS MOTHER STOP ADVISE INTERMENT BUENOS AIRES STOP HER TOMB DESIGNED BY YOURSELF ERECTED BY ME SPOT SHE FOUGHT FELL GLORIOUSLY WILL BECOME HISTORIC CENTRE PIONEERS BAHAI ACTIVITY STOP MOST WELCOME ARRANGE AFFAIRS RESIDE HAIFA STOP BE ASSURED DEEPEST LOVING SYMPATHY SHOGHI

And from Bahjí, on the same day, Rúḥíyyih Khánum wrote the following letter to her father:

Bahjí,
March 2nd, 1940.

My dearest Daddy:

No words between us can ever convey either the sense of loss we feel or the sympathy we long to express each to the other. It is as if our very heart had been plucked from our breast – because in a way that one human being rarely is to another, Mother was our all-in-all.

From your own sense of inconsolable loss you can fathom my feeling. To know I shall not hold her in my arms again, nor confide all I had of joy to tell her – not even ever receive another letter from her living hand is almost unbearable. But I have been in the Holy Shrine reciting those words of the prayer for the dead: *We all verily render thanks unto God, we all verily are patient in God!* and I <u>did</u> render thanks Daddy that the one we loved the most had attained to her own greatest desire – because I remember that at that very Threshold she had supplicated God for Martyrdom. I am patient in His decree, so sad for me, but so glorious for her.

As Shoghi Effendi said she went like a meteor! She rose to the zenith and became extinguished at her highest point! Would we have chosen it otherwise for her? The essence of true love is sacrifice, and I know neither you nor I would have withheld from Mother such a happiness, such a luminous end, even if we had foreseen it!

I had always hoped that Mother would pass away in my arms,

who love her so dearly, so desperately! But then this glory could not have been hers – the ease of the bosom of our family is not the plane of martyrdom! and loving we must always sacrifice! And so dearest you see I have taken the cup and drunk it that God has held out to me and I lean on you and 'leaning find my strength'.

It is only right that after such a loss we should be together. I feel you too will be longing for the solace as I am and I suggest you put your affairs in order, rent or place a caretaker in our home, and come make Haifa your base. It does not mean you can't go back again. But at least now come and live here and make it your centre. How could we bear now, all alone, to have the war separate us? It is unthinkable and I think it would kill you and sadden me till the end of my life.

Ah Daddy, Daddy! Death is always with us and yet we always think of life! It is not that I am not happy over her happiness – it's just I longed so terribly to see her again!

The Guardian sustained me in my hour of need most tenderly and wonderfully. All the telegrams came at once. One even from Mother! But fortunately he managed to withhold the news she had passed on until he prepared me and showed me how great her death was and how befitting after her life. The ways of God are not the ways of man and we must rely on His Mercy and Love.

Please, for my sake, don't let yourself be too grief stricken over this sudden and terrible loss! Remember you had her so many years longer than I! including the last three years. Now you must take her place as well as your own to me.

I am writing Jeanne. Poor girl! This must have been a terrible thing for her just after losing Unkie. But it comforts me very much to know they are together – Mother and Unkie.

I never knew any family that had the deep love, understanding and unity we three had, and will <u>always</u> have. We must be grateful for all our blessings and not the least of these is that Mother's own consuming desire has been fulfilled. So many achieve but never crown their achievements – Mother has done both gloriously and we share it with her, bitter as it is to our bereaved hearts, and derive comfort from the thought that even had we known she went to her death, from such a death we would not have withheld her selfishly!

Daddy, dearest, dearest father, I kiss you tenderly and am waiting with longing and impatience for you to join me. There is nothing

left to hold you there now, and you can go back for visits whenever you want to – to our beloved home, so sacred in its memories.
Your own child, Mary.
(Rúḥíyyih Rabbani)

And written on the left margin:

> P. S. I forgot to say that in the East if you love and admire someone a great deal it is common to erect their grave. I wanted you to fully understand dear Shoghi Effendi's motive in suggesting this. We must feel so honoured and happy, Daddy, that she will rest in the grave you design and the Guardian builds. It must be very beautiful!

Pasted inside this letter, apparently by Mr Maxwell, is a one-page yellow sheet on which is written in Rúḥíyyih Khánum's handwriting:

> Copy of the cable that Shoghi Effendi sent the National Spiritual Assembly. He also sent a wonderful cable to Persia.

Her handwritten copy of the Guardian's cable is then included, followed by:

> And I cabled the National Spiritual Assembly the following:
>
>> Humbly grateful beloved Mother answered Guardians call turned southward sacrificed life Holy Faith beg prayers daughter may follow her footsteps.
>
> Daddy dearest we two should be very happy that our love, in the last days of her life, did not prove a selfish bond. That we let her go – like a bird to wing its way alone – to its eternal home. After such a life as hers of burning love for God and for His Cause, no other death would have been worthy of such a soul. As the Guardian truly told me, she had everything in this life and in the next! She had a husband who adored her, a daughter who idolized her. She attained the highest honour any Mother could in this world by giving her child to the Guardian and then she went off and on and up! and got a martyrs crown! and all her physical sufferings are now at an end!

LATE YEARS 1937–1940

* * *

Condolences came pouring in. In response to one sent to the Guardian from Lee and Margot Worley, Bahá'ís in Brazil who had had the privilege of meeting May in Rio de Janeiro just two weeks before her death and who described her as '. . . one of the finest characters and shining lights in the Bahá'í world', Shoghi Effendi wrote:

> May the beloved of our hearts aid you to work as devotedly and unremittingly as our dearly-loved and valiant pioneer, Mrs. Maxwell, and aid you to carry on the work for which she gave her life, and thus set so noble an example to those who will labour after her in the Divine Vineyard.
> Your true brother, Shoghi

In response to another letter from the Bahá'í community of Philadelphia, Amatu'l-Bahá wrote on 6 April 1940:

> Dear Bahá'í brothers and sisters:
> I was deeply grateful for your loving letter of sympathy. The love of the friends has been so wonderful to me at this time and helped me so much! Although it was a great shock to lose my beloved Mother so suddenly and so far away from me – yet I could never be anything but grateful to God for conferring on her such a blessing at the end of her life of service to this Cause.
> It is as if the 'Horn of Plenty' had been emptied upon her! She must have had something very wonderful in her soul that attracted such rich blessings upon her! I think it was her single-hearted adoration of her 'Beloved'! So often she used to say 'this Cause is my life'. When she was ill . . . and we would remonstrate with her about taking care of her health and not going out to a meeting or exerting herself in some way we thought dangerous for her health, she would always say she could not live without the friends, that to go and serve would cure her – and it often did! . . . She learned . . . (t)o be happy while suffering! . . . If more of us could learn to live this way we would be able to help our fellow-men so greatly!
> Surely the path has been made very clear to us American Bahá'ís by our dear ones – Lua, Keith, Martha, Mother and many, many

others. We must all work together to follow them on it and I do hope you will all pray for me that I may grow to be like them!
Much love to you all, in our Guardian's service,
Rúḥíyyih

In contrast to all the accolades and eulogies, Sutherland expressed his loss with a characteristic simplicity that plumbed the depths. Writing an account of May's passing to Mason Remey, on 16 March 1940, he ends his letter:

> It is different now with me, but it's the same just, such a happy experience with such a being can have no ending. Affectionately
> Sutherland

How different it was for him can only be imagined. To be alone in 1548 Pine Avenue was not an unusual experience for W. S. Maxwell. He had been alone there all through the time that his wife and daughter had been travelling in Europe five years before, and had been frequently alone since. But there would have been quite another depth now to the silence in the stairwell, to the solitude in the hall. There must have been another resonance to the vacant rooms still filled with May's belongings. After her death, the house on Pine Avenue was not simply emptied of bustle and activity, but haunted by an absent presence, by the memory of prayers chanted in the room where the Master Himself had prayed, by the echo of laughter in the living room where the youth had always gathered, by that beloved voice to which they had listened in rapt attention.

In the days and weeks that followed her passing, Shoghi Effendi evoked the spirit of May Maxwell in many of his letters. And as the fourth year of the Seven Year Plan began, he wrote a powerful challenge to the National Spiritual Assembly of the United States and Canada, dated 25 April 1940, evoking her spirit in conjunction with those of Martha Root and Keith Ransom-Kehler:

> The sudden extinction of the earthly life of that star-servant of the Cause of Bahá'u'lláh, Martha Root, who, while on the last lap of her fourth journey round the world – journeys that carried her to the humblest homes as well as the palaces of royalty – was hurrying

homeward to lend her promised aid to her fellow-countrymen in their divinely-appointed task – such a death, though it frustrated this cherished resolution of her indomitable spirit, steeled the hearts of her bereaved lovers and admirers to carry on, more energetically than ever, the work which she herself had initiated, as far back as the year 1919, in every important city in the South American continent . . .

And now as this year, so memorable in the annals of the Faith, was drawing to a close, there befell the American Bahá'í community, through the dramatic and sudden death of May Maxwell, yet another loss, which viewed in retrospect will come to be regarded as a potent blessing conferred upon the campaign now being so diligently conducted by its members. Laden with the fruits garnered though well-nigh half a century of toilsome service to the Cause she so greatly loved, heedless of the warnings of age and ill-health, and afire with the longing to worthily demonstrate her gratitude in her overwhelming awareness of the bounties of her Lord and Master, she set her face towards the southern outpost of the Faith in the New World, and laid down her life in such a spirit of consecration and self-sacrifice as has truly merited the crown of martyrdom.

To Keith Ransom-Kehler, whose dust sleeps in far-off Isfahan; to Martha Root, fallen in her tracks on an island in the midmost heart of the ocean; to May Maxwell, lying in solitary glory in the southern outpost of the Western Hemisphere – to these three heroines of the Formative Age of the Faith of Bahá'u'lláh, they who now labor so assiduously for its expansion and establishment, owe a debt of gratitude which future generations will not fail to adequately recognize.[6]

On the following day the memorial service requested by the Guardian was held in the House of Worship during the National Convention. It was described by Agnes Alexander:

> Memorial Service held in the Temple, Wilmette, Illinois
> For the beloved maidservant of God, May Maxwell,
> April 26, 1940
>
> The Temple foundation room was filled to capacity. The service began at 9 p.m. and lasted until about 10:30 p.m. A quietness and

---
6 Shoghi Effendi, *Messages to America 1932–1946*, pp. 39–40.

reverence seemed to pervade the entire audience. As one of the nine who took part in the service, I was unconscious of anything but the quietness of the room. The service was spontaneous and only planned in the later part of the afternoon of that day. Marion Holley was the guiding spirit in planning the program. There was no personality in the service, each one in his or her turn arising without any names being announced and speaking.

After it was over I heard it said that it was the most wonderful gathering, or service ever held in the Temple. A young man from Portland, a new believer, told me he had never in his life attended such a meeting and he was especially impressed with the impersonality of it. Mr. Solon Friedman said it was not only the most wonderful meeting ever held in the Temple, but the most wonderful meeting he had ever attended in his life, and he wished me to convey to our dear Rúḥíyyih Khánum his loving greetings. First Jessie Revell read a prayer.

2. The first speaker, Mr. C. M. Remey told of the early days in Paris and how he first met May Ellis Bolles and of her beauty.
3. Juliet Thompson also spoke of how she came into the Cause in Paris and told of the time when May sent for her to come to Green Acre and assist in the raising of the Peace Flag there.
4. Philip Sprague read the cablegrams which came from the Guardian relative to May's passing in Buenos Aires. Also he read portions from the booklet, "An Early Pilgrimage".
5. Agnes Alexander mentioned briefly her meeting with May in Paris in 1901, and then in Haifa in 1937, and read a portion of a Tablet to her which spoke of May, also from one of May's letters and from a letter she had received the evening before from May's daughter, our beloved Guardian's wife, which spoke of the passing of her adored Mother. In this way it seemed a providence that our beloved Rúḥíyyih Khánum herself took part in that gathering.
6. Marion Holley read some extracts from Tablets to May and also from one to May's Mother in praise of her daughter. Also some words of May's daughter referring to her Mother.
7. Mrs. Frances Stewart spoke of May's last days in South America.
8. Mr. Ernest Harrison of Montreal repeated words from a Tablet to him referring to May and then, facing the East, he recited most touchingly the Prayer revealed by 'Abdu'l-Bahá for Canada.

9. Ali Kuli Khan closed the service by chanting in Persian a Prayer for the dead by Bahá'u'lláh.

This is a very inadequate account of that glorious service. It was planned that afternoon, April 26th, with eight speakers, then later, surely by divine providence, Mrs. Frances Stewart arrived making the nine.

Agnes B. Alexander

In his message to that Convention, dated 24 April 1940, Shoghi Effendi once again mentioned Mrs Maxwell and immortalized her as one of the triple heroines binding together the spiritual destiny of the Americas:

> INTERCONTINENTAL CRUSADE THROUGH PATH BROKEN MARTHA ROOT AND SEAL SET MAY MAXWELLS DEATH YIELDING DESTINED FRUIT GALVANIZED PERMANENTLY SAFEGUARDED TOGETHER WITH KEITH THEY FORGED THROUGH SACRIFICE TRIPLE CORD INDISSOLUBLY KNITTING COMMUNITY NORTH AMERICAN BELIEVERS TO CRADLE FAITH EVERY CONTINENT OLD WORLD AND LATIN AMERICA

And finally, four years later, in his sublime epic *God Passes By*,[7] he paid tribute to May Maxwell and her fellow heroes and heroines for the last time. No words but his could bring to a befitting close the story of so ardent a life:

> Nor was this gigantic enterprise destined to be deprived, in its initial stage, of a blessing that was to cement the spiritual union of the Americas – a blessing flowing from the sacrifice of one who, at the very dawn of the Day of the Covenant, had been responsible for the establishment of the first Bahá'í centers in both Europe and the Dominion of Canada, and who, though seventy years of age and suffering from ill-health, undertook a six thousand mile voyage to the capital of Argentina, where, while still on the threshold of her pioneer service, she suddenly passed away, imparting through such a death to the work initiated in that Republic an impetus which has already enabled it, through the establishment

---

7 p. 400.

of a distributing center of Bahá'í literature for Latin America and through other activities, to assume the foremost position among its sister Republics.

To May Maxwell, laid to rest in the soil of Argentina; to Hyde Dunn, whose dust reposes in the Antipodes, in the city of Sydney; to Keith Ranson-Kehler, entombed in distant Iṣfahán; to Susan Moody and Lillian Kappes and their valiant associates who lie buried in Ṭihrán; to Lua Getsinger, reposing forever in the capital of Egypt, and last but not least to Martha Root, interred in an island in the bosom of the Pacific, belong the matchless honour of having conferred, through their services and sacrifice, a lustre upon the American Bahá'í community for which its representatives, while celebrating at their historic, their first all-American Convention, their hard-won victories, may well feel eternally grateful.

A few days after May's funeral Jeanne Bolles wrote to Rúḥíyyih Khánum telling her some of the details about the funeral:

Dearest Rúḥíyyih,
    There are so many, many things to tell you, that it is hard to know where to begin.
    I hope, my dearest Cousin, that you are recovering from this terrible shock, and that your health has sustained the difficulties of these days . . .
    Whenever I think of the beauty of living and in living I like to think of your dearest Mother – oh how beautiful she made your home life – from day to day and hour to hour in so many sweet and beautiful little ways. How generous she always was, how she loved everyone – showered them with love.

Shoghi Effendi had already cabled Mr Maxwell, in the difficult months immediately following his wife's passing, asking for photographs of May for the next volume of *The Bahá'í World*. It was at a critical time, when everything posted had to pass through the censor and could easily be lost en route, but it was the only time that this task could be done, for W. S. Maxwell was arranging to leave the house at 1548 Pine Avenue indefinitely. He was going through his wife's personal belongings, making plans to quit his position in the firm, and organizing his travel to the Holy Land at the Guardian's invitation. He sent the prints to Shoghi Effendi on 12 April 1940, with the following brief note of explanation for the censor:

> The photographs are of my wife who died while visiting Buenos Aires, on March 1st, 1940. They are for Shoghi Effendi Rabbani whose father-in-law I have the honour to be. Thanking you, W. S. Maxwell, Architect, Montreal.

His letter to Shoghi Effendi was labelled as being 'from Mrs. Rabbani's father' and was written by hand:

> My dear Shoghi Effendi
>
> Your cable asking for five photographs of May was received yesterday. I enclose five smooth prints and they show May in 1900 and as she was in different succeeding years.
>
> The large 1928 head is from a snapshot Mary took in our garden of May, Princess de Broglie and myself. In it May is in her most robust period and the Montreal Friends all love it. I have many others not all of which are satisfactory and there is a very nice one of her holding Mary, who is about one year old, in her lap.
>
> I did forward Marion Holley a lot of eight or nine which I understand are to be forwarded to you along with her article on May's life. I sent Marion ten pages of data to assist her and I expect her article will be beautiful.
>
> I did not think I would have time, before the airmail closes, to do other than cover the data about the photographs, but happily I have a few minutes to spare.
>
> I thank you from my heart for the inspiring and consoling messages your cables to me contained.
>
> Your messages to Jeanne Bolles helped her to carry on and attend to the many matters she was faced with. She has been greatly helped and wishes to remain in South America for some time. She went to Santos in Brazil to recuperate from the strain of carrying on after May's passing.
>
> It has been a great happiness to me that May and I carried out your wish that we visit the friends in different Centres and both speak to them.

Had this not been done I would have been very unhappy. May's next activity was her glorious visit to Rio de Janeiro and Buenos Aires and your description of its significance is sublime.

Your decision to put up a monument to May, and your permission to me to design it, calls forth my humble appreciation of the great honour and my heartfelt gratitude.

I am well and conscious of being surrounded with May's spirit and love, so there is no grief in my heart.

My love and greeting to your Mother and Father and the Family and to you and Rúḥíyyih, I send all love and devotion.

Sutherland Maxwell

The design for May's memorial was completed in Haifa, one year after Sutherland took up residence there. The Guardian asked Mrs Amelia Collins,[8] a close friend and for many years a co-worker of May on the National Spiritual Assembly of the United States and Canada, to oversee the construction of the monument in Buenos Aires. In a letter written to her two years later, on 14 April 1943, Sutherland defined the significance of this memorial to him and to his daughter:

> The memorial to May is an expression of appreciation and love for one whose life was consecrated to the Bahá'í Faith. It is not a family affair – as memorials usually are, it is the embodiment in concrete form of the New Spiritual Ideal that will transform this careworn stricken world. When you write the sculptor please let him know that Rúḥíyyih Khánum and I convey our appreciation of his splendid work in making the model. He had to do the upper decorative portion largely from photographs of the small original model which was made in Haifa; you will recall that Rúḥíyyih Khánum modelled the wings and I did the rest of the decorative and plain parts.

When she visited her mother's grave in Buenos Aires for the first time in December 1967, in the company of her beloved cousin Jeanne Bolles Chute, Rúḥíyyih Khánum confirmed the manner in which her father's beautiful plans for the monument were finalized by the Guardian and by herself in the course of that year:

---

8 Appointed a Hand of the Cause of God in 1951.

Christmas, 1937, in the home of Edward Maxwell, 3480 Peel Street, Montreal. May and W. S. Maxwell with some of Edward's family, as well as the family of Randolph Bolles, May's brother

In her memoirs, Amatu'l-Bahá Rúḥíyyih Khánum writes about this photograph: 'Mother is shown with two pillars rising up behind her and a lion by her side . . . on the steps of the Hotel Rockingham in Portsmouth, New Hampshire . . . But if one looked the world over one would not find anything to better epitomize Mother's character and her faith and her service to the Cause, than these two symbols – the lion and the pillar, for she was lion-like in her courage and a true pillar of the Faith in every way.'

May Maxwell with her niece Jeanne Negar Bolles (later Chute), probably in Rio de Janeiro in February 1940

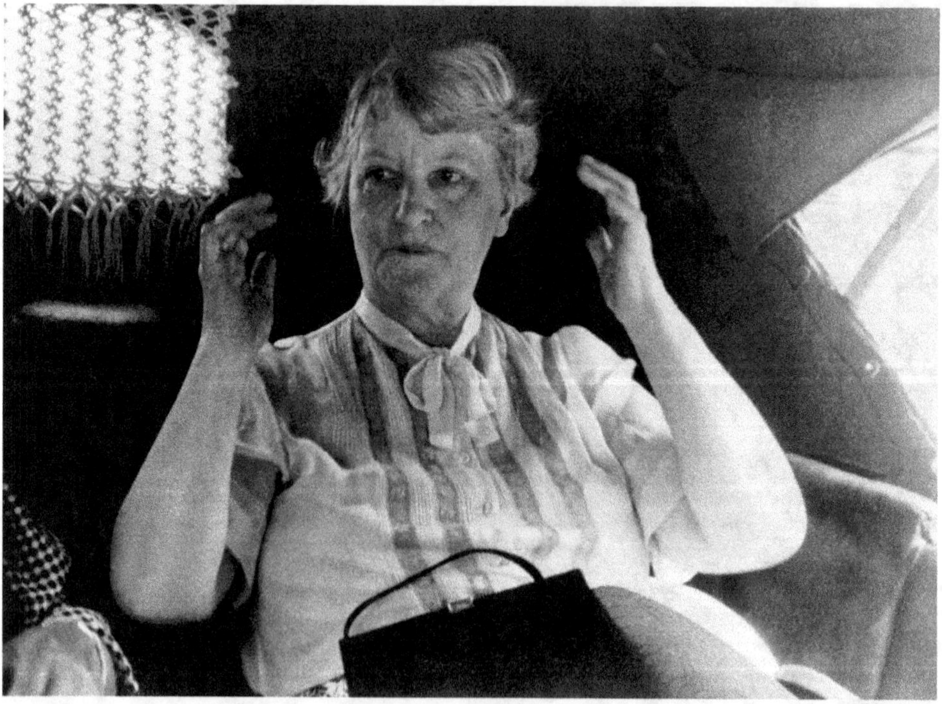

May Maxwell, shortly before her passing, 1940

Friends at the funeral of May Maxwell, 13 March 1940, Quilmes, Argentina

Jeanne Bolles, Leonora Holsapple (Armstrong) and Haig Kevorkian at the graveside, March 1940

The completed monument, designed by W. S. Maxwell. The wings were Rúḥíyyih Khánum's suggestion, for which she made the models

Amatu'l-Bahá Rúḥíyyih Khánum at her mother's graveside, Quilmes, Argentina, end of December 1967 or January 1968

I don't think the friends know how this monument came to be, how my father designed it. The whole central design is his. I always believed that mother should have wings on her grave. Since we are not Christians it could not be an angel. If there was ever a spirit with wings, it was the spirit of my mother. I sculptured the wings; this is my work. Father made the model (of the central portion) in <u>plasticine – it was very beautiful – and I made the wings. It was sculptured from this model.</u> Father's original design did not have the things on the sides. Shoghi Effendi said that it was incomplete and that it needed something on the sides. The vases, which add so much to the design, were Shoghi Effendi's suggestion.

Just before leaving Canada for Haifa around mid-May of 1940, Mr Maxwell received a letter from the National Spiritual Assembly of the United States and Canada, dated 15 April 1940, asking him 'to consider the important matter of a design for the memorial to be constructed at the grave of Martha Root in Honolulu'. Mr Maxwell's response to this letter has not come to light, but more than likely his imminent departure to live in Haifa and all the arrangements such a move would entail made it impossible for him to accept the honour attached to this request, especially since the letter stated: 'The hope is to have the design in hand by July.'

It is clear, however, that William Sutherland Maxwell had every intention of practising his profession outside Canada, for he left with a letter of introduction from the Association of Architects of the Province of Quebec, dated 1 May 1940, signed by the President, Jean T. Perrault, and addressed: 'TO WHOM IT MAY CONCERN':

> Mr. W. S. Maxwell, F.R.A.I.C., F.R.I.B.A., R.C.A., Past President of the Province of Quebec Association of Architects and Past President of the Royal Architectural Institute of Canada is going to Europe and Palestine for a visit. He is a member in good standing of our Association and any courtesies or facilities extended to him will be appreciated.

His departure for Europe and then Haifa, in the middle of a world war, did not pass unnoticed in Montreal society. There were several events connected with it in the course of April and May of 1940, the last of which was a formal farewell dinner given by the Montreal Arts Club on Friday, 3 May. One of his fellow architects, Frank R. Foster, who could not attend this event, wrote an apology to Mr Maxwell the evening before:

> May I take this opportunity of telling you how often I have thought that your example of enthusiasm and thoroughness in anything you have undertaken in the cause of the Arts has been an inspiration to us all. For many reasons and for the high personal esteem in which we all hold you, it is somewhat unnecessary for me to say how much you will be missed in Montreal. I shall always hope that we may meet again in our 'old age' at the Arts Club, which you so materially helped to inaugurate and have so willingly and unselfishly supported.

Sometime around 11 May, Sutherland left Montreal aboard the *S. S. Rex*, and sailed for Genoa, Italy. Years later, in her *In Memoriam*[1] article about her father, Rúḥíyyih Khánum was to write with characteristic forthrightness:

> ... May suffered a heart attack and died.
> The first act of the Guardian was to invite Sutherland, now entirely alone, to come and live in Haifa. From 1940 until his death in 1952 may be said to be the true years of burgeoning in this distinguished man's life.

---

1 *The Bahá'í World*, vol. XII (1950–1954), p. 661.

1940–1952

The story of W. S. Maxwell's meeting with his daughter and the Guardian in Italy in the middle of World War II, of their heart-stopping journey across war-torn France to London at the height of the blitz, and of their subsequent voyage together across the torpedo-infested waters round the coast of West Africa to Cape Town has already been told by Amatu'l-Bahá Rúḥíyyih Khánum in her incomparable book *The Priceless Pearl*.[1] It is so vivid that it bears repeating:

> ... we therefore left Haifa on 15 May in a small and smelly Italian aquaplane, with the water sloshing around under the boards our feet rested on as if we were in an old row-boat. A few days later we arrived in Rome and I went to Genoa to meet my father who arrived on the last sailing the *S. S. Rex* ever made as a passenger ship ... [W]e ... left Italy for France, passing through Menton on 25 May and proceeding to Marseilles. Within a few days Italy entered the war against the Allies.
>
> It is hard to describe the period that followed. The whole episode was like a brilliantly lit nightmare – a personal nightmare for us and a giant nightmare in which the whole of Europe was involved. As our train made its way to Paris every station was crowded with thousands of refugees fleeing before the rapidly crumbling Allied front in the North. There was no way of getting any accurate information, chaos was descending. In Paris we discovered to our dismay that all ports to England were closed and the last hope of reaching that country – a hope diminishing hourly – was to go down to the little port of St Malo and see if we could still get a boat from there. We, and hundreds of other people trying to get home to England, had to wait a week before at last two boats succeeded in calling at St Malo

---

1   pp. 177–81.

... At last we embarked on the first of the two boats that came during the night of 2 June to evacuate the people stranded in St Malo and we sailed in total darkness for Southampton, where we arrived on the following morning. It was the day after we left, as I remember, that the Germans marched into St Malo. We had almost as much difficulty getting out of England as we had had in getting into it. It was the time of the great 'evacuate the children' drive which had top priority and it was only due to the position of Shoghi Effendi, and my father's friendship with the man who was Canadian High Commissioner in London, that we succeeded in getting passage for South Africa, sailing for Cape Town on the *S. S. Cape Town Castle* on 28 July.

But the tale told from Mr Maxwell's point of view is less well known and much less dramatic. It is only between the cracks of dates and places recorded in his sketch books and a few cables and letters to his daughter between 21 August and 4 October 1940 – sent from Johannesburg, Cape Town, and Durban, South Africa; Cairo, Egypt; and finally Tel Aviv – that we can catch a glimpse of his own historic journey. We find in this correspondence references to Rúḥíyyih K͟hánum and Shoghi Effendi in Victoria Falls, Southern Rhodesia; Johannesburg, South Africa; Stanleyville, Belgian Congo (now Kisangani); Elizabethville, Belgian Congo (now Lubumbashi); Juba, Sudan; and Cairo, Egypt. Some time in May or June 1940, when they were waiting interminably for their passage to England, he made a sketch of St Malo, on the west coast of France. He sketched the Groote Schuur Estate in Cape Town on 17 August and made about eight other drawings of architectural landmarks in the city when the *R. M. S.*[2] *Cape Town Castle*, on which they were all sailing, docked there five days before. His sketch books also contain a drawing of the Art Gallery in Durban where he remained for some weeks alone in a hotel, designing May's tombstone, as Rúḥíyyih K͟hánum tells us in *The Priceless Pearl*, 'pending his ability to secure air passage' to Cairo. Shoghi Effendi was very concerned about Mr Maxwell's frail health, and did not want him to attempt the overland trip through the heart of Africa.

When he bade farewell to the Guardian and Rúḥíyyih K͟hánum in Durban, he had been given only the most general instructions; he had

---

2 Royal Mail Ship (recorded in *The Priceless Pearl* as S. S.).

simply been told to make his way to Palestine by air and wait for their arrival in a hotel in Nazareth. He had no idea when he would see them again once they parted company and Shoghi Effendi and Rúḥíyyih Khánum set off on their overland journey through the Belgian Congo to the Sudan; and they had no idea either where he was during the course of their excursions. But his daughter has left us an immortal word sketch of the miracle of seeing his dear familiar figure emerging from the darkness of a suffocating Khartoum evening and walking towards the lights of the hotel porch where she was sitting with the Guardian after dinner.

It must have been the greatest balm for Amatu'l-Bahá, who surely felt her mother's absence most poignantly during this period, to be granted the presence of her dear father. What a blessed relief he must have been for her, what a vital reminder of that very different world of the Maxwells of Montreal, that far-away but dearly familiar world, that physical and emotional refuge of her childhood as well as the bedrock of her faith, that place protected by a loving mother and understanding father.

The isolation during these years of cataclysm on a global scale and within the Faith of God meant that they were continuously in each other's company at this time. Indeed, they had no one to rely on but each other. Cut off from kith and kin and surrounded by the increasing insecurity of the streets of Haifa, Mr Maxwell was invited by Shoghi Effendi to take his meals upstairs in the Master's House with him and Rúḥíyyih Khánum. Their intimacy was precious to all three. The Guardian was very fond of Mr Maxwell and expressed his love in a thousand personal and tender ways. On one occasion when they were eating upstairs, Rúḥíyyih Khánum recalled, he took a choice morsel of food from his plate, leaned across the table and popped it into her father's mouth. The expression on Sutherland's face at that moment, she used to say, was simply radiant!

Rúḥíyyih Khánum would also recount another story about her father and 'attar of rose' which classically illustrates his relationship with the Guardian. Shoghi Effendi was much given to using this heady perfume, and like many oriental men, was sprinkled with it liberally. After placing a few drops of 'attar' on his fingers, he liked to trace them across his cheeks and his moustache as well. Once, in a gesture of affection towards Sutherland, he did the same to him. Rúḥíyyih Khánum said she would never forget the look of mingled horror and delight on her father's face! To be daubed with perfume was hardly in keeping with the habits of a Scotsman, but to have his cheeks caressed by his beloved Guardian was more than he felt he deserved. Caught between deference and distaste, he was overwhelmed by confusion.

There was another instance which Rúḥíyyih Khánum fondly remembered with regard to her father's character and his relationship to Shoghi Effendi. Once, during summertime, when the Guardian had left Sutherland responsible for all practical affairs in Haifa during his summer absence from the Holy Land, Sutherland was asked to oversee the payment of all the workers and gardeners. He was so anxious to avoid making mistakes and so concerned to make sure he kept records of every penny spent that he divided the money he was giving them each week into separate envelopes. Instead of giving the Guardian a list of accounts on his return to Haifa, he presented him with a cardboard box brimming with empty envelopes all covered with scribbles! Rúḥíyyih Khánum often recalled Shoghi Effendi's combination of delight and despair at what she called her father's 'envelope system'.

Sutherland's transparently cultural limitations and his profound respect for the Guardian endeared him to Shoghi Effendi. The Guardian loved him very much, and later, recalling those harsh, yet happy and deeply intimate times, Shoghi Effendi stated that Mr Maxwell had brought light to his heart 'DURING DARKEST DAYS MY LIFE'.

In the middle of the war, on 2 February 1942, W. S. Maxwell's older sister, Amelia Johan Maxwell Hutchinson, died in Montreal. She had been his last living sibling and the wife of one of his closest friends since his days in Paris. Had it not been for his daughter and the Guardian, he would have had no immediate family left. And had it not been for him, they too would have had no one.

Some years later, on 25 May 1946, Rúḥíyyih Khánum in her diary drew a moving portrait of her father which depicts his dignity, his saintliness and his nobility during his late years, and his invaluable services to Shoghi Effendi at that time:

> My mind is tired but for a long time I have wanted to write many things here. First let me say I think my father is wonderful – really I am often absolutely astonished at his faith and beauty of character; mother always said 'Your father always rises to big things'. This is so

true – he is really a pillar of strength to me. So surprising, for outwardly he has grown so slow, so timid with the touching timidity of age . . . now it is years he has been here; since 1940 he has never left the country, had practically no change or vacation. The first few years he spent a few weeks in the summer with Shoghi Effendi and me in Jerusalem. But as he [Shoghi Effendi] did not want to make his family jealous the time was short. Since then he has been on the job here all the time, last summer doing <u>everything</u> and he was very tired when I came home in February. He is very anxious to go home to settle our affairs, left in a mess when he rushed over after Mother's death . . . and to see home and family once more. But it has been impossible. Shoghi Effendi and I have no one left now but Daddy; he is everything and does everything: he attends to all the banking, mails all letters, sends all the telegrams, goes on all the errands that are confidential – for visas, government matters, City Hall, etc. – and consults and designs, etc., all this at the age of 71. He is doing the work of Ali Askar, Riaz and Hussein. He never complains, but he has said he wants to get home to attend to his affairs – I, loving him so dearly – suffer very much that I cannot take better care of his old age. I neglect him, his clothes need mending and cleaning, he would enjoy and needs the right diet, but I have no time for him . . . I feel it very keenly. I want him to be made happy, I mean to go home for a change – so it is very hard to see all the work fall on him, and now Shoghi Effendi and I have been talking about our plans; he says we must go to . . . Switzerland. It seemed so terribly hard to have to leave Daddy, old and tired, once again with all the work of the Cause and no rest or respite. But when I talked to him today he was marvelous, said he can manage everything, not to worry over him, that everything will be all right. I can't put into words, being so very tired, (I've had 3 good cries today) how wonderful his spirit is. So unassuming yet so very noble and heroic. How often I feel how utterly inferior I am to both my parents, they are so noble, so refined in spirit; and gentleness and breeding of the true sort so characterizes them. Sometimes I feel all of my generation is inferior to its parents.

In a letter written by Rúḥíyyih Khánum to her father on 6 August 1942 she expresses her deep love and affection for him:

My beloved Daddy,

I just feel I want to tell you a few thoughts I have which I found it hard to put in words.

I hate to be separated from you and have to leave you in Haifa all alone – but for the first time since you came to Haifa, indeed since the Guardian bestowed such a great and undeserved blessing on us as to choose me to be his companion – you are able to render him and the Cause a very helpful and much-needed service by being worthy of his complete trust and confidence and enabling him to have his much-needed rest and opportunity to regain his strength for the trials that will lie ahead. I have felt so keenly these last few days the closeness of Mother and I believe Daddy dear her heart is grateful and rejoices that you are given this opportunity to help lift Shoghi Effendi's load. I am grateful too and proud that you are worthy to serve him.

Lately since we are all alone, so to speak, and I have been with you more than ever before in my life, I have come to realize more clearly why Mother so greatly loved you and valued you so highly, as she did.

You have an uncomplaining acceptance of your lot, a sweetness of character, and loyalty and high-mindedness, that I have come to see more clearly and admire with all my heart!

I just want you to know this Daddy, and to know that I love you more than I ever did before.

Please don't feel too lonesome!! Go and look up that fellow you met in the art gallery once, you told me about.

We will be seeing each other fairly often anyway.
          All my love,
          Your chick,
          Mary

* * *

William Sutherland Maxwell was a man of deeds rather than words. But when he did express himself, the emotion was palpable. His spirituality, like his grief, was not of the voluble sort, but profoundly felt and simply expressed. In a letter written to the National Spiritual Assembly of the United States and Canada on 14 March 1944 he admitted:

> [W]e miss May's presence but are so frequently conscious of her being with us in spirit and in our thoughts and it is a source of happiness to us that she is also a source of inspiration to many others.

> He had the ability of genius not only to grasp but also to express the most profound ideas with absolute purity of line.

Rúḥíyyih Khánum noted that her father had submitted his first studies for the superstructure for the Shrine of the Báb to Shoghi Effendi by 1942. She often spoke about the remarkable manner in which her father and Shoghi Effendi worked together and wrote about the nature of their partnership in *The Priceless Pearl*. She told how the Guardian would describe to Sutherland what he wanted, and Mr Maxwell would go away and make a scaled drawing of it. She recorded how the Guardian would then take his pencil and, with one or two deft strokes, make certain amendments to the drawing to make it reflect more accurately what he imagined. Sometimes Sutherland's drawings so perfectly rendered the Guardian's inner vision that there was nothing for him to add. Rúḥíyyih Khánum often used to tell a story about her father's design for the main gate leading to the Shrine of the Báb. When Sutherland finished the drawing, she carried it up to Shoghi Effendi's room. He was in bed at the time and took the piece of paper from her, gazed at it wordlessly for a few moments and then suddenly said: 'It's not fair.'

She was terribly worried at his words. She thought he was displeased with the design.

'Is it not what you had wanted?' she asked anxiously. But the reverse was in fact true.

'Why,' the Guardian replied, admiringly, 'no one can resist anything when it looks as beautiful as this!' For the drawing by W. S. Maxwell depicted with uncanny accuracy exactly what Shoghi Effendi had conceived. In fact, he was so delighted with it that he had this drawing framed and kept it on the wall of his room to the end of his days. At other times, he would ask Sutherland to make him a 'maquette' or model of the final concept so that he could literally see it. They worked together so beautifully, as Rúḥíyyih Khánum describes in *The Priceless Pearl*, that they were like a handle and a knife: Shoghi Effendi was the cutting edge of the blade, knowing precisely what was required; W. S. Maxwell was the handle, fitting perfectly in the Guardian's palm, and enabling him to achieve exactly what he wanted. This is how Sutherland was able to work on the plans for the Shrine of the Báb in close conjunction with the Guardian's wishes; this is how he miraculously realized Shoghi Effendi's vision for this most exquisite monument in honour of the Prophet-Herald of the Bahá'í Faith. In 1944, his design for the superstructure was completed and appeared as the frontispiece in *The Bahá'í World*, volume IX (1940–1944).

Amatu'l-Bahá often reassured her father with letters expressing the deep love and appreciation of the Guardian, as well as that of herself. In her letter of 18 October 1944 she rejoiced in the acceptance by the Guardian of the design for the Shrine of the Báb:

> . . . really Dad you should be the happiest man on earth – Shoghi Effendi is <u>so</u> delighted with your design for the Shrine. He keeps looking at the photograph of it and you know when he likes a thing how persistently and consistently he enjoys it! To think that you should have been given the chance, during war, after all hopes of a big future for your work in Canada were over, because of the building slump etc., to do the best piece of work of your life – and for such a Figure as the blessed Báb! It is really, to me, still too wonderful to be true, almost.

Other letters full of warmth and love followed over the course of the years. On 24 December 1945 she wrote:

> Shoghi Effendi and I were talking about you tonight and I assure you it was with the greatest love. You have helped us both so much Daddy, in so many ways, and in what will perhaps be seen in future as the hardest days of our life. Whenever we talk about you and what you have and are accomplishing in serving the Cause in Haifa, Shoghi Effendi always says: 'How your Mother must rejoice!'
>
> You know how much she loved you, how she never felt any other man held a candle to you! Well you can guess how proud she is now of her 'Sutherland'!
>
> When your cable came suggesting Shoghi Effendi accept at once your scheme for the two vases, he read it and decided to wait for the sketch before accepting. But about 3 hours later he took it out and re-read it, and said: 'You can see he is a man who is used to and knows how to tantalize his clients; he puts it in such a way that it

grips you' . . . or words to this effect, and then he promptly accepted by cable. So you should feel very flattered.

During this period, Mr Maxwell wrote a letter to his devoted secretary A. M. Parent, on 2 April 1943, providing her with news of his own activities and requesting her assistance in financial matters. It is revealing that although the indomitable 'AMP' never became a Bahá'í, she was entrusted with the most intimate financial matters in the Maxwell family, including their contributions to the Bahá'í Funds:

Dear A. M. P.,

I am cabling you to forward funds, same as last installment. I am going in the near future to take a couple of weeks off and go to Tel Aviv and Jerusalem where I shall go into the subject of Palestine Architecture, call on some architects and take photographs of some new work that interests me. I shall then be able to prepare the work on 'Palestine Architecture' as requested by the Royal Architectural Institute of Canada – at least I shall have made a start. In 1937 I took a lot of snapshots of work in Tel Aviv and Jerusalem but the negatives and prints are in Montreal and since that date a good deal of new work has been completed . . .

I have had my spell of shopping looking for material for a suit and a pair of trousers. The usual custom is to buy the cloth and take it to your tailor who charges to make it. I finally went to a tailor who is, of the opinion of Mary's dressmaker and her woman's husband, ranked number one. He is making me a two piece suitable for spring and summer cost £17½ and a pair of worsted trousers, cost £5. The cloths are really first class English goods . . .

The Bahá'í Garden, the one with the white marble monuments, is now practically completed. The uphill part has been carried about 80 yards to the right of the small photograph I sent you of the new Entrance. It is all the work of Shoghi Effendi's creative genius and has been carried out under his direction. He makes no drawings but visages what he considers the right thing to do and the results are very original and individual – in fact they are the best in Palestine. They are open daily in the afternoons and visited by many . . .

There is one matter that Mary and I want you to attend to on our behalf. The Centenary of the Bahá'í Faith will be celebrated in

May 1944. The Baháʼí Temple, in so far as the exterior is concerned, has been completed in Wilmette which is a suburb of Chicago and is beautifully situated on the shore of Lake Michigan. We want to make, on our behalf, in Canadian Funds a contribution to the fund, for teaching in Canada. Send the money to Fred Schopflocher, who is the treasurer and as you know lives in Montreal. Our preference is that the money be paid each month but if it is more convenient, the payments, starting on receipt of this letter, can be made every three months in advance. They are to terminate in May 1944. Our contribution is to be at least $60 per month and not over $100 per month and we prefer to give as near to the higher amount as financial circumstances permit. Use your good judgement in this matter . . .

Long before Mr Maxwell came to Haifa to live, Rúḥíyyih Khánum had expressed a heartfelt wish as early as 14 November 1937:

My own dearest Dad:
    Your letters, plans, and all the signs of your love and forethought for me have brought me happiness. I feel as if I were often with you in your office and our home – no sense of separation at all! You have done so much to beautify my wonderful new life and I feel in me increasingly the traits of both you and Mother – as if they were woven into the pattern of my being, and this were Daddy and that were Mother in me! It is most astonishing and more vivid than ever before in my whole life.
    I often wish you could help Shoghi Effendi with the work on terraces, plans, etc. But someday, God willing, maybe you will. Now you have other work to do for him and for the Cause. I told him you were sending your plans of the Temple and he was very pleased and said he would be interested to see them. But they are not, alas, representative of what you <u>could</u> do!

Two years later, on 11 October 1939, writing on behalf of the Guardian, she conveyed the following:

Dearest Daddy:
    I am writing you on behalf of the Guardian who has something he wants me to ask you to consider for him and make your plans for

it as your idea might prove to either be just what he wants or give him something to work on. He is about to build the last terrace of the Shrine on Mt. Carmel and although in an unforeseen future it might need to be changed or added to, he expects it for the present to be the permanent entrance to the terraces. Enclosed are a photograph of the present state of the terraces, a plan of the ones built and where the projected one will come and the property limits, and a cross section map showing the inclination of the mountain and the terraces.

Now the whole thing is this: What should the entrance, marked by me in elegant red ink with the letters 'XYZ', look like? That is where your work comes in. As you perhaps remember you discussed it here with Shoghi Effendi and he showed you a model that had a huge flight of circular steps opening out of the smaller flight that led up through the wall of the terrace to the higher level? He does not like this design and leaves it to you to propose one or more different ways. Also he is not absolutely fixed in the idea of using the big wrought iron gate, the design of which you also saw, in that position. So that gives you carte blanche except for the rather narrow and unfavourable approach to this entrance and the incline of the mountain itself. Unfortunately, as you can see from the enclosed photo, the houses are just fronting the as yet unfinished road that leads up to the terrace end. That makes a wide view of it impossible, I mean nice flanking gardens, etc. Also the incline is very steep. The projected stairs could come as near the boundary of the Bahá'í property to the RIGHT of the XYZ line as you think would look nice.

Shoghi Effendi says that as mails are so slow and uncertain now and the distance so great he wants you to not make a detailed plan as that would take too long and be a waste of your time. Make two or three tentative plans in the form of sketches with rough dimensions attached. He has a fairly good engineer who can carry it out. And above all don't try and ask me more details and wait for the answer as by that time probably summer will be here! At the present rate of mails!

And four months later, at the time her mother was en route to Buenos Aires, Rúḥíyyih Khánum wrote to her father on 17 February 1940:

Shoghi Effendi shows a marked determination to keep a stiff eye on mother so she won't get stuck in Buenos Aires! – as you can see from the enclosed letter which I have left open so you can read it and then forward it to mother. We can be at rest on this score as the only person mother is scared of is the Guardian! It's lucky for us she is! . . .

Somehow I feel and hope that some day you are going to be able to do something really nice for the Guardian here at the World Center. I do so hope so! You should pray that the opportunity will be given you because with your years of accumulated experience and knowledge and love of beauty, you should be able to do a piece of your best work, perhaps better in a way than the Chateau. Who knows?

In what would turn out to be Sutherland's last letter to his wife, he wrote to May on 26 February 1940:

Dearest

Your letter of February 19th greeted me on my arrival this morning and it was welcome.

I completed all drawings for Shoghi Effendi by midnight Sunday and they are in the hands of the printer – will be returned at four – and tonight I shall write my description.

There are 14 sheets in all, many of which are studies of detail with more than one sketch.

I have numbered all sheets and will be able to supply duplicates at any time and to correspond intelligently.

Saturday I decided to sketch a curved stairway plan and also made a coloured perspective – so the envoi is a fairly comprehensive one – agreeably presented. The cost of sending it air mail will be something – but it's the only way . . .

Well, that's all – a good hug and a kiss to you – time hasn't changed your youthful and rigorous outlook – thank goodness.

                            Ton Sutherland

In April of 1943, to their great joy, Sutherland and his daughter received photographs of May's memorial in Buenos Aires. They were sent by Mrs Amelia Collins, who had undertaken to ensure that it had been built according to the specifications sent by Mr Maxwell. On 14 April he replied to her letter:

Dear Millie,

The photographs you sent of May's monument arrived and Rúḥíyyih Khánum and I were thrilled with them. You will be pleased to know that Shoghi Effendi approves of them in every way and of the great service you have so efficiently rendered in the Cause. Rúḥíyyih Khánum and I recognize your good judgement in selecting the right man to do the work and from the beauty of the full size model you had him make, we feel sure that the executed work in marble will be still more beautiful than the model indicates.

Personally I doubt if I could have done as well as you did in attending with such skill to all the artistic and business matters involved in carrying out the monument. You certainly have all the qualifications essential to a practicing architect – and your success in getting the extra plot in Quilmes Cemetery was a stroke of genius, for it was really needed. There is nothing else that I can think of that could render more complete the arrangements you have made. I do think of May as having followed your every action with astonishment and love, for you always occupied a number one place in her affections and as for Rúḥíyyih Khánum and me, there is only one Millie Collins and our love and gratitude go out to you for what you have done for May and for us . . .

I seem to be installed here for the duration of the war; this has its recompenses – which I deeply appreciate. When circumstances permit I shall return to Canada and then go to Buenos Aires. When there my thoughts and my appreciation will inevitably go out to you and Philip Sprague for what you both have done for May and for us.

Shoghi Effendi and Rúḥíyyih Khánum are well, notwithstanding the pressure of work and the supreme importance of the work Shoghi Effendi has in hand for the Centenary of the Bahá'í Faith.

The 'work' Shoghi Effendi had in hand for the Centenary of the Bahá'í Faith was of course not only his immortal *God Passes By* but the design for the Shrine of the Báb on which Mr Maxwell worked through the war years. Amatu'l-Bahá Rúḥíyyih Khánum confirms that the completed design, in model form, was accepted by Shoghi Effendi in 1944 and 'exhibited to the Bahá'ís gathered on the One Hundredth Anniversary of the Declaration of the Báb's Mission, in the precincts of His resting-place'. Her wonderful story of its construction is recorded in *The Priceless Pearl* and will not be repeated here.

There are however, numerous letters written by, or to, and shared amongst Mr Maxwell, Rúḥíyyih Khánum and the Guardian, of which only a few examples are cited here. On Wednesday, 6 August 1947, Mr Maxwell wrote to Rúḥíyyih Khánum:

Dearest

Greetings and love to Shoghi Effendi and you.

All is getting along nicely here and all are well.

First of all – the Shrine – really good progress has been made and some days ago I met the Engineer who had been recommended to me by Mr. Ratner, who is the head of the Technical Institute Architectural Department (and was the Eden Hotel Architect) – and he recommended Professor Neuman who is the head of the Engineering Department of the Technical Institute and also is the head of a technical testing laboratory in Haifa. I had him call on me last Saturday and showed him a series of large scale plans I had prepared in order that he could have every opportunity to see everything to scale and see the limitations imposed by the Shrine rooms.

I had allowed a sufficient space directly over the Shrine roof, in order that a transmission of loads from the octagon level to columns below could be arranged. Prof. Neuman said this was the right thing to do, and I gave him, to assist him, a series of plans and elevations – in all a total of 14 items: plans, elevations, photos etc.

Today Professor Neuman brought in a drawing to a large scale, showing the construction carefully worked out and I was pleased and satisfied with it. His scheme is less costly than mine and avoids any changes or interruption to the existing Shrine of the Báb or the Shrine of 'Abdu'l-Bahá.

Professor Neuman goes to England leaving on August 13th and returns on Oct. 1st. The plans and elevations and necessary drawings to take to Italy will be ready to take there within the 3 month period that starts from the time you left for abroad –

Well, I am busy and the draughtsman is quite useful. His home in Italy was in Milan. It's a bit late and I want to be fresh for the morning's work.

Good hug and a kiss to my Darling, Your Dad

Just over two months later, on 17 October 1947, Mr Maxwell sent additional details to Rúḥíyyih Khánum:

> Dearest
>
> Love and greetings to Shoghi Effendi and to my Darling – Well I have been working hard and can report as follows. The plans are well advanced but my draughtsman is now working 2 hours a day because he is going to the Technical Institute, attending the course in architecture. Of course this is not satisfactory from my point of view. Fortunately the drawings he is making are well advanced. Prof Neuman is back in Haifa – and soon I shall have him over again.
>
> I have made many studies of the decorative work to a scale of 1–10 & this will enable the technical and artistic work to be gone into intelligently with carvers etc. I have coloured the details – my next drawing will be the diagonal view particularly the cartouch at the parapet level.

In the summer (August) of 1948, when the Guardian and Rúḥíyyih Khánum were away, Sutherland, in both a personal letter and a progress report wrote:

> Dearest Ones
>
> I am behind in my correspondence due largely to the weather which old timers say has been the hottest in their experience . . .
>
> I am not attempting to cover the same ground as Gladys and Ben. We are fortunate in having them. Ben has been a marvel at getting consignments of stone delivered at the site and placed where they should be, pending requirements of the mason, etc.
>
> The north-east corner has the pilasters set in position, and a goodly part of the facing cut stone and the backing stone is set. Work on two of the other corners is advancing. I am not attempting to make a report on progress at the site; Ben will do that. I do visit the site whenever I am needed by the others and when special decorative work arrives and is to be set in position . . .
>
> Yesterday I visited the work at the Shrine and to see the corner panels, and we were all very pleased – particularly with the carved borders of the corner panels. The design and execution of the carved borders is quite satisfactory; of course the bottoms and an amount

of the sides only, is set. It is very well finished and unusual in composition. The pilasters, in granite, are very agreeable in colour. Well to me, a promising start has been accomplished and the setting work is well done. We are not up to carved caps level – but from the boxes containing capitals etc. that have been opened I think this work will scale well and look well from the ground level. Well the contractor for the setting is doing his work very well and skilfully, so there is nothing to worry about.

Again, in the late summer of 1949, on 10 September, while work on the Shrine of the Báb was proceeding, Rúḥíyyih Khánum wrote to her father:

Dearest Daddy mine:
... Now, dearest, Shoghi Effendi and I want to impress something on you <u>very</u> <u>strongly</u>.

As the contract for the parapet is now signed and we want the work to go ahead steadily so as to <u>be sure</u> it is all done for the Centenary of the Báb's martyrdom in July 1950, there is no time to lose.

On the other hand you must not tire yourself out and over work as you are more precious to us than anything.

As far as I can see what is required is the exact specifications for the masonry. The designs you have made, Daddy, are so perfect – even though not full scale – that they are more than enough for the <u>extremely</u> capable and gifted Italian workers to go by. There is no doubt that Bufalini has first class carvers and what they have done so far proves they are in the swing of your style and feel exactly what you want. In view of this Shoghi Effendi and I beg you not to hold up the work and tire yourself by making more detailed drawings of the ornamentation. Send them the specifications and the masonry drawings. The mosaic, we all already approved of from the samples received from Italy. There is no doubt the parapet will be a <u>dream</u> of beauty . . .

. . . the work on the Shrine is at a point where you, with your great experience, are indispensable to it.

When your letter came, saying you were satisfied, Shoghi Effendi heaved a sigh of relief and said 'one word from your father I attach more importance to than any amount of praise by the engineers' because he knows how critical you are and how excellent a judge.

We both send our dearest love, and don't exhaust yourself – your Mary – hugs & kisses.

The beginning of the actual work and the critical task of ordering and delivering the marble for the Shrine's construction coincided with the outbreak of yet another war, between the Jews and the Arabs in Palestine. Marion Jack was quite correct in her assessment of the Shrine as Mr Maxwell's greatest architectural achievement. This undaunted and heroic pioneer in Sofia, Bulgaria, whom 'Abdu'l-Bahá had called 'General Jack', wrote the following letter to Mr Maxwell on 30 June 1945, celebrating the exquisite manner in which his design for the Shrine honoured the blessed Báb. She had been one of May's dearest spiritual children and was very fond of Sutherland:

> Our darling May once rather lamented that you were in a sense overshadowed by your brother. Now, at last, you have come into your own, and will be world famous... Now I rejoice with you and for us in Canada that such a beautiful design has come from one of our dearest and finest of Bahá'í brothers of our country – Bravo for you, Maxy dear...
>
> I have often laughed to myself over your lamentation of many years back in that you never had been spiritual and were not then – I think you got a spurt forward by the fear of an eternal separation from our darling May. Anyhow, thank God she lived to see the day when no one could put that tag on the back of her beloved Sutherland – and I believe you are one of her proudest successes, although she would have been the last to claim any great hand in the spiritual growth of her dear one – and how proud she was Maxy. She told me long ago how much higher you stood in her estimation than some of our most distinguished Bahá'í brothers of America and that she would not give you up for the very best of them... How 'Abdu'l-Bahá blessed you when He gave you that heavenly soul – and prayed for your sweet little daughter! He must have foreseen the wonderful future of that little trip.
>
> I do hope some day you may come this way with a message from our beloved Guardian. We so need the visit of the Bahá'í friends, and as our darling May could not come, maybe you will come in her stead – I know it would rejoice her heart.

What is all the more remarkable is that Mr Maxwell attained the height of his artistic and spiritual power in his seventies, when he was already an elderly man. As Amatu'l-Bahá noted in the *In Memoriam* article she wrote about him after his passing:[3]

> By 1946 – for a period of about one year – Sutherland found himself in charge of the Guardian's outside work. Mail, visitors, Government contacts, errands were managed single-handed by this white-haired man of seventy-two. He did a good job, but it was too much for him – a blood vessel broke in his ear and left him totally deaf on one side, shaken and dizzy for weeks on end.

Mr Maxwell kept meticulous notes and records throughout his life and made periodic reports of work at the World Centre, leaving a unique record of the planning and construction of the Shrine of the Báb, along with the ancillary work connected to these developments. Moreover, they provide a glimpse of the life of the small Bahá'í community in Haifa. A sampling of these reports from the mid-1940s serves as an invaluable document in describing the rhythm of Haifa days, and of the tasks undertaken in service to the Guardian.

> *December 8th, 1945*
> I have been swamped with work – Arrivals of mail, etc. have been coming in, in quantities . . .
> The Ascension of 'Abdu'l-Bahá was well attended – and the spirit shown by all was one of deepest devotion and respect. Readings, and good chanting by adults and young boys were reverently given. In fact the conduct of the large attendances was exemplary in every way. I saw to it that Hossein Ekbal was given a position, and readings to deliver – all in keeping with his position as a senior representative member of the Guardian –
> The Birthdays of the Báb and Bahá'u'lláh were observed [on the lunar calendar] in the same spirit. Roses were placed on the Thresholds and before the Friends entered the Shrine I sprinkled Attar of Rose Perfume on the threshold of the Shrine of the Báb (the inner threshold) using perfume the Guardian gave me two or three years ago and for the Threshold of Bahá'u'lláh the Attar of Rose was

---

3   *The Bahá'í World*, vol. XII, pp. 657–62.

furnished by G. After chanting & readings on the lawn and the usual cakes and fruit, the Shrine was visited. (I almost forgot to tell you that the chair where the Guardian sits, occupied its usual place on the lawn and symbolized His Presence in our midst.)

A visit was made by all of us to the room of Bahá'u'lláh in the Mansion. I returned to Haifa, accompanied by Mansur – before the curfew expired – I am sure that all who attended, on the three occasions were greatly benefitted.

December 29th & 30th

I have just finished the drawings for the Vase supports and have an appointment at 5 p.m. tomorrow with Roth and the contractor, shall have prints ready so a price can be arranged.

Klapholz is painting the gates and the foundation work will start in about a week.

Sent an airmail to Crowther as we can't cut the stones for the new work until he cables me the exact diameter of the bases of the vases.

Had an interview with Glovaski and Levy on Friday. Everything went smoothly and on Monday at 10:30 I am to be at the Land Registry Titles office and everything will be signed etc. – all as per contents of the telegram received on Dec. 28.

I have been very busy but in a few days the pressure will be eased.

January 20th, 1946

At the Shrine the excavation work is well advanced –

I got via telegram from Crowther the exact diameter of the base of the lead vases. This enabled me to make the final pedestal drawings and that gave the last information needed by the mason – and also enabled the final foundation lines to be determined.

The electric fixtures for the top of the gate piers are being made, and the iron worker is doing a splendid bit of work. I had luck in getting 3 globes – size 35cm – so there is now everything in hand – or being made to do a complete job – except gold leaf – but that can wait until the rainy season is over because we have not located enough gold leaf of the desired colour at a fair price.

Inspected the excavation work today at about 12:40 a.m. – Sand, crushed stone etc. are delivered . . .

The help situation is now rearranged and operating.

... The gardens look well, but, as you know not many varieties of flowers are in bloom at this time.

Inspected work on the 'Crown' fixtures this morning. The quality of the work is tip-top and the design appeals to me.

[To Amatu'l Bahá:] Glad you had that feeling in retrospect: 'You and Mother gave me such a wonderful childhood'. Why not? You were worth it and I have been repaid thousands of ways – and times.

November 23rd, 1946

Apart from the deafness in one ear, I am quite able to go out alone, but I still use Abdul Raouf as a safety measure – crossing streets etc. Trouble in Palestine is nearly all outside the Haifa district – and the Persian Colony is one of the really tranquil spots.

I am happy in being able to render service, particularly at this most important period and I want you to know that it is just as easy to function now as it was before – and there is nothing to worry over.

December 23rd, 1946

This morning I got the six vases passed for free entry—a deposit will be made—as usual.

The balance of the Schopflocher gold has arrived. I expect tomorrow to get it passed, free of charge. The parcel is marked 14-carat.

I have got the city at work, at last—on the sidewalk. The street drain was recently completed and that removed the obstacle to the road or sidewalk being delayed. There is a great amount of truck and other traffic on Mountain Road, mostly military vehicles.

Much earlier that year, Mr Maxwell had the matter of the construction of a new sidewalk on his mind. His handwritten 'Memorandum' dated 29 April 1946 and entitled: 'Visit to Municipal Building 9.30 to 11.40 to see Mr Prushonsky' was a record of a request made by Mr Maxwell on behalf of the Head of his Faith to the Municipality of Haifa for a new sidewalk to be built opposite the property that was situated on what was then called the Mountain Road, in Haifa, on which the superstructure of the Shrine of the Báb was to be constructed.

I explained the willingness and desire of the Bahá'í community to have the sidewalk started at once.

Mr. P. entirely favourable and will help in every way he can.

Mr. P. said that the present decision of the City Council, put into force some time ago, requires total cost to be paid by the Bahá'í Community.

Mr. P. said that an application to the City Hall (City Council) should be made by the Bahá'í Community, requesting that this present arrangement be cancelled and the Bahá'í Community be given back the rights they are entitled to as an officially recognized Religious Body, entitled to certain exemptions such as being charged, and paying 50 percent of the cost of a new sidewalk opposite Bahá'í Shrine property situated on Mountain Road, Haifa, and the Municipality paying the other half.

Mr. P. said the City Council meets about twice monthly, and that he is favourable to the construction of the proposed sidewalk. I explained to Mr. P. some of the various building projects contemplated, and that the constructions are made possible by contributions from Bahá'ís in almost all parts of the world. Explained also the constructive economic value to Palestine labour etc.

Although his tasks were multiplying in the Holy Land and the pressure of work was great as the time for the construction of the Shrine drew near, W. S. Maxwell did not lose touch with his professional contacts in Canada. Indeed, as will be shown, he used them for his work in Haifa. He also kept in close touch with A. M. Parent, who wrote him on 24 December 1946 to inform him that

> ... the Knox Crescent Church on Dorchester St. was burned down some weeks ago. It happened in the middle of the night. The walls are still up but the roof came down with a crash. The registers and vestments were however found intact. The memorial window to your father's memory has suffered greatly. The talk is that they cannot afford to rebuild ...
>
> I will deliver your message to Mr. Gagnon;[4] he appreciates your

---

4 Clarence Gagnon (1881–1942), a fellow artist and friend of W. S. Maxwell, was a full member of the Royal Canadian Academy of Arts and is best known for his rural Quebec landscape paintings and the illustrations for Louis Hémon's novel *Maria Chapdelaine*. He received the Trevor Prize of the Salmagundi Club of New York (a centre for fine artists from New York and around North America providing exhibitions of paintings, sculpture and photography), and was an award-winning printmaker as well as an active promoter of Quebec handicrafts.

kind thoughts of him deeply . . . with love to you and Mary, I am always your old pal – Amanda

Miss Parent had not only been left in charge of the Maxwell finances but also the house at 1548 Pine Avenue, together with Dorothy Ward who was overseeing its care. On 4 July 1947, the Spiritual Assembly of Montreal wrote to Mr Maxwell with questions regarding the use of the Maxwell house for Bahá'í purposes, and in answer to this letter Amatu'l-Bahá also wrote to Dorothy Ward on 11 July:

> Everyone tells me how beautifully you take care of our home, and as you know my father and I have the greatest confidence in you. We feel sure that you will keep it exactly the way it always was. As you know, Daddy still considers it his home, and if it were not for all the work he has to do here, which is more important than anything else, he would have gone home for a visit by now. He wants it kept just as it was when he left, and if anyone wishes to make any changes, they must consult him first . . .
> Much love to you, and Daddy sends his kind regards. We both thank you for all you are doing. Rúḥíyyih

In the spring of 1947, Mr Maxwell went to Cyprus for a short vacation. He had a very relaxing time there and visited Nicosia and other ancient sights. As usual he made several sketches, and wrote of them in this exchange of cables and letters with Rúḥíyyih Khánum:

Stamped in Haifa: 12 May 1947

> ENJOYED BELLEPAIS ALSO KYRENIA CASTLE STARTED SKETCH FROM BEDROOM WINDOW ALSO COLOURED LINENS ATTRACTIVE VISITING NICOSIA MUSEUM SOON HEALTH EXCELLENT LOVE ALL CHEERIO = MAXWELL

Stamped in Haifa: 20 May 1947

> FINE DRIVES VISITED ST HILARION MAY GO NICOSIA STAY 2 DAYS TOMORROW WELL LOVE ALL = MAXWELL

26th May 1947
My Dearest Daddy:

Every day I have been going to write 'tomorrow' but it just never came, as you know from personal experience, evidently! I can feel you are having a grand time ... at least I hope the waves of peaceful contentment that are flowing over the sea from Cyprus are not all in my fond imagination?

I am with you in thought every day and wish with all my heart we were having this vacation together, but if that cannot be I at least have the satisfaction of knowing you are getting a much deserved and needed rest. Things are going well here and Shoghi Effendi says to tell you he has lots of surprises for you on Mt. Carmel of a pleasant nature and which require no more exertion on your part than just contemplating them leisurely! He also sends you his 'dearest love'.

30th May 1947
Dearest

Well I made one sketch only, sky and water – not good so did them in gouache ...

Of course I have visited many astounding semi decrepit ruins – but I liked best, the little church and monastery at Lambousa, Byzantine – Greek Catholic – 2 monks only – Russian Ikon paintings, nice gilded carvings. Russian Ikon paintings etc. condition = good -

I deeply appreciate Shoghi Effendi's message and news – of course he is wound up and active all the time and he even breaks the speed limit in Garden Production. But his last work – almost completed when I left, is a very original and beautiful piece of work.

So Gladys went to Jerusalem. Congratulations – hope it may result in a new car. The trip required – nerve. . . .

Well chicken – that's all this morning.

To Shoghi Effendi I send deepest love and appreciation.

To Gladys – Congratulations & love on safe return from her 'Dime Novel Experience' and to you, Snooper in Chief

A hug a kiss and love from Dad

Less than a year later, on 14 April 1948, a joyous cable was received in Haifa from the Local Spiritual Assembly of Montreal, addressed directly to W. S. Maxwell:

> FIRST HISTORIC CANADIAN CONVENTION PLANNED YOUR HOME PLEASE CABLE APPROVAL AND BLESSING LOVING GREETINGS MONTREAL ASSEMBLY

Mr Maxwell's reply was immediate:

> DELIGHTED HAVE HISTORIC CONVENTION HELD 1548 PINE AVENUE REGRET VERY MUCH INABILITY ATTEND BUT FEEL VERY PROUD CANADAS ACHIEVEMENTS GREETINGS TO ALL SUTHERLAND MAXWELL

The joy and excitement felt by father and daughter, the two remaining Maxwells, can be palpably felt through the cables sent by Amatu'l-Bahá in honour of this event on 19 April 1948. The first is addressed to the Canadian National Bahá'í Convention:

> OUR HEARTS WITH YOU ALL JOYOUS TRIUMPHANT OCCASION LAUNCHING CANADIAN INDEPENDENT SERVICE BELOVED FAITH ASSUMPTION PRECIOUS RESPONSIBILITY MAY YOUR LABOURS BREAK ALL RECORDS CARRY OFF THE PALMS LOVING GREETINGS BEST WISHES ALL IN WHICH MAY SURELY JOINS US RUHIYYIH SUTHERLAND

The second cable to Emeric Sala states:

> DADDY MYSELF BEGINNING MAY INSTRUCTED MISS PARENT PAY CANADIAN NATIONAL FUND SEVENTY DOLLARS MONTHLY ONE YEAR PLEASE YOURSELF GIVE HER NAME TREASURER AFTER ELECTION BOTH WITH YOU ALL HISTORIC OCCASION LOVE RUHIYYIH

The third cable was addressed to Rosemary Sala:

> WE WOULD DEEPLY APPRECIATE YOUR MAKING ARRANGEMENTS SERVE DELIGATES FRIENDS EITHER A BANQUET OR BUFFET IN

> OUR HOME TOKEN MAXWELL JOY OCCASION CONVENTION PLEASE TAKE EXPENSES FROM MISS PARENT DEEPEST LOVE RUHIYYIH

And the fourth, addressed to Miss Parent, confirms the above instructions:

> DADDY SAFELY ARRIVED ROME STOP ASKED ROSEMARY SALA COLLECT EXPENSES BANQUET GIVEN OUR HOME FROM YOU STOP ASKING MR SALA GIVE YOU NAME TREASURER CANADIAN NATIONAL ASSEMBLY TO RECEIVE MONTHLY CONTRIBUTION ALL WELL DEAREST LOVE MARY

The reference to Rome in this last cable provides a glimmering of all that W. S. Maxwell was doing at this time. Although the formation of the new National Spiritual Assembly of Canada was the source of immense pride and joy to him, his heart and mind were in Haifa, for the construction of the superstructure of the Shrine of the Báb had started and his work and responsibilities had doubled as a result. The years from 1948 on were exciting as well as stressful times for all concerned. The Shrine of the Báb was being built during the height of chaos and confusion in Palestine when internal wars had erupted which would eventually culminate in the birth of the State of Israel. Although the details of this period have been brilliantly portrayed by Amatu'l-Bahá Rúḥíyyih Khánum in *The Priceless Pearl*, the crucial role played by her father can also be traced in the family files.

By 1948, Gladys Cotton was called to serve at the World Centre and Ben Weeden, whom she later married, followed soon afterwards. After that, Mr Maxwell had some help in the process of negotiating with government officials, but his presence was crucial when the first contract was made for the stone work of the Báb's Shrine. Since it was a time of such turmoil and insecurity in Palestine, during the War of Independence the journey from Haifa to the airport in Tel Aviv was quite a risky venture and Mr Maxwell not only travelled in an armoured vehicle, but, for security reasons, also went armed with a letter written and signed by Shoghi Effendi:

Haifa, Palestine
April 11th, 1948
To Whom it may Concern:

    This is to introduce Mr. W. S. Maxwell, F.R.I.B.A., who is a member of the Bahá'í Community and has been residing in Haifa with me since 1940. He is my father-in-law and is proceeding to Italy in connection with work to be carried out on one of our Bahá'í Shrines on Mt. Carmel.

    He is accompanied by Mr. Benjamin Weeden, a Bahá'í from the United States of America, who is likewise occupied here in Haifa in serving the Bahá'í Faith at its World Centre. Mr. Weeden is proceeding to Italy to assist Mr. Maxwell in his work there.

    I, as Head of the Bahá'í Faith, would appreciate every assistance being rendered to these two gentlemen in discharging their tasks and in facilitating their journey and safe transit through Palestine territory.

        Shoghi Rabbani, Head of the Bahá'í Faith.
            House of 'Abdu'l-Bahá
              7 Persian Street,
                  Haifa

On 2 April Shoghi Effendi cabled Dr Ugo Giachery about this historic trip:

> MR. MAXWELL ACCOMPANIED BENJAMIN WEEDEN ARRIVING ROME APRIL THIRTEENTH PLANE BRAATHENS SOUTH AFRICA FAR EAST AIR COMPANY STOP PURPOSE PLACE CONTRACTS COMPLETION SHRINE BAB STOP WEEDEN AMERICAN SUBJECT OWING CONDITIONS HERE UNABLE OBTAIN ITALIAN VISA JERUSALEM STOP APPRECIATE MEET THEM AERODROME ARRANGE FOR WEEDEN OBTAIN VISA ON ARRIVAL OTHERWISE HE MUST PROCEED SAME PLANE GENEVA STOP MR MAXWELL BEING BRITISH REQUIRED NO VISA STOP KINDLY CABLE RECEIPT THIS CABLE STOP LETTER FOLLOWING STOP DEEPEST LOVING APPRECIATION

The flight was postponed from the 13th until the 16th, and on April 19th Shoghi Effendi finally sent a cable addressed to 'MAXWELL WEEDEN CARE UGO GIACHERY':

DELIGHTED SAFE ARRIVAL STOP PRAYING SUCCESS STOP LOVE FRIENDS SHOGHI

In his report to Shoghi Effendi written on 26 April 1948, W. S. Maxwell gave a vivid picture of his trip to Rome and his investigations with Mr Weeden regarding the acquisition of the correct stone, the quality of the carving and other details connected with this commission. Interestingly enough, Mr Maxwell used the letterhead of the Royal Institute of British Architects, of which he was a Fellow in British Mandate Palestine, instead of the Canadian Institute, as had been his wont:

Dear Shoghi Effendi
Rome, April 1948
   I was to write you and to telegraph frequently. I have not lived up to the bargain as consistently as I should have done, for which I apologize.
   Ben is the ideal person for mailing and telegraphing and a good part of what he sent to you was after consultation with you & me. Our armoured car travelling was a novelty to us. We encountered no villains and have not heard any gunshots except for a few in Tel Aviv at night time.
   The time lost by cancellation of planes was trying, but we were rewarded by a very interesting night trip in a splendid four-engined Norwegian plane, American made and capably staffed by capable Norwegians. There is nothing in particular to dwell upon, other than say it was quite interesting to be one of forty or more passengers in an up to date plane.
   We had a few hours of flying amid clouds in the early morning, with an occasional pinpoint or so of mother earth to let us know that there was some hope of arriving. Well our capable young captain finally came down over the River Tiber and it was not long before we landed and there was Mr. Giachery cheerfully greeting us, bless his heart – he must have been there for hours.
   A letter from Alberto Bufalini awaited us, saying he could go to Rome or meet us in Milan. We consulted together – Ben + Giachery + W. S. M. asking him to come to Rome. The reason for this decision was the prime importance of finding a stone for the carved work.

Returning yesterday from a visit to the Chief of police, regarding getting a form filled out, I asked Mr. Giachery if there was a government geological museum in Rome. He said yes and this morning we met there and had the good fortune to be personally conducted by the Curator, who is the expert and is also the Professor in the university. I showed the sample of the Palestine stone and he said they had the same stone. We inspected it and it is a splendid stone, just what we require for the caps and carving etc. This is the reason for having Bufalini come to Rome and the key matter governing the possibility of having carving etc. done in Italy. It is desirable to have Bufalini's acceptance of the stone and it smoothes the way for action and estimating etc.

Well things look bright now. You may not be aware how the elections yesterday and today have affected progress – all shops factories closed etc.

By the way, the Curator told me that the firm that is to supply the granite etc. – Guido M. Fabbricotti and Bufalini etc. is the best firm in Italy, so the guidance from my Canadian friend Mr. Allen has been just what is wanted; also the Curator spoke highly about Bufalini and I am very pleased.

Well it's getting late, so I report we are all well and happy about the progress made and about the future.

A great deal of love to you and Mary, Affectionately,
     Sutherland

By the way, it was a great pleasure to see Mrs. and Mr. Giachery and they are doing splendid work. Mary will get all this detail from Gladys.

* * *

There had always been, from the early years of Rúḥíyyih Khánum's marriage, a cordial relation with General McNeil and his wife Lilian, who was a Bahá'í. The following letter from Sutherland to Rúḥíyyih Khánum in August of 1949 refers to the passing of Mrs McNeil as well as the answer he received from the General.

Dearest

I am enclosing a letter from General McNeil to me. It explains itself and I am astonished – that the General, at his age, writes so clearly and well. I always liked him and Mrs. McNeil and her visits to see you in the past – when she came to Haifa – were a pleasant break in the routine of life in the East.

From Brig. General McNeil
Kasu Mazra'a
Nahariya
19.8.49

Dear Mr. Maxwell

I wish to thank you for so kindly sending flowers for my dear wife's funeral and for attending yourself. I feel sure that Shoghi Effendi and his wife will be very grieved at the sad news. My wife had been failing steadily during the past month and was practically speechless towards the end. So we must regard her very peaceful passing as a happy release.

With my best regard & thanks,
Believe me – Yrs sincerely
Angus McNeil

Step by step, Shoghi Effendi guided, encouraged and supported W. S. Maxwell in realizing the crown of his life's work. As the superstructure of the Shrine of the Báb rose, day by day and month by month, before the eyes of a wondering world, he drew on the most refined essence of Sutherland's experience – his architectural know-how, his artistic talent, his love and devotion – for the completion of that blessed building. This edifice symbolized the apex of Mr Maxwell's accomplishments in the field of architecture. It was quite literally the crown of his whole life's work. Begun at a time when he was already old and frail, this monumental task was to become his most glorious achievement and he persevered in it until he reached the limit of his powers.

The Guardian also urged Ben Weeden to write a series of detailed articles on the day-to-day progress of the building of the Shrine of the Báb which were serialized in the American *Bahá'í News* in the March and October 1949 and August and September 1950 issues.[5] When the building of the arcade was completed, Shoghi Effendi asked Horace Holley to write about the Shrine for *The Bahá'í World*.[6] Dr Ugo Giachery also made the following reference to W. S. Maxwell's work in an article in volume XII:[7]

> Many are familiar with the beautiful color plate giving the architect's design of the Shrine as it appears in Volume IX of *The Bahá'í World* as the frontispiece. But only a few have seen the countless accurate and detailed drawings of this unique building, a mighty work done by one man.
>
> The Italian architects who have had the opportunity to examine these plans have expressed their admiration, with the highest words of praise, for the conception, the style, the elegance, and the exquisite intricacy of the decoration which characterizes the entire project.

Amatul-Bahá later wrote in her *In Memoriam* article about her father:

> In spite of failing strength he continued his detailed and working drawings right up to the night when his health broke down . . .

But Shoghi Effendi must have already been concerned about Sutherland's increasingly fragile physical condition when he sent him the following cable from Europe in August 1949, during the hottest month of the year in Haifa:

> URGE YOU TAKE UTMOST CARE AVOID POSSIBILITY SUNSTROKE WHILE INSPECTING SHRINE STOP AS WORK PROGRESSES YOU ARE INCREASINGLY PRECIOUS TO US ALL STOP AIRMAIL COPY PHOTOGRAPH SHRINE MODEL NOT TOO SMALL LOVE

On 5 April 1950 Mr Maxwell collapsed, and the flood of cables and letters about his precarious health from 1950 through to the end of

---

5 The series was also included in its entirety in *The Bahá'í World*, vol. XII (1950–1957), pp. 246–52.
6 ibid. vol. XI (1946–1950), pp. 16–18, as part of the International Survey of Current Bahá'í Activities in the East and West.
7 ibid. vol. XII (1950–1954), p. 240.

Painting by W. S. Maxwell of a seaside scene in Kyrenia, Cyprus, showing a church steeple and a lighthouse, May 1947. The original is in brilliant colour and very beautiful

Original structure of the Shrine of the Báb, built by 'Abdu'l-Bahá

The Shrine of the Báb. The superstructure, designed by W. S. Maxwell, was completed in 1953

Rúḥíyyih Khánum with her beloved father William Sutherland Maxwell, in Torquay, England, 1948

W. S. Maxwell with his brother's granddaughter Mary Yates Walker, at the Maxwell home, 1548 Pine Avenue, Montreal

Monument on William Sutherland Maxwell's grave, Mt Royal Cemetery, Montreal, Canada. Amatu'l-Bahá Rúḥíyyih Khánum wrote of it: 'My father designed this stone for his brother-in-law Randolph Bolles and he told me he "would not mind" having it for himself too; so I gave him the same design.' (Photo by Lorraine Goh)

1951 offer a glimpse of this painful period. Amatu'l-Bahá Rúḥíyyih Khánum described it in the *In Memoriam* article she wrote about her father as follows: 'He suffered ups and downs, recovery followed collapse, collapse recovery. It was a heart-breaking two years for those who loved him.'[1] Since she herself has written amply on this period in *The Priceless Pearl*, it simply suffices to say here that Mr Maxwell was suffering from enlarged gallstones, which, due to the limited medical means available at the time, could not be removed and caused him excruciating pain. The morphine required to enable him to endure the pain only exacerbated his condition further and rendered him confused and disorientated. It was a very difficult period for Rúḥíyyih Khánum. On 11 May 1950, Shoghi Effendi cabled Amelia Collins:

> SUTHERLAND GRAVELY ILL ONLY HOPE TRANSFER HIM EXPERT CARE DOCTOR GENEVA STOP TURNING AGAIN YOU HAVE GREAT NEED STOP COULD YOU FLY GENEVA NEXT WEEK IF NECESSARY MATTER STRICTLY CONFIDENTIAL DEEPEST LOVE

And on 14 May, having received her reply in the affirmative, he cabled again:

> PROFOUNDLY TOUCHED RESPONSE WILL INFORM YOU DEVELOPMENTS ABIDING GRATITUDE

On the same day, on a copy of a cable addressed to Swissair, in Athens, which states 'RELEASE THREE SEATS 17/5 SR 331 URGENTLY NEEDED FOR EMERGENCY CASE LYD/GEN. SWISSAIR', Amatu'l-Bahá wrote the following:

> This is more than historical, it's miraculous – we got answer at 4 o'clock the 16th and caught the plane.

Several excerpts from letters dated 23 June, 28 June and 5 July 1950, written by Amatu'l-Bahá on behalf of Shoghi Effendi to the National Spiritual Assemblies of Canada, Australia and New Zealand, and the United States, also give us a glimpse of the distress that was being experienced in Haifa at this time:

---

1 ibid. p. 661.

[S]ince the beginning of April my dear father, Mr. Maxwell, has been dangerously and desperately ill. The anxiety this caused us all, and the constant coming and going of doctors and nurses, and two periods in hospital, have necessitated putting aside all correspondence for months. Now, however, thank God, Mr. Maxwell is slowly improving and the threads of normal existence can be taken up by us all.

Mr. Maxwell, the architect of the Shrine, at the beginning of April became desperately ill, and for ten weeks absorbed the anxious care and attention of us all, as his condition was seemingly hopeless.

It is only the last two weeks that he [Shoghi Effendi] has been able to take up the question of his mail, due to the fact that the very serious illness of my father, since April 5th, has kept us all in a condition of confusion and suspense for months. As it was seemingly a hopeless condition, and one most agonizing for us all to have to watch, it was impossible to concentrate for the time being on anything else.

Thanks however to the Mercy of Bahá'u'lláh and the iron determination of the Guardian not to allow the builder of the Shrine to pass away at this time, Mr. Maxwell is now recovering and our lives are getting back to normal.

In a statement entitled 'An Enterprise Transcending any National Institution' quoted in his *Messages to the Bahá'í World, 1950–1957*, Shoghi Effendi wrote with regard to the Shrine of the Báb, 'My gratitude is deepened by the miraculous recovery of its gifted architect, Sutherland Maxwell, whose illness was pronounced hopeless by physicians.'

In fact, in defiance of such gloomy prognostications, the Guardian had arranged to send Mr Maxwell to Switzerland where he could benefit from a more healthy diet and be under the treatment of their own homeopathic doctors. On his return to Haifa on 13 January 1951, Amatu'l-Bahá cabled Doctor Pierre Schmidt in Geneva to say: 'FATHER PERFECT HEALTH SINCE ARRIVAL'.

* * *

As Amatu'l-Bahá has stated in her father's *In Memoriam* article, his 'cherished wish' was to visit Montreal again, and since his health seemed to have improved so much in Switzerland, arrangements were made for him to pass the summer of 1951 in his own home, attended by his devoted nurse. He was to return to Haifa in the autumn but by then it was evident that if he did so, he might easily have a relapse due to the acute food shortages during the early years of Israel's independence. 'He remained in Canada,' Rúḥíyyih K͟hánum wrote, 'longing for the day he could return to his home in the Holy Land.'

In May of 1951, Rosemary Sala in Montreal wrote Amatu'l-Bahá a touching description of her father's return to Montreal:

> I know how eager you must be to learn all the details of your father's arrival. Emeric and I took Millie to the airport with us to meet him. Mr. Pitts came but he, through pull, got right into the place where the passengers entered while we were in the wire enclosed 'cage' outside! You must know how our hearts fluttered watching for his figure to appear. When at last it did, our joy and shock was terrific – I shook so while Mrs. Yates and I couldn't help but weep. He stumbled so and wandered away until a guide took him by the arm – the nurse was so heavily laden with rugs and bags etc. We didn't speak to him then; we thought the excitement and meeting the others was sufficient. We had to go out of town for the day. When we came back we phoned Dorothy. She said he knew her and kissed her on both cheeks, took her arm, and went right into the living-room. The first thing he picked up was a photograph of the monument on May's grave which Dorothy had framed and placed on the small table near the window seat. He held it, nodding his head, then he touched each object giving its date and period. He saw the balcony, which Dorothy had fixed up with a small couch, two summer chairs and window boxes. He smiled and went over to the couch, lay down for a moment, and it has been his favourite spot ever since!
>
> On Saturday we had an NSA meeting, but called to pick up Millie for dinner. I went on to the porch to meet your father, kissed him and said, 'Rosemary'. He took my hand and held it and said, 'Emeric?'. When Emeric appeared, he immediately knew him and said how much he had enjoyed reading his book . . . The other members wished to meet him . . .

The following excerpts are from a letter of Dorothy Ward, the caretaker of the Maxwell home, who also wrote to Amatu'l-Bahá about her father:

> I have tried to do my best all summer since your Father arrived; it has been rather difficult as I do not speak French [his Swiss nurse spoke only French]. We have had a cleaning woman once a week and of course Nurse has done everything for your Father. She has marvelous physical strength, I don't know how she has kept going since June, without any relief, how marvelous! to have that strength . . . Your father looks a lot better but his memory is still the same. Some days he knows me, some days he does not . . . Lovingly, Dorothy Ward

It was at the end of that year, on 25 December 1951, that Shoghi Effendi's thrilling message cabled on 23 December reached Montreal, appointing W. S. Maxwell as a Hand of the Cause:

> MOVED CONVEY GLAD TIDINGS YOUR ELEVATION RANK HAND CAUSE STOP APPOINTMENT OFFICIALLY ANNOUNCED PUBLIC MESSAGE ADDRESSED ALL NATIONAL ASSEMBLIES STOP MAY SACRED FUNCTION ENABLE YOU ENRICH RECORD SERVICES ALREADY RENDERED FAITH BAHA'U'LLAH

Two days later, on 27 December, he received the following cable from his daughter:

> CONGRATULATIONS DADDY DEAREST ON YOUR APPOINTMENT BY BELOVED GUARDIAN STATION HAND CAUSE ALL MY LOVE MARY

And on Christmas Day 1951 Rosemary Sala wrote a letter to Amatu'l-Bahá describing the circumstances in which her father registered this overwhelming news. Her portrait gives us a glimpse of the true humility of W. S. Maxwell:

> It is late, but in spite of two busy days and an early start for Winter School tomorrow, I cannot sleep without telling you of our precious visit this afternoon with your father! He has not been too well lately as you know; the doctor comes again tomorrow but he has said his blood pressure is worse than his heart condition.

We found him quite feeble dear. He greeted us lovingly but did not speak too coherently. The telephone rang – the cable office – & Mlle. Bovay [his nurse] asked me to take the message. It was the wonderful cable from the Guardian to your father!

I returned to the library and told Emeric and the nurse of the message – your father was sitting, half-sleeping. The nurse then showed us the cable which had arrived that morning but she had hesitated to show it to him for fear that it would agitate him. She then gave it to your father but he couldn't grasp it. Then Emeric wrote in large letters, 'Shoghi Effendi has appointed you a Hand of the Cause'. Your father read it slowly aloud. Then it was so beautiful to see the light and life come into his tired face, yet such a touching humility. He sat silent a moment then said, 'But I didn't do it all alone. There were so many others to help me!' We felt so blessed and privileged to be with him at that moment. I had been rubbing his cold hand and I could not resist kissing his hand as Emeric explained to the nurse the great honour and distinction that had been bestowed on her beloved patient. Tears came to her eyes; she was so touched and she said: 'Je suis contente, je suis tres contente, il le merite'.

It was amazing to see the change in your father – the weariness left him, and he came with us to the door as we left and remained to wave us off with such a sweet smile. We recalled how your mother so often told us that the Master had said Mr. Maxwell would perform a great service for Canada.

With so much love and gratitude – Rosemary

* * *

He was not destined to see his daughter again. He remained for the next two winter months in 1548 Pine Avenue, increasingly fragile, a semi-invalid, the last and sole occupant of a house that had seen so much life and vitality over the previous four decades. The thought of him there alone must have seared the heart of his daughter in the Holy Land. She must have agonized over this separation that was destined to be the final one. In an effort to reassure her over her parting from her father, Rosemary Sala wrote to Rúḥíyyih Khánum on 11 April 1952:

Truly, your decision to satisfy his longing to be back in Montreal has bestowed an everlasting bounty on Canada. Never doubt this. His happiness in being in his own home would have satisfied you. Of course he asked for you and the Guardian; he would search for his coat & hat and say he was going to meet you. Then he would be distracted, and within an hour or so talk of you as though he had seen you and as if you had gone upstairs for a moment . . .

On 21 March, Naw-Rúz of 1952, Mr Maxwell received the following cable from Haifa:

> DEAREST LOVING THOUGHTS SURROUND YOU OCCASION NAWRUZ BOTH WELL SHOGHI MARY

In that same letter of 11 April, Rosemary Sala shared with Rúḥíyyih Khánum a last glimpse of Mr Maxwell; she had seen him a brief week before Naw-Rúz:

> Emeric and I had seen your father about ten days before. We had taken him for a drive, and he was the brightest we had seen him for some time, pointing out homes he had built or houses of people he knew. This continued for over an hour, though by the time he arrived home for tea, he had tired. On that following week, I had to visit Ottawa and didn't see him, though Nurse told me he weakened and fell . . . in the Master's room . . .

Apparently this fall was too much for his already weakened body, and four days after Naw-Rúz he passed away. Rúḥíyyih Khánum's aunt, Jeanne Ruhanguiz Bolles, described the circumstances in a letter she wrote on 12 April:

> As you know now your beloved father was only (very) ill 3 days. Dear Stirling and a believer[2] were with him, also his faithful nurse all night before he 'left' for the Kingdom. God be praised! Bahá'u'lláh did not let him suffer.

---

2 Stirling Maxwell, his favourite nephew, and René Roy, brother of Mrs Marie Bolton of Australia.

By the time Rúḥíyyih Khánum received the news of her father's critical condition and was making her preparations to go and be with him, it was already too late. On 25 March the late edition of *The Montreal Daily Star* printed his picture under the headline: 'W. S. Maxwell, Well-known architect, dies'. The subtitle stated:

> William Sutherland Maxwell, prominent Montreal architect, who died today at his home, 1548 Pine Avenue West. He was 78. Funeral arrangements will be announced later.

The Guardian cabled the Bahá'í world immediately that same day, 25 March, with an announcement of his passing that was simultaneously a resounding accolade of his achievements and a tribute to his nobility of character and distinctive station:

> WITH SORROWFUL HEART ANNOUNCE THROUGH NATIONAL ASSEMBLIES HAND CAUSE BAHAULLAH HIGHLY ESTEEMED DEARLY BELOVED SUTHERLAND MAXWELL GATHERED GLORY ABHA KINGDOM STOP SAINTLY LIFE EXTENDING WELL NIGH FOUR SCORE YEARS ENRICHED COURSE ABDULBAHAS MINISTRY SERVICES DOMINION CANADA ENNOBLED FORMATIVE AGE FAITH DECADE SERVICES HOLY LAND DURING DARKEST DAYS MY LIFE DOUBLY HONOURED THROUGH ASSOCIATION CROWN MARTYRDOM WON MAY MAXWELL INCOMPARABLE HONOUR BESTOWED HIS DAUGHTER ATTAINED CONSUMMATION THROUGH HIS APPOINTMENT ARCHITECT ARCADE SUPERSTRUCTURE BABS SEPULCHER AS WELL AS ELEVATION FRONT RANK HANDS CAUSE GOD STOP ADVISE ALL NATIONAL ASSEMBLIES HOLD BEFITTING MEMORIAL GATHERINGS PARTICULARLY MASHRIQULADHKAR WILMETTE HAZIRATULQUDS TIHRAN STOP INSTRUCTED HANDS CAUSE UNITED STATES CANADA HORACE HOLLEY FRED SCHOPFLOCHER ATTEND MY REPRESENTATIVES FUNERAL MONTREAL STOP MOVED NAME AFTER HIM SOUTHERN DOOR BABS TOMB TRIBUTE HIS UNIQUE SERVICES SECOND HOLIEST SHRINE BAHAI WORLD STOP MANTLE HAND CAUSE NOW FALLS SHOULDERS HIS DISTINGUISHED DAUGHTER AMATULBAHA RUHIYYIH WHO ALREADY RENDERED STILL RENDERING MANIFOLD NO LESS MERITORIOUS SELF SACRIFICING SERVICES WORLD CENTRE FAITH BAHAULLAH

On 26 March he cabled the Hand of the Cause Siegfried Schopflocher with instructions regarding the funeral:

> HEARTFELT APPRECIATION SYMPATHY STOP ADVISE ENSURE BEFITTING BAHAI FUNERAL STOP APPOINT YOU AND ANOTHER HAND CAUSE UNITED STATES ACT MY REPRESENTATIVES FUNERAL STOP APPRECIATE YOUR ARRANGING TWO WREATHS FLOWERS BEHALF MYSELF RUHIYYIH PLACE HIS COFFIN STOP URGE AS MANY NATIONAL ASSEMBLY MEMBERS BELIEVERS ATTEND FUNERAL PAY TRIBUTE FOREMOST HAND CAUSE STOP NON BAHAIS ALSO WELCOME ATTEND STOP ADVISE PROCURE LARGE BURIAL PLOT BEFITTING HIS STATION DEEPEST LOVE KINDLY CABLE HOUR FUNERAL

The Guardian appointed the Hand of the Cause Horace Holley to be his other representative at the funeral service and interment at the Mount Royal cemetery. A memorial issue of the *Canadian Bahá'í News* dedicated to W. S. Maxwell included the details of the programme of the funeral, held on 29 March. A Negro Spiritual was sung by Eddie Elliot at the special request of Mr Maxwell's daughter. An attendant at the chapel where the service was held later commented that it was the most impressive he had ever witnessed.

Some months later, in Shoghi Effendi's letter of 8 June 1952 to the National Spiritual Assembly of the Bahá'ís of Canada, in which he appealed to them to focus 'on the dire necessity of multiplying the number of pioneers, the rapid formation of groups and the conversion of groups to Assemblies', he challenged the Canadian community to forge on and win their goals, '[i]nspired by the example and the accomplishments of those of its members who have distinguished themselves in the Holy Land, on the European continent and in both the northern and southern continents of the Western Hemisphere', and paid the following unique tribute to the three Maxwells of Montreal:

> One more word in conclusion. The passing, at this juncture, of one who, through a long career of distinguished service to the Cause of Bahá'u'lláh, not only since the birth of this community but in more recent years in the heart and centre of the Bahá'í World, has left an indelible mark on the annals of the Faith, has evoked not only the

deepest sorrow but the utmost regret at a time when this community is beginning to reap at long last the first fruits of its stewardship to the Cause of God, and the whole Bahá'í World is on the eve of celebrating one of its greatest Jubilees. By reason of his own saintly life, his self-effacement, gentleness, loving kindness and nobility of soul; by virtue of his remarkable endowments which he so devotedly consecrated to both the embellishment of the slopes of God's holy mountain and the creation of a befitting design for the second most holy Bahá'í Edifice embosomed in its very heart; and because of his kinship, on the one hand, with a wife whom posterity will regard, not only as the mother of both the Canadian Bahá'í Community and of the first Bahá'í centre established on the European continent but also as one of the foremost pioneers and martyrs of the Faith and, on the other with a daughter, whose unfailing support to me as my helpmate, in the darkest days of my life, has earned her the title already conferred on her father – Sutherland Maxwell has left a legacy, and achieved a position excelled by only a few among the supporters of the Faith of Bahá'u'lláh throughout the eleven decades of its existence.[3]

After Sutherland Maxwell's passing tributes poured in. They included many from his colleagues and from professional organizations with which he had long been associated, and to which he had made significant professional contributions in their development during his long and brilliant career in the fields of art and architecture.

A memorial booklet from the funeral, as well as a list of floral contributors, was sent to Rúḥíyyih Khánum by Siegfried Schopflocher. It included:

> A typed, formal list of those attending the funeral, including:
> (1) Representing the Royal Architectural Institute of Canada:
>   J. Roxburgh Smith, President; H. H. Simmonds, 1st Vice-Pres.
>   Harold Lawson, Hon. Sec.   R. S. Morris, Hon. Treas.
>   Executive Committee: Maurice Payette, O. Beaule,
>   A. J. C. Paine, Louis N. Aude,
>   J. C. Meadowcroft, Chas. David,
>   A. J. Hazelgrove
>   Executive Secretary: C. J. Carroll.

---

3 Shoghi Effendi, *Messages to Canada*, pp. 31–2.

Also a hand-printed card: (with a wreath)	IN TRIBUTE from The Council & Members of The Royal Architectural Institute of Canada [signed] J. Roxburgh Smith. President
(2) A handwritten card from: (with a basket of flowers)	The President and Council and Members of the Arts Club

The Royal Institute of British Architects, over the signature of C. D. Spragg, sent a letter of condolence on 20 June 1952, and enclosed a copy of its published obituary in honour of Mr Maxwell. The letter was addressed to the office of Maxwell and Pitts, 1158 Beaver Hall Square, Montreal:

Dear Sirs,

The sad news of the death of Mr. William Sutherland Maxwell, a Fellow of the Royal Institute of British Architects, was announced to the Council of this Institute at their last meeting. The Council unanimously: –

'RESOLVED that the regrets of the Institute for the loss it has sustained by the decease of Mr. William Sutherland Maxwell be entered in the minutes of this meeting and that a vote of sympathy and condolence be passed and communicated to his relatives.'

I was directed to convey to you this expression of their sorrow and sympathy which, though framed in the terms of a formal resolution, represents the personal and individual feelings of the officers and members.

Yours very truly,

C. D. Spragg

On the margin of the enclosed published obituary is written: *The Journal of the Royal Institute of British Architects Vol. 59 – November 11 – September 1952*. Attached to the copy is a printed article by J. Roxburgh Smith, from the October 1952 *Journal of the Royal Architectural Institute of Canada*; the article is quoted in full in this obituary:

William Sutherland Maxwell [F] past President of the Royal Architectural Institute of Canada and one of Canada's most distinguished architects, died in Montreal on 25 March. He was 78.

Mr. Maxwell, who was born in Montreal, was educated at the Montreal High School, at Tucker's School and at the École des Beaux Arts, Paris. He began his architectural career as draughtsman with his brother, Edward Maxwell, in 1890. He subsequently spent some years with a Boston firm, working on large office buildings and hotels, and later travelled and studied in France, Switzerland, Italy, England, Asia and Egypt. In 1902 he formed the partnership[4] of Edward and W. S. Maxwell and on the death of Edward Maxwell in 1923, the partnership Maxwell and Pitts.

Among his various buildings throughout Canada are the Parliament Buildings, Regina, Saskatchewan; several hospitals in Montreal and the Montreal High School; the Church of the Messiah, Montreal; the Palliser Hotel, Calgary; the Chateau Frontenac, Quebec; and a number of private residences.

Mr. J. Roxburgh Smith [F], Past President of the Royal Architectural Institute of Canada, writes of Mr. Maxwell as follows:

'Due to his long absence abroad in more recent years and his unfortunate illness upon returning home, he was perhaps not too well known by many members of the present generation. However, in spite of the lapse of time, there are still quite a few active members in the profession who were fortunate enough to come under his influence and who retain appreciation for the benefits derived from the association. To some it has been in the form of a prized heritage which has proven its worth, amid the ever-changing tempo of our diversified age.

'His extensive travels and studies in France, Switzerland, Italy, England, Asia Minor and Egypt provided him with a broad outlook which was reflected in all his artistic efforts. His ceaseless activities in the draughting room were an inspiration and his meticulous attention to detail, a not-to-be-forgotten lesson. The effects of this important faculty can be clearly discerned, by the discriminating observer, in all his works.

---

4 Information in letters of W. S. Maxwell as well as in Yates, 'The Artistic Achievements of William Sutherland Maxwell' in volume I, Appendix II confirms that the firm was formed by his brother Edward in 1892 and that W. S. Maxwell was made a partner in 1901; on the death of Edward in 1923 George Pitts joined the firm.

'His great interest in the "Atelier Maxwell", connected with the Beaux-Arts Institute of Design in New York, of which he was the guiding spirit, should be recorded among his professional efforts, along with his enthusiastic activities in the creation of the Arts Club in Montreal. His devotion to the Institute and its *Journal* in the early years of their development, are matters of professional history. He was fortunate in the opportunities presented during his day – hotels, railway stations, parliament buildings, schools, art galleries, office buildings, banks and numerous large houses for wealthy clients, etc., etc., all came to his hand and with their many qualities remain today as monuments to his outstanding abilities.

'He was Past President of the Quebec Association of Architects; a Fellow and Past President of the Royal Architectural Institute of Canada; a Fellow of the Royal Institute of British Architects; Vice-President of the Royal Canadian Academy in 1938 and associated with many other Societies related to the Arts.

'In his passing, the profession loses a distinguished gentleman and his country a talented son.

J. Roxburgh Smith
Royal Architectural Institute of Canada'

And from the Beaux-Arts Institute of Design in New York:

BEAUX–ARTS INSTITUTE OF DESIGN
115 East Fortieth Street, New York 16, New York

BOARD OF TRUSTEES
[Names of the 11 Trustees are listed across the top of the letterhead]
17 July 1952

Maxwell & Pitts, Architects
1158 Beaver Hall Square
Montreal 2, Canada
Gentlemen: Attention: A. M. Brooks

We are most appreciative of your consideration in sending us the newspaper clipping reporting the death of Mr. W. S. Maxwell. His passing will be regretted by our members as he was long an interested and a constant supporter of our educational efforts in which he shared in the early days of his career.

Please convey to the members of Mr. Maxwell's family our sympathy and express to them the deep respect and high esteem which his fellow members had for him.

Sincerely yours,
Kenneth K. Stowell, Secretary

Nine years after his passing Rúḥíyyih Khánum received the following letter dated 4 January 1961 from the President of the Arts Club of Montreal, honouring her beloved father:

Dear Madam:

One of my last duties as retiring President of the Arts Club is to forward a photograph of the bronze plaque placed on the fireplace mantle which I trust you will place among your Canadian souvenirs.

Council has asked me to express our sincere appreciation for the fitting manner in which you unveiled the bronze plaque commemorating our first president. We shall long remember the loving tribute to your father and the charm of your presence on this occasion.

With kind regards,
H.A. Valentine
Immediate Past President

The plaque reads:

WILLIAM SUTHERLAND MAXWELL
F.R.A.I.C. F.R.I.B.A. R.C.A.
1874–1952
A DISTINGUISHED ARCHITECT
WHO DESIGNED THIS ROOM
WAS A LEADING SPIRIT IN THE
FORMATION OF THE ARTS CLUB
AND BECAME ITS FIRST PRESIDENT
MAY HE LONG BE REMEMBERED
AND FUTURE GENERATIONS
APPRECIATE HIS QUALITY
AND HIS OUTSTANDING
CONTRIBUTION
TO THE ARTS

Several decades later, Amatu'l-Bahá Rúḥíyyih Khánum made two gifts of precious art and architecture books from Mr Maxwell's library: in 1985, a donation of books to McGill University, Montreal, Quebec; and in 1990 a similar gift to the University of Victoria, British Columbia. Acknowledgement of these two generous gifts came from each institution. The Director of the McGill libraries wrote:

> 19 September 1985
> Mrs. R. Rabbani
> On behalf of McGill University I wish to extend sincere thanks to you for the recent donation to the Canadian Architecture Collection, held in our Blackader–Lauterman Library, of the very important parts of the archives of your late father, Mr. W. S. Maxwell.
> My colleagues in the Library have studied the lists of materials involved and assure me that these items represent a very valuable addition to our collection. I do wish to thank you for your thoughtfulness and generosity at the same time as I assure you that the material will be well looked after and made available to scholars and the interested public in the near future.
> Your willingness to donate these documents is very much appreciated.
> With sincere good wishes,
> Yours,
> Dr. Hans Möller
> Director of Libraries

And from the Curator of the Maltwood Art Museum and Gallery at the University of Victoria:

> March 12, 1990
> Dear Madame Rabbani:
> Further to our communication confirming the safe arrival of the 25 cartons containing the architectural archival material of William Sutherland Maxwell, we would like to thank you for this generous donation. I can assure you that from what I have so far seen this does indeed constitute a rare find and will match very well our collecting emphasis in the North American and European Decorative Arts area.

We plan to hire an academic research assistant this summer to begin the work of sorting, documenting and physically arranging the material for reference use by faculty and students here at the University...

I will continue to keep in touch as we work on the collection further,

>Martin Segger
>Director/Curator
>Maltwood Art Museum and Gallery.

A further note reporting on work done on the collection by the University staff states:

> The Rabbani Papers is a large collection and also an important one, reflecting as it does the art world in the early twentieth century... [It] must be preserved for the future use of students and scholars.

In 1953, after the Intercontinental Conference in Wilmette and the inauguration of the House of Worship, at which Amatu'l-Bahá was the Guardian's representative, Rúḥíyyih Khánum went to Montreal and visited her father's grave. She had requested that the same monument be raised on his tomb in North America as he had himself designed for her mother in South America. But before leaving Haifa, she had told the Guardian that she wanted to give the house on 1548 Pine Avenue to the National Spiritual Assembly of Canada. This building, which had been so clearly identified by the Master as His home and had for so many decades housed the spirit of the Maxwells, belonged, in her mind, to the Faith and not to her. Shoghi Effendi was deeply pleased with her decision. While in Montreal, she legalized this transfer of the title deeds officially and it was shortly thereafter that Shoghi Effendi blessed her action with the wonderful announcement naming this building a 'Shrine' for the first time. His letter of 20 June 1953 to the National Spiritual Assembly of Canada, written on his behalf, states:

> To this institution [the national headquarters] you will soon be adding the Maxwell Home in Montreal, which should be viewed in the nature of a national shrine, because of its association with the beloved Master, during His visit to Montreal. He sees no objection

to having one room in the house being used as a little museum associated with Mr. and Mrs. Maxwell.[5]

So although the Maxwells of Montreal were there no longer, the house at 1548 Pine Avenue was to be forever associated with their names. Rosemary Sala, in her letter of condolence to Amatu'l-Bahá Rúḥíyyih Khánum, written on 11 April 1952 soon after Mr Maxwell's passing, expressed not only the feelings of her own generation but also the emotions felt by all who would in years to come visit this spot:

> The first thing I did was to go in by myself into the drawing-room to say a prayer, facing 'Akká, on his behalf and for you, dear Rúḥíyyih Khánum. The house was filled with that same beautiful peace – it is peace – which filled it when we prayed for May, twelve years and three weeks ago. Emeric then told me that the house had the atmosphere of the Shrine on Mount Carmel. Now the home is to be our first Canadian Shrine! I think we have all had premonitions of this on those occasions when we have loved one another, and therefore the Cause sufficiently to be aware of its atmosphere. Your home was our womb, dear, if it is not sacrilegious to call it so, as it was for so many others. Nurtured in that atmosphere, with your blessed mother and father, how can we be so limited?

* * *

There is an end to everything, even the most beautiful. And it invariably contains the seeds of new beginnings. The Maxwells fulfilled their separate destinies and departed, one by one, and the story of their family has also come to an end. But in reading their letters, it is difficult not to feel a sense of kinship with them and a responsibility towards those bright lights they circled round. It is impossible not to ponder our own lives and ends in light of theirs. How can we avoid seeing ourselves in the mirror of this last page, or evade the challenge they pose to each subsequent generation?

Since we began with Rúḥíyyih Khánum's own words, it seems befitting to bring this story to a close with them too. In her earliest notebooks written during World War II, she meditated on the fleeting nature of

---

5   Shoghi Effendi, *Messages to Canada*, p. 38.

the present in relation to the future and the past. Her thoughts are not original, but they are universal. They are familiar to each and every one of us and their simplicity makes them immediately accessible. It may have even been her intention to end this book with ideas such as these, for they occur at the end of her first black notebook, which is dedicated to her mother's memory and concludes with the unequivocal words:

> Life is divided into two parts: the part when you are always looking forward and the part when you are always looking back! A child lives in the moment, largely, but that moment is always filled with dreams and plans and make-believe of the future. 'Let's pretend! . . .' that we are grown up, that we have a house, that we are married, that we have a child, that you are a doctor and I a patient . . . always what we will do in that glorious thing the future! Even beyond adolescence it lasts, even into the twenties. 'When I am married' or 'When I graduate from college' or 'When I get promoted' – that surely will be the time, the time when I live every moment full and free and the future is realized.
>
> But suddenly we find a metamorphosis has taken place, how, when, why – we don't know. But we begin to remember. The looking back has started! When I was a little girl . . . that day we went to the mountains . . . those carefree years of early youth . . . the colours of the autumn leaves as we scuffled happily among them on a brilliant October day . . . we have passed the point. One half of longing for things to come, one half of tender brooding over things that have been – that seems to be life. It really has no present at all.
>
> The present is too fleeting – too swift and illusive, we touch it and it is gone – for a moment it danced before us in the glorious garb of hopes – things seen as in a vision, and then it was laid away in the store of inanimate memory – things that shall never be again, a strange residue that forms all of life – the past. The dear dead past!
>
>> Yesterday is but a dream,
>> Tomorrow but a vision –
>> But today well lived makes
>> Every yesterday a dream of happiness,
>> And every tomorrow a vision of hope.
>> Look well, therefore, to this day!   (Sanskrit Proverb)

Two thoughts bring me infinite rest and comfort. One the infinitude of the stars, the other the infinitude of the atoms. When I feel restless, troubled, harassed – haunted by fear sometimes of my own failure – I look up at the stars and think of their vastness, their unbounded limits, their glorious nebulae, and my own smallness fades away. The vast universe is there, it will go on. It is beautiful and pure, God rules over it forever. There are better beings than I, if I fail. And so with the atoms, with all their radiant activity, their swiftness, their infinitesimal life. Forever building up the universe, forever changing, sifting in and out of forms – eternal of themselves.

If anybody wants to strengthen his religious belief, let him study the ways and nature of this creation we live in. It breathes fresh life into one's faith and seems to present a thousand subtle testimonials to the things of the spirit.

The ways of the Maxwells too, as well as their individual natures, breathe life into one's faith. If Amatu'l-Bahá Rúḥíyyih Khánum wished to bequeath the story of her family to us, perhaps it was because it bears witness to 'the things of the spirit'.

BIBLIOGRAPHY

'Abdu'l-Bahá. *Abdul Baha on Divine Philosophy*. Comp. I. F. Chamberlain. Boston: The Tudor Press, 1918.

Alexander, Agnes. 'May Maxwell – A Tribute', unpublished enclosure in a letter of 28 May 1940. Research Department of the Universal House of Justice; from the Hawaii Bahá'í National Archives.

Bahá'í News, no. 1 (December 1924). Wilmette, IL: National Spiritual Assembly of the Bahá'ís of the United States and Canada.

Bahá'í Prayers: A Selection of Prayers Revealed by Bahá'u'lláh, The Báb, and 'Abdu'l-Bahá. Wilmette, IL: Bahá'í Publishing Trust, rev. ed. 1991.

The Bahá'í World. Wilmette, IL: Bahá'í Publishing Trust. Vol. IV (1930–1932); vol. VI (1934–1936); vol. VII (1936–1938); vol. VIII (1938–1940); vol. XI (1946–1950); vol. XII (1950–1954); Haifa: Bahá'í World Centre. Vol. XIX (1983–1986).

Freeman, Dorothy. *From Copper to Gold: The Life of Dorothy Baker*. Oxford: George Ronald, 1984.

Garden of the Heart, The. Comp. Frances Esty. East Aurora, NY: Roycrofters, 1930.

Giachery, Ugo R. 'An Account of the Preparatory Work in Italy', in *The Bahá'í World*, vol. XII (1950–1954), pp. 240–46.

Hogenson, Kathryn Jewett. *Lighting the Western Sky: The Hearst Pilgrimage and the Establishment of the Bahá'í Faith in the West*. Oxford: George Ronald, 2010.

Holley, Marion. 'May Ellis Maxwell', *In Memoriam* article in *The Bahá'í World*, vol. VIII (1938–1940, pp. 631–42.

Nabíl-i-A'zam (Muḥammad-i-Zarandí). *The Dawn-Breakers: Nabíl's Narrative of the Early Days of the Bahá'í Revelation*. Wilmette, IL: Bahá'í Publishing Committee, 1932. London: Bahá'í Publishing Trust, 1953.

Rabbani, Rúḥíyyih. *The Priceless Pearl*. London: Bahá'í Publishing Trust, 1969.

— *A Spiritual Assembly's Growing Pains*. New Delhi: Bahá'í Publishing Trust, n.d; Bahá'í Publishing Trust Australia, 1976.

— 'William Sutherland Maxwell', *In Memoriam* article in *The Bahá'í World*, vol. XII, pp. 657–62.

Shoghi Effendi. *The Advent of Divine Justice* (1939). Wilmette, IL: Bahá'í Publishing Trust, 1984.

— *The Dispensation of Bahá'u'lláh* (1934). Wilmette, IL: Bahá'í Publishing Trust, 1970. Also in *The World Order of Bahá'u'lláh*, pp. 97–157.

— *God Passes By* (1944). Wilmette, IL: Bahá'í Publishing Trust, rev. ed. 1974.

— *Messages to America 1932–1946*. Wilmette, IL: Bahá'í Publishing Committee, 1947.

— *Messages to the Bahá'í World, 1950–1957*. Wilmette, IL: Bahá'í Publishing Trust, 2nd ed. 1971.

— *Messages to Canada*. National Spiritual Assembly of the Bahá'ís of Canada, 1965.

— *The World Order of Bahá'u'lláh: Selected Letters by Shoghi Effendi* (1938). Wilmette, IL: Bahá'í Publishing Trust, 2nd rev. ed. 1974.

Spierckel, Pierre. 'Lucienne Migette', *In Memoriam* article in *The Bahá'í World*, vol. XIX (1983–1986), pp. 610–11.

Star of the West: The Bahai Magazine. Periodical, 25 vols. 1910–1935. Vols. 1–14 RP Oxford: George Ronald, 1978. Complete CD-ROM version: Talisman Educational Software/Special Ideas, 2001.

Townshend, George. *The Heart of the Gospel: Being a Restatement of the Teaching of the Bible in Terms of Modern Thought and Modern Need*. London: Lindsay Drummond, 1939; New York: Bahá'í Publishing Committee, 1940; Oxford: George Ronald, 1951.

Weeden, Ben D. 'Reports on the Construction of the Arcade', in *The Bahá'í World*, vol. XII (1950–1954), pp. 246–52.

INDEX

Abbas Effendi *see* 'Abdu'l-Bahá
'Abdu'l-Bahá
   and Administrative Order 206, 271, 346–7
   Ascension (commemoration) 398
   on Bahá'í life 99, 156
   Centre of the Covenant 22, 289, 346–7
   on education of children 30
   family of 63, 82, 309
   and Germany 218, 240
   on happiness as cause of development 96, 148
   on prayers for departed souls 136
   House in Haifa 5, 17, 31, 32n, 142, 308, 383
   imprisonment in 'Akká 105
   on martyrdom 175, 250
   passing 3, 18, 24
   and pilgrims 64–5, 164, 299
   on racism, 186, 191, 346, 348
   in Ramleh, Egypt 14
   and Shoghi Effendi 32–3, 310, 346
   on studying the Hidden Words 125
   Tablets and writings 109, 120, 165, 263, 274, 365
      of the Branch 347
      to May Maxwell 4-5
      prayer for Canada 374
   Shrine of 66, 394
   on spiritual awakening of France 247
   on spiritual life 146
   station of 347
   on teaching and service 94, 96, 113, 148, 342
   on tests 132, 152
   visit to North America 20, 83, 94, 165n, 194
      Montreal 160, 167–9, 193, 247, 344–5, 372, 425
      New York 24–5, 94, 115, 347
      Philadelphia 130–31
      San Francisco 165
      Temple dedication 198
      Washington 131
   Will and Testament 124, 127, 147, 151, 206, 345–6

World War I 249
for individual believers see separate entries
Abdul Baha on Divine Philosophy 175
'Abdu'l-Karím-i-Ṭihrání 111
Abdul Raouf 400
Abramson, S. H. 211
Absolute Scientists 51
Adams, Evangeline 177
Administrative Order *see* Bahá'í Administrative Order, *also* Bahá'í administration; Committees; Convention; Spiritual Assembly (Local, National); World Order
Advent of Divine Justice, The 322, 325
Afnan, Ruhi 83, 86
Africa 381, 382–3
Ahrens, Captain 213
Aix-en-Provence, France 280
'Akká (St Jean d'Acre) 67, 105, 165, 244, 259, 426
Alaska 80
Albertson, Alma 165n
Alexander, Agnes 206, 272, 300, 316–17, 318–19, 348, 373–5
Alexandria, Egypt 9–10
Ali Kuli Khan 194, 375
Alizadeh, Teddy Edwards 161
Allenby, Lord and Lady 77
Amatu'l-Bahá Rúḥíyyih Khánum
   letters to parents on behalf of Shoghi Effendi 275, 298–30, 304–6, 320–21, 326–7, 331–5, 344–5, 360, 390–91, 410–11
   and superstructure Shrine of the Báb 397–8, 390–97
   wife of Shoghi Effendi 275–8, 283, 286, 289–90, 292–6, 306–8, 310–14, 331, 335–6, 338, 361
   see also Maxwell, Mary
America, Americans 18–19, 27, 105, 120, 131, 186, 192, 215, 217, 223, 238, 244, 253, 271, 301, 311–12, 320, 331, 340, 358, 367, 375, 401n, 424, 425
   Bahá'í community 17, 21–2, 28, 43, 50, 75, 81, 111, 115, 148, 158, 166, 175, 177, 192, 195–78, 210, 250, 270–71,

287–8, 299, 310, 311–12, 322–3, 340, 347, 352, 371–3, 375–6, 397
  Seven Year Plans 300, 304–5, 307, 354, 367, 372
  spiritual destiny of 375
  see also Maxwell, May; Latin America; South America; youth
Ames, Sir Herbert 76
animals 7, 9–10, 15, 17, 31, 36–9, 57–8, 60, 86, 132
Apostles (of Jesus) 247, 248
Arabs 231, 308–9, 339, 397
Arab Revolt 283, 308, 326
Argentina 221, 354–7, 361–8, 375–6 see also Buenos Aires
Armstrong, Lily (Perry) 174, 181–2
Arts Club, Montreal 380, 402, 422–3
  Ball 44, 71
attar of rose 22, 280, 383–4, 398
Atlantic City, NJ 184–5
Australia 354, 376, 416n
  National Spiritual Assembly 411
Austria 232, 256
  National Spiritual Assembly 241
Auxiliary Board 304
Azízu'lláh Khán 89

Báb, the 187, 207, 229–30, 248, 348
  Birthday 398
  see also Shrine of the Báb
Baghdadi, Zia 282
Bahá'í administration 11, 17, 20, 22, 25, 28–9, 73, 121–3, 147, 151, 156, 166–7, 173, 187, 191, 218–19, 220, 228, 239, 252, 300, 315, 323, 346
Bahá'í Administration (book) 189, 201
Bahá'í Administrative Order 21–3, 24, 28–9, 44, 121–3, 125, 151, 153, 157, 191, 220, 237, 270, 301, 304, 346
  see also Bahá'í administration; Committees; Convention; Spiritual Assembly (Local, National)
Bahá'í Fast 296–7
Bahá'í Funds 110, 112–13, 115–16, 118, 275, 276, 389–90, 404
  see also Bahá'í Temple
Bahá'í Gardens, Haifa 389–91, 400
  terraces 390–91
Bahá'í Magazine 176
Bahá'í News 43, 140, 163, 270, 284, 409–10
  Canadian 418
Bahá'í Shrines see individual entries
Bahá'í Temple, Wilmette, Illinois 11, 50, 84, 115, 116, 118, 165, 176, 190, 196, 197, 198, 202–3, 220, 300, 309, 317, 346, 348, 373–4, 390
  Fund 110, 112–16, 117–19, 150, 192–197, 390
Bahá'í World, The (Year Book) 163–72, 207, 230, 232, 257, 272, 276, 283n, 337, 376, 380, 388, 398, 410
Bahá'í World Centre 398, 405–6, 417
Bahá'ís 217
  in Palestine 309
  Western and Eastern 295
  work and service a necessity for 156
  see also America; Argentina; Brazil; Canada; England; Europe; Haifa; Lyon; Germany; Paris
Bahá'u'lláh
  Ascension of 68
  Birthday of 88, 263, 398
  bounty and blessings of 221, 274, 318, 412, 416
  devotion and service to 142, 251, 307, 332
  faith in 216, 243, 314, 337
  family of 309, 361
  power of 98, 117, 121, 127, 140, 146, 180, 187, 198, 256, 282, 314, 325, 347, 350
  prayer to 317
  Revelation, Cause, Faith of 229, 346, 355, 373, 414, 418–19
  teachings 9, 17, 95, 97–8, 99, 105, 113, 122, 125, 153–5, 177–8, 187, 201, 237, 250, 348
  thankfulness to 231, 274, 318
  Writings 109, 157, 340–41, 375
  see also Covenant; Mansion of Bahá'u'lláh; Shrine of Bahá'u'lláh
Bahá'u'lláh and the New Era 143, 232
Bahjí 6, 16, 196, 259–60, 263, 365, 368, 399
Baker, Dorothy 242
Baker, Louise (Matthias) 242
Baldwin, Katherine 324, 337–8
Balkans 253, 256
Baltimore 118, 195
Banani, Samíheh 308
Barney, Laura see Dreyfus-Barney
Barton, Wilfred 363
Barwick, Doreen 30–31
Bean, W. Worth, Jr 175n
bear (as domestic pet) 57, 60, 132
Beaux-Arts Institute of Design, New York 422
Beaver Hall Square 56, 420, 422
Belgian Congo 382, 383
Belgium 210–11, 213, 227–8, 230, 235–8
Belgrade 241
Benjamin, Romeyn 112
Bergson, Henri 355
Berlin, Germany 219, 241, 257
Bessborough, Earl and Countess 171
Bible 94, 138, 307, 321

INDEX

Black Thursday 105
Blackader-Lauterman Library 424
Blakely, Julie Russell 161
Bley, Edna 213
Blomfield, Sara, Lady 19
Blum, Alvin and Gertrude 288–9
Board of Trade (Montreal)
Boger-Shattuck, Dr Martha Isabel 203, 347
Boigharian family 367
Bolles, Jeanne Negar (cousin of Rúḥíyyih Khánum) 233, 241, 278, 287, 318, 357–66, 369, 376–8
Bolles, Jeanne Ruhangiz (aunt of Rúḥíyyih Khánum) 31, 57, 216, 233, 278, 287, 328, 332, 335, 416
Bolles, Randolph (brother of May Maxwell) 11, 31, 33, 57–9, 90, 138, 180, 207, 211, 258, 260, 272–3, 282, 285, 369
  and Shoghi Effendi 327–9, 334–5
Bolton, Marie 416n
Bolton, Stanley and Mariette 354
Booker, Mr 188
Borel, Madame 246, 253
Bosch, John and Louise 65, 205, 329–30
Boston 42, 52, 54, 55, 57, 89, 118, 155, 168, 209, 421
Bourgeois, Louis 118
Bovay, Mlle 415
Brazil, Brazilians 358, 360, 362, 371, 377
Brazil, S. S. 357
Breakwell, Thomas 80n, 164–5, 276, 337
Bremen, Germany 211
Bretton Woods 101
Brierly, Walter 46–7
Brindisi, Italy 263
Britain, British 20, 250, 271, 326, 406
British Empire Exhibition (London) 49
British Hospital, Port Said 64
British Mandate 283, 308, 407
British Progressive League 80
British Women's League 51
Brittany 55–6
Brittingham, Isabella 167, 205
Bromsgrove Guild 212
Broadway, New York
Broglie, Princesse de 77, 171–2, 236, 377
Brown, Bishop 194–5
Browne, Edward Granville 20
Budapest, Hungary 269, 273, 278
Buenos Aires 355–7, 361–8, 374, 377
  memorial to May Maxwell 368, 378–9, 391–3
  Spiritual Assembly 367
Bufalini, Alberto 396, 407–8
Burke, Athala 3, 4, 10, 12, 14, 15–16, 108
Burlington 37–8
Burnett, Mr 78

Bushrui, Badi 68
Cairo, Egypt 9, 12–13, 111, 382
Calgary, Alberta 207, 412
California 40–41, 56, 62, 144, 199, 201–5, 209, 210, 300, 345, 349
Cambridge, England 47, 210
Campbell, Helen 205
Canada 12, 29, 55, 202, 209, 254, 292, 302, 339, 388, 401–2, 413, 415–16, 419–22
  Baháʼí activities and communities 12–13, 17, 28–9, 50, 65, 71, 72–3, 77–9, 81, 142, 169, 178, 207, 209, 277, 284, 300–03, 316, 354, 390, 397, 404–5, 417, 425–6 *see also* individual cities
  Baháʼí Convention, first Canadian 404–5
  history of Baháʼí Faith in 160, 169, 375
  prayer revealed by ʻAbduʼl-Bahá for 374
  Tablets from ʻAbduʼl-Bahá about 5, 32n
  World Unity Conference 72, 75
  visit of ʻAbduʼl-Bahá 160, 167–9, 193, 247, 344–5, 372, 425
  Youth Movement 148n, 159, 160–61 *see also* Montreal
  see also Committees; Conventions; hotels; Spiritual Assembly (Local, National)
Canadian Academy of Arts 401n
Canadian Baháʼí News 418
Canadian Civil Liberties Union 302–3
Canadian Pacific Railway 12
Canadian Parliament 12, 74, 76, 421, 422
Carmel *see* Mount Carmel
Cape Town Castle, R. M. S. 382
Cape Town, South Africa 381–2
Carlyle, Thomas 224
Catholicism, Catholics 129, 160, 179, 403
  see also Christianity
Centenary
  of Baháʼí Faith (1944) 389–90, 393
  of martyrdom of the Báb (1950) 396
Century of Progress Exposition 196
Champney House, New York 24–5
Chanler, Julie 122–7, 305, 315, 349
Chase, Thornton 166
Chateau Frontenac 10, 11–12, 392, 421
Chicago 27, 32–3, 72, 84, 88, 116, 118, 144, 190, 196, 200, 202, 224, 235, 315–17, 390
Chicago Jewish Forward 340
Christianity, Christians 99–100, 108, 125, 207, 342, 353, 379 *see also* Catholicism; Jesus
Christmas 9, 36, 107–9, 146, 257, 414
Church of the Messiah (Montreal) 169, 421
Cleveland, OH 165, 177
Clock, Dr 167
Cobb, Stanwood 166, 184, 188, 190, 258
Cole, Helen Ellis 165

Collins, Amelia, Hand of the Cause 378, 392–3, 411, 413
Columbia University 43, 74
Columbus, S. S. 211, 213
Committees 44, 74, 98, 150
   Amity C. 188, 189
   Bahá'í Publishing C. 26
   Convention C. 72–4
   Finance C. 11
   History of the Cause in America C. 25, 176
   Inter-Racial C. 189
   Green Acre C. for Plays and Pageants 207
   Green Acre Program C. 25, 176
   Green Acre Publicity C. 25
   Music Arts Exhibitions C. 11
   National Teaching C. 22, 25, 28–9, 50, 75, 84–6, 88, 113, 114, 140, 156–7, 167, 176, 301, 354
   Publicity C. 75, 112–13
   Religious Congress C. 128
   Resolution and By-Laws C. 25
   Reviewing C. 172–3
   Star of the West C. 27
   Teaching C. (Montreal) 11, 25
   Teaching C. (Washington DC) 184
   Temple C. 11, 118
   Ways and Means C. 11
   World Unity Conference C. 75
   Year Book C. 167
   Youth C. (Montreal) 157–9, 217
conscience 133, 155–6, 256
Continental Boards of Counsellors 304
Conventions, Annual Bahá'í 21–2, 26–7, 50–51, 64–5, 71–3, 78, 80, 84, 105, 114–16, 138, 144, 178–9, 203, 223–4, 231, 271, 297, 315–17, 322, 339, 348, 354, 373–6
   first Canadian 404–5
Cook, Coralie Franklin 189
Coolidge, President 42–3
Cooper, Ella Goodall 93, 160, 205
Coristine, Elizabeth (Libby) 32, 93, 149
Coristine, Mary 32, 97
Corot 224
Cotton, Gladys *see* Weeden
Covenant 22, 60, 102, 120–27, 129–30, 154–5, 293, 297, 309–10, 375
   Centre of 22, 289, 293, 309–10, 347
Covenant-breaking 120–27, 262, 309–10, 349
Cowles, Elizabeth 78
Cropper *see* Thornburgh-Cropper
Crowther, Mr 399
Cyprus 402–3

Daird, Mr 78

Dawn-Breakers, The 149–50, 301, 327–8, 335
de Livi, Liv 78
Depression *see* Great Depression
de Tremblay, Mr 34, 39
Detroit 118, 177, 340
Dewing, Edward, 161, 184
Dispensation of Bahá'u'lláh, The 206, 325
Divine Plan 32n, 93, 276
Díyá'íyyih Khánum, 262, 269, 270, 285
Dodge family 81–2, 165
Dominion Express Building, Montreal 12
Dresden, Germany 219, 241
Durban, South Africa 382
Dreyfus-Barney, Hippolyte and Laura 3, 50, 227–9, 243–4, 278
Dunn, Hyde 376

Early Pilgrimage, An 374
Ecole des Beaux-Arts, Paris 421
economics 67, 91, 104–6, 156–7, 223
Eddington, Archie 167–9
Egypt 3, 8–15, 18–19, 30, 31, 64, 111, 259, 281, 376, 382, 421
Edell, Ethel 209, 310
Edward and W. S. Maxwell, architects 12, 421
Elizabethville (Lubumbashi) 382
Elliot, Eddie 78, 161, 418
England 18, 45, 48–9, 163, 226, 286, 381–2, 394, 421
   Bahá'ís in 19–20
Englewood, NJ 286, 355, 366
Esperanto 339, 340
Esslemont, Dr John 19, 27–8, 340
Esslingen, Germany 213, 216–18, 237, 239, 240, 242
Estall, Rowland 149, 161
Estall, Stella Dean 287
Este, Rev. 342
Esty, Frances 177
Europe, Europeans 77, 121, 223 *see also* Maxwell, Sutherland: journeys
   Bahá'í activities and communities 27, 210, 218, 239, 375, 418–19
   Central 255 *see also* individual cities
   France 236, 239, 245–2, 255, 275–6
   Germany 218, 239, 255 *see also* Maxwell: Mary, May
   travels of Shoghi Effendi in 8–9, 27, 36, 51, 54, 275, 381–2, 384, 395
   and war 101, 210, 214–15, 223, 225–6, 230–31, 282–3, 320, 325, 339, 381–2
Evanston, IL 84, 116, 196, 316–17, 348 *see also* Bahá'í Temple

fascism 101, 139, 210, 226
Farmer, Sarah 43, 166
Fazel, Jenabe 14, 68, 347

INDEX

Ferry, Mrs Mansfield 77
Fitzgerald, Scott 101
Foreign Policy Association 145
Formative Age 373, 417
Foster, Frank T. 380
France 58, 62, 81, 153, 209, 223, 226–31, 234, 236, 239, 242–55, 260, 276, 278–82, 339, 364, 381–2, 421
Frankfurt, Germany 215, 238, 241, 258
Friedman, Solon 374
French, Gloria 108
French, Janet 78
French, Nell 69, 167, 168, 171, 205, 230, 276
Frothingham, Rev. O. B.
fundamentalism 139–40

Gagnon, Clarence, 401–2
Gail, Marzieh (Khan) 351
Garden of the Heart, The 109
'Gate of Dawn, The' 207
Gaudreaux, Maud 181
Geneva, NY 94, 98, 124, 140, 146, 177
Geneva, Switzerland 406, 411, 412
Genoa, Italy 380, 381
Germany 119–20, 121, 210–27, 231–42, 250, 253, 255, 282
  Bahá'í youth in 159, 214–15, 234, 240
  National Spiritual Assembly 241
Getsinger, Lua 9, 13, 70, 111, 113, 165, 175, 371, 376
Geyserville 65, 204, 205
Giachery, Ugo, Hand of the Cause 406–8, 410
  Mrs (Angeline) 408
Gillies, Rosemary *see* Sala
Gilman, Lucius 204
Glendale, Calif. 205
God Passes By 375, 393
Goodall, Ella *see* Cooper
Goodall, Helen 205
Gordon, Rena 161
Graham, Leah 347
Grand, Helen 141
Grand Mufti of Jerusalem 283
Grapes of Wrath, The 102
Grassle, Alfons 229, 228, 232
Great Depression 101, 103–5, 115–16, 192, 223, 325
Greatest Holy Leaf 13, 21–2, 51, 61, 65, 118, 173–4, 183, 186, 264, 361
Great Gatsby, The 101
Green Acre (Maine) 22, 25–6, 40, 42–3, 45, 48, 51, 62, 68, 103, 144–5, 160, 162, 176, 183, 207, 288, 318–19, 374
Green Amber 184–5
Greenleaf, Elizabeth 51, 54–5, 65, 79–80
Gregory, Louis G., Hand of the Cause 84

Guardian (of the Bahá'í Faith) *see* Shoghi Effendi
Guido M. Fabbricotti and Bufalini 408
Guthrie, Dr 82
Gyp (dog) 10, 60, 86

Haifa, city of 231, 292, 326, 383, 394, 400, 405, 410
  Bahá'ís resident in 68, 162, 398–9
  Mountain Road 400–01
  Municipality 400–01
  Persian Colony 5, 17, 66, 400, 406
  port 258, 263, 339, 381
  see also Monument Gardens; Mount Carmel; Pilgrim House; Shrine of the Báb
Hakim, Dr Lotfullah 4
Hall, Albert 165
Hamburg, Germany 219, 231–4, 257
Hands of the Cause of God 121, 304 *see also* individual entries
Haney, Mariam 24, 166
Haney, Paul, Hand of the Cause 31
Hannan, Joseph 166
Harris, Hooper 82
Harrison, Ernest 374
Harrison, Mary 41, 58
Harrison, Thomas 67
Harvey, Mr and Mrs 51
Hearst, Phoebe Apperson 164–5
Hearst, William Randolph 68
Heart of the Gospel, The 353
Hédévary, Mme de 227
Heidelberg, Germany 220
Hemmion, Dr 105
Hémon, Louis 401n
Herran, Audie 78
Herrman, Brenetta
Hidden Words 125, 201, 340, 348
Hitler, Adolf 225, 325, 335
Hoagg, Emogene 81, 165n, 361–2
Hofman, David 78, 161, 162, 163, 293, 347, 353–4
Hofman, Marion *see* Holley
Holley, Grace 204
Holley, Horace, Hand of the Cause 72, 170, 182, 199, 323, 410, 417, 418
Holley, Marion (Hofman) 204–5, 210, 211, 250, 257, 283–4, 317, 374, 377
Holocaust 325, 339
Holsapple, Leonora (Armstrong) 80, 221, 262, 264, 359, 360, 362, 363
Holy Family 6, 19, 20, 21, 27, 63, 65, 66, 80, 169, 258, 272, 279, 285, 356, 359
homeopathy 203, 212, 237–8, 273, 347, 360, 412
Honolulu 324, 337, 379
Hope Street, Montreal

Hopper, Marie 93
Horn, Edith 213, 241, 258
Hossain, Syud 145
hotels
   Alvear Palace (Buenos Aires) 362
   Azour's Ritz (Tel Aviv) 274
   Barbizon Plaza (New York) 329, 355
   Bancroft (Worcester) 132
   Burlington (Washington DC) 188
   Chateau Frontenac (Quebec City) 10, 11, 12, 392, 421
   City (Buenos Aires) 363–4
   Constance (Pasadena) 205
   Gloria (Rio de Janeiro) 358, 359, 360, 362
   Jousten (Buenos Aires) 363
   King Edward (Toronto) 171, 209
   Marquardt (Stuttgart) 240
   Mayfair (Los Angeles) 202
   Nordland (Rostock) 219
   Orrington (Evanston) 316
   Palais (Brussels) 213
   Palliser (Calgary) 421
   President (Atlantic City) 184
   Ritz (Tel Aviv) 274
   Ritz-Carlton (Montreal) 43
   Rockingham (Portsmouth, NH) 162
   Roosevelt (New York) 97
   Sir Francis Drake (San Francisco) 206
   Vancouver 51
   Westminster (Toronto) 209
   Windsor (Montreal) 72, 73
Houde, Mayor (of Montreal) 107
House of 'Abdu'l-Bahá (Haifa) *see* Master's House
Ḥuqúqu'lláh 111
Hutchison, Amelia Maxwell 269, 384

individual, life of 22, 98, 100, 112, 125–6, 154–5, 167, 188, 201, 237, 261, 271, 304–5, 428
Intercontinental Conference, Wilmette 425
International Art Exhibition (Brussels) 210–11
International Monetary Fund 101
International Teaching Centre 304
Ioas, Leroy, Hand of the Cause 114, 205, 354
Irwin, Frank and Mary 286–7
Israel, 32, 405, 413 *see also* 'Akká, Haifa, Jerusalem, Nazareth, Tiberias
Italy, Italians 18, 210, 226, 234, 380, 381, 394, 394, 396, 406–8, 410, 421
Ives, Mabel 177, 301
Ives, Howard Colby 83

Jack, Marion 80–81, 258, 397
Jackson, Dr Josephine 200, 204

James, Lillian 116–17
Jerusalem 283, 385, 389, 403, 406
Jesus 125, 207, 247, 248 *see also* Christianity
Jews 46, 108, 144, 160, 219, 231, 283, 308, 339–41, 397
Joan of Arc 246, 247
Johannesburg, South Africa 382
Johnson, Nora 78
Jones, Helen H. 324, 338
Jones, Mr 78
Josselyn, Elizabeth 43–4
Juba, Sudan 382

Kahlke, Agnes 116
Kemp, Evelyn and Stanley 76–7, 128, 207
Kevorkian, Haig 364, 367
Khan, Ali Kuli 194, 375
Khan, Marzieh (Gail) 351
Khartoum, Sudan 383
Kilgore, Mrs Joseph 141
Kinney family 82, 115, 181, 281, 287–8
Kisangani (Stanleyville) 382
Kitáb-i-Aqdas 111
Knobloch, Mrs 166
Knox Crescent Church, Montreal 401
Kyrenia, Cyprus 402

Lagne, Mr 78
Lambousa, Cyprus 403
Latin America 365, 375–6 *see also* South America
Leach, Mr 78
Leacock, Stephen 106–7
League of Nations 11, 50, 75, 101, 232
League of Women Voters 75–6
Lee, Lena L. 93
Lee, Ruth 78
Leipzig, Germany 219, 241
Libby, Elizabeth *see* Coristine
Liverpool 46
Loeding, Sophie 196–7
Lohse, Doris 190
Lohse, Walter 159, 302, 333
London, England 19–20, 49–50, 121, 213, 238, 381–2
Los Angeles 176, 200–1, 202, 205
Lou Helen ranch 206
Lubumbashi (Elizabethville) 382
Lunt, Alfred 22, 282
Lyall, Laura Muntz
Lyon, France 213–14, 228, 230–31, 235, 236, 242–7, 251, 252–4, 260, 275, 278–82, 285
   Spiritual Assembly 243, 246, 275

Macphail, Agnes 74–6, 159, 169
Maltwood Art Museum and Gallery 424–5

INDEX

Manucher Khan 68
Marseille, France 3, 246, 277–80, 282, 381
Marsh, Carrie 115
Marshall, Mr 78
martyrdom, martyrs 66, 78, 175, 199, 250, 341, 347, 365, 367, 368–9, 370, 373, 417, 419
Mashriqu'l-Adhkár *see* Bahá'í Temple
Masson, Jean 166
Master's House (Haifa) 5, 17, 31, 32n, 142, 308, 383
Mathews, Loulie 114
Matthias, Hubert 241–2
Matthiesen, Bertha 220
Mauretania, R. M. S. 63
Maxwell, Edward (brother of W. S. Maxwell) 10, 11–13, 269, 421
Maxwell home *see* Pine Avenue West
Maxwell, Libbie 269
Maxwell, Mary
  Bahá'í activities
    Canada & United States 135–50, 156–7, 183, 185–90, 207
    Germany 119–20, 211, 214–26, 231–5, 237–42
  education 29–42, 56–8, 89–92, 105, 135–7
    spiritual 33, 92–111, 131 146, 154–5
  love of animals 9–10, 17, 36–8, 57
  Notes, 1937 in Haifa 315–25, 330, 332
  pilgrimages 3–10, 14–19, 60–70, 257–60
  relationship with parents
    May Maxwell: when young girl 4–7, 15–17, 30–41, 56, 61–70, 82, 87–101, 102–4, 107–11, 117–19, 121, 124–5, 127, 128–34; when adult 138–58, 168, 171–3, 177–9, 183–95, 201–2, 209–10, 221, 214, 216–17, 226, 231–42, 253–4, 257, 260, 262–4, 271–3, 275, 277–8, 283–97, 299, 308, 309–110, 311–15, 341–4, 349–51, 355–6, 358–9, 368–9, 371, 378
    Sutherland Maxwell: when young girl 10, 13, 32, 39, 49–50, 56, 58, 60–61, 78, 87; when adult 36–7, 216, 221–3, 225–6, 235–6, 239, 263, 265, 297–8, 308, 309–10, 311, 314–15, 331, 355–6, 368–70, 378, 383–6, 388–98, 402–3, 410–11, 414–16, 423–5
  sculpture 36–7, 40
  and Shoghi Effendi 5–6, 66–70, 134–7, 149, 172–3, 183, 191–2, 217–20, 255–6, 260, 307
    marriage to 260, 262–5, 269–71, 284–9

writing 39–40, 119, 132–3, 172–3, 184–5, 188, 209
see also Amatu'l-Bahá Rúḥíyyih Khánum
Maxwell, May
  and 'Abdu'l-Bahá 3–5, 7, 11, 51, 64–5, 92, 94–6, 99–100, 125, 131, 160, 212, 226, 247, 289, 344–5
  Bahá'í service
    Bahá'í World, The 163–72
    Canada & United States 20–29, 50–55, 72–6, 79–80, 83–5, 113, 120–27, 138, 140, 142–4, 156–8, 176–87, 190, 200, 204–8, 209, 300–02, 304–5, 316–17, 346–8, 354
    France 226–9, 235–6, 242–50, 252, 253
    Germany 217, 237, 239–41
    radio 177–182
    South America 354–60
    Temple, Wilmette 110–12, 115, 117, 118, 192–9, 202–3
  Bahá'í youth 101, 141–62, 191, 197, 204–5, 227
  bonds, spiritual, with individuals 76–8, 81, 117, 128–9, 139, 142, 162 *see also* Maxwell, Mary
  correspondence 18, 28–9, 80 *see also* individual names
  finances, funds 102–4, 107–17, 121
  Greatest Holy Leaf 13, 51–2, 118, 173–5
  health 3, 7–8, 12–14, 51–3, 85, 199–200, 203–4, 212–14, 216, 237–8, 272–3, 326, 364–5
  home in Montreal (Maxwell house) *see* Pine Avenue West
  Mary Maxwell, *see also* Amatu'l-Bahá Rúḥíyyih Khánum; Maxwell, Mary
    marriage 262–5, 271–5, 282–3, 284–9
    Notes, 1937 in Haifa 315–25, 330, 332
  monument, Argentina 368, 370, 378–9, 392–3
  passing 364–70, 380
    memorial service and messages 357, 373–6
    named as martyr 367, 370
  pilgrimages 3–20, 251–60
  Shoghi Effendi, correspondence from Haifa 3, 5, 7–8, 13–14, 17–19, 260–62
  North America 20–29, 43, 51–5, 63, 67, 69, 93, 95, 100, 102, 112, 114–16, 122–7, 164–72, 174–5, 183, 185–6, 190–92, 197–9, 206
  travel teaching in Europe 210–11, 213–14, 216, 228–9, 236, 239, 250–57
  after marriage of Mary Maxwell

437

271–5, 277–30, 282–3, 301–6,
318–21, 326–7, 331–5, 343–4,
346–7, 360, 365, 366–8, 372–3,
375–6, 390–91, 410–11
Sutherland Maxwell
  correspondence with 3, 6, 9, 14, 25–6,
30, 35, 42, 44–9, 52–3, 55–60, 69,
71–4, 81–3, 85–7, 103, 200–01,
121–13, 223–6, 229–30, 235–6,
237–9, 259, 260, 345–7, 355–6,
358–9, 362, 365
  relationship with 13, 43–4, 47–8,
55–6, 59–60, 71, 78–9, 85, 88,
103, 221, 223–6, 235–6, 254, 272,
297–8, 314, 365–6, 397
Maxwell & Pitts Co. 11, 12, 281, 420, 421, 422
Maxwell, Stirling 416
Maxwell, William Sutherland
  Bahá'í service
    administrative 11, 42–3, 56, 69–70,
72–4, 223–4, 254, 343, 404
    Green Acre 26, 42, 207
    Haifa 36, 272, 361, 384–6
    Shrine of the Báb, architect superstructure 299, 387–9, 391–401, 405–10
    Temple, Wilmette 11, 115, 117–18
  books 39, 424
  character 43, 44, 59, 78, 87, 114–15, 314, 383–5
  Haifa, move to and life there 369, 376, 380–410
  Hand of the Cause of God 44, 414–15
  illnesses 329–33, 410–12
  last months and passing 412–23
    monument 425
  journeys to
    Cyprus 402–3
    Europe 45–50, 210–12, 278–9, 381–2
  Keith Ransom-Kehler, monument 175–6
  Mary Maxwell *see* Amatu'l-Bahá Rúḥíyyih Khánum; Maxwell, Mary
    marriage of 262–3, 269, 271, 279, 284
    Notes, 1937 in Haifa 315–25, 330, 332
  May Maxwell *see* Maxwell, May
    passing of 365–70, 372, 387
  Parent, A. M. 273, 278, 281, 389–90, 401–2, 405
  photography 117, 164, 169–71, 272, 376–7, 389
  Pine Ave. West, home 43–4, 56, 372, 376, 402, 404, 413–16
    named as shrine 425–6
  professional life 10–12, 86, 171, 212, 281, 376, 379, 401, 421
  sculpture 36–7

Shoghi Effendi 169–71, 194, 262–3,
276–7, 278–80, 285, 288, 297–8,
302–4, 330–31, 333–4, 343, 357,
361, 365, 367–8, 376–9, 380,
414–15, 416, 417–19
  and residence in Haifa 381–98, 406–8
McCracken, Dr 90
McDaniel, Allen B. 184
McGill Daily 72
McGill University 59, 74, 91, 105–6, 212, 424
McGregor, Norman 161
McNeil, General Angus 408–9
McNeil, Lilian 408–9
McNeil, Marjorie 78
Menton, France 381
Messages to the Bahá'í World, 1950–1957 412
Meyer, Richard 62
Migette, Lucienne, 243–51, 260, 279–81
Milan, Italy 394, 407
Mills, Mountfort 11, 50, 80, 181
Mírzá Mihdí (Purest Branch) 359, 361, 363
Möller, Hans 424
Moncton, New Brunswick 301
Monet, Claude 224–5
Montessori education 29
Montreal
  Arts Club, 44, 71, 380, 420, 422–3
  Bahá'í activities, community 11, 17,
32n, 33, 42, 50, 54, 65, 68, 72–5,
78–81, 93, 100, 118, 140, 144, 152,
162, 173, 178–80, 196–7, 224, 226,
300–3, 346, 354, 377, 390, 402,
412–16, 418, 425–6
  city 12, 29n, 43–4, 46, 59, 71–2, 75, 83,
102, 107, 169, 203n, 209, 212, 258,
300, 303, 379–80, 417, 419–22, 424
  clubs *see individual entries*
  Spiritual Assembly of the Bahá'ís of 11,
42–3, 71–4, 78, 81, 113, 141, 158,
217, 256, 300, 302–3, 402, 404
  visit of 'Abdu'l-Bahá to 160, 167–9, 193,
247, 344–5, 372, 425
  Youth Group, Movement 62, 65, 75,
147–8, 150–60, 170, 204, 217, 372
  see also Pine Avenue West
Montreal Gazette 12, 43n, 74, 149
Montreal High School 12, 421
Montreal Daily Star 43, 121, 168, 333, 417
Montevideo, Brazil, 361, 362
Montroyal, S. S. 46
Monument Gardens, Haifa 361, 363, 389
Moody, Susan 376
moral values 97, 99, 133, 154–6, 237
Moranville, Chevalier de 228
Morton, Florence 113
Morton, Mrs 16, 42

Mount Carmel 112, 299, 356, 361, 363, 391, 403, 406, 426
Mount Royal, Montreal 117, 418
Mullá Ḥusayn 191
Munich, Germany 119, 214, 220–21, 228, 232, 238–9, 240
Munich Agreement 339
Munírih Khánum 67, 272
Mussolini 158
mysticism 138, 145–6, 346
Mysticism Congress 145

Naples, Italy 257
Napoleon Bonaparte 238–9
National Socialist (Nazi) Party 210, 340
National Spiritual Assembly *see* Spiritual Assembly
Navváb 359, 361, 363
Nazareth 272, 273, 277, 383
Nielsen, Kay 39
Negro Club (Montreal) 75
Negro Forum Group 190
Neuman, Prof. 394–5
New History Society 120–28, 150
New Thought 51, 80
New York 32, 43, 81–2, 99, 115, 117, 130, 145, 165, 181, 197, 201, 229, 258, 287–8, 298, 300, 328, 341, 351, 401, 422
  'Abdu'l-Bahá's visit to 24–5, 94, 115, 347
  Covenant-breaking 120–27
  May Maxwell in 27, 31, 34, 37, 43–4, 54, 64, 71–2, 77, 82, 84–6, 91–2, 94, 97–8, 115, 120–27, 128–9, 140–41, 146, 161–2, 163, 166, 174, 177, 181–2, 186, 188, 242, 250, 287–9, 292–3, 295, 316, 323, 347, 349, 351, 353, 355
  shopping 107–8
New Zealand 30
  National Spiritual Assembly 411
Nicolas, A. L. M. 229–30
Nicosia, Cyprus 402
Nobbs, Professor 46
Norway, Norwegians 324, 338, 407
Nova Scotia 183–4
Nuremberg, Germany 212

Ober, Grace and Harlan 88, 93
Obouhow, M. 236
Oldham, Rev. G. Ashton 145
Olga, Miss, piano teacher 32
Omaha, Nebraska 324
Orleans, France 251
Orlova, Mme 206
Ortenberg, Michel 78
Overstreet, Prof. Henry A. 145
Oxton Hall, Tadcaster 48

Padlock Act 302–3
Page, Katherine 165n
Page, Lorne and Bobby 108
Palestine 265, 273, 283, 308–9, 339, 351, 379, 383, 389, 397, 400, 401, 405, 407–8
  architecture 389
Panama–Pacific International Exposition
Parent, Amanda M. (AMP) 273, 278, 281, 389–90, 401–2, 404–5
Paris, France 3, 49–50, 53, 240, 243–4, 245, 260, 275, 381, 384, 421
  early Bahá'í community 80, 116, 160, 164, 241, 243–4, 364, 374
  1930s visits of May Maxwell 221–2, 226–30, 251–3, 278–82
Paris World Exposition 278, 281–2
Paris, S. S. 3
Parliament Building, Regina 12, 421
Parsons, Agnes 345–6
Pasadena, Calif. 148, 199, 201, 204–5, 209
Patterson, Col. & Mrs 141
Peeke, Margaret Barton 165
Pen and Pencil Club 87
Perrault, Jean T. 379
Persia 27, 66, 150, 175, 198, 230, 271
Persian Colony, Haifa (Persian St.) 5, 17, 66, 400, 406
Persian language 62, 68, 262, 270, 320, 356, 358, 361, 375
Persian Wife, The 172
personality, over-emphasis on 286, 310–12, 314–15, 374
Philadelphia 118, 130–31, 166, 344, 352, 355, 371
pilgrimage, pilgrims 64, 164, 165, 173, 261, 272, 296, 299, 308, 326, 339
  pilgrims' notes 68–9, 261–2, 315–17, 319, 321–2
  see also Maxwell, Mary: Notes 1937
Pilgrim House, Haifa
  'old' 4, 5, 17, 21
  Western 112, 263–5, 271
Pine Avenue West, Montreal (Maxwell home) 56, 77–8, 79, 153–4, 167, 193–4, 241, 260, 300, 372, 376, 402, 404, 414–5, 417
  Bahá'í shrine 425–6
  visit of 'Abdu'l-Bahá 160, 167–9, 193, 247, 344–5, 372, 425–6
Pitts, George 10, 12, 86, 207, 212, 281, 413, 421
Poland, Polish 227, 335, 339–41
Pomeroy, Mrs 33
Pompeii 11
Popliger, Mr 78
Portland, OR 59, 206, 374
Port Said, Egypt 9, 12, 14, 18–19, 64, 281

Portsmouth, NH 30, 51, 89, 162, 167, 169, 211, 340
Portugal 242
Prague 241
prayer, stages of 95
Prenidas, Mr 78
Priceless Pearl, The 27, 148n, 264–5, 269, 271, 381–2, 387, 394, 403, 411
Prichard, Rev. A. Adye 145
Progressive Education Association 54
Promulgation of Universal Peace, The 157
Prosser, Seward 292–3
Prushonsky, Mr 400–01
Purest Branch 359, 361, 363

Quackenbush, Dr 78n
Quebec, Province of 302–3, 324, 354, 379, 401
    Association of Architects 324, 379, 422
Quilmes cemetery, Argentina 366, 368, 378–9, 391–3
Quinlan, Della 340
Qur'án 5, 246

Rabbani Papers 425
radio 174, 177–82
Rackham, Arthur 39
racism 177, 184–91, 219, 348
Ramleh, Egypt 9, 14–15
Randall, John Herman 43, 74
Randall, William (Harry) 33, 166
Ransom-Kehler, Keith, Hand of the Cause 53, 82, 84, 113–14, 115, 175–6, 199, 205, 371, 372–3, 375–6
Ratner, Mr 394
Remey, Mason 176, 184–90, 195, 197, 203, 209, 352, 372, 374
Revell, Ethel 353
Revell, Jessie 166–7, 351–3, 374
Rex, S. S. 380, 381
Rexford, Orcella 84
Rhine, Rhineland 212, 214–15, 225, 232, 325
Rhône valley 243
Rickman, Poppie 78
Rio de Janeiro, Brazil 358–60, 362, 363, 371, 378
Robert, Mr 78
Robeson, Paul 119, 238
Robin 62, 66, 68
Roddick, Mrs 342
Rome, Italy 257, 381, 405–8
Romer, Annie B. 26
Root, Martha, Hand of the Cause 141, 178–81, 205, 309, 337–8, 341, 371, 372–3, 375–6, 379
Rosenzweig, Simon 364, 366

Rostock, Germany 219, 233, 257
Roxburgh Smith, J. 419–22
Roy, René 416n
Royal Architectural Institute of Canada 171, 203, 379, 389, 419–22
Royal Canadian Academy 171, 401n, 422
Royal Institute of British Architects 407, 420, 422
Royal Victoria Hospital, Montreal 12, 332
Rushton, Sir Andrew 46
Rye, NY 37–8, 77

sacrifice 19, 25, 28, 64, 81–2, 88, 99, 102, 109, 113–19, 123, 133, 187, 191–4, 195–8, 250, 289, 294, 308, 312, 316, 336–7, 343, 352–3, 357–8, 367, 368–9, 370, 373, 375–6
saints, saintliness 78, 261, 342, 384, 417, 419
Sala, Emeric 78, 149, 161, 292, 302, 333, 404–5, 413, 414–15, 426
Sala, Rosemary (Gillies) 78, 141, 149, 161–2, 207, 291, 301–2, 333, 404–5, 413, 414–16, 426
Sanderson, Edith 6, 50, 228–30, 278, 281
San Francisco 51, 110, 137, 165, 191, 205–6
San Mateo 206
Santa Maria del Casale 263
Santos, Brazil 351, 377
Sarah Farmer Inn *see* Green Acre
Sarah Lawrence College 90–91
Saskatchewan Legislature (Parliament) 12, 421
Saturday Evening Post 323
Savage, Anne 11, 33, 80–81
Seattle 51, 59, 207
Scheffler, Carl 87
Schepens, Dr 237–8
Schopflocher, Lorol 13, 83, 184, 193, 196, 231, 232, 235
Schopflocher, Siegfried, Hand of the Cause 17–18, 78, 193, 196, 303, 390, 400, 417–9
Schubarth, Johanna 324, 338
Schulman, Rabbi Samuel 145
Schweizer, Friedrich 241
Schwerin 240, 257
science 130, 134–6, 234
Scotland, Scots 34, 46, 110, 114, 224, 271, 384
Scott, Sir Walter 4
Security for a Failing World 232
Segger, Martin 425
Seven Year Plans 300, 304–5, 307, 354, 367, 372
Sherman, Mrs 132
Schmidt, Dr Pierre 412

Shoghi Effendi, Guardian of the Bahá'í Faith
  Bahá'í administration and institutions
    17, 20, 24, 29, 112, 121–4, 151, 173,
    191, 201, 218, 239, 270, 304–5, 322,
    331, 418–19, 425
  Bahá'í World, The (Year Book) 163–72,
    366–7, 388, 410
  Covenant-breaking 120–27, 309–10
  Europe 26
    France 236, 239, 245–2, 255, 275–6
    Germany 218, 239, 255
    travels in 8–9, 27, 36, 51, 54, 275,
      381–2, 384, 395
  God Passes By 375–6, 393
  Greatest Holy Leaf 174
  home in Haifa (Master's House) 31, 383
  letters to North America 18–19, 26, 102,
    115, 118, 149, 163, 189, 192, 201,
    356, 362–3, 372–3
  and Mary Maxwell 5–6, 66–70, 134–7,
    149, 172–3, 183, 191–2, 217–20,
    255–6, 260, 307
    marriage to 260, 262–5, 269–71,
      284–9 *see also* Amatu'l-Bahá
      Rúḥíyyih Khánum
  and Maxwell family *see* Bolles, Randolph;
    Maxwell, May; Maxwell, Sutherland
  Migette, Lucienne 245–51, 260
  overwork 27, 54, 256, 356
  pilgrims' notes 261, 319, 322–3
  plans 151, 276, 300, 304–5, 367, 375
  prayer 95, 317
  Shrine of the Báb and terraces 387–93,
    396, 403, 406–8, 409–10, 412, 417
  station of 22, 117, 120, 121–27, 261–2,
    270–71, 286, 290, 291, 293–7, 300,
    308, 309–10, 313–14, 317, 346–7
  suffering 21, 31, 66, 174, 309–10, 312,
    356
  Temple, Wilmette 192–9
  World Order of Bahá'u'lláh 17, 21,
    122–3, 191, 270–71, 346
  'World Order' letters 118, 206, 325
  youthfulness 5–6, 21, 148n, 287, 362
Shrine of the Báb 27, 61, 65, 66, 252–3,
  299, 366, 374, 398, 426
  superstructure and terraces 387–8,
    391–401, 405–10, 412, 417
Shrine of Bahá'u'lláh 7, 27, 61, 65, 67,
  252–3, 259–60, 261, 264, 335, 368,
  398–9
shuffle-board 46–8
Simms, Alberta 78, 143, 144
Sluter, Gerrard 78, 161
Smith, Mr 46–7, 48
Smythe, Marguerite (Daisy) 61–4, 65, 66, 69
social sciences 67, 91, 105–6, 135–6, 156–7

Society of Architects (Boston)
Soghomanian, Mrs 279, 280
Sohrab, Ahmad 120–27, 305, 315, 349
South Africa 382, 406
Some Answered Questions 157
South America 221, 250, 354–68, 371, 373,
  374–6, 377, 425
snakes 7, 10, 15, 36–9, 57
Sofia, Bulgaria 232, 258, 397
Soroptimist Club 51, 80
South Africa 382, 406
Southampton, England 382
Spain 210, 211, 234, 325
Spanish Civil War 211, 226
Spendlove, George 161
Spierckel, Pierre 244n
Spiritual Assembly (Local) 228–9, 300–2,
  323
  Buenos Aires 367
  Hamburg 234
  Lyon 243, 246, 275
  Milwaukee 324–5
  Montreal 11, 42–3, 71–4, 78, 81, 113,
    141, 158, 217, 256, 300, 302–3, 402,
    404
  New York 210
  Paris 228–30
  Pasadena, California 205
  Philadelphia 166
  Vancouver 51
  Visalia, California 204
  Washington DC 186–9, 190–91, 205
  see also Spiritual Assembly (National)
Spiritual Assembly's Growing Pains, A 188
Spiritual Assembly (National)
  Australia and New Zealand 411
  British Isles 163
  Canada 302, 405, 418, 425
  Germany and Austria 241
  United States and Canada 22, 24–5, 29,
    74–5, 77, 85, 112–13, 116, 118, 121,
    123, 138, 163, 177, 182, 190, 191,
    196–7, 269, 284, 318, 322, 341, 367,
    370, 372, 378, 379, 386
spiritual life 71, 95, 98, 125, 146, 147, 153,
  201, 301, 306
Spragg, C. D. 420
Sprague, Philip 190, 194–9, 202, 204–5,
  258, 259–60, 341, 374, 393
Square Mile, Montreal 2
Squires, Marie *see* Hopper
St Lambert 301–2
St Malo, France 381–2
Stanleyville (Kisangani) 382
Stanford University 205
Star of the West 27, 165
Steinbeck, John 101–2

Stewart, Frances 362–5, 366, 374–5
Stewart, Mary 33, 167
Stewart, Mrs H. E. 75
Stowell, Kenneth K. 423
Stuttgart, Germany 80n, 212, 213–14, 218, 220, 240, 258
Sudan 382–3
suicide 43–4, 136, 234, 248
Switzerland 54, 274–5, 296, 385, 412–14, 421
Sydney, Australia 376

Tablets of the Divine Plan 32, 93
Tadcaster, England 48
Technical Institute (Haifa) 394–5
Tel Aviv 274, 275, 382, 389, 405, 407
Ten Year Crusade 304
Thomas Cook & Son 62, 111, 355, 358-60
Thompson, Juliet 24, 60–64, 69, 93, 281, 346–7, 374
Thornburgh-Cropper, Virginia 19
Tailhard, Dr 280
Tiberias, Galilee 68
Tiepolo 197
Tombs, Laurence 232
Tormo, Mr 364
Toronto 54, 65, 72, 79–81, 112, 150, 171, 209, 331-2, 354
Townshend, George 353
Treblinka 341
Trevor Prize 401n
Trieste, Italy 256, 257, 260
True, Edna 6
Tucker's School 421
Turner, Robert 165

United States *see* America; Spiritual Assembly (National)
Universal House of Justice, The 121, 304
United Nations 101

Valentine, H. A. 423
Vancouver, BC 51, 54, 79, 128, 137–8, 207, 354
Van Horn, Miss 281
Versailles, Treaty of 101
Victoria, BC 59, 424
  University of 424–5
Victoria Falls 382
Vienna, Austria 241

Wall Street 101–2, 104
Walsh, Jim 232
Wade, Dorothy and Glen 161
Ward, Dorothy 78, 141, 402, 413, 414
Warnemünde, Germany 219
War of Independence (Israel) 162
Warsaw, Poland 340–41

Washington Conference for the Limitation of Armaments 145
Washington DC 94, 111, 150, 176–7, 184–91, 195, 203, 205, 207, 258, 352, 355
  visit of 'Abdu'l-Bahá 131
Weeden, Ben 161, 395, 405–7, 409
Weeden, Gladys (Cotton) 161–2, 290, 403, 405
Westmount, Montreal 102 *see also* Pine Avenue West
Weston School 36
White Mountains, NH 161–2
Wiesbaden 241
Wilhelm, Roy 82, 195, 277
Wilmette
  construction of Temple 112, 116, 178, 192–9, 300, 390, 425
  Conventions and conferences 84, 316–17, 339, 348, 373–4, 425
Winnipeg 51, 354
Women's Canadian Club 75
Worcestershire Regiment 339
World Bank 101
World Order of Bahá'u'lláh 17, 21, 122–3, 191, 270–71, 346
'World Order' letters 118, 206, 325
World's Fair 196
World Unity Conference, Movement 50, 72, 74–5, 93
World War I 101
World War II 101, 148, 162, 293, 315, 324–6, 335, 339, 344, 379, 381–2, 426
Worley, Lee and Margot 360, 371
Wright, Louise 209

Yagorski, Madame 227
Yates, Mrs 413
Yates, Nancy 421n
Yazdi, Rahim 62
Yazdi (in Lyon) 246, 281
York, England 47, 48
Young People's Conference 157–9
youth 62, 65, 93, 135, 148, 155, 163, 190, 197, 220, 247, 249, 283, 392, 427
  in Germany 159, 214–15, 234, 240
  in Montreal and Canada 62, 65, 75, 147–8, 150–60, 170, 204, 217, 372
  in North America 146–7, 160–61, 191–2, 204
  of Shoghi Effendi 5, 148, 287

Zabih, Izzatu'lláh 214, 242–3
Zamenhof, Lidia 236, 339–41
Zamenhof, Ludovik 340
Zoroaster 351
Zugspitze 221–2, 238

www.ingramcontent.com/pod-product-compliance
Lightning Source LLC
Chambersburg PA
CBHW051802230426
43672CB00012B/2601